ELIZABETH HERVEY,
THE HISTORY OF NED EVANS (1796)

Chawton House Library Series: Women's Novels

Series Editors: Stephen Bending
                     Stephen Bygrave

Titles in this Series

1 *The Histories of Some of the Penitents in the Magdalen-House*
edited by Jennie Batchelor and Megan Hiatt

2 Stéphanie-Félicité de Genlis, *Adelaide and Theodore, or Letters on Education*
edited by Gillian Dow

3 E. M. Foster, *The Corinna of England*
edited by Sylvia Bordoni

4 Sarah Harriet Burney, *The Romance of Private Life*
edited by Lorna J. Clark

5 Alicia LeFanu, *Strathallan*
edited by Anna M. Fitzer

6 Elizabeth Sophia Tomlins, *The Victim of Fancy*
edited by Daniel Cook

7 Helen Maria Williams, *Julia*
edited by Natasha Duquette

Forthcoming Titles

Sarah Green, *Romance Readers and Romance Writers*
edited by Christopher Goulding

Sarah Green, *The Private History of the Court of England*
edited by Fiona Price

Marie-Jeanne Riccoboni and Frances Brooke, Françoise de Graffigny and Rose
Roberts, *Translations and Continuations*
edited by Marijn S. Kaplan

Elizabeth Hervey,
The History of Ned Evans (1796)

EDITED BY

Helena Kelly

LONDON AND NEW YORK

First published 2010 by Pickering & Chatto (Publishers) Limited

Published 2016 by Routledge
2 Park Square, Milton Park, Abingdon, Oxfordshire OX14 4RN
711 Third Avenue, New York, NY 10017, USA

First issued in paperback 2016

Routledge is an imprint of the Taylor & Francis Group, an informa business

© Taylor & Francis 2010
© Editorial Material Helena Kelly 2010

All rights reserved, including those of translation into foreign languages.
No part of this book may be reprinted or reproduced or utilised in any form or
by any electronic, mechanical, or other means, now known or hereafter
invented, including photocopying and recording, or in any information storage
or retrieval system, without permission in writing from the publishers.

Notice:
Product or corporate names may be trademarks or registered trademarks, and
are used only for identification and explanation without intent to infringe.

BRITISH LIBRARY CATALOGUING IN PUBLICATION DATA

Hervey, Elizabeth, ca. 1748–ca. 1820.
The history of Ned Evans. – (Chawton House library series.
Women's novels)
1. Social classes – Ireland – History – 18th century – Fiction.
2. Ireland – Politics and government – 1760–1820 – Fiction.
I. Title II. Series III. Kelly, Helena.
823.6-dc22

ISBN 13: 978-1-138-23569-4 (pbk)
ISBN 13: 978-1-8519-6637-0 (hbk)

Typeset by Pickering & Chatto (Publishers) Limited

CONTENTS

Acknowledgements	vi
Introduction	vii
Select Bibliography	xx
Note on the Text	xxii
Ned Evans	1
Endnotes	345

ACKNOWLEDGEMENTS

I am very grateful to Stephen Bygrave, who has been behind this project from the beginning. Thanks are also due to Dr James Shanahan of Trinity College Dublin, to Colin Harris of the Bodleian Library and, finally, to David Armstrong and to Anna Luedecke, for making me smile.

INTRODUCTION

The History of Ned Evans, published anonymously in 1796, has been attributed to three very different individuals – Jane West, the conservative author of *A Gossip's Story* and *A Tale of the Times*, a Waterford clergyman by the name of Robert Elliott, and Elizabeth Hervey. The attribution to West is the least plausible of these because, despite its frequent references to Biblical passages, *Ned Evans* is certainly not a conservative text. In addition to criticizing the upper echelons of the church and the practice of educating girls for a purely domestic role, it is openly sympathetic both to the aims of the American Revolution and to emergent Irish nationalism. In *Ireland in Fiction 1650–1900*, Rolf and Magda Loeber identify a certain 'Revd Robert Elliott of Waterford' as the author, relying on the evidence of a note in the flyleaf of a single copy of the novel in a private collection. There were two men called Robert Elliott who were clergymen in the dioceses of Waterford and Lismore, but the first must have been dead by 1796 while the second was only appointed curate in the 1820s, suggesting that he was still a child at the time of the book's publication. The book's cheerful endorsement of illegitimacy and frequent jabs at the clergy scarcely read like the work of a clergyman. The final and most credible candidate is Elizabeth Hervey. She is named as the author of the 1810 London edition of *The Mourtray Family*, an 1803 edition of which was published in Dublin as being 'by the author of Ned Evans'; not clinching evidence given the questionable accuracy of pirated editions, but the strongest for any of the three candidates. She was married to a Colonel in the Guards which would have given her the experience of military life which the author of the novel seems to have possessed, she had numerous connections among the Irish nobility, and she was reputedly the mistress of a man whose revolutionary sympathies brought him into close contact with Lord Edward Fitzgerald, one of the foremost members of the nationalist United Irishmen.

Elizabeth Hervey was born in 1748, the daughter of Francis Marsh or March, whose money came from Jamaica, and Maria Hamilton, granddaughter of the sixth Earl of Abercorn. Elizabeth's father died around 1752, and in 1756 her mother married William Beckford of Fonthill, giving birth to a son, William, the

viii   *The History of Ned Evans*

future author of *Vathek*, in 1760. While Elizabeth was still in her early teens, she was married to one of her stepfather's Jamaican business associates, a man called Alexander Harvie. He died in 1765, leaving Elizabeth a widow at the tender age of seventeen. Her personal fortune (£1,200 per annum, secured on the estate of Oldfield's Bog, in the south of the island of Jamaica) was caught in the quagmire of debt and legal wrangling which Harvie and his brothers had built up. Nearly ten years later we find Elizabeth still litigating about the matter, though to no avail (see S.D. Smith, 179). In 1777 the property left to her by her father ended up in the hands of Daniel Lascelles, who had been one of her trustees.[1] Elizabeth's next foray into matrimony was with Lieutenant Colonel William Thomas Hervey, illegitimate but acknowledged son of Lady Hanmer by the Hon. Thomas Hervey, uncle to the third and fourth Earls of Bristol and, according to Samuel Johnson, 'though a vicious man ... one of the genteelest men that ever lived'.[2] The pair married at St George's, Hanover Square, on 5 May 1774. Todd's *Dictionary of British and American Women Writers* states that the Colonel died in Liège in 1778, leaving two sons and a mass of debt.[3] Horace Walpole, however, speaks of Colonel Hervey as being still alive in 1789.[4] If the Colonel was still living, he was estranged from his wife, for by the late 1780s Hervey seems to have been established at Brussels as the mistress of Robert Merry, the poet Della Crusca.[5] According to Hester Thrale, the pair nearly married, and remained close friends even after Merry married another woman in 1791.[6] Hervey published her first novel, *Melissa and Marcia, or The Sisters*, in 1788, with *Louisa* following in 1790. A silence of six years was broken by the publication of *The History of Ned Evans* (1796) and *The Church of Saint Siffrid* (1797). *The Mourtray Family* appeared in 1800 and her last novel, *Amabel, or Memoirs of a Woman of Fashion* in 1814. We catch a glimpse of her in 1818 at Madame de Stael's Swiss salon, when, as Byron relates in a letter, 'Mrs. Hervey (she writes novels) fainted on my entrance' but I have found no later reference so it is possible that she died not long afterwards.[7]

   Ned Evans is very different from Hervey's earlier works, *Melissa and Marcia* and *Louisa*, which clearly owe much to Burney, and which were commonly assumed to have provided her brother William Beckford with some of the targets for his parodies on sentimental novels, *Modern Novel Writing* (1796) and *Azemia* (1797).[8] In some ways Ned is a typical romance hero – beginning the novel in rural isolation with his impoverished foster-parents he is revealed by the end as the rightful heir to a noble title and estates – but this narrative arc becomes complicated and eventually even seems to fracture. Hervey deliberately pushes the family recognition scenes to the point of absurdity. In Volume III Lord Ravensdale comments on the resemblance between his late nephew and Ned (see p. 197) while in Volume IV, when Ned is at the house of his unknown grandmother after being rescued from a shipwreck, he is not only declared to be the image of his mother, but even to sound like her, 'O Jenny, he is so like my

Lætitia! – His eye, his manner, nay his voice brings her so strongly to mind' (see pp. 281–2). The grandmother's companion dismisses her suspicions as 'romantic' and requiring evidence 'much more convincing than the mere circumstance of resemblance and co-incidence of name' (see p. 282).[9] Nor is the revelation of his true name and title straightforward. Ned's foster parents are Welsh, and he is adopted by an American Indian woman before discovering his true Irish or Anglo-Irish identity only in a series of scenes which recall the complexities and confusions of the denouement of Henry Fielding's *Joseph Andrews* (1742). Throughout the novel the reader encounters characters whose identities are labile (Ned himself, women whose marriages are suspect or repudiated, an Irish thief who constantly changes his name) or whose places can be filled by another person (as among the Agigua). Nothing is quite solid.

The novel appears to have been written quickly, giving the same names to a number of unconnected minor characters (there are two Patricks and three Mollies) but is at the same time self-consciously literary rather than merely derivative, referring repeatedly to *Paradise Lost* and Virgil's *Aeneid*. It borrows a Fieldingesque flavour for its first volume, noted by early critics, and has a number of similarities to *The Old Manor House*, a 1793 novel by Charlotte Smith, chief among which is the fact that both novels send their heroes to fight in the American Revolutionary War, where they are kidnapped by American Indians. Hervey may also have taken aspects of Smith's first novel *Emmeline, or The Orphan of the Castle* (1788), whose eponymous heroine, like Ned, attains exquisite social graces while being raised in rural Welsh isolation, and is cheated out of her birthright by an uncle. Unlike Smith, who has frequently been ridiculed for the Canadian savannahs and magnolia trees which appear in *The Old Manor House*, Hervey did at least some research for her Indian episodes, lifting much of the material almost unaltered from James Adair's *The History of the American Indians*, published in 1775. She may have collected details such as names from her husband's uncle, the Hon. William Hervey, who had spent many years with the army in Canada and who often stayed with her.[10] Choosing as her motto for the book the words, 'O'erstep not the modesty of Nature!',[11] part of Hamlet's speech to the players, in which he claims that the 'end' of acting is 'to hold as 'twere the mirror up to Nature', Hervey also draws a large part of her inspiration for the novel from real life. Not only do her characters spend a verisimilitudinous amount of their time eating, drinking and sleeping, but several of them represent real individuals, her hero being a thinly-disguised portrait of Lord Edward Fitzgerald, a younger son of the first Duke of Leinster and energetic proponent for Irish independence who was to become one of the leaders of the United Irish uprising in 1798.

Lord Edward, born in 1763, was a fifth son, the twelfth of nineteen children born to the Duke and Duchess of Leinster. He was destined for the army, and joined a regiment which was leaving for America. In 1781, still in his teens, he

x *The History of Ned Evans*

was seriously injured in the battle of Eutaw Springs. His survival was due to the intervention of Tony Small, a runaway slave who rescued him from the battlefield and nursed him back to health. In a decision probably motivated as much by pragmatism as by sentiment, Small chose to go with Fitzgerald as a servant rather than risk being returned to his former owner by the Revolutionary forces.[12] At the end of the 1780s, Lord Edward changed regiments to enable him to return to North America, where he travelled from Canada to New Orleans through the back-country and was adopted into one of the Sioux tribes. Returning once more to Europe he began to move in radical circles, becoming a personal friend of Thomas Paine, with whom he lodged when he visited Paris in 1792. Caught up in the increasingly fervid political climate, he joined the United Irishmen, the society which had been founded by Paine, among others, he left off using his title, becoming Citizen Fitzgerald, and at the end of 1792 married Pamela, the putative daughter of Louis-Philippe Egalité – the former Duc d'Orléans – and Madame de Genlis. After their return to Ireland, the Fitzgeralds became increasingly radicalized. Pamela often went to society balls wearing 'radical' clothing or ribbons around her neck alluding to the guillotine and Edward gave a speech which so offended the other members of the Irish Parliament that he was forced to apologize before they would allow him back into the house. In 1798, as the United Irish uprising in which he had been so closely involved was about to begin, Lord Edward was betrayed to the authorities, and after a short and bloody struggle, during which one soldier was fatally stabbed and Fitzgerald was shot and beaten, he was arrested and died in prison a few days later, allegedly from the neglect of his injuries.[13]

Hervey's sometime lover Robert Merry moved in the same circles as Fitzgerald in Paris in 1792–3 and, like Fitzgerald, was much caressed by the French revolutionary government.[14] I have not been able to discover whether Hervey ever met Fitzgerald herself, but her decision to include in her novel a character based on him indicates that she intended it to be read as an avowedly political work. There is one minor character who might be meant for a portrait of Hervey's half-brother William Beckford, with whom she enjoyed a sometimes fraught relationship (see note 55 to Volume I, p. 349, below), but the majority of Hervey's thinly-veiled portraits of real individuals are of political figures connected with the struggle for Irish independence. Walter Hussey Burgh, the politician and Irish patriot who in 1779 resigned from his position as head of the governmental party in order to support Grattan's opposition, appears *in propria persona* in Chapter 25 (pp. 136–7). Lord Ravensdale, Ned's great uncle, is plausibly meant for the second Duke of Leinster, Lord Edward Fitzgerald's eldest brother, while the 'Bishop of Limerick' who makes an appearance in Volume IV, seems from his intimacy with the Ravensdale family intended to serve as a portrait of the Bishop of Derry, Hervey's husband's cousin, who was a political ally of Leinster. Lord Squanderfield, the unsuccessful suitor of Lady Cecilia, may be Charles Manners, the fourth Duke of Rutland, who was made Lord Lieutenant in February 1784 and who attempted unsuccessfully to implement Pitt's plans for Union between Britain and Ireland.

The political aspect of the novel was apparent to the publisher of the Dublin edition of 1796, where it is asserted that 'The History of Ned Evans' is 'interspersed with moral and critical remarks; anecdotes of many persons well known in the polite world and incidental strictures on the present state of Ireland'. Despite its setting in the early 1780s, the novel is very much preoccupied with the state of Ireland in the 1790s and Hervey includes a potent symbol of 1790s Irish nationalism, the harp. At the beginning of the eighteenth century, Irish harp music had been relegated to a lowly status, while the harp itself had been adopted as a symbol of Ascendancy rule.[15] By the early 1790s, in imitation of other Celtic cultures which had 'rediscovered' their national music and poetry, the Irish harp was being reclaimed as a nationalist symbol by the United Irishmen, a group whose membership was predominantly Anglo-Irish and either Presbyterian or non-Catholic. Thuente demonstrates that many of the founding members of the United Irishmen were strongly interested in Irish antiquarianism and culture, and that a number of United Irish songs were set to traditional Irish tunes.[16] Barra Boydell notes that Maria Edgeworth's father paid Irish harpers to play for the family on a regular basis, while the first harp festival was held in Belfast in 1792.[17] The harp is used as a symbol of the United Irish programme on the title page of John Corry's *Odes and Elegies*, published in 1797, pictured next to a poem which reads, 'Delightful Love! my Soul inspire, / Teach me to tune Ierne's Lyre / To social Amity'. There was also, during the late 1790s, a United Irish newspaper published in Cork which was called the *Harp of Erin*.

Ned's excellence on the harp – an instrument on which he fast outstrips his teacher – reinforces his connection to the United Irishmen, but at the same time insists on its artificiality as a nationalist symbol. The Irish-bred Cecilia is astounded on hearing the Welsh harp played for the first time, remarking that she has, 'sometimes heard it played upon in Ireland ... commonly by some blind woman, but either from its own defects, or the want of skill in the performer, I did not think it much preferable to a dulcimer' (see p. 53). Ned has been taught to play the harp by John Price, whose history is narrated at some length. In his youth, 'addicted ... to poetry and music, talents not uncommon in Wales' John 'enlisted in a marching regiment', 'served his country', and finally 'returned to his native soil, to subsist on a small pension which the bounty of his country allowed him' (see p. 52). Here he composes 'ballads on his achievements and misfortunes, which he set to the ancient music of his country, and sang, accompanied with the harp, on which he played with tolerable skill'. John's nationality seems to slip, and his 'country' to change between Wales, England and Britain according to context. John's daughter Molly is the mother of Ned's illegitimate child, who shares his name, meaning that Ned is never permitted to enter fully into his Irish identity. The name which he is known by for the majority of the novel, Edward Evans, was shared with a nonconformist minister, poet and harpist who was a popular and well-known figure in Glamorgan and who was lauded as an 'ancient British bard' in the *Gentleman's Magazine* of November 1789. Though his Welshness never vanishes entirely, Ned is shown to be almost endlessly adaptable to new circumstances and new national and social identities. Kidnapped after the battle of Eutaw Springs and, still suffering from the injury to his leg, forced to march for hundreds of miles on hardly any food or sleep, to witness bloody raids on European backwood settlements and, once he finally arrives in Indian territory, to watch some of his fellow prisoners tortured and killed, Ned settles down quite happily to Indian life. He becomes an excellent hunter and tracker and lives among the Agigua for almost two years before orchestrating his escape. In Indian territory he is an Indian; in Wales he is Welsh; once he has returned to Ireland we find him making Irish 'bulls', those supposedly hilarious, supposedly typically Irish, nonsensical sayings (see p. 285). When Ned first arrives in Dublin, no one knows his nationality, or rather they think they do but they are mistaken. The Irish maids at the inn say that Ned 'has the best legs that ever I saw with an Englishman' (see p. 117), but the ragamuffin boys on the street identify him as Welshman; 'hur is a Welchman, hur Welch plud is up! Ah! When did hur cross the ferry, agrah! And did hur leave St. Taffy, and who milks hur grandmother's goats, now hur is away?' (see p. 118). At the end of the novel it emerges that Ned's first set of foster parents were Irish Catholics who marked the back of his neck with a cross before leaving him in the garden of the family with whom he grew up, from which one might infer that Ned might as easily have grown up to be a Catholic tinker as the good Anglican son of a curate, as easily an Indian hunter as an Anglo-Irish aristocrat (see pp. 314–15). Hervey emphasizes that identities – and loyalties – are complex and almost endlessly mutable. In America, Ned and his loyal Welsh servant encounter Scotsmen who have been driven out of the Highlands but continue to identify with the British cause (p. 241), and an Irishman who is at one and the same time American – a fervent supporter of the rebels – and Irish, but who is willing to shelter a British soldier (p. 259).

Hervey's treatment of nationality as a fluid concept complicates the marriage between Ned and Cecilia. Representing as it does a reconciliation between the two sides of the Rivers family, their union could be a forerunner of the 'national marriage' which concludes Lady Sydney Morgan's *The Wild Irish Girl* (1806), and features in several of Edgeworth's later Irish novels, or, conversely, a purely Irish marriage illustrating Ireland's ability to stand alone and independent, but

Ned's compromised identity – he is not wholly Irish, English, Anglo-Irish, or even Welsh – means that the symbolism fails on either count.

Nor does Hervey ever seem quite clear in her own mind as to the symbolism which should attach to Ravensdale, the estate which Ned eventually inherits. There was a real Ravensdale, but it was located near the coast in County Louth, whereas Ned's Ravensdale is, fittingly enough, in the centre of Ireland, on the banks of the Shannon. In Volume II the estate is described in terms which recall two widely differing texts; the description of Eden in Milton's *Paradise Lost* and the description of Carton, the country estate of the Fitzgeralds, in Arthur Young's *Tour through Ireland*, published in 1780;

> the celebrated Shannon, whose lordly tide might bear a navy on its bosom, wound round the demesne: when expanding itself into a lake, it formed a sheet of water full thirteen miles in length and half as much in breadth ... the banks of this liquid mirror presented the richest and most diversified scenery – sometimes level lawns, the fertile pastures which feed the West-Indies, and all the navies of Europe – sometimes towering rocks, the inaccessible aeries of eagles and of hawks, sometimes groves, whose venerable shades embrowned the rocks, and seemed to grow downwards to the bottom of the lake ... towers were not wanting, the venerable remains of ruined monasteries; nor here and there the rising smokes of cheerful cottages ... oh happy plains of plenty and of peace.[18]

Arthur Young, the crusading agricultural improver and proselytiser, visited Ireland three times between 1776 and 1778, and wrote with breathless admiration about 'his grace's seat at Cartown';

> the park ranks among the finest in Ireland. It is a vast lawn, which waves over gentle hills, surrounded by plantations of great extent, and which break and divide in places, so as to give much variety. A large but gentle vale winds through the whole, in the bottom of which a small stream has been enlarged into a fine river ... there is a great variety on the banks of this vale; part of it consists of mild and gentle slopes, part steep banks of thick wood; in another place they are formed into a large shrubbery, very elegantly laid out, and dressed in the highest order, with a cottage, the scenery about which is uncommonly pleasing: and farther on, this vale takes a stronger character, having a rocky bank on one side, and steep slopes scattered irregularly, with wood on the other.[19]

Young appreciates the picturesque elements of Carton but, in a finesse often used in his work, he transfers that admiration from the aesthetically to the morally and practically pleasing, and his greatest enthusiasm is reserved for the productiveness of the landscape;

> On one of the most rising grounds in the park is a tower, from the top of which the whole scenery is beheld; the park spreads on every side in fine sheets of lawn, kept in the highest order by 1100 sheep, scattered over with rich plantations, and bounded by a large margin of wood, through which is a riding. From this building his Grace

xiv *The History of Ned Evans*

> has another sort of view, not every where to be met with; he looks over a great part of 60,000 acres; which lie around him nearly contiguous; and Ireland is obliged to him for spending the revenue on the spot that produces it.[20]

A Tour in Ireland is in general highly critical of the prevailing rural status quo, and alert to the resentment it encourages. Young expatiates in particular against that aspect of anti-papist legislation which entirely undermined any meaningful or secure system of land tenure. Catholics were unable to hold a lease for more than thirty-one years, and Catholic freeholders were barred from entailing their property, ensuring that their land and houses were gavelled – that is, equally distributed among all the sons in a family, a practice which soon reduced the descendants of the great Irish families to penury and meant that the great houses passed into the hands of Ascendancy landowners.[21] Any convert to the Church of Ireland automatically became sole heir to freeholds and leaseholds, immediately reducing their parents to the status of tenants-for-life. Young saw that these measures were retarding agricultural progress in Ireland, creating a system in which rackrenting middlemen – 'the most oppressive species of tyrant that ever lent assistance to the destruction of a country' – flourished and undertenants continued, 'the barbarous custom of having the whole farm laid waste at the end of a lease, and every inch ploughed up'.[22] There was simply no incentive for the vast majority of tenant farmers to invest in their land and even if they did improve it, they risked losing it, since anyone who reported that a tenant was paying substantially less rent than the land was worth was entitled to take over the remainder of the tenancy. Cotters, who held their land on a even more tenuous basis, were still worse off, and Hervey notes the parlous situation of such families in Volume II (see pp. 166–8). As Young asked, 'where is there a people in the world to be found industrious under such a circumstance?'.[23]

Like Maria Edgeworth's *Castle Rackrent* (1800), *Ned Evans* uses Young's *Tour through Ireland* to comment on Irish society and Irish politics. Young is far from certain that Ireland is in safe hands under the Ascendancy and while he approves the efforts of improving landowners, he criticizes those who, far from aiming to imitate English parkland or demesne, seem to be succumbing to native ways, 'the residence surrounded by walls, or hedges, or cabbins; and the lawn enclosure scattered with animals of various sorts, perhaps three miles off' with a garden of 'five, six, ten, and even twenty Irish acres ... but generally double or treble what is necessary'.[33] As the proximity of great house and 'cabbin' suggests, these landowners are dangerously close to turning native, and with their haphazard, wasteful notions, are hardly ideal custodians of the landscape. The estate owned by Hervey's Nettlefield, is an example of just such disastrous Ascendancy land management.

Introduction xv

his estate lay about five miles from Ravensdale, and the demesne might have very properly been called after the name of its proprietor. The nettles and other weeds which were spread over what they called the lawn, might have furnished specimens to the botanists of all the baneful vegetables that were to be found in these climates among which a few haggard-looking kine ... were picking their dangerous and scanty food ... the house stood solitary in the midst ... part of it seemed in ruins

(see p. 162).

Young Nettlefield has so far abandoned his Anglo-Irish roots as to agree to be married by a Catholic priest in order that he can later abjure the marriage (see p. 146). When, at the end of the novel, he agrees to manage his estate as Ned directs, the reader should understand that the worst excesses of the Ascendancy are being checked by the wise and benign rule of Irish nationalism.

There is another episode in the novel which requires a familiarity with Young's *Tour through Ireland*. During a jaunt to a local panoramic beauty spot – a 'level plain on top of a mountain' – Lord Squanderfield, who is spoken of as a future Lord Lieutenant of Ireland, loses control of his horses when young Nettlefield decides to scare them. Squanderfield and Cecilia, whom he is driving in his carriage, are only saved from a serious accident by the quickness of Ned (see pp. 174–6). If Cecilia represents Ireland, as women in Irish literature so often do, then the symbolism of this averted accident is complex.[24] Ireland – Cecilia – is endangered by the malice of a certain type of Ascendancy landowner and the incapability of England and only the enlightened nationalist, the representative of the United Irishmen in the figure of Ned, can save her.

The incident takes place on an open space on top of a mountain, a space which Hervey describes with care; 'the top of this mountain is a level plain, containing about fifteen acres of ground, and which is as smooth and as richly covered with a short pile of velvet grass, as if it had been formed for a bowling green' (see pp. 174–5). This plain, with its preternaturally smooth surface, measured in acres, must evoke the image of a drained bog. Despite his confusion of Irish landscape terms, Young is clear that bogs can lie on high ground; 'all such bogs ... with a fall from them for draining, might very easily be improved into excellent meadow'.[25] The treatment which he advocates for improving them would produce just such a surface as Hervey describes;

the surface should be leveled and burnt, and I would advise nothing to be done for a year or two but rollers as heavy as might be, kept repeatedly going over it, to press and consolidate the surface ... probably the draining and rolling would bring up a fresh surface of vegetables ... sheep ... would encourage the white clover and grasses to vegetate strongly.[26]

xvi *The History of Ned Evans*

Young's *Tour through Ireland* is, in fact, obsessed with bogs. Early in Volume I, Young visits the farm of a Mr Rowley who 'keeps a very considerable domain in his hands; adjoining to it is a black turf bog of admirable use for firing'. This bog Young describes at length;

> I viewed it attentively, and am clear, that all such bogs as this with a fall from them for draining, might very easily be improved into excellent meadow. The surface is covered with heath about a foot high, and under that eight or nine feet deep of puffy stuff, which when burnt yields no ashes; then the bog turf ten feet deep cuts like butter, and under that a Marley limestone gravel. They have found at 14 feet deep evident marks of the plough in the soil at bottom, also remains of cabbins, cribs for cattle, mooses horns, oaks, yews, and fir'.[27]

What 'might very easily be improved into excellent meadow' has clearly already *been* excellent meadow once before. Irish history moves in circles, and Young himself circles back to the problem later in the text, reiterating the fact that, 'under some bogs of considerable depth there are yet to be seen the furrows of land once ploughed'. Young seizes on the remains of trees often discovered under bogland, noting that some, 'seem broken off, others appear to be cut' and others show 'the marks of fire on them' and concluding that:

> a forest cut, burnt, or broken down, is probably the origin of a bog ... the native Irish might cut and burn their woods enough for the tree to fall, and in the interim between such an operation, and successive culture, wars and other intestine divisions might prevent it in those spots, which so neglected afterwards become bogs ... the places where the traces of ploughing are found, I should suppose were once fields adjoining to the woods, and when the bog arose to a certain height it flowed gradually over the surrounding land.[28]

Yet even this solution raises the possibility that the same thing might happen again, that the draining and improvements which Young's *Tour* encourages will be swallowed up by a new tide of incompetent land management, followed by another round of 'wars and other intestine divisions'.

The spectre of 'wars and other intestine division' haunts *Ned Evans* too. As well as Young's encomium on Carton, the description of Ravensdale recalls Milton's description of Eden in *Paradise Lost*. Hervey returns to the poem over and over again, as she does to Virgil's *Aeneid*. Both these works are narratives of civil war and of the destruction and bloodshed attendant on every attempt at nation-building and Hervey's references to them were to prove prophetic. The image with which the novel closes – the paradise of Ravensdale under United Irish rule – would soon become blurred, vanishing altogether in the aftermath of the failed 1798 Uprising. For another century and more, the dream of Irish independence would remain in the realm of romance, along with wicked uncles, outrageous coincidences and fairytale endings.

Introduction xvii

Notes

1   S. D. Smith, *Slavery, Family, and Gentry Capitalism in the British Atlantic* (Cambridge: Cambridge University Press, 2006), p. 179, 203. *Slavery, Family and Gentry Capitalism* also has much more detail on Harvie and his brothers, and on Lascelles and Maxwell, who were Elizabeth's trustees.

2   Boswell, *The Correspondence and other Papers of James Boswell Relating to the Making of the Life of Johnson*, ed. M. Waingrow (1969), vol. 2 of *The Yale editions of the private papers of James Boswell*, p. 341. In 1741 Thomas Hervey published *A Letter from the Hon. Thomas Hervey to Sir Thomas Hanmer*, a scurrilous and vituperative attack on the former husband of his mistress which became notorious.

3   J. Todd, *Dictionary of American Women Writers* (Totowa, NJ: Rowman & Littlefield Publishers, Inc., 1985), p. 163.

4   'I return your ladyship the Herveyan letter, which is a more proper word than frantic: it did not surprise me at all: his father was always attempting to excite compassion by the most virulent abuse on his nearest relations. Besides, I have seen and received parallel epistles. I had one a year and a half ago: I made no answer, but told Mrs. E. Hervey, his mother's and his most kind friend, that I could not refuse giving a little money to a man of quality, with whose family I had been so much acquainted all my life; and did give her five guineas for him. He, I know from Lady Ailesbury, has grossly abused Mrs. E. Hervey since to whom he has had great obligations. He wrote to me again this spring; I threw his letter into the fire, and sent no reply. I would not hinder Lord Ossory's charity, but he certainly had better not write, for when a gentleman can beg in that abject manner, he would probably print the letter, like many of those worthless beings whose flattery and scurrility are employed indifferently for half a crown' (Letter of Horace Walpole to Lady Ossory, 12 December 1789, 412). Mrs E. Hervey was the Colonel's unmarried aunt, to whom Elizabeth Hervey the author was very much attached. Lady Ailesbury was a close friend, often mentioned in Elizabeth Hervey's letters. Hervey's eldest son cannot have been more than fourteen at the time and it seems unthinkable he would have been writing begging letters to Walpole, so it would appear that the Colonel was still alive in 1789.

5   W. N. Hargreaves-Mawdsley, in *The English Della Cruscans and Their Time, 1783–1828* (Martinus Nijhoff: The Hague, 1967), twice mentions the affair; 'nor had Merry been long in solacing himself for the loss of one mistress by acquiring another. This was Mrs. Hervey' (p. 143); 'the erratic life, the visits to Brussels, where the open liaison with Mrs. Hervey continued, had become public talk. On 20th February 1788 Lord Pembroke writes to Lord Herbert, agog to hear whether the rumours are true and that Merry has married, or is about to marry Mrs. Hervey, Beckford's half-sister he notes' (pp. 167–8).

6   'I have seen Mrs. Hervey the Woman whom della Crusca had Thoughts of marrying while they lived much together at Brussels; he wrote me word once I remember, yt "He should soon be married or go to Smyrna; & that he run about equal Chance of catching the *Plague* either way." He who could so express himself did wisely to let the first Project dye away; & I now do believe it was *his* Fault; for the Lady seems Lovesome, & I fancy lends him Money from Time to Time. She is born a Hamilton, has been Wife to the Bastard Boy yt Lady Hanmer brought Tom Hervey, which Intrigue gave rise to the famous Pamphlet so attentively preserv'd for Love of its Obscenity -- & She is Authoress of a Novel called Louisa. I think 'tis pity the affair went no further – such an Adventurous Dame was fit for Della Crusca; & She has an agreable person enough, tho' no Pretensions

xviii *The History of Ned Evans*

to Beauty. Mrs. Lewis & I call her the little Faery Instruction from Miss Talbot's Tale for Babies' (*Thraliana: the Diary of Mrs. Hester Lynch Thrale, 1776–1809*, ed. K. C. Balderston, 2 vols (Oxford: Clarendon Press, 1942), p. 762).

7   Byron, *Letters and Journals of Lord Byron with notices of his life*, ed. T. Moore (Paris: Galignani, 1830), p. 298. The Countess of Westmorland, describing Hervey as 'a little old lady of sixty eight, full of cleverness', explains that she was a friend of Byron's wife's mother and that she only 'nearly fainted', *The Correspondence of Priscilla, Countess of Westmorland, 1813–1870*, ed. Lady R. Weigall (London: 1909: reprinted by Kessinger Publishing Ltd., n.p., n.d.), p. 22.

8   In October 1818 Thomas Moore notes in his journal that he, 'talked of Beckford's two mock novels, Azemia & The Elegant Enthusiast, which he wrote to ridicule the novels written by his sister Mrs. Harvey (I think) who read these parodies on herself quite innocently, & only now & then suspecting they were meant to laugh at her' (*The Journal of Thomas Moore, Volume 1*, ed. W. S. Dowden, B. Bartholomew, J. L. Linsley (Brunswck NJ, London and Mississauga, Ontario: Associated University Presses, 1983), p. 70).

9   The *OED* cites a passage from Hervey's 1800 novel *The Mourtray Family* as one of the earliest uses of the word 'romantic' to mean 'fantastic' or 'impractical' and a similar use seems meant here. *Ned Evans* is cited ten times in the current edition of the OED online.

10   See William Hervey's *Journals of the Hon, William Hervey, in North America and Europe, From 1755 to 1814, Suffolk Green Book*s, no. 15 (Bury St Edmund's: Paul & Mathew, 1906). He left keepsakes both to Hervey and to one of her sons in his will.

11   *Hamlet*, III.ii.16–34.

12   Simon Schama's *Rough Crossings: Britain, the Slaves and the American Revolution* (London: BBC Books, 2005), notes the experience of former slaves who joined the British army during and immediately after the American Revolutionary War (pp. 113–162).

13   The details of Lord Edward's life given here are drawn from S. Tillyard, *Citizen Lord: Edward Fitzgerald 1763–1798* (London: Chatto & Windus, 1997) and K. Whelan, 'New Light on Lord Edward Fitzgerald', *History Ireland* (Winter 1999), pp. 40–4.

14   See J. Mee, '"The Magician no Conjuror": Robert Merry and the Political Alchemy of the 1790s' in *Unrespectable Radicals? Popular Politics in the Age of Reform*, ed. M. T. Davis and P. A. Pickering (Aldershot: Ashgate, 2008) pp. 41–96.

15   As it still appears in certain Northern Irish Unionist imagery.

16   M. H. Thuente, *The Harp Restrung: the United Irishmen and the Rise of Irish Literary Nationalism* (Syracuse, NY: Syracuse University Press, 1994), pp. 26–35.

17   B. Boydell, 'The United Irishmen, Music, Harps, and National identity' in *Eighteenth-Century Ireland/Iris an dá chultúr*, 13 (1998), pp. 44–51, p. 46.

18   *The celebrated Shannon ... of peace*: A. Young, *A Tour in Ireland: with General Observations on the Present State of that Kingdom. Made in the Years 1776, 1777, and 1778, and brought down to the End of 1779,* 2 vols (Dublin: James Williams, 1780), vol. 2, pp. 34–5. Compare with:

> A happy rural seat of various view;
> Groves whose rich trees wept odorous gums and balms
> Others whose fruit burnished with golden rind
> Hung amiable, Hesperian fables true
> If true, here only, and of delicious taste.

Betwixt them lawns, or level downs, and flocks
Grazing the tender herb, were interspersed
Or palmy hillock or the flowery lap
Of some irriguous valley spread her store,
Flowers of all hue and without thorn the rose.
Another side umbrageous grots and caves
Of cool recess, o'er which the mantling vine
Lays forth her purple grape and gently creeps
Luxuriant: meanwhile murmuring waters fall
Down the slope hills dispersed, or in a lake,
That to the fringed bank with myrtle crowned
Her crystal mirror holds, unite their streams.

(Milton, *Paradise Lost*, IV.247–63)

19 Young, *A Tour in Ireland,* vol. 1, p. 23.
20 Ibid., pp. 23–4.
21 Under the Irish version of gavelling or gavelkind, 'the inferiour Tennantries were partible amongst all the Males of the Sept, both Bastards and Legittimate' (OED).
22 Young, *A Tour in Ireland*, vol. 1, p. 49.
23 Ibid., p. 48.
24 See Thuente for a discussion of the symbolism attached to Irish women in Irish literature (35 ff.).
25 Young, *Tour through Ireland*, vol. 1, p. 30.
26 Ibid., p. 74.
27 Ibid., p. 30.
28 Ibid., vol. 2, p. 73.

SELECT BIBLIOGRAPHY

Adair, J., *The History of the American Indians* (London, 1775).

Beckford, W., *Modern Novel Writing, or the Elegant Enthusiast* (1796).

—, *Azemia, a Novel: Containing Imitations of the Manner, both in Prose and Verse, of Many of the Authors of the Present Day; with Political Strictures* (London, 1797).

Boydell, B., 'The United Irishmen, Music, Harps, and National identity' in *Eighteenth-Century Ireland/Iris an dá chultúr*, 13 (1998), pp. 44–51.

Coleridge, S. T., *Critical Review: or Annals of Literature*, 18 (November 1796), p. 341

Fielding, H., *Joseph Andrews* and *Shamela*, ed. D. Brooks and M. C. Battestin (Oxford: Oxford University Press, 1970, 1999).

Fulford, T., *Romantic Indians: Native Americans, British Literature, and Transatlantic Culture 1756–1830* (Oxford: Oxford University Press, 2006).

Hargreaves-Mawdsley, W. N., *The English Della Cruscans and Their Time, 1783–1828* (The Hague: Martinus Nijhoff, 1967).

Hervey, E., *Melissa and Marcia, or The Sisters* (London, 1788).

—, *Louisa* (London, 1790).

—, *The Church of Saint Siffrid* (London, 1797).

—, *The Mourtray Family* (London, 1800).

—, *Amabel, or Memoirs of a Woman of Fashion* (London, 1814).

—, MSS. Beckford c.32 fol. 88–122 and fol. 123–49. Bodley, Special Collections.

Hervey, T., *A letter from the Hon. Thomas Hervey to Sir Thomas Hanmer* (n.p., 1741).

Hervey, W., *Journals of the Hon, William Hervey, in North America and Europe, From 1755 to 1814*, Suffolk Green Books, no. 15 (Bury St Edmund's: Paul & Mathew, 1906).

Loeber, R. and M. Loeber, *Ireland in Fiction, 1650–1900* Dublin: Four Courts Press, 2006).

Mee, J., '"The Magician no Conjuror": Robert Merry and the political alchemy of the 1790s' in *Unrespectable Radicals? Popular Politics in the Age of Reform*, ed. M. T. Davis and P. A. Pickering (Aldershot: Ashgate, 2008), pp. 41–96.

Milton, J., *Paradise Lost*, the poems of Milton, ed. J. Carey and A. Fowler (Longman: London, 1968; Norton, New York, 1972).

Moore, T., *The Journal of Thomas Moore, Volume 1*, ed. W. S. Dowden, B. Bartholomew, J. L. Linsley (Brunswck NJ, London and Mississauga, Ontario: Associated University Presses, 1983).

Richards, E., *Debating the Highland Clearances*. (Edinburgh: Edinburgh University Press, 2007).

Sadleir, M. 'Elizabeth Hervey and Some Anonymous Novels', *Notes and Queries*, 153 (1927), p. 350.

Smith, A. E., '"Julias and Louisas": Austen's *Northanger Abbey* and the Sentimental Novel', *English Language Notes*, 30 (1992–3), pp. 1, 33–42.

Smith, C., *Emmeline, or The Orphan of the Castle* (1788), ed. L. Fletcher (Ontario: Broadview Editions, 2003).

—, *The Old Manor House* (1793), ed. J. Labbe (Ontario: Broadview Editions, 2002, 2005).

Smith, S. D., *Slavery, Family and Gentry Capitalism in the British Atlantic: the world of the Lascelles, 1648–1834* (Cambridge: Cambridge University Press, 2006)

Thrale Piozzi, H., *Thraliana: the Diary of Mrs. Hester Lynch Thrale, 1776–1809*, ed. K. C. Balderston, 2 vols (Oxford: Clarendon Press, 1942).

Thuente, M. H., *The Harp Restrung: the United Irishmen and the rise of Irish literary nationalism* (Syracuse, NY: Syracuse University Press, 1994).

Tillyard, S., *Citizen Lord: Edward Fitzgerald 1763–1798* (London: Chatto & Windus, 1997).

Todd, J. (ed.), *A Dictionary of British and American Women Writers, 1660–1800* (Totowa, NJ: Rowman & Littlefield Publishers, Inc., 1985).

Virgil, *Aeneid*, ed. R. D. Williams (1973; Bristol: Bristol Classical Press, 1998)

Whelan, K., 'New Light on Lord Edward Fitzgerald' in *History Ireland* (Winter 1999), pp. 40–4.

Young, A., *A Tour in Ireland: with General Observations on the Present State of that Kingdom. Made in the Years 1776, 1777, and 1778, and brought down to the End of 1779*, 2 vols (Dublin: James Williams, 1780).

NOTE ON THE TEXT

I have used the Chawton House Library copy of the first edition of *The History of Ned Evans* (G. G. and J. Robinson, London 1796) as the copy text and have altered very little. The text appeared in two volumes in a (presumably pirated) Dublin and Philadelphia edition in 1796, reprinted in 1797 and in 1805. A second authorized London edition, again in four volumes, appeared in 1797 and a four-volume French translation in 1800, under the title *Histoire de Ned Evans* (Paris: Michel, Billois).

Spelling, punctuation and capitalization (or lack thereof) remain unchanged, except for letters, which appear in modern style. Obvious errors have been silently corrected. The original pagination is indicated by the symbol '/'.

THE HISTORY OF NED EVANS.

THE

HISTORY

OF

NED EVANS.

'O'erstep not the modesty of Nature!'[1]
Shakespeare.

IN FOUR VOLUMES.

VOL. I.

LONDON:

PRINTED FOR G. G. AND J. ROBINSON,
PATERNOSTER-ROW.
M.DCC.XCVI.

THE HISTORY OF NED EVANS.

CHAP. I.

In one of those beautiful and retired valleys which abound in the country once known by the general name of Snowdon, and which now forms a part of the country of Caernarvon, was seated the humble but hospitable dwelling of the reverend Evan Evans.[2] The high mountain of Penmanmawr defended this little mansion from the chilling blasts of the north east; whilst a stream purer/ than crystal ran murmuring among the rocks which time and the winter's torrents had separated from the neighbouring mountains, forming a series of successive water-falls before his windows, and clothing its banks with an eternal verdure. Thousands of sheep, whose fleeces might vie with snow in whiteness, were the happy tenants of this peaceful vale; whose innocent bleatings, being echoed by surrounding woods, and mixed with the songs of birds and the murmurs of the brook, formed a concert of natural and soothing music, which art can seldom equal, and never excel. Here Mr. Evans had resided for upwards of eighteen years, and exercised the pastoral office literally over his sheep, and figuratively over a numerous parish in a manner that won him the hearts of all his congregation.

The reader must not imagine however that Mr. Evans was a beneficed clergyman.[3] He had indeed long fulfilled the/ duties of one with respectable abilities, and with conscientious and unceasing diligence; but the emoluments were reaped by a gentleman who had never seen the parish but once, when he quarrelled with the parishioners about his tythes,[4] and had therefore resolved never to come among them again. It is possible however they had no great loss, for the trust was faithfully executed by the worthy Evans for the small salary of 201. a year, which, with the profits of a few acres round his little dwelling, and which could hardly be estimated at above 201. more, was all the income he possessed in the world. But though fortune had dealt thus hardly by him, nature had been more benignant; for from her he inherited an excellent constitution both of body and mind, and, what was still more valuable, a heart overflowing with kindness, and replete with every virtue that could ennoble and exalt a man.

4 *The History of Ned Evans*

Mr. Evans moreover was happy in an excellent wife, whom he had/ married in his youth from the uncommon motive of pure affection, without any view either to interest or fortune; and which was inspired by the equally uncommon quality of unalterable sweetness of temper, which gave her a look of benignity surpassing beauty, and which she now retained in full perfection at an age when beauty (if she ever had any) would have been considerably impaired. She had now lived with her husband upwards of thirty years in happy wedlock; and I heard her declare, that in all that time she had never differed with him but once, and that too was on a point about which it might be presumed he had no right to interfere. It was soon after he took her home to a little house he had in the neighbouring diocese of St. Asaph (where indeed he was born, and where he first served a cure,[5] before he removed to his present dwelling) that the good woman was employed on her first brewing of ale; a matter of very considerable/ importance to a Welch housewife, and of no less moment to a Welch parson; and honest Evans, being an adept in the art, and a perfect connoisseur in the true smack of cwrw (as ale is called in his country), took the liberty to find fault with his wife's management; which it must be confessed was a tender point, and what no husband ought to presume to do. It is therefore not to be wondered at if the good lady for the first time in her life was a little off her guard, and defended her undoubted prerogative of managing her drink as she thought fit; it is much more to be admired, that this was the last time as well as the first that she ever differed from her husband. And indeed she had candour enough to declare, that it was the event of this quarrel which confirmed her in perfect submission ever after; for certain it is, the ale proved sour, which she wisely ascribing to the tartness of some speeches she chanced then to let fall, determined from/ that time forth that no ill humour of hers should ever again be the cause of a domestic calamity – a resolution which she has inviolably kept ever since, and which I should most heartily recommend to all those good wives who may chance to peruse this story.

Mrs. Evans, while she resided at St. Asaph, had borne to her husband one daughter, whom they named Winifrid, from a lady of illustrious beauty and virtue in those parts, whose name has long since been enrolled amongst the martyrs and saints in heaven; and indeed the cherub countenance and the opening virtues of the little terrestrial Winifrid[6] filled her parents hearts with the fond and pleasing hope that she would one day rival the saint in every excellence both of body and mind; but Providence thought fit to determine otherwise, and took her to himself in the seventh year of her age. The afflicted parents sustained their loss with that meekness and resignation/ which true wisdom, and a just sense of religion never fail to inspire. They were however so far infected with human weakness that their home became disagreeable to them. They could not bear the walks in which they no longer saw their little darling: and the neat bit of garden before the house in which she used to play, and where with transport they so often beheld her tying up the flowers, and with artless innocence displaying taste even in her most careless diversions, for ever recalled her to their mind, and filled their eyes with a fountain of perpetual sorrow, too tender and too distressing for hearts so susceptible as theirs to endure. It was this melancholy event which first determined them to quit St. Asaph; and the cure in Caernarvonshire soon after offering, they gladly removed to it; but not before Heaven had assuaged their sorrow by sending them a son, who at the opening of this history was in the nineteenth year of his age. This/ darling boy, whose name was Edward, and in whom all their cares and all their hopes were now centered, was every way worthy of their tenderest affection. His beauty was of that manly kind where robust strength is united to perfect elegance: the blushes of the morning seemed to be lighted up in his cheeks, which glowed with health, and which were shaded by his thick and glossy hair, that played about his neck in natural curls; whilst wit tempered with good nature beamed from his dark eyes, whose fire was softened without being concealed by a pair of long eye-lashes of the deepest brown. There was, besides, a grace and majesty in his figure that would have bestowed dignity upon a clown, and which was far surpassing any thing that could be expected from the son of a Welch curate.

Nor was the mind of this amiable youth any way inferior to his person. It had been the delightful task of Mr./ Evans to form his heart from the first dawn of opening reason, and nature had been so kind as to give him a heart, than which a worthier was never planted in a human breast. Under the care of this kind instructor he had acquired a competent knowledge of the Latin and Greek languages; and having an elegant turn for music and painting, which indeed the scenes about him had naturally inspired, he had improved those talents merely by the dint of industry and genius in a wonderful manner, and had acquired many accomplishments that adorn the gentleman, to a degree infinitely beyond what could be expected from the humility of his station and the lowness of his finances.[7] For this he was indebted to a happy disposition of nature, which drank instruction more greedily than it could be offered; and as the excellent character of Mr. Evans made every thing that belonged to him an object of regard, young Edward found no difficulty in being admitted/ to the best companies in the neighbourhood, where his own good qualities were soon known and admired, and every where established him a general favourite. In these societies his good sense soon taught him to distinguish what was most estimable; and though he never remembered to have been fifty miles from the sequestered habitation in which he dwelt, yet neither his figure nor his manners would have been reckoned awkward in any drawing room in Europe.

Such was Ned Evans, the subject of the following memoirs; for whose welfare and success the author confesses himself deeply interested, and to whom he trusts the reader is already not wholly indifferent; and he hopes that, in the course of his future history, he will never be found to act unbecoming his character, nor give occasion to forfeit that good opinion which his first appearance generally inspired./

CHAP. II.

It was one night in the month of November in the year 1779,[8] that our good curate and his amiable wife had sat down to regale themselves over a mug of ale and a plate of toasted cheese; when they were suddenly startled by a bright flash of lightning, which was instantly followed by a tremendous clap of thunder. Mrs. Evans was naturally timorous, and more afraid of thunder than of any thing else in the world; and though her husband was not subject to this weakness, yet the uncommon loudness of the peal, and the season of the year when thunder is but a rare phenomenon, hindered him to be altogether at case; especially as it was not long before that a house in the neighbourhood had been set on fire by lightning, and much mischief done, though/ the family had the good fortune to escape. But it was not for his house, nor for himself, that his fears were alarmed on this occasion; the morning had been uncommonly fine, and he had taken advantage of it to send Ned as far as Bangor, about nine miles off, on some business he had with the register of the diocese; and Ned, being stout, and unwilling to tire his father's only horse, had taken an oaken staff in his hand, and trusted to his own legs for the journey; in which indeed his wisdom was as conspicuous as his humanity; for it is certain that his own two were much better and safer to be relied on than the other's four. Be that as it may, he was not yet come back, though it was long past the hour he had been expected; and as he was not accustomed to stay on any errands, and the night was now set in with all its horrors of storm and of darkness, we may forgive our worthy curate, if he began to be disturbed by some rising fears; which however he/ endeavoured to suppress out of compassion to his wife, who was now in such an agony of terror as could not support itself under any addition. Long did they listen with attentive and expecting ears, hoping to hear the welcome tread of Ned's active and nimble feet; the ale and the cheese (now cold) were suffered to stand neglected on the table; whilst the good man holding his wife's left hand in his right, while her head rested on his bosom, spoke not to her, but looked unutterable tenderness and affection. He was supporting her in this tender attitude, and endeavouring to soothe her fears, when Towser,[9] who was Ned's favorite dog, and was lying on the hearth, set up a loud and melancholy howl; which was presently followed by the

8 *The History of Ned Evans*

trampling of horses, and the sound of many voices at the gate. Poor Mrs. Evans, who had long been wound up to the highest pitch of terror, could not support this new alarm, and immediately/ fainted in her husband's arms; who was himself in a condition not much better, bawling in vain to their only maid to come to her mistress's assistance; but she had long since crept into her bed, terrified at the thunder, where she lay smothering under the clothes, incapable of hearing, and afraid even to draw her breath. The noise now grew louder, and approached the house, when Mr. Evans distinctly heard Ned's voice calling for assistance, and begging him to open the door. The agitation the poor man was in is not to be described; his wife still senseless in his arms, and his boy, for aught he knew, about to be murdered at the gate. He had presence of mind however to lay her gently in an arm chair which happily stood by him, and then endeavouring to spring to the door, he unluckily overthrew the table, with his ale and his cheese, and, what was far more unfortunate, the candle, which was extinguished in the fall. All was now darkness and/ confusion, Ned still thundering at the door, and calling on his father. 'What, in the name of God, has happened to you?' said he, as he endeavoured to unbolt the lock; 'Nothing to myself,' cried Ned, 'but every thing that is disastrous to two unhappy ladies, one of whom is in my arms.' 'Thank God! Thank God!' replied the honest curate, not considering what he said, but rejoiced to find that Ned at least was safe; when continuing to fumble about the lock, the youth's patience was exhausted, and driving his foot against the door with all his force, he burst it open with such violence, that it laid the old gentleman sprawling on the floor. Ned then came in, supporting the lady, who was altogether senseless; and finding his father on the ground, 'My dear Sir,' said he, 'I hope I have not hurt you: I heartily beg your pardon; for, on my soul! I meant you no disrespect, but the situation of this unhappy lady must excuse me.' 'It does, it does, my dear/ boy, were it ten times worse; I am not hurt, and if I was, the joy of seeing you safe would cure me.' He now rose from the floor, and groping into the kitchen, discovered Molly in her covert,[10] whom he quickly unlodged, and set about endeavouring to recover a light. A candle at length was brought, and discovered a spectacle of sorrow, the extent of which was not known before; Ned, wet to the skin, supporting in his arms a beautiful creature of about seventeen, dressed in a travelling habit of the most elegant fashion: her hair dark as the wing of the raven, was floating all dishevelled, over her lovely bosom, which just heaved with breath; and her cheek all pale as ashes, lay reclined upon his neck; her eyes seemed closed in death; and she was wholly unconscious where she was, or how there, or what had happened. Behind were two postillions bearing in the body of another female, dressed with the same elegance, but advanced in/ years; whilst blood was streaming from a wound which she had received in her breast. Poor Evans stood motionless with horror and astonishment; wholly regardless of his wife, who was now come to herself, but equally entranced with terror and surprise. At length he found utterance; and clasping his hands together, 'Oh! Ned,' he cried, 'who is this angel you have brought here, and what has befallen her?' 'Alas! Sir,' said he, 'I cannot tell – all I know, I shall relate. As I was coming home from Bangor (where, as it now turns out, I was fortunately detained), about a hundred yards beyond the turning to the house, I met a post chaise and four on the turnpike road: it had globes with lights in them, by the glimmering of which I saw it suddenly attacked by two highwaymen on horseback; one of whom stopped the foremost postillion, whilst the other went to the window of the chaise. I soon after heard a female shriek, when springing/ forward to give them what assistance I could afford, I was lucky enough to knock the scoundrel at the window down with the oak stick I had in my hand; which the other fellow seeing, immediately quitted the postillion, and discharged a loaded blunderbuss, as I believe, into the chaise. The unfortunate lady whom you see killed, said, 'Oh God!' and instantly expired. This angel, whom you now see senseless in my arms, fell into them in this condition. The wicked perpetrators of this horrible act took advantage of the darkness and confusion, and have escaped. The postillions are no way to blame; they behaved as well as lads in their situation could do: they have preserved the trunks and the effects; and the wretched authors of all this mischief have no other prey but the life of this innocent and unfortunate lady. I trust that the lovely object in my arms has no other hurt but fright, and I rejoice that Providence has so ordered it/ as to bring me to her assistance, and that the misfortune has happened so near the house which can afford her an asylum in her present comfortless and forlorn situation.' 'And I rejoice, too,' said honest Evans, 'and I bless my God, who has inspired you with courage and resolution to fear no danger in succouring the distressed, and who has given me this humble habitation to be a comfort and refuge to this fair unfortunate. Go, my dear,' said he, turning to his wife, who was now wholly recovered, 'go and see what cordial, or other thing you can find, that can help to restore her to her senses.' He now turned to the postillions, who were standing all this time, bearing the body of the murdered lady between them; and having assisted them to dispose it decently on chairs set for the purpose, he desired them to tell him all they knew of the matter. They said they were wholly ignorant who the ladies were, but they certainly were people of condition – /that they had come from London, and had crossed the ferry at Conway, about four o'clock – that they were on their way to Ireland, of which country they believed they were natives, and wishing to overtake the packet, which sails tomorrow from the Head, they were in haste to get on to Bangor this night; and had therefore, late as it was, taken a chaise and four at Conway for that purpose; that they had come on very well notwithstanding the storm till the highwaymen stopped them – and that all the rest was just as Mr. Edward had described it.

10 *The History of Ned Evans*

Mrs. Evans now returned, with the remains of a bottle of Hungary water,[11] which was the only thing she had in the house that was like a cordial (for she was not one of those good women, who, under the pretence of weak nerves and windy stomachs, are for ever taking drams disguised with the name of cordial waters); and with this she bathed the/ lady's temples, while her husband held a bottle of salts to her nose, Ned Evans still supporting her in his arms. In a little time she fetched a deep sigh; and soon after raising her languid eyes, which still shone, though with diminished lustre, 'Where am I?' said she, 'and into what 'hands am I fallen?' – 'You are fallen into honourable hands,' replied Evans; 'into hands that shall be exerted to the utmost to administer to you every comfort and consolation they can procure, and which your appearance and situation so justly demand.' 'Whoever you are, Sir,' said she, 'I thank you; greatly, greatly do I thank you.' 'Dear lady,' said Ned, 'let me support you to this arm chair; sit down a little and endeavour to be composed, till we can get you some refreshment.' She now raised herself upon her feet, when turning to be led, and beholding the body of her companion where Evans and the postillions had laid it out, she sprang to it with renewed strength,/ and throwing herself on her knees and embracing it in her arms, 'Oh! Mrs. Melville,' said she, 'my dear, my faithful, my parental friend, have I lost you for ever!' She kissed the corpse with an intense fervor, and turning up her eyes to Heaven, she burst into a violent flood of tears.

Mrs. Evans and Ned would have gone to her and endeavoured to force her to the chair; but Mr. Evans forbade them. 'Let her alone awhile,' said he; 'her heart is agitated to the last degree, and tears will be the speediest and most effectual relief.' They suffered her then to remain unmolested; and she continued in the same posture, and with the same unceasing flow of sorrow, for about a quarter of an hour: at length she stopped, and rising from the body, 'It is enough,' said she; 'you are gone, and you are a blessed inhabitant of heaven. I am left on earth to deplore the best and most beloved of friends.' Ned now stepped/ forward, and offering her his hand, she suffered herself to be led to the arm chair, and composedly sat down. A deep silence was kept for some minutes. At length Mr. Evans ventured to speak: 'I lament, Madam,' said he, 'with the deepest and most unfeigned sorrow, the fatal event which has procured me the honour of seeing you in this house: nevertheless, it is a consolation to me, that my son here has been the means of affording you some relief, and of conducting you to this humble habitation; and I promise you, both for my wife and for myself, that you cannot oblige us more than by considering yourself at home, and making use of such accommodation as it affords, as long as it may be necessary or agreeable to you to stay.' 'Yes, indeed, Madam,' said Mrs. Evans, 'both my husband and I will think it the happiest incident in our lives to accomodate you on this melancholy occasion; and we only lament that our entertainment cannot be equal/ to what, from your appearance, you have certainly been accustomed to: but, such as it is, we hope you will accept it.' 'Yes, Madam,' replied the lady, 'I will gladly and thankfully accept it; and I think myself happy that when so sudden and so dreadful a calamity came upon me, Providence has graciously conducted me to such hospitable and benevolent minds as yours.' Then, turning to Ned, she said, 'I find it is to you, young gentleman, I am indebted for this generous deliverance. I beg your pardon, I ought indeed to have recollected it before; but the sad confusion of my thoughts and hurry of my spirits must plead my excuse. I am glad, however, that I now know you for my protector and deliverer; and you may assure yourself that my gratitude shall cease only with my life.'

Ned's face was covered with blushes; but presently recollecting himself, 'Dear lady,' he said, 'your condescension overwhelms/ me; you owe me no gratitude: I did nothing but my duty, and what was the duty of every man on the like occasion; and had my life been the forfeit of it, I should gladly have given it to rescue yours.' 'That you have ventured it indeed,' said the lady, 'is abundantly apparent, and I should be unworthy of the protection you have afforded me, if I should ever forget it.' She now asked for a glass of water, which being brought her, Mr. Evans told her that he was extremely sorry it was out of his power, at that time, to ask her to qualify it with any better liquor. 'I have indeed,' said he, 'some excellent ale of my own brewing, which, if you ever taste that liquor, I can venture to recommend: but as for wine, Madam, I am but a poor curate, and never was master of a dozen in all my life; though, could I have foreseen the honour of having you for my guest, I should have taken care not to have been wholly unprovided.' She thanked him with an obliging smile, and told him that/ at that time no liquor whatever was so agreeable to her as pure spring water. 'I am sorry, indeed,' said she, 'for your own sake, that fortune has not bestowed on you whatever is thought comfortable in life: but for myself, I entreat you will not give yourself the smallest uneasiness. I trust that in a few days I shall be able to continue my journey to Ireland, where my friends live, and where I am extremely anxious to be; in the mean time I must be indebted to you for the protection of your house, which is all I stand in need of at present, and shall cheerfully and thankfully put up with your own fare, whatever it may be.'

Mrs. Evans then asked her if she could not be prevailed on to eat a bit of something; 'there is very good butter and cheese in the house,' said she, 'and if you could fancy it, I could get you a Welsh rabbit[12] in a few minutes:' the lady assured her that she could not taste any thing, but would be obliged to her, if, as soon as was convenient,/ she would shew her to her chamber. The good woman replied, that she believed her room was by that time ready; that she would go and see; and when it was, would immediately come back and conduct her to it. In a short time she returned with a candle; and the lady rising, curtsied to the two gentlemen, and wished them a good night. As she passed the body of her departed friend, she stopped for about a minute, and contemplated it in silence;

12 *The History of Ned Evans*

she then took one of the hands, and, stooping down, kissed it with impassioned tenderness; her eyes swimming in tears were raised to heaven, and her lips seemed to say something, though her voice was not heard. She then rose, and wiping her tears with a cambrick handkerchief, withdrew.

The two gentlemen who were standing followed her with their eyes, and bowing as she went out of the room, remained fixed in thought for some time afterwards. Evans at length broke silence – 'Go, my dear boy,' said he to Ned, 'into the/ kitchen, and see that all the baggage of these unfortunate ladies be brought into the house: let the horses be taken care of as well as they can, and let the poor lads have a good fire, and plenty of ale to comfort them after this sad adventure.'

Ned immediately went, and found things already taken care of in the manner prescribed. There was a lad at the house, one David Morgan, the son of a man who had lived as a farm-servant with Mr. Evans ever since he had come to that part of the country; this lad was much about Ned's age and size, a sturdy well-looking fellow as any of his station in the country; and as they had been brought up boys together, there subsisted a friendship and attachment between them, which made David a frequent inmate of the house, though he was not a regular servant in it. This lad was entertaining the two postillions, after having helped them with their horses, and trunks, &c. and extolling his young master's prowess and his own. 'Ah!' says he, 'if I had/ been there with young maister,[13] those scoundrel robbers should not have escaped.' 'Why, what would you have done?' said one of the postillions. 'We would have lent them such a flick,' said David, 'as they would never have been cured of but by the gallows.' 'Mayhap you would have found yourselves mistaken,' said the other; 'why they had fire arms with them, and what could you have done then?' 'Why the same as maister did with one of them,' said David. 'Damn them and their firearms together! if the Devil had been with them, with a pistol as big as Bangor steeple, I would na ha fear'd 'un, provided I had a prayer-book in my pocket, and young maister at my back.' 'Hut you fool you,' said Ned just then entering, 'hold your tongue, and drink your ale: it is not a week since I saw you frightened almost to death by farmer Watkins' white horse.' 'True, maister,' said the other, 'but then I took him for a ghost! I own I's woundily[14] afraid of dead men, but I do/ not fear any living man that ever wore a head.' 'Then,' said Ned, 'you are just the reverse of me; for I do not fear any dead man; but I will not be so vain as to assert that no living man could alarm me. But that is neither here nor there – are all the things brought safe out of the carriage, and are the horses fed?' Being answered in the affirmative, he told them they might sit on then and drink their ale, but charged them to make no noise, left they should disturb the poor lady who had gone to her repose; and so saying, he returned to the parlour.

It was now growing late, and as there were but two beds in the house, one of which the lady occupied, Ned asked his father if he would not come and sleep with him; for, as for Mrs. Evans, she slept upon a pallet[15] in the same chamber with the lady. Mr. Evans replied, that the sad adventure of the evening had driven all sleep out of his head. 'Besides, my dear,' said he, 'you know decency requires that some person/ should sit up with the corpse. Go, then, my dear boy, go you to your bed; you cannot be otherwise than fatigued; but as for me, I shall sit here until the morning.'

Ned then retired to rest; where we will leave him to that sound and refreshing sleep which innocence of mind, and health of body, never fail to bestow. Mr. Evans spent the greatest part of the night in prayer, as was his custom when any unusual accident beset him; and when he was not on his knees, he relieved himself by reading 'Sherlock upon Death,'[16] a book which he extremely admired, and which of all others seems best calculated to give comfort and consolation to an afflicted heart./

CHAP. III.

NED rose as soon as it was day; and being impatient to hear something of the lady, went immediately to the parlour to his father. 'Well, Sir,' said he, 'what tidings have you heard of our unfortunate lodger, and do you know how she has passed the night?' 'I have not heard a word,' said Mr. Evans, 'nor seen a creature but the maid, who has just been here to make up the fire; but go, my dear, and bid her tap at the door, and ask your mother how she is.' Ned did as directed, and then went out to see about the horses and postillions: they were up getting ready to go away. He desired them to go into the house, and get some cheese and ale for their breakfast, and not to go away without seeing his father. He then returned to the parlour, where he found Mrs. Evans sitting/ with her husband; when asking about the lady, 'Alas!' said she, 'poor soul, she has not closed her eyes the whole night, and indeed I am greatly alarmed for her health. She complains of a violent pain in her head and back, and is continually shivering with cold, though to the touch she is like a coal of fire. I am going to make her a little warm tea, which perhaps may throw her into a perspiration, and be of service to her.' 'Do, my dear,' said Evans, 'and I think it would be prudent to send to Conway for Doctor Jones, for God knows how her illness may turn out.' This thought was highly approved of, and Ned said that he would be himself the messenger, in order to be sure to bring him, let him be where he would; and now going out to order the horse, the postillions told him he should be welcome to a seat in their chaise, and they would engage to carry him quicker than any other conveyance. This was accepted of; and Mr. Evans finding the chaise had been/ paid for by the ladies at Conway, gave the lads half a crown each, in reward for their activity and attention; and Ned hastily taking off a bowl of milk, and eating a crust with it, set off at full speed with them. He got to Conway in little more than an hour, and was lucky enough to find Doctor Jones at home. The doctor was not a regular physician,[17] but had long practised as a surgeon and apothecary with good reputation. He was a benevolent and humane man; qualities which are peculiarly necessary in his profession, and which often do more in curing a patient than the drugs he swallows. When the doctor heard the tale, it awakened all his feelings: 'I will go with you, my friend,' said he, 'in ten minutes; I will only order

– 14 –

other horses for expedition, and I will take back the chaise at my own expence; for, exclusive of the lady who calls for all tenderness and attention, I would go to the world's end to serve your father or any of his family.' Ned thanked him/ for his kindness; and now finding that a chaise was to carry him back, he took care to get a dozen of the best wine that could be had in Conway, that the poor lady might want no comfort that could be procured for her. The rumour of the robbery and murder had reached Conway the night before; but now that Ned and the postillions appeared, every body crowded about them to hear the particulars. He satisfied them as concisely as he could, and then set off with the doctor for his father's, accompanied with the praises and the blessings of all who had heard the story. The lads drove at a good rate, and when Mr. Evans heard the chaise, guessing by its return that the doctor was come, he went out to meet him. 'My dear doctor,' said he, as he was alighting, 'I always am glad to see you, but never did your presence give me so much pleasure as at this instant; I am infinitely obliged to you for the haste you have made to visit my unfortunate guest, whose situation/ is so distressing, that all the tenderness and attention we can pay to her is not equal to her claim upon us for it.' 'Her situation is deplorable indeed', replied the doctor, 'and her claim for attention and tenderness as great: it is a consolation, however, to know that she has happened among those who can fully feel for her; and whose sympathetic hearts will do every thing that can alleviate her distress. Does she know,' continued he, 'that I have been sent for, or was it only a mere motion of your own?' 'She knows nothing about it,' replied Mr. Evans; 'my wife represented her to me to be in such a situation as I thought alarming; and as I know that in all distempers much may be done in the beginning, which, if that opportunity be lost, may never be able to be done afterwards, I took the liberty to send for you of my own head, without consulting her on the subject, which might perhaps have alarmed her more, and could answer no good end that I can see.' 'You have/ done wisely,' replied the doctor; 'it is of no consequence who sent for me, nor did I ask the question with any other view than merely to know the fact before I speak to herself; it is enough for me that she is in distress, and that she wants medical assistance; and I shall be happy, my dear friend, to go hand in hand with you in giving her that and every other assistance that the may happen to want. 'You speak like a gentleman and a christian,' replied Evans, 'and I only pray that our assistance may be effectual.' Mrs. Evans now came down; and the doctor, after the first salutation, enquiring about the lady, she told him she was just then in a doze, but it did not seem like one that would refresh her; she breathed hard, and started often, and sometimes muttered something which she could not understand. 'Will you step up yourself, doctor, and look at her? and you will be better able to judge.' 'No, my dear madam,' replied the doctor, 'I will not go to her till she is apprised of my coming./ If she happened to wake while I was at her bed-side, there is no saying what effect the seeing a stranger in her

16 *The History of Ned Evans*

room might have upon her in her present weak condition. Be you so good as to return to her, and sit by her till she wakes; and then tell her, that seeing her out of order, you took the liberty to send for me, as I lived in the neighbourhood, and ask her leave to bring me to her.' 'I believe indeed you are right,' replied Mrs. Evans; 'her spirits are so fluttered that she could not bear surprise of any kind; I will go and do as you bid me, and return again as soon as I am authorised.' Mr. Evans then offered the doctor some refreshment; and he said he would take a bit of dry toast and some mulled ale, for the day was cold, and he had come off without any breakfast. They talked of indifferent matters while this was preparing; and when it came, Ned's stomach was so complaisant as to enable him to assist the doctor very effectually in demolishing the ale and toast, together/ with half a dozen eggs that they got boiled. They had scarcely finished when Mrs. Evans came down, and acquainted the doctor that the lady had waked, and readily consented to see him. He immediately followed her up stairs; when he came to the bed side, and beheld the lovely object he came to see, he could not suppress the emotion her beauty and her distress inspired – he was obliged to turn aside his head to conceal the manly tear which trembled in his eye. The voice of the lady recalled him to himself. 'I am obliged to you, Sir,' said she, 'and to this kind gentlewoman, for the tender concern you seem to take for my health: I was in hopes to have been able to continue my journey home; but alas! I am very unable even to speak; and if Providence designs to make this my home, his will be done; I think I am content.' 'Oh, my dear madam!' replied the doctor, 'I trust you have many many years of health and happiness before you yet. It is natural, and/ what might be expected, that the violent shock your spirits have received should have an effect on your health, but I trust there is no reason to apprehend but that rest and a little time will perfectly restore you.' The lady gazed on him with a languid eye for a little time: at length the spoke again. 'Oh! Mrs. Melville – Sir – my dear Mrs. Melville – have you seen her? The robbers did not kill her – they could not kill her – has she slept, Sir? – do tell me, has she slept?' The doctor now perceived that she was raving, and that the dreadful accident of the night before had brought a fever on her spirits: he felt her pulse; and finding them extremely low, he told Mrs. Evans, that, for the present, there was nothing to be done but to keep her quiet – that rest was of the greatest importance to her – that the least sudden noise might prove fatal, or drive her into madness – that she must be soothed, and crossed in nothing; and for nourishment she might give her a little wine whey,[18] acidulated with/ juice of lemon, or a little cream of tartar; but that bleeding, or any thing of that kind, was highly improper. 'All that can be done at present is to keep her quiet, and endeavour to support her strength. I will call again to-morrow,' said he, 'and even stay with her, should it become necessary.' He now left the room totally unobserved by the lady, who indeed was not in a condition to observe any thing.

When he came to the parlour, Mr. Evans saw by his countenance the situation of the lady; he was anxious, yet afraid to ask him what he thought of her. The doctor relieved him from this embarrassment: 'It is happy, my dear friend,' said he, 'that you sent for me; vastly fortunate that I chanced to be in the way. This poor lady is in a most alarming situation, in a fever of the most critical and dangerous kind; it is not, however, infectious, nor need you fear that your humanity will be any otherwise wounded than in seeing this unfortunate lady die.'/

'What!' interrupted Ned in an agony of distress, 'is she dying?' 'No, no!' replied the doctor, 'I do not say that – God forbid! – I only mean that her illness is of a very dangerous kind, and her symptoms at present unfavourable. I do not despair, however, but that, with the blessing of God, she may come through.' 'May God Almighty graciously bestow that blessing upon us!' said Evans – 'and I trust he will, since it surely was by his inspiration that I sent for you.' The doctor then repeated to Mr. Evans the directions he had given above stairs to his wife, and when he mentioned wine whey, 'Good God!' said Evans, 'how forgetful I am! I protest there is not a drop of wine in the house. Oh! that I had thought of sending for it in the morning to Conway!' 'Do not be uneasy on that head, my dear Sir,' said Ned; 'I have taken care of that, and brought in the chaise a dozen of the best I could get.' 'Have you indeed?' said Evans; 'I rejoice at that, and/ cannot but admire and love that attention which I have always seen you pay to every person in distress.' 'Oh!' said Ned, 'this lady's distress is enough to awake attention in a stone.' 'It is indeed,' replied the doctor; and now finding the day advanced beyond the moon, he said his other patients required his attendance, and he must therefore return to Conway, but promised to be back again the next day. 'To-morrow,' said Mr. Evans, 'is Sunday, and therefore I shall be engaged all the morning; but do, my dear friend, contrive matters so as to stay and eat a bit of my own mutton with me; I shall be grieved if, when I come from church, I should find you gone.' The doctor said he could not promise for staying, as it depended upon his other patients whether he could do it with propriety or not; but that if he could, he would. So saying, he took leave; and Mr. Evans and Ned attending him to the door, he got into the chaise and drove off./

The rest of the day passed off in a thoughtful and serious manner, which, on Mr. Evans's part, was not uncommon, as he usually dedicated the evening of Saturday to the contemplation of his important duty the following day: but Ned's spirits were not used to be depressed; and indeed it required something very solemn and affecting to keep him serious half an hour together, for his heart by nature was turned to gaiety, which he had neither art nor necessity to conceal, and which diffused an air of cheerfulness over his countenance that did not at all accord with gravity and sedateness. In the evening, preparations were made for paying the last sad office to Mrs. Melville, who was still lying in the same spot where the postillions had deposited her. It was intended to inter her the fol-

18 *The History of Ned Evans*

lowing evening after prayer. Mrs. Evans therefore took care to have her properly dressed for the grave, and laid by her other clothes, and particularly her pockets, without examining their contents, in a place/ where they would be secure. When her coffin came home, Mr. Evans had her removed to an out-house, that the melancholy sound of nailing her up in it might not reach the ears of the lady above stairs, who was not able to bear noise of any kind, and least of all that which, if she suspected the occasion, would probably fit her for the same sad service. With regard to her situation, there was no material alteration in it. She continued extremely low and languid, sometimes in her senses, and sometimes wandering. She scarce ever spoke, except for a little drink. She did not appear to sleep, which, if it could be procured, was the best thing for her, but which hitherto she had not been able to do, at least in that quiet and composed manner which alone could tend to restore her. At night Mr. Evans and Ned sat down to their supper, and finished the most silent and thoughtful meal they had ever eaten together. Soon after they retired to the same bed to rest./ Youth and health soon procured Ned the blessing of quiet sleep; but Mr. Evans, notwithstanding his having sat up the night before, continued the greatest part of this night also in meditation and prayer./

CHAP. IV.

THE morning rose, and with it both the gentlemen. Ned was first dressed, and hastening up to the lady's apartment, tapped, with a timorous heart, at the door. Mrs. Evans opened it, and told him she could not perceive any material alteration; that she had been for the most part quiet, but without any refreshing sleep. If at any time she chanced to slumber, it was only for a few minutes, when she awoke in a terror; and she thought these slumbers did her more hurt than good. Poor Ned received the intelligence with a downcast look, and communicated it to his father, who partook of his sorrow. 'Yet let us not be altogether cast down, my boy, it is possible she may yet do well: and I shall, this day, in the church, offer up the prayer of the congregation, to beseech Almighty God to spare her to us.'/

They now went to breakfast, which on Ned's part was bread and milk, to which the parson (especially on Sunday) added a piece of cheese and a pint of warm ale. Cheese and ale are to a Welchman nectar and ambrosia; and our good curate, who loved hospitality as far as his circumstances would allow, took care to be always provided with plenty of both, and that the best of their kind.

When breakfast was over, he retired to prepare himself for church, whither he went as soon as he was dressed; but Ned staid at home that he might be in the way to receive the doctor when he came, and to execute any directions he might leave in case he could not stay dinner. The church was about half a mile from the house; and well attended by many genteel families in the neighbourhood, as well as by a numerous congregation of inferior note; all of whom respected Evans as a father, and could not fail to be virtuous as far as they followed either his precepts or/ example. His sermons were of that plain and natural kind which were suited to every understanding, and always upon topics which came home to every man's heart. He did not dwell on those abstruse doctrines, which, after all that can be said of them, must for ever remain inexplicable; but he enlarged on those important duties in which all christians are agreed, and which the divine Author of our religion has prescribed, in order to adorn and exalt our nature – to soften and correct the heart; that every man being guided by the dictates of right reason, and by faith in the promises of God, might regulate his life accordingly,

20 *The History of Ned Evans*

and thereby ensure himself respect in this world, and everlasting happiness in the next.

These discourses he delivered in a distinct and not ungraceful manner; and he must be either a very abandoned or very inattentive hearer indeed, who could be present at them without being affected by them. On this day he chose for his subject/, the shortness and extreme uncertainty of life; and spoke upon it with an unusual degree of eloquence and fervor. He alluded to the fatal and recent example which was at that time in his own house; and the whole sermon was a kind of funeral oration on the unfortunate Mrs. Melville, whose obsequies were to be performed in the evening. When service was over, most of the congregation crowded about him to ask about the unfortunate lady at his house, and to inform themselves of all the circumstances of the melancholy event: he had the pleasure to find Ned's conduct universally approved, and his praises echoed by every tongue; and he had likewise the satisfaction to receive many friendly offers of assistance on this occasion, and some of them of a very generous kind; a pleasing testimony how much he was esteemed and beloved by his people, and that his preaching had not been in vain. These offers, however, as they were not necessary, he politely declined; but not without warm/ commendations of their benevolence, as well as thanks for their kindness; and, mounting his horse, returned home, followed by the blessings and the prayers of his parishioners.

When he got to his own house, Ned met him at the door, and informed him that the doctor had not yet come, and that the poor lady was in the same way. This intelligence neither surprised nor disappointed him; he was rather pleased the doctor had not arrived, as it gave him greater hopes of his staying; and, at any rate, he would be glad to hear from himself his opinion of his unfortunate patient. In about a quarter of an hour he came; and, after first sending for Mrs. Evans, and consulting with her, he followed her up stairs to the lady. Evans and Ned remained below, in silent and pensive expectation of his return. At length he came down with the comfortless intelligence, that she was certainly no better, but rather otherwise; 'though not so much so,'/ said he, 'as to make me despond altogether. It is the nature of these nervous fevers to be slow and lingering, and to keep us long in suspense; I have sometimes seen patients so reduced as to appear altogether dead, yet afterwards recover and do well. I have brought here some medicines in my pocket, which you will cause to be given to her as directed.' Here he took out some phials, the contents and operations of which it is unnecessary here to relate. 'The best medicine,' said he, 'for her, is quiet and composed sleep; which if we could procure from nature, I should not wholly despair; but it must not be forced.' Mr. Evans promised that all his directions should be punctually followed; and Ned's face, which was the picture of distress before, began to resume its usual serenity, merely on the slender comfort that he did not wholly despair.

The doctor now endeavoured to divert them to other topics; and, among the rest, told them, that a suspicious fellow, who/ could not give a very good account of himself, had been taken up at Conway the night before, and was then in the jail – he had been examined before a magistrate, but nothing appeared that could convict him. He then said he thought Ned had better see him, as he might possibly know him again, or might embarrass him with questions that might tend to a discovery. Ned said he had no objection in the world to see him, and would go to the end of the earth to bring the villains to justice; but at the same time confessed he should be very tender how he swore any man's life away, or even gave suspicions of his character. 'In the present case,' said he, 'I fear I can be of little use; for unluckily it was so dark that I have not the smallest idea of the face or persons of the villains who attacked the chaise. All I know is, I knocked one of them down, and I am sure I hit him on the head. I'll warrant he bears the mark of the stick; and if this man you talk of has any such mark, it/ will be at least a good reason for detaining him in custody. To-night,' said he, 'I must attend the funeral of Mrs. Melville; but I will go to Conway in the morning, and, if you are at leisure, we will go together to the prison.' The doctor replied, he should be happy to attend him, and asked him to come early in the morning and breakfast with him, and bring him a particular account of the lady; and when they had done with the prisoner, they would return together to Mr. Evans's.

Dinner was now brought in, which consisted of a leg of mutton and turnips. The parson's pudding, which he usually indulged himself in on Sunday, was obliged to be omitted; because Mrs. Evans, who always made it, and who understood the composition of a pudding as well as any woman in England, was too much engaged in her tender and humane attendance on the unhappy lady, to admit of her absence for a moment, or her occupying herself with any other business: its place was supplied with/ a double allowance of toasted cheese; a fare not less agreeable either to the parson or physician; and which, accompanied with excellent ale, was given by Evans, and accepted by the doctor, with all the good humour which the most open hospitality and the truest friendship could inspire.

Oh! ye great ones of the earth![19] ye who are clothed in purple and fine linen, and who fare sumptuously every day! ye who worship Luxury, and make your vows before her golden shrine! – know that ye are far from her! – Would you discover her true residence, leave your luxurious feasts, and idle pomp! seek her in the humble dwelling of contentment! find her in the simple meal which cheerful hospitality bestows, where health sits smiling at the table, and appetite produced by temperance gives relish to every food!

Such was the meal which our good curate and the doctor now enjoyed; and which, after returning thanks to the great bestower (a ceremony now generally

22 *The History of Ned Evans*

omitted/ where much has been bestowed), they washed down with a temperate glass of ale; socially conversing on various subjects, in which Ned bore his part, till the hour of evening prayer approached, which on this day was rather earlier than usual in order to give time for performing the last rites to Mrs. Melville.

The doctor attended Mr. Evans to the church, which in compliment to the lady was uncommonly full; and after the service was finished, she was interred in the body of the church, as you approach the steps leading to the communion-table, in the spot where Evans himself intended to be laid whenever it should please God to take him! The awful and affecting service appointed for this occasion he read with a becoming dignity; and though the unfortunate deceased was so unhappy as to die among strangers, and to have her last rites performed by persons wholly unknown to her, and uninterested in her concerns, yet it is a doubt whether in any situation her funeral would have been/ more respectably attended, or her remains deposited with a greater effusion of sincere and heart felt sorrow,

When all was finished, the doctor went home to Conway, not without reminding Ned of his promise to be with him in the morning, who assured him he should not forget it; and then he and Mr. Evans returned to the house. The rest of the day was spent, as Evans always spent his Sunday evening, in sober and religious conversation; in reading sermons of the most approved authors; and in instructing Ned in that most useful of all knowledge, the knowledge of himself and of his Maker.

Ned listened to his instructions, not only with attention but delight: for, though he was by nature of a gay and lively disposition, and of a constitution of body active and vigorous in the highest degree; though he loved diversion, and excelled in all those exercises with which young men of his age are usually delighted, yet the acquisition of knowledge had charms for him/ still more attracting. His understanding was clear and penetrating; his heart warm and affectionate. Every thing that was grand and sublime interested the one, every thing delicate and refined touched the other. The history of the gospel, therefore, which eminently unites whatever is sublime and whatever is beautiful, could not fail to affect his heart: he loved Christianity because it is indeed lovely, and he practised it because it was congenial to his feelings, without hypocrisy, and without enthusiasm.[20] I would not have the reader imagine, however, that he was an angel or a saint. Alas! he was human, and, as all human creatures do, he erred. His errors, however, were not those of a bad or a corrupt heart; not such as disgraced his honour or his sentiments: they were the failings of nature, under temptations sometimes too powerful to be resisted, yet always repented of, and always atoned for, as far as he was able.

While Mr. Evans and his son were thus piously and instructively employed, they/ were interrupted by the arrival of two visitors, who sometimes came to drink tea on a Sunday evening with Mrs. Evans. Tea was a luxury that did not suit with their finances to indulge in every day; but as Mrs. Evans was fond of it, though far too prudent to allow herself any gratification which their income was not fully equal to, the use of it was confined to Sunday evening, and to such occasional times as they happened to be visited by any person whose situation in life made it necessary to offer it to them.

The visitors who now arrived were Mrs. Watkin and her daughter, the wife and only child of the farmer in the neighbourhood, whose white horse, as we have before noticed, was taken for a ghost by David Morgan. Mrs. Watkin was one of those good kind of women who are not to be met with every day. Her education and understanding were on the ordinary level of those of her rank; her temper was good, and her disposition meek and submitting: and happy was it for her that it was so, for she was/ yoked to a very imperious and severe husband. Watkin was a man between fifty and sixty years of age, of a large person and austere countenance; his temper was answerable;[21] severe and unaccommodating; yet, on some occasions, he appeared not wholly divested of good nature. He had the reputation of being scrupulously honest, and of possessing great skill in his business. His greatest fault was the love of money, to which he sacrificed every thing except integrity; and as he had long been in possession of a lucrative farm, which he managed with superior skill, it was universally supposed that he was worth a round sum. His wife however, and his daughter, were for the present but little benefited by it. His pride indeed always furnished them with decent clothes to appear in when they went abroad; but this was a pleasure he seldom allowed them, as he hated company himself, or whatever else was in the smallest degree expensive. He had indeed a respect for Evans, as every body had who knew him,/ and he would sometimes relax so far as to drink a can of ale at his house, and give him one in return; but this was very seldom; and for the most part he staid at home, minding his own concerns, and never troubling himself about other people's. The daughter was a sensible and a good-humoured girl, but rather plain in her person; her education was confined[22] to reading and writing, plain needle-work, and, above all, domestic concerns. She had, however, a sensible and feeling heart, with great sweetness and openness of temper; was about twenty years of age; and, as she was an only child, and her father rich, she was thought to be a desirable wife for almost any young man in the neighbourhood.

As soon as Mr. Evans saw them, he welcomed them in the kindest manner; he laid by his spectacles and his book, and stirred the fire, while Ned handed them chairs, and assisted them in taking off their cloaks and laying them by. Mr. Evans enquired after his good friend Mr. Watkin, and then told/ the ladies he was afraid his wife would not be able to quit the poor lady's apartment, where she constantly attended both day and night; 'but if you can endure me,' says he,

24 *The History of Ned Evans*

'I will endeavour to be as agreeable as I can: or, if you like a young man better, as may possibly be the case, I can answer for Ned's doing every thing he can to entertain you.' Ned said he was never so happy as when employed in the service of the ladies; that he would step up and tell his mother; and if she could not come down, he would endeavour to supply her place himself, provided Miss Watkin would make tea. Miss Watkin bowed consent; and Ned immediately went up stairs.

Mrs. Evans told him that the lady was then quiet, and had been so some time; that she would go down and see Mrs. Watkin and her daughter; and leave the maid in the room till her return, with directions to come to her if the lady should want any thing. Ned sent the maid up stairs, and returned to the parlour, whither he was/ soon after followed by Mrs. Evans, who had a great regard both for Mrs. Watkin and her daughter, and was always very glad to see them.

Mrs. Watkin told Mrs. Evans, that her visit was not altogether intended as a visit of mere ceremony or curiosity; 'nor indeed,' said she, 'should I have come at all, at this time, knowing how much you must be engaged, but with the hope of giving you some relief. I hear that you watch continually in the poor lady's apartment, and that you have not been in bed these two nights. My daughter and I have been exceedingly anxious for your own health, and she made me come here this evening to offer you her assistance as far as she is able.' – 'Yes, indeed, Madam,' said Miss Watkin, 'you cannot oblige me more than by allowing me to stay with you for a little time, and relieve you in sitting up with the lady; and my father too was very willing I should come, and do any thing for you that I could.' Mrs. Evans said she had been extremely/ obliged to them all upon many occasions, but upon none more than the present; – she thanked her in the warmest manner for her kind attention, and accepted the offer with the greatest gratitude. Evans too was heartily rejoiced, who, by this means, would sometimes see his wife again, whose company he never liked to be long without; and Ned too was not displeased to have a third person, to enliven those serious *tête-à-têtes* he had with his father. All parties were pleased; and the introduction of tea, and an enormous plate of toast swimming in butter, contributed to make this evening much more agreeable than the two last, particularly as they were now rid of the awful spectacle which before occupied great part of the room: and the poor lady above having been more composed than she had hitherto been, they gave way to the pleasing hope that she was on the mending hand.

They spent a couple of hours together, cheerfully and innocently, without being interrupted/ by any message from above stairs; and then Mrs. Watkin rising to go home, Ned said he would attend her. She had a boy and horses with her; but this did not prevent Ned from seeing her to her own house. He rode the horse which carried Miss Watkin, who remained at his father's; and having delivered Mrs. Watkin safe into the hands of her husband, he left the horse and returned home on foot.

Mr. Evans always concluded Sunday evening with family prayer. Miss Watkin and Mrs. Evans went up as soon as it was over; and he retired with his son to bed, where in a few minutes they were both found asleep.

CHAP. V.

THERE is a great affinity between the chapters of a novel and the acts of a play – they are so many pauses in the narration, which should always be determined by similar pauses in the story they relate or represent. I do not, indeed, think it necessary, as some great critics, and particularly the French, pretend, that the whole story of a play should be confined, with respect to the possibility of its happening, to the exact space and time of the representation; at the same time I confess, that the liberties which the immortal Shakespear often takes, of crowding years into minutes, and hurrying us from one country to another, are equally unnatural and disgusting.[23]

I could admit almost of any liberty in this respect, provided there is a pause in the representation. The judicious distribution of plays into five separate acts, and/ the music which intervenes, relieves the attention, and enables the poet to take advantage of that circumstance to carry the audience where he will, without shocking probability, because I can allow any time to pass while the representation is suspended; and, at the beginning of a new act, it is equal to me whether I am set down in England or in France. – It is the same way in novels, which indeed, being read and not represented, admit of greater latitude as to the unities of place and time than plays, yet are not wholly free from restraint, but to be agreeable must be natural, and never shock the mind by any thing highly improbable, nor distract it by too often shifting the story from one country to another; – and wherever this is necessary to be done, it should be contrived in separate books or chapters, where the narration naturally pauses, and suffers nothing by the interruption.

I have been led into this digression by reflecting on the conclusion of my three last/ chapters or acts, wherein I have judiciously laid all my actors fast asleep; and if the events I am relating have not sufficient merit to interest the attention of my readers, I heartily and sincerely wish they may have the power to lay them in the same condition; since, next to being usefully employed, or agreeably entertained, I know no state more delightful than sound sleep – and, indeed, I have heard some, who very seldom could procure it, say they preferred it to any entertainment whatsoever. If any of my readers, therefore, should experience this benefit, let them not on that account decry the work – but, with due gratitude to the author, recommend it to others as an opiate, full as effectual, and far more safe than laudanum or poppies.[24]

It is now time for Mr. Edward to shake off his poppies, and accordingly we must now behold him rising early in the morning, and carefully getting out of bed, left he should disturb his good father, who was still snoring. As soon as he was/ dressed, he went out to the stable, to get the horse ready to go to Conway. Ned loved horses, and was as fond of handling them himself, and as skilful in every thing that belonged to them, as if he had been bred a groom. He combed and curried old Blackbird, till he made him look as spruce and as glossy as the bird whose name he bore; and having got Morgan to black his boots, and to clean his plated spurs, he seemed as neatly equipped for the saddle as any young man need to be. He then returned to the house in order to enquire about the lady, and, if his father was awake, to ask if he had any commands to Conway. He went up to his mother's room, and tapping at the door, it was opened by Mrs. Evans. From her he learned that the lady had been composed most of the night, and she hoped had got some sleep; but that she never spoke except when once or twice she had asked for a little drink. He now went down with the intention of seeing his father; but before he approached the door,/ he was informed by the music of his nose that he was still asleep; wherefore, unwilling to disturb him, he went to the stable; and taking out old Blackbird, who had just finished a good feed of oats, he patted him awhile on the neck, and then, vaulting into the saddle, rode off.

When he came to Conway, he found the doctor and his wife ready to receive him; the tea-things were spread upon the table, and they only waited his arrival to bring in the kettle, which was followed by a large plate of toast and butter, and another with boiled eggs. After mutual compliments and enquiries about the lady, they sat down to breakfast, where Ned, whose appetite was increased by his ride, did due honour to what was provided for him: he demolished, indeed, more than half the toast, together with four of the eggs, and washed them down with a proportionable quantity of tea.

When breakfast was finished, the doctor and Ned proceeded to the jail, to see the/ unfortunate man who was confined there, and to try to discover if he was one of the villains who were the authors of the tragical event that happened a few evenings before. This was the first time in his life that Edward had ever been within the doors of a prison; and though he had nothing to apprehend from it for himself, yet his feelings were too delicate, his heart too tender, to suffer him to enter it without concern. This was much increased when he was introduced into the room where the man was confined. The wretched and gloomy look of this receptacle of guilt and misery struck him with a universal horror.[25] It was a small room dimly illuminated by a diminutive and dirty window, raised

28 *The History of Ned Evans*

high from the ground, and secured by an iron grating within and without. The few gleams of light which were able to penetrate through the crust of filth with which the glass was covered, served only to discover sights of woe. The walls were bare plaster, which, in most places, was mouldering/ away; they had once been white-washed, but smoke and damp had everywhere so discoloured them that nothing like white could be seen. There was, indeed, a fire-place in the room, with a few small rusty bars by way of a grate; but not a spark of fire, nor any appearance of there having been any for years, though the season of the year and the dampness greatly required one. An old and broken truckle bed, with some straw in it, lay in a dark corner; and on this was the miserable object whom they came to see stretched, shivering under a tattered blanket, when they entered the room. 'Good God!' thought Ned in his own mind, 'should this man be innocent, what amends can be made to him for placing him in this miserable situation?' Again the supposition that he fired the guilty shot, by which an innocent lady was already dead, and another in imminent hazard of her life, suppressed these tender emotions, and raised a conflict in his mind, which was strongly pictured/ in his countenance, but which would be extremely difficult either to paint or to describe. The doctor, to whom scenes of horror were more familiar, approached the bed, and, calling to the prisoner, told him there was a young gentleman that wished to see him. The man raised himself on his arm, and discovered a face on which calamity was deeply engraven. His appearance was sordid and filthy, for he had not been washed since he was committed: he had on a black wig, that seemed not to fit him, and to be much the worse for the wear; and then rolling his gloomy eye-ball upon Edward, he asked, in an indignant and surly tone, what business he had with him?

Ned was somewhat staggered with the question: – but soon recovering himself, replied, that perhaps he might have no business at all with him, and he sincerely wished it might be so; but that depended on his own innocence or guilt: – that a few evenings before, a most barbarous and atrocious murder had been committed on an unhappy/ lady by two highwaymen; and that another lady, who had been with her, was then in great danger of her life: – that Providence had brought him to their assistance, and that he had himself given one of the villains such a blow on the head as brought him to the ground, though he afterwards escaped; and that, hearing a suspicious person had been taken up, he had desired to see him, to know whether he could recollect him. 'Well,' said the fellow, 'what do you know of me, now you see me?' 'Why I confess,' said Ned, 'I cannot say that I know any thing of you.' 'Then by what right is it that I am kept here starving with hunger and with cold? Since you know nothing about me, you should go to the man that put me up here, and desire him to release me, and pay me besides for the injury I have suffered in being put here: – but, damn you and him together! you are both of you greater rogues than I am, or you could not have done so to an innocent man.' 'Friend,' said/ Evans, 'I have nothing to do either with your commitment or release: – if you are indeed an innocent man, you have nothing to apprehend, and doubtless a satisfaction will be made you; but let me tell you, that the intemperance of your tongue does not look like innocence, which, shielded by its own rectitude, disdains so weak and so indecent a defence: the magistrate who committed you is a man of equal integrity and humanity, infinitely above the reach of any aspersion that such a tongue as yours can level at him; he shall be sent for to examine you further while I am here, and he is the only person authorised to decide on the propriety of releasing or detaining you.

Whilst Ned was thus haranguing the prisoner, the doctor had slipped out of the room, and now returned with the jailor. They then questioned the jailor respecting the want of food and other comforts, which the prisoner had complained of. The jailor replied, that as for fire there was no/ provision made for it by the county, and that the man had refused to pay for any, and therefore he wanted it; but that for food he had sent him some of his own dinner, which the other, in a fit of sullenness, had also refused, and damned the person that carried it to him; so that if he wanted necessaries, it was entirely his own fault. To all this the prisoner made no reply, but sat sullen on the bed-side; the jailor approaching him, said he had better wash and shave himself. 'You shall have a shirt of my own,' he said, 'while yours is washed; and if you will give me your wig here,' said he, 'I will get it combed.' This he said by agreement with the doctor, and at the same time attempted to take it off his head; but it was tied under his chin. The fellow, upon feeling the attempt upon his wig, got up in a rage, and, clapping both his hands to it, 'Damn you!' said he, 'have you a mind to rob me of the little I have left? There's ne'er a one of you, by G –, shall take my wig, without/ taking my life first.' The jailor was not at all discomfited by this declaration: 'As for your wig,' says he, 'I care nothing about it; but, by G –, I'll see what colour your hair is of.' And so saying, he pulled harder at the bob,[26] which, however, was too well fastened to give way; which the doctor observing, he, in an instant, cut the string with a pair of his anatomical scissars, and transferred the wig from the head of the prisoner to the fist of the jailor; and then, indeed, was discovered what was suspected before – the large and very visible marks of a recent contusion. 'Hey!' said the doctor, 'what is the matter here? Why, here's a large wound. How have you got this desperate bruise, and why have not you applied for assistance?' The fellow seemed a good deal confounded; but replied, that he had got it by a fall from his horse; and as for doctors, he never applied to them, for he hated them, and every thing that belonged to them. 'They are obliged to you,' replied Jones; 'nevertheless/ I will mend this broken head for you, and it shall cost you nothing neither.' He then offered to examine it; but the fellow positively refused, and desired him to stand off, for he should not lay a finger near it. 'Well,' said

30 *The History of Ned Evans*

Jones, 'you may do as you please just now; but the justice who committed you will soon be here, and then, in his presence, and in the presence of his attendants, I will examine it whether you will or no.' The doctor and Ned then left the room, and adjourned to the jailor's apartment, when they sent for the justice, and told him all the circumstances that have been related; as well those respecting the robbery, as those relative to the suspicious conduct of the prisoner. After about an hour's conversation, they agreed to go in and re-examine the prisoner, attended by some of the inferior officers of justice, in case any assistance of theirs might be necessary. This precaution, though prudent, was now unnecessary; for whether awed by the consciousness of guilt, the new/ circumstance against him that had been discovered, the solemnity of the appearance of the magistrate, or the natural depression of his spirits, the prisoner had now lost every appearance of opposition, and sat on the bed-side in a state of utter despondence. The justice observed his weakness; and, being a man of the tenderest humanity, he asked him if he was ill? The prisoner said, he was ill indeed; for he had not tasted food for two days. The justice told him, that no advantage should be taken of him; and though he came to examine him, he would wait till he was more composed. He then withdrew again to the room he had left, and ordered the jailor to carry to the unfortunate prisoner some bread and a pint of warm wine. After he had taken this refreshment, and some time had been allowed him to recollect himself, the justice (attended as before) and the gentlemen went in to him.

I shall not now trouble the reader with his examination, or his answers, which were/ evasive and unsatisfactory. The doctor after examining the wound, pronounced that it could not have been got by a fall from a horse, as it was on a part of the head on which it was next to an impossibility to pitch by such an accident: but it might very well have been got by a blow of a stick, which it resembled much more; and as such a blow had been given to one of the persons concerned in the robbery, there was the greatest reason to believe the prisoner was that person. The justice summed up the incongruities in his account of himself; and further added, that his horse was in custody as well as himself, and that, in all probability, such further evidence would in a short time appear as would effectually condemn him if he was guilty; and it was already so strong as to make it impossible for him to release him from prison. He therefore seriously and earnestly exhorted him, if he knew himself guilty, not to deprive himself of the merit of making a full and voluntary confession;/ which would turn out greatly to his advantage, and which, he pledged himself, he should not lose the benefit of. 'If,' says he, 'you are the person who was knocked down, it is evident you are not the person who fired the shot, and if you will give such information as can bring that murderer to justice, you shall be admitted evidence for the crown, and obtain his majesty's pardon.'

Volume I   31

This last promise had the desired effect. The unhappy man, whose heart was now softened, and who had seemed infinitely touched by the tenderness and the humanity of the justice, now burst into a flood of tears; and, with a tremulous and broken voice, confessed he was the person who was knocked down. 'You have done well to confess it,' replied the justice: 'and now remember that you tell fairly and fully who you are, and who the wretch is that was confederated with you, that he may be brought to justice; for on the faithfulness/ of this confession, and the truth of your report concerning your accomplice, depends your own life, and my power of making good the promise I have given you.'

CHAP. VI

'My name,' said the unfortunate man, 'is Andrew Collins; I am the only child of my mother, and she is a widow. I was born at Chester, and am, or rather lately was, servant to Mr. Nicholson, an eminent cloth-merchant there. Mr. Nicholson is an Irishman by birth, but is settled at Chester, and is at present in London. When he first came to live at Chester, about ten years ago, he brought with him a young lad from his own country, to live with him as a servant, and he did every thing he could to make him a faithful and a skilful one. For some years he did pretty well; but as he grew up to be a man, he became idle and negligent, then drunken and extravagant, and at last wicked and abandoned in every respect.

'His master bore with him till it was not possible to bear him any longer; and at/ last, about six months ago, he turned him out of his house, and would have nothing more to say to him. I happened to be hired in his place; and if I had had any grace or fear of God, I might have been happy; but, alas! I have been seduced to ruin – seduced against my sense, nay almost against my will, and all by that wicked servant, for he it is that was my tempter and my accomplice. His name is Patrick Reilly; but he sometimes calls himself Maguire, and sometimes Flanagan, but his real name is Reilly. He is of a very strong make, a very daring courage, and of a fierce and bloody temper: though he will do any thing to get money, yet he cares little about it when he has it, but spends it in idleness and debauchery, with a show of generosity; and, alas! it was this show that has undone me.

'I never knew any thing about him till I unfortunately succeeded him in his place: he soon after contrived to get acquainted with me, and, instead of hating me as I expected, he seemed to be fond of me, and/ used to praise my master and own his own faults; and he often gave me good advice how to please him, and how to get about him, as he called it, which I always found successful, and I thought him the best friend I had; – but all this was to serve his own end, and his revenge.

'When he had got me to love him and think well of him, he would often, when there was an opportunity, treat me to liquor, and sometimes he would introduce me to some of his female acquaintances, and even give me money to pay for the favours those despicable wretches were to grant; in short, he won me

– 32 –

to his purposes, first by affection, and then by fear: – for twice or thrice I saw him give very stout men, who had offended him, such desperate beatings, that I own I felt myself like nothing before him, and did not dare to contradict whatever he might propose. I observed he was always flush of money, though I could not tell how he came by it, nor did I ever dare to ask him; but he had from time to time given me so much, that I began to/ think, if he should happen to ask me for it, that my whole wages would not be sufficient to repay it. This gave me great uneasiness; and, from the moment that I felt myself in his power, I lost my peace, my happiness, and at last my innocence.

'I resolved to disentangle myself from him as soon as I could, but I did not know how to do it; and once that he began to grow angry at my refusing to go with him, he terrified me into instant obedience, and obliged me to ask his pardon, though I knew not for what. From that moment I was lost. He saw my condition, and did not fail to take advantage of it.

'About a week ago my master went up in the coach to London, and left the two maids and me to take care of the house; he is not expected back this fort-night to come. The day after he went, Reilly called upon me, and asked me if I could let him have the money he lent me, for he had a sum to pay, and was in great want. I was thunderstruck at his demand; and assured him I had not half a guinea in my possession;/ but I told him that, as soon as my master came back, I would ask him for some, and that I would give him every shilling I got. 'Oh, damn your master!' said he, 'that won't do for me; he mayn't come this month! – I want my money tonight! Don't think to put me off with that flam; but get me the money, or the money's worth, by eight o'clock to-night, for by G – I must have it! and you may expect to see me then for it. So saying, he went off, and left me in a condition that if the earth had opened and swallowed me up, it would have rejoiced me. I knew it was impossible to get the money, or any thing like it – and indeed I never went about it; but I passed all the rest of the day in a state of stupid terror and distress that it is impossible to describe. At length eight o'clock came, and soon after I heard a knock at the door, which I knew to be Reilly's; and I went to open it with a heart beating against my breast, so that I could hardly breathe./

'When I let him in, and he saw the condition I was in, he burst out a-laughing – 'What is the matter with you, man?' said he, 'You look as if you saw a ghost!' I was not able to give him an answer. 'Is it because I asked you for the money,' said he, 'that you are so frighted?' 'Why yes,' said I, in a faltering voice; 'I have it not, nor do I know where to get it; but if you leave me the clothes on my back, which are my master's, you may take every thing else I have in the world.' 'No, damn it!' said Reilly, 'I'll not be so hard-hearted as that neither; you are an honest fellow, and I love you as my friend; and as for the money, you will pay me when you can. I have got a supply for the present, I did not expect; and I came to tell you the

34 *The History of Ned Evans*

good news, and to ask you to come to my lodging and to drink a bowl of punch with me, where, if you are an honest cock,²⁷ and my friend, I'll shew you how to make us both happy all our days.' It is not possible for words to express what I felt at this speech./ The suddenness of the relief, the surprise and joy that flowed in upon me, was more than I was able to bear; and I should have fallen to the floor, if Reilly had not caught me in his arms. As I hung upon his neck in a transport of joy and gratitude, I told him I would serve him with my life, and go with him to the end of the earth.

'Oh, fatal folly! Oh, dreadful and irremediable guilt! It is not yet a week since I slept in innocence and peace! – a little week since my hands were pure, and my character unstained! Alas! my mother! my aged, my helpless, my widowed mother! It is not yet a week since you saw your child in freedom, in guiltless freedom, and gave him your blessing. What will you do when you hear that in one hour he is become a robber and a murderer? – a disgraced and deserved outcast from all society!'

This affecting apostrophe brought tears into the eyes of the humane justice, and seemed to make some impression even on the/ stony hearts of those subaltern myrmidons of the law,²⁸ by whom he was surrounded. The unhappy man himself seemed to be in an agony not to be described; and Ned stood with his hands folded together, contemplating him with a silent and a sorrowing eye.

The justice first broke silence. – 'Your guilt and your misfortunes,' said he, unhappy man, are great; but if I can judge of others by myself, they will not be thought unworthy of compassion. It is your happiness that your career in wickedness has been cut short by an early detection; and if you have the grace to be sorry for your sin, and to forsake it, you may be yet restored to some degree of comfort even in this life. In the mean time, it is your duty, as well as your interest, to proceed faithfully in your narrative, which is the best atonement you can make to your country, and which, as far as I have heard, seems candid and deserves credit.'

The prisoner then continued his narrative:/ 'In an evil hour I consented to go with him: he soon got a good supper, with plenty of spirits and wine, and plied me with both till he had got me well warmed for any business he had to propose. At length he ventured to break the affair; he told me his father and mother lived in Ireland, where they had a good farm; and that he had a sister who was a great beauty; that my master was a great rogue, and was worth a deal of money, which he made by wronging other people; that he knew very well where he kept a large sum; and that if I would only keep out of the way, and give him the key of the iron box in which the plate was kept, and of which he knew I had the charge, he would contrive to carry off the whole; and that it could never appear that I had any hand in it whatever; and that then he would carry me to Ireland, where

Volume I 35

I should marry his sister, and he would give me half of the spoils to set me up with.

'Had this been proposed to me in my/ sober senses, I believe I should have had virtue enough to withstand it: even as it was, it both terrified and shocked me. I told him I could not think of joining to rob a man who had never done me wrong; and though I might be so lucky as to escape the gallows, yet I could not conceal my wickedness from God, who would surely judge me for it in the next world, if not in this. He laughed at the idea of the next world, and said he did not believe there was any such place; 'but if there is,' said he, ''tis easy enough to make peace there. God knows your master is a great rogue, so do I; and perhaps he may put this into my head to be a means of punishing him, and then we are only his instruments; – and besides, your master is a protestant and a heretic, and it is no sin to rob a heretic; and indeed I might be afraid myself, but I know, if there is any truth in religion at all, that the church has power to forgive sins – not your church, which is a heretic church – but the old and true church, the church of/ Rome; and I know that Father Dogherty, as good a priest as ever lived, will give me absolution for half-a-crown;[29] and he will do the same for you if you will be a good catholic, so that you will not only make your fortune, but save your soul too.'

'I was not so drunk, nor yet so ignorant, but that I could see the weakness and the wickedness of this argument. Reilly perceived too that I was not satisfied: 'I'll tell you what', said he, 'to cut the matter short, I am determined to do the thing. I love you, therefore I offered you to give you share of the booty; and as an earnest of it, I forgive you what you owe me, and here are ten guineas more for you in your fist. But remember that you do as I desire you; for I have trusted you with my secret; and if you don't do as I bid you, by the living G – I will take care of you, and put you where you can tell no tales; and I shall get absolution for that too.'

'This last threat, which I fully understood, harrowed up my soul. I saw myself/ wholly in his power, and do not make the smallest doubt but that he would really have murdered me as he threatened, if I had any longer refused him: so with an aching and an unwilling heart I consented. He was too cunning to let me cool upon it; he detained me with him the whole night, and at length put me into his own bed in a state of complete intoxication.

'In the morning he did not fail to make me renew my promise, as he did his threat in case I failed: and I went to my master, sick both in body and mind. The eldest of the maids saw I had been drinking, and chid me severely for staying out; and said she would tell my master if ever I did so any more. I promised I would not; but I said I was so sick I was afraid I was going to have a fever, and that I would go home to my mother, and if I was better, I would return the next day.

36 *The History of Ned Evans*

They both endeavoured to dissuade me from this; but it being my purpose to be out of the way, I persisted, and went./

'I called on Reilly, gave him the key, and told him where to find me. I then went to my mother, and staid there all night. – How I passed that night I cannot describe, nor never shall forget. Every time I looked at my mother, the consciousness of my guilt stung me to the soul. Her tender assiduities wrung me to the heart, when I thought of the sorrow and the shame I was preparing for her grey hairs! When the hour came in which I knew the mischief would be doing, my agony was inexpressible, and such as I can never again suffer, though I should be executed for the crime.

'Early in the morning I called on Reilly, but he was not at his lodging. I then went home to my master's, where I found all in confusion. The two maids were at their wit's end – they told me all that had happened, and upbraided me with being out of the way; and the eldest did not scruple to say that she was sure the villain Reilly was the author of it; and that, as I was his companion of late, she did not doubt but I had/ gone out of the way on purpose. This last accusation, so just and so direct, shocked me like a stroke of lightning. I saw my folly to its full extent, and felt it to my soul. I cursed and swore, indeed, and denied it; but my guilt was in my face, and might be discerned by a less penetrating eye than hers. I knew indeed she could not prove it, but the suspicion was too just not to set me on providing for my safety.

'I soon after went to Reilly's again; and having informed him of what was said, and my fears about it, he agreed with me that it was not safe to remain, and that we should both set off that very day for Ireland. I did not hear a word of dividing the spoil; I don't know what he got; and I never received a shilling more. He went out, desiring me to remain where I was till he came back. In about an hour he returned, and told me he had two horses ready saddled and bridled, and desired me to go off with him directly. I had now no other choice left; so off we went together, intending/ to go across the country, and by round-about ways, till we came to the Head; and there to embark for Ireland.

'Nothing remarkable happened to us till last Friday evening. The day was very bad, and we had stopped at Conway to refresh ourselves and our horses. Looking out at the window, we saw a post-chaise stop, with two ladies in it, and no servants attending. We soon found they were going on for the Head, notwithstanding the stormy night; and their defenceless situation first put it into Reilly's head to rob them. I was absolutely at his disposal; he ordered me therefore to get ready, and that we should ride on before to meet them, as it were, when it was dark. He desired me to attack the women, and as I had no arms, he gave me a pen-case,[30] which he said was just as good for them; and as for himself, who had a blunderbuss, he said he would take care of the postillions, that they should be no interruption. All that happened in consequence you know. I found myself/ knocked down, and I heard the shot go off; but murder was no part of my plan. I got nothing. In the darkness and confusion I escaped for that time; and recovering the horse, I returned to Conway in search of Reilly: but I have never seen nor heard of him since; nor do I know whose the horses are, nor any thing about them.

'This, gentlemen, is my whole story, and I will seal it with my dying words. I am thankful that I have been early detected, and that I am rescued from the tyranny of Reilly, even by the gallows. But if his majesty should vouchsafe to extend mercy to me, the rest of my life shall be spent in prayers for him, and in endeavours to atone to my country for my great transgression.'

The justice told him, he was glad to see that his misfortunes seemed to have made a proper impression on him: that it was necessary for him to be detained in custody, but that he should not want either for compassion or necessaries while he was there. He applauded/ the candour of his confession, and desired him to commit it to writing, and to sign it; and that he himself would take care it should redound to his advantage. He then returned to his own house, and Edward went with the doctor to his; from whence they soon after set forward together on horseback for Mr. Evans's.

CHAP. VII.

WHEN they arrived at the gate, that worthy man went out to meet them with his accustomed hospitality: he welcomed the doctor, but with a chastised pleasure, and so visible a discomposure of countenance as greatly alarmed both him and Ned. 'Has any thing happened?' said the doctor; 'and how is my unfortunate patient?' 'She is alive,' said Evans, 'but, I fear, fast approaching to her dissolution.' The doctor said no more, but went up immediately to her chamber; whilst Ned, with an aching heart and trembling steps, followed his father into the parlour. 'What,' said he, 'my dear Sir (after sitting a little while), 'what new symptom has arisen since I went away, that makes you despair of the poor lady's recovery?' 'Alas, my child!' said he, 'she is, I fear, past all recovery. God is going to take her to himself, and/ to reward her sufferings in a better world. I have seen her,' continued he – 'seen her lie all senseless and forlorn, wholly unconscious even of existence; she has been in this state the whole day, and could not be roused to the smallest sensibility even for a moment. I am glad the doctor is come; for though I have no hope that his skill can avail any thing, yet it will be a consolation to have him in the house, and I do not mean to let him go till all is over.'

Ned's eyes witnessed to his feelings by some silent drops which trickled on his cheeks. He then gave his father a particular account of all that has been already related respecting the prisoner at Conway; which Mr. Evans heard with much satisfaction, particularly Collins's contrition, and trusting that it would be the means of bringing the arch-villain Reilly to condign punishment. 'In all my time,' said he, 'I never knew, nor heard of, murder escaping unpunished. God seems to have marked this dreadful crime for particular/ vengeance even in this life; and let it be perpetrated ever so cunningly or secretly, it always is discovered. Should other means be wanting to find it out, there have been instances where the wretched perpetrators themselves, unable to bear the stings of conscience, and the horrors of remorse, have voluntarily surrendered themselves to justice; and fled to death itself, and a public execution, as a refuge from the terrors of their guilty minds. How gracious is God! and what a proof of his wisdom and mercy does it afford, when we consider that this unerring monitor is implanted in every breast! that we cannot deviate in the smallest degree from our duty, without feeling its checks, and being sensible of the divinity within us! While you live then, my dear boy, listen to this sacred advice; it is the voice of God speaking to your soul, which, if you will obey, will always speak to you peace and comfort, and, in the end, conduct you to ineffable happiness and glory.'/

Whilst Evans was thus moralizing with his son, Miss Watkin came down stairs to get something the doctor wanted. Neither of the gentlemen could muster up courage enough to ask about the unfortunate lady; but Ned, whose tenderness was extreme, and who could no longer bear the suspense he was in, stole after her up stairs, and went with her into the room. He stood for a while motionless at the foot of the bed, silently contemplating its pale inhabitant. Her eyes were half open, but they saw nothing; the paleness of death sat upon her countenance, which nevertheless was still beautiful; and a soft complacency was diffused over all her features, as if she was happy in the prospect of being soon in heaven. 'Whoever thou art,' said he, 'unfortunate young lady! earth never bred a fairer form, nor sent to heaven a more unpolluted soul than thine.' He took one look at her, which he firmly believed to be the last; and, without saying a word to any person in the room, retired to his own/ chamber, to give vent to that sorrow which was visible in his eyes, and which a much less feeling heart than his could not suppress.

Here he remained fixed in meditation till the maid came to summon him to dinner. He would gladly have been excused going; but, thinking it would look particular, he went into the parlour, and partook of a cheerless meal, at which little was said and less was eaten. When the cloth was removed, and a glass or two of ale had gone round, Ned ventured to ask the doctor if it was possible for the lady to recover. He replied, that nothing was impossible to God; and that while there was life in her he would continue to do every thing in his power for her; but he confessed he had very little hopes, for, in all his practice, he had never seen any one in a more alarming situation. Mr. Evans then requested the doctor would not leave the lady till all was determined one way or other. The doctor said he would not; and that he would sit up/ with her himself this night, to watch the operation of blisters[31] which he had put on several parts of her body.

When night came, the doctor and the ladies retired to the sick apartment; and Mr. Evans and Ned continued sitting in the parlour. The anxiety of their minds had banished all thoughts of sleep; and though Mr. Evans pressed Ned to go to his bed, yet that amiable youth would not quit his father, but chose to sit up with him to endeavour to cheer him through the silence of the night, and to receive in his turn the consolation and instruction which he knew he should find in the conversation of his father on this solemn occasion. For several hours they sat without hearing the smallest stir; their conversation turned, as might be expected, on the sublime truths of Christianity, the nature of death,

40 *The History of Ned Evans*

the immorality of the soul, and the several proofs of it that might be drawn from reason, exclusive of revelation. In this serious and instructive manner did they/ pass the greatest part of the night, without any interruption: the clock struck four, and soon after they heard the room-door open, and the doctor's foot upon the stairs.

All their apprehensions were now awakened; they longed, though they dreaded, to see him enter the parlour; and in this awful moment of suspense, a by-stander might have seen, that neither philosophy, nor even religion itself, could wholly subdue the feelings of nature. Notwithstanding their sublime conversation, and their thorough belief of the great gain that death is to the virtuous, they were struck with terror when the door opened, and were unable for a while even to speak. At length Evans found his tongue: 'Is all over?' said he. 'I hope all is over,' replied the doctor. 'The lady lives – and I can pronounce her better. The blisters have risen; and she has recovered sense – she has just asked for drink, and taken some wine whey, and I could not delay communicating to you these happy tidings.'/

The joy that now flowed in upon them, was equal to the despondence with which they were before oppressed. Ned's eyes, which were always the ready interpreters of his heart, bore witness to his satisfaction; whilst the venerable Evans, referring this blessing to the Bestower of all blessings, poured out his thanksgivings on his knees. And, indeed, it was the constant custom of this truly pious and excellent man to be take himself to his Maker on every occasion of importance, whether of joy or sorrow. He had a thorough faith, that all the events of this life were guided by an all-disposing Providence, though not absolutely predetermined so as to supersede the freedom of the will: but he believed that the Lord of nature, who at one view could comprehend the whole universe, and direct all the movements in it, did often, if not always, interpose his providence, although in doing so he made use of second and natural causes; and where men were studious to recommend themselves to him, and faithful/ enough sincerely to rely on him, he did further believe that all events were directed for their real interest; and though they might appear ever so untoward, yet in the end they would be conducive to lasting happiness. And indeed it would not be easy for the most acute philosopher to disprove this doctrine; for it must be allowed that the comfort and satisfaction which good men would derive from this belief, would diffuse over their whole lives such contentment and tranquillity as all the storms of adversity could never destroy. And such indeed was the influence it had on the mind of Evans, who, according to the common opinions of the world, might well be reckoned a man of sorrows and acquainted with grief, but whose internal comforts arising from integrity of heart and purity of faith were so great, that they were ever visible both in his countenance and temper; and it may well be doubted if there was really a man in the kingdom more truly happy

Volume I 41

than himself. Certain it is, he was completely so at this/ moment: his satisfaction arose from the purest source, the most open and unbounded benevolence; and now being relieved from the great anxiety which depressed them in the beginning of the night, he and Ned retired for the remainder of it to rest, and the doctor returned to his attendance on the lady./

CHAP. VIII

I HOPE my readers, if they have had patience to come to the beginning of this chapter, are by this time somewhat interested in the story, and that they are longing to know who the unfortunate lady is, that I have endeavoured to recommend to their attention, and for whose recovery all that were about her seem so much concerned. She is as yet unknown even at Mr. Evans's, and perhaps it may be her desire to continue for some time longer in obscurity; though certainly no young lady whatever has less reason to shun the public eye, as none could surpass her either in beauty or virtue. The only motive she can have for wishing to be some time longer concealed, arises from the very cause that would make a lady less delicate and considerate ambitious of declaring herself, namely, her rank./ But though this might be a reason to a mind like hers, to keep Evans in the dark, because she hated to give trouble, or to oppress her inferiors with the splendour of her title, yet it can be none with me to deny that satisfaction to the reader; – and I shall therefore take this opportunity, while the venerable curate and his family are asleep, and are therefore in no danger of overhearing us, to disclose the secret.

Lady Cecilia Rivers was the only daughter of the Earl of Ravensdale, in Ireland, and had at this time nearly completed her eighteenth year. To Nature she was indebted for a form absolutely perfect, and for a mind every way suited to such a form. To her father she was obliged for a most finished education. His lordship was born a younger brother, and, having married early in life, was once blessed with a numerous family of children. He succeeded to the title on the death of his elder brother, about fourteen years before the commencement of this history./

The late lord had an only son, who had the misfortune to displease his father by marrying contrary to his consent; on which account he never would see him afterwards. He died, as his wife did also, about five years before his father, leaving a new-born son, who was said to have also died at nurse; and, on the demise of the late lord, Lady Cecilia's father succeeded of course. He had a clear landed estate of 16,000l, a year, which he enjoyed with dignity and œconomy, and was universally supposed to possess as much honour, humanity, and virtue, as any

– 42 –

nobleman in the kingdom. He had the misfortune to lose his lady soon after his accession to the title, when Lady Cecilia, who was his youngest child, was yet an infant; and of all his numerous family there now remained only her ladyship and two brothers. Her eldest brother, Lord Rivers, who was heir to the title and estate, was at this time about twenty-five years of age; and her second brother, about twenty-two, was a captain in the army./

The death of Lady Ravensdale, when her daughter Lady Cecilia was little more than four years of age, was a great blow to her lord, who tenderly loved her, and would have been severely felt by the children, had it not been for the tender and parental care of Mrs. Melville, the unfortunate conclusion of whose life we have already related.

This lady was a near relation of Lady Ravensdale, to whom she was extremely attached: she had been married to a gentleman of small fortune, but great accomplishments; and whilst they lived together, they were universally considered to be one of the happiest as well as the most elegant pairs that ever love had united in matrimony. But alas! this happiness was of too short duration, and Mr. Melville, at an early period of his life, fell a sacrifice to his affection for his wife. It happened that they were one night at the theatre, when, towards the end of the entertainment, there was an alarm in the house, of fire![32] In a short time/ the flames were seen bursting out among the scenes; and the dreadful confusion that ensued, by every body crowding to get out, was the occasion of many lives being lost which might otherwise have been saved. They happened to be in the stage box, and Mr. Melville, whose presence of mind never forsook him in danger, was well aware that it was impossible to escape by the ordinary passages to the boxes; he took therefore the desperate resolution of jumping on the stage with his wife in his arms, and bore her through the flames to the back of the house, which he knew communicated with the manager's dwelling, and was fortunate enough to deposit her in a place of safety without any material injury from the fire. But the terror, the heat, and the hurry of his spirits, together with being obliged to walk home in the night, neither his own nor any other carriage being to be got in the confusion, threw him into a fever, of which he died, to the inexpressible affliction of his disconsolate widow, who it was thought for a long time would nor/ be able to survive him. At length however she recovered, and possessed a jointure from her husband of 300l. a year, [33] which, as she had no child, was in Ireland a sufficient income for a single woman of fashion to live tolerably comfortably on, especially as she had many friends to whose houses she was ever a most welcome guest.

Her summers she usually spent with Lord and Lady Ravensdale, at their seat in the country; but the winters she passed in Dublin, where she had a small but very neat house in one of the new streets in the neighbourhood of Merrion-square.[34]

44 *The History of Ned Evans*

Some time after Lady Ravensdale's death, she was prevailed upon by my Lord to supply her place to her infant children; and Lady Cecilia, the youngest, coming more particularly under her care, she transferred the affection she had for the mother to the daughter, and really felt for her a parental tenderness: under her forming hand she grew perfect in every polite attainment, whilst the excellence of her understanding,/ and the native sweetness of her disposition, gave additional lustre to the surpassing beauties of her person.

Lord Ravensdale had a sister, Lady Elizabeth Belmont, who was married to an English gentleman of large fortune, and who lived wholly in that kingdom. This lady had not seen her niece since she was a child; but hearing much of her beauty and accomplishments, she wished exceedingly for that pleasure, and to introduce her into the first circles, and to all the splendid amusements of the metropolis of the empire. She had therefore, in the autumn, written pressingly to Lord Ravensdale, and also to Lady Cecilia, inviting her to spend the winter with her in London; and she wrote at the same time to Mrs. Melville, requesting her to accompany her. Lord Ravensdale could not refuse this request, so proper in itself, and which promised to be so agreeable to Lady Cecilia also. The two ladies therefore had accepted the invitation, and gone over in the month of September. Lord Rivers,/ Lady Cecilia's brother, had escorted them all the way, and delivered them safe to Lady Elizabeth Belmont, at her house in Berkeley-square;[35] but his attendance in the Irish parliament (where he was a commoner) being necessary, he was obliged to return soon after to Dublin.

Lady Cecilia and Mrs. Melville were received by Mr. Belmont and Lady Elizabeth with all the affection and politeness they could desire; and perhaps if Lady Cecilia had had less beauty, or her aunt had lived in a less splendid circle of gaiety and fashion, they might have passed a very agreeable winter, and the amiable Mrs. Melville been still living. But Providence, who from causes the most common, and seemingly the most trivial, often deduces the most important consequences, thought fit to determine otherwise. For some time, indeed, the novelty of the scenes amused; and Lady Cecilia, who was the very soul of elegance, could not fail to find in London whatever could delight her fancy, or improve her taste. Had she been/ in her own house, or her amusements left to her own choice, this would undoubtedly have been the case; but in her aunt's house she was under the necessity of conforming to her mode of living, and of choosing her amusements and her company by her direction, which, as their education and sentiments were widely different, were not always entirely such as Lady Cecilia approved. She could not all at once divest herself of her love of tranquillity, and of those calm and soothing pleasures which an elegant and refined mind seeks within itself, and enjoys most when it is alone, or in the company of a few and select friends. The eternal round of dissipation, however fashionable, and the perpetual return of the same amusements, however splendid, though they pleased at first, soon lost their charm, and at length grew fatiguing: – just like the insipid amusement of Ranelagh,[36] where all are astonished at the splendour and magnitude of the room on their first entrance; but after passing a few hours, they find it little/ better than an enormous cock-pit, and are as much amused with the dull round of the circle as a horse in a mill. Even the theatres, where she might reasonably hope for entertainment, miserably deceived her; not indeed from any fault in them or the managers, but solely from the fashion; for she soon found that fine ladies go to the theatres not to see, but to be seen; that the side-boxes, where they are condemned to sit, though favourable for the exhibition of themselves, is not so for seeing the play; that the company talk as much there as at any other assembly, and, except in a few instances, return home as ignorant of the entertainment as those who had never been at it.

After a few weeks therefore of fashionable dissipation, her curiosity was satisfied; the pleasures of London ceased to be agreeable when they were no longer new. She was not formed for the thoughtless hurry of what is called high-life: she was bred in retirement notwithstanding her rank, and/ she longed to return to the elegant but tranquil amusements which used to employ her at her father's house. But it was not the being satiated with London alone, which induced her so earnestly to long for the time of her return: she dreaded the addresses of a young nobleman, to whom her aunt had introduced her, and whose praises she was perpetually sounding in her ears; yet in whom she could never see any thing to admire, but, on the contrary, had conceived a contempt for his person, his manners, and his sentiments.

As this nobleman was become a constant party in all Lady Elizabeth's entertainments, and as all his attentions which he did not bestow on himself were directed to Lady Cecilia, she found herself under the most disagreeable restraint; while her respect for her aunt, and for the rank of her guest, obliged her to endure the society of a man whom she despised, and even to feign complacence in his company, that she might not discover her contempt. Her mind was of/ that generous openness, and her sense of honour and truth so delicate, that she could not bear any thing like dissimulation, even where the intent was praise-worthy; and her situation would probably in a short time have become very disagreeable, had not a fit of the gout in the stomach, with which her father was attacked, furnished her with an excuse for quitting London long before the time she had originally intended. Her aunt pressed her to stay, and would have persuaded her that the fit would go off in a few days, as it had often done before: she was really sorry to part with her so soon, for she was justly proud of the sense, the beauty, and the virtues of her niece; but Lady Cecilia would not hear of any delay, the reasons already mentioned co-operating with her filial affection to make her long to throw herself into the bosom of her father.

It was in pursuance of this intention that she left London, after taking an affectionate leave of Mr. Belmont and Lady Elizabeth; and Mrs. Melville returning with her, they/ pursued their journey without any molestation, till that unhappy evening when that amiable woman lost her life, and the tender and affectionate Lady Cecilia, overwhelmed with grief and consternation, was conducted, by Ned's courage and activity, to the poor but friendly mansion of his father./

CHAP. IX.

In the morning the family assembled together to breakfast; and a visible joy was expressed in every countenance, when the doctor assured them that his patient was out of danger. As their anxiety for her life was now over, their next curiosity was to discover who she was. Various were their conjectures on this head; some of them wide, and some not very remote from the truth: they all however agreed that, let her be who she would, she was an angel both in form and disposition; and Evans, whose joy for her recovery knew no bounds, thanked Heaven for the accident that brought her to his house, and made him any ways instrumental to her comfort and satisfaction. The doctor told them that nothing would be now necessary for her, but nourishing food and exercise; that her/ mind must be made as cheerful as possible; and for this reason, all enquiries about her family or situation, or any thing that could agitate her spirits, must be wholly let alone. 'It is perfectly immaterial who she is,' said he; 'she is in distress, and moreover she is certainly a gentlewoman, and in every respect entitled to all that can be done for her. I would, therefore, ask her no questions, but leave it to herself to disclose her situation or not as she thinks proper.' Mr. Evans entirely agreed with the doctor in all these sentiments; and the women were obliged to acquiesce, though it must be owned their curiosity was not a bit abated.

After breakfast the doctor took his leave, as his attendance was no longer necessary; but he promised to come frequently to see her, and to be ready in a moment if he should be wanted. Ned saddled his horse, and rode a part of the way with him; and the worthy Evans betook himself to his garden, which he had not visited before since this disastrous event took place. A/ garden, to an elegant and philosophical mind, is one of the greatest amusements in the world; every beneficent and amiable passion is gratified in it; and it also answers the noblest moral purpose, when it lifts up the heart in gratitude and admiration to that great and benevolent Being, who there so profusely gratifies the senses of his creatures. Our Saviour himself suggests this to us, when he desires us to consider the lilies of the field; which, though they neither toil nor spin, yet surpass Solomon himself in the beauty of their raiment. Mr. Evans was extremely sensible of this beauty, and had from his earliest years addicted himself to the study of

48 *The History of Ned Evans*

Nature, and to the pleasing and rational amusement of cultivating and adorning her wherever he had opportunity. Next to the improvement of the mind, he thought nothing more becoming than that of his garden, which he considered as the primitive employment of mankind, prescribed to our first parents by God himself, and therefore every way suitable to our nature, and to/ pure unadulterated taste. His skill in the science was consummate; not only in the theory but practice, for he wrought in it himself, which he considered as a wholesome and pleasant exercise, in which his son often joined him when not employed in more important concerns.

The spot which he now possessed was beautifully situated for the purpose: it contained only about three acres, but was so agreeably diversified by the inequality of the ground, and by the winding walks which he had formed through it, as to appear of much greater extent; and you might walk miles in it without being tired, and even without being conscious that you were treading the same ground. All the flowers which our climates produce to perfection were here profusely scattered, and in such a manner as to appear the work of Nature, though in fact they were attended with the nicest care, and disposed by the most artful management, so as to contrast their colours, and set off their beauties to the best advantage./ There were no walls to this garden; for Mr. Evans did not go to the unnecessary expence of raising foreign fruits: he was contented with those which could bear the climate, without artificial heat; and he had abundance of these of all kinds, and in the greatest perfection. His garden was nevertheless well fenced; for it had high and close hedges, where holly formed a verdant and impenetrable wall, and where sweet brier and woodbine spread their delicious odours all around. His esculent herbs,[37] such as cabbages and the like, which, though of most use, are the least ornamental, he disposed in such a manner as not to be seen unless purposely visited: they were concealed in large and irregular plots, surrounded by flowering shrubs, and various kinds of fruit-trees, both standards and espaliers, among which the walks were formed; which were perpetually covered with a short and verdant grass, kept closely mowed and rolled, where not a weed was to be seen. A large wood/ of forest trees sheltered it from the rigours of the north and eastern wind; and from among these trees issued the river we have already spoken of, which murmured through the bottom of the garden, the banks of which Mr. Evans had every where adorned with violets, cowslips, primroses, and lilies of the valley, which thriving under the shade of some weeping willows, that he had also planted there, formed a delicious and elegant seat, not to be equalled by the most pompous and elaborate work of the most skilful architect. To this place he now came; and though it was a season in the year the least favourable to rural pleasures, yet the fineness of the day conspiring with the tranquillity of his mind, and with the recent joy which the recovery of his fair lodger had created, he fell into a train of rapturous sensations, which at length broke forth into the following soliloquy:

'How happy are these shades! How beautiful is Nature! 'T is now the depth of winter; yet the luxuriant verdure of you/ laurestinus, the rich crimson of the fruit of yon arbutus glowing through the deep green of its surrounding leaves, seems to take from summer the proud boast of vegetation, since it cannot produce any thing more beautiful. Hark! the sweet note of yon robin redbreast – he sits upon that naked currant bush, and warbles his song from amidst its leafless branches. Do you remember, little rogue, how often you regaled upon its fruit? Do you expect to find the like entertainment now? Or rather, do you come, in the generosity of your little heart, to visit it in its distress, and, thankful for the delicious meals it has afforded you, to cheer it with your song, and comfort it for its departed verdure? Yes! sweet warbler, you follow the voice of Nature, and raise your tuneful song in gratitude to him that feeds you. Shall man then be silent? Shall he to whom most is given be the last to acknowledge? – O! thou sovereign and almighty Goodness, whose care is over all thy works: Thou who kindlest/ the sun, and directest the planets in their orbs; who findest food for the young ravens, and protectest the embryo of a worm: Thou who art above all things, and before all things, and who nevertheless carest and providest for the meanest of thy creatures: Oh! grant me a heart to feel and to adore thy goodness, who hast made me what I am, and so much happier than I deserve to be! – Oh! give me gratitude to acknowledge thy spontaneous mercy, and let it produce in me a like feeling to my fellow creatures, that, humbly imitating thy great example, I may impart to them some of that good which thou hast so liberally bestowed on me!'

Such was the train of thinking which the sight of a robin redbreast on a currant bush excited in the mind of the humble and the virtuous Evans: and where a mind is formed like his to virtue, and trained up in the exercise of piety and devotion, there is scarce an object in nature that is not productive of improvement, no sensation of/ pleasure that does not at the same time abound with virtue. O happy and enviable feeling! O exalted and sublime sentiment! This is true religion, equally removed from enthusiasm and superstition – this is that small still voice which follows us into our inmost retirement, which speaks in secret to our soul – the gentle key by which the affections of all virtuous hearts are tuned, and which affords them on earth no mean resemblance of the eternal harmony of heaven.

In this train of soothing and sacred meditation did Mr. Evans remain until Ned returned from his ride. As soon as he had put his horse in the stable, and set a good lock of hay before him, which he never neglected, he went into the garden to his father, in order to assist him with any work in which he might happen to be engaged – a pious duty, which was always agreeable to Ned, who loved him

50 *The History of Ned Evans*

at once with all the affection of a child, and all the manly warmth of a friend. He revered him for his virtues, loved him for the sweetness/ of his temper, admired him even in his weaknesses, and felt for him every thing that the most dutiful affection or the most impassioned friendship could suggest. Evans again felt all these sentiments for Ned, with four-fold force; so that perhaps in the whole circuit of nature there was not another father and another son so linked together by every tie of reciprocal duty and affection. The sight of Ned soon roused Mr. Evans from his meditations, and they both went seriously to work for some hours, in correcting all that had gone amiss since they had last wrought together, and in doing such other business as the season of the year allowed. Let not my readers think this detail uninteresting, or smile with contempt on the humble labours of Evans and his son. If they can inspire one breast with a taste for those pure pleasures, if they can induce one pair of idle hands to occupy themselves in the same innocent and delightful employment, these pages have not been written in vain./

The hour of dinner gave respite to their labour, and their labour gave them appetite; a sauce more luxurious than is to be found in the whole system of cookery, and which indeed it is not in the power of any thing but labour to bestow. Their meal to-day was particularly enlivened by the presence both of Mrs. Evans and Miss Watkin, who indulged their native gaiety and good humour without restraint, since the happy change in their fair patient's complaint; and Lady Cecilia herself had sat up the greatest part of the day, and had so far indulged their curiosity as to tell them her name was Cecilia Rivers, and that she was the only daughter of a gentleman of distinction in Ireland: but she did not tell them that her father was an earl, thinking the splendour of a title would embarrass them; and besides, while she remained in Wales, she wished to be entirely at ease, without being known or visited only by the good family she was in, and their particular friends. Every thing indeed conspired to/ make retirement at this time as pleasing to her as it was necessary; and she only waited the return of a little strength, to pursue her journey to Ireland, where her heart and her affections were now wholly centred. This was the first time that she had ever been out of it; and it had so happened that she had hardly ever passed a truly pleasant day since she left it. The dreadful event which deprived her of her dearest female friend completely disgusted her with travelling, and she longed with impatience for the time that was to restore her to her country, her friends, and the endearing embraces of her father. Her impatience, however, did not get the better of her wisdom; she knew she was in no condition to travel, and she determined to wait the restoration of her health, before she would attempt it: for the rest, she was perfectly satisfied with her, present situation; she was pleased with the attention of Mrs. Evans and Miss Watkin, and was fully sensible that, since the fatal accident did happen, she could no where/ have been placed more to her satisfaction. Mrs. Evans and Miss Watkin, on the other hand, thought and spoke of her as if she was more than human. Her elegance, her youth, her beauty, her distresses, and above all her piety and resignation, had raised in them sentiments of the highest admiration; and as no object is more interesting than beauty in distress, especially where that beauty is heightened by virtue, it is no wonder if the amiable Mrs. Evans grew enamoured with Lady Cecilia, and if, next to her husband and Ned, she loved her better than any thing else in the world. This really was very soon the case; and if Lady Cecilia's affections had not been so deeply and so recently wounded, by the loss of Mrs. Melville (a loss which she will never cease to deplore but with her life), it is highly probable she would have felt an equal attachment to Mrs. Evans. As it was, she felt all that gratitude could inspire; which is every thing in a heart susceptible like hers, formed both by nature and education to be the/ dwelling of every noble and exalted virtue. Being thus, therefore, equally satisfied with each other, Mrs. Evans did every thing in her power to contribute to the ease and amusement of Lady Cecilia; and her ladyship, supported by religion, submitted to a calamity which could not be cured, and, daily recovering health and strength, with them recovered her usual cheerfulness and serenity of mind./

CHAP. X.

In the neighbouring village, not far from Mr. Evans's house, there dwelt a poor man whose name was John Price: in his youthful days he had addicted himself to poetry and music, talents not uncommon in Wales; but finding, like other poets, that the Muses seldom could maintain their votaries, he listened to the noble trumpet of ambition, and enlisted in a marching regiment, in the twentieth year of his age. He served his country with courage and fidelity for several years, though he found Mars a severer master, and almost as bad a patron as Apollo. At last having received a wound in the head at the unfortunate battle of Fontenoy,[38] which ended in a defluxion,[39] by which he lost his sight; he was discharged the service, and returned to his native soil, to subsist on a small pension which the bounty of his country allowed him./

Here he returned to his first mistresses the Muses, and composed ballads on his achievements and misfortunes, which he set to the ancient music of his country, and sung, accompanied with the harp, on which he played with tolerable skill. The charms of his music and of his pension got him a wife, and they between them got a daughter, who was now grown a rosy, buxom girl, with hazel eyes, and auburn hair, whose curling tresses used to ensnare the hearts of all the young fellows who came to listen to her father's music, and enjoy a pot of ale; for the good housewifery of the wife brewed excellent ale, which, accompanied with their music, they retailed in the village, and, to say the truth, it was an entertainment not altogether inelegant. Even Ned himself was charmed; and though he never descended to sit with the company that usually resorted there, yet he loved the old man, and used to go at times, when he knew the country people were otherwise engaged, to hear his tales and his songs, and to play/ himself upon the harp – on which he soon made such proficiency as to touch it with far more delicacy and taste than Price himself.

One evening when Lady Cecilia had recovered so far as to partake of the family meals below stairs, after the tea-things had been taken away, and the company were chatting about the fire, Miss Watkin asked her ladyship, if she was fond of music? 'I love it passionately,' replied Lady Cecilia, 'and think music well performed the most rapturous entertainment upon earth.' 'It is indeed,' said Mr.

Evans, 'the most affecting of all entertainments; but it is only rapturous when employed in its first and noblest destination, the praises of the great Creator.' 'Your observation is just,' replied Lady Cecilia, 'and I will not contend for the propriety of my expression; though I confess I have felt such pleasure at some concerts, as I have no idea of being transcended by any thing on this side of heaven: – but, to be sure, music, when employed/ in religious worship, receives a grand addition of sublimity, nor can the feeble praises of man be offered up in any way more suitable to the inconceivable dignity of the great Being to whom they are addressed.' 'I fully agree with you in this sentiment,' said Mr. Evans; 'and I cannot but regret that custom has banished from our churches all instruments except the organ; which, though I allow it to be the grandest of all instruments, and the best suited to religious worship, is yet not the only one that might be so employed; and is besides of such cumbrous and expensive structure, as cannot be attained by any churches except cathedrals, or such as have very large revenues annexed to them.' 'It is a pity, indeed,' said Lady Cecilia, 'that organs large enough for a church are so very expensive; but I know of no instrument that could supply its place. The harpsichord is too feeble; and though I greatly admire a violin in a room, yet I could not endure to see a fiddler's elbow/ shaking in an anthem, or a trumpeter puffing out his cheeks in the solemn praises of the Deity.' Evans smiled – 'I confess,' said he, 'these objects would be rather ludicrous; but what think you of the harp? This is a solemn instrument, and not liable to those objections.' 'It is an instrument I am not very well acquainted with,' said Lady Cecilia: 'I have sometimes heard it played upon in Ireland,' said she, 'commonly by some blind woman;[40] but either from its own defects, or the want of skill in the performer, I did not think it much preferable to a dulcimer.'[41] 'You have never heard the Welch harp, then?' said Mr. Evans. She replied that she had not. – 'Would you like to hear it?' said he. 'Extremely,' said Lady Cecilia – 'have you one in the house?' 'No, madam,' said Mr. Evans, 'but there is a poor old fellow in the neighbourhood, who was a soldier, and who lost his sight in the service of his country, but who, having some knowledge of playing on the harp, now follows it as/ a profession; and if you have a mind to hear it, I will send for him, and order him to bring his harp with him.' Lady Cecilia said, 'By all means; it would give me a great deal of pleasure.' So the maid was immediately dispatched for honest John.

The poor fellow was however unable to come; he had got a fall two days before, by trusting too much to his knowledge of the way, and walking without his dog, who commonly was a faithful guide; and he was now lying in bed, unable to get out of it, from the bruise he had received. – These tidings were a great disappointment to the whole company, and Lady Cecilia could not conceal that she was affected both by the loss of the entertainment, and much more by the accident which occasioned it. Ned perceived her emotion – 'I am sorry,'

54 *The History of Ned Evans*

said he, 'for poor John's mischance; he is an honest and a good-natured old man; and deserved a happier lot in life than has fallen to his share: however, that Miss Cecilia (as he called her) may not be wholly disappointed,/ I will go and fetch the harp myself, and endeavour to strum upon it a little for her entertainment.' Lady Cecilia now recovered her spirits, and said, he was always doing obliging things; but begged, if it was far to fetch, or troublesome to carry, that he would not undertake it, as she could wait with patience till another time. Ned said it was neither far to fetch nor troublesome to carry, at least he should think nothing troublesome that could contribute to her entertainment; and he immediately went for it.

When he left the room, Lady Cecilia observed to Mrs. Evans, that her son had the most natural politeness of any young man she ever saw. 'My obligations to him are great,' said she; 'great indeed, never to be forgotten! – (here a tear trembled in her eye) – yet he is always contriving to add to them by those little attentions which are the test of good manners, and which receive additional grace by the way in which he performs them.' Mrs. Evans replied,/ 'You are very good, madam, to think so favourably of my son: he is indeed an excellent lad, with a kind and a tender heart; but you over-rate the services he has done to you, which are only those of duty, and which I know he thinks the happiest incident of his life.'

Miss Watkin bore her testimony to the amiableness of Ned's manners and disposition; and assured Lady Cecilia, she would have no loss of the harper, for that Mr. Edward played upon that instrument with far greater delicacy of taste and power of execution.

Ned soon after returned with the harp upon his back; which when Lady Cecilia saw, she was confounded indeed at giving him so much trouble; for she had no idea of its size from the harps she had seen in Ireland. This was one of the best of its kind, and so tall, that when Ned had reared it, and placed it in its proper position, the top of it almost touched the ceiling of the room. The Welch harps, besides the great/ difference in their size, are all strung with catgut, which gives them a vast advantage over those of Ireland, which are not only diminutive in comparison, but have fewer strings, and those of wire, which never have the softness nor expression of the cat-gut strings. Ned now called forth all its harmony – his fingers flew over the chords with rapid velocity, yet touched them with such lightness that the sound at first seemed like the breath of some solemn and melodious voices wasted by the air from a remote distance; then, swelling by degrees, appeared to approach nearer, till, rising to its highest pitch, it warbled for some minutes, like the sweet notes of the sky-lark singing at the gates of heaven; then all at once descended in a full stream of the richest melody, that overpowered the soul, and drowned the senses in a rapturous elysium.

Lady Cecilia listened to it with astonishment – her breath seemed to keep pace with the notes through all their variations; and when he came to the close, she was almost/ exhausted, and, like Strada's nightingale,[42] had well nigh expired on the strings.

She was infinitely delighted with the entertainment, and confessed she had never heard any stringed instrument like it, and for sweetness of expression she thought it superior even to the organ itself. Evans said he was happy that she was pleased, and that she gave her sanction to his judgment.

'This,' said he, 'madam, is our national music, and perhaps I am partial to it on that account: I love it for another reason, and even hold it as something sacred; for this is the instrument in which we are told that holy David delighted, and for whose music he composed those sacred and divine hymns whose beauty and sublimity excel all the poems in the world.' He then made Ned play several anthems, and accompanied them with his voice; in which he himself joined with considerable grace and propriety.

When all was finished, he asked Lady/ Cecilia, if she did not think that instrument might be admitted into a church? 'Yes, Mr. Evans,' said she, 'I think it might be admitted into heaven; and if any thing on earth can without profaneness be compared to heaven, it is such an entertainment as you have this night given me. – A family linked in the closest bonds of unity and affection, dealing benevolence on all around them, and hymning the praises of their Creator to the most melodious of all instruments – I can conceive nothing on earth to exceed this, and it has made an impression on my heart that I think I shall be the better for all the days of my life.'

She then expressed a desire to try if she could make out a tune upon it. She was a perfect mistress of the harpsichord and the guitar; but never having touched a harp before, she could not be expected to do much on it at first. Ned Evans, however, shewed her the manner of touching the strings, and, leaning over her chair, assisted her in holding the harp. She very quickly accomplished/ several tunes, and accompanied one or two of them with her voice. Miss Watkin whispered to Mrs. Evans, that Miss Cecilia put her in mind of a beautiful print she had once seen, where her celebrated namesake, St. Cecilia, the patroness of music, was represented playing on a harp; and that Mr. Edward looked like the angel that had come down from heaven to listen to her. This observation was made in the purity and innocence of her heart; but the elegance and aptness of the allusion surprised Mrs. Evans, knowing that Miss Watkin, though perfectly amiable in her disposition, was, from her confined education, rather vulgar in her conceptions.

From that moment however she suspected that Ned had made an impression on her heart; and as it would certainly be an advantageous alliance for him, she was not at all displeased at it. Morgan was now called, to carry the harp back to

56 *The History of Ned Evans*

its owner; and as he went out of the room, Lady Cecilia followed, and, slipping a guinea into/ his hand, desired him to give it to the poor man, and to bid him bring his harp again as soon as he was able to come with it: and she charged him not to say a word to any body else about the money. He promised faithfully to obey her: nevertheless, in two hours, it was known to the whole house. Though this action could not raise Lady Cecilia in the esteem of the Evanses where she already held the highest place, yet it served to confirm them in a just opinion of the goodness of her heart, and also in that of her being a lady of distinction./

CHAP. XI.

Miss Watkin's attendance not being now necessary, she returned home to her father, who indeed could not do very conveniently without her, and who (considering his temper) had submitted with wonderful patience and good humour to want her so long. She left Lady Cecilia with infinite regret; and though it was but a small distance from Mr. Evans's to her father's, yet she shed as many tears at parting as if they never were to meet again: but Lady Cecilia, who had a sincere regard for her, and thought herself much indebted to her for her attendance, made her promise to come as often as she could, while she should still be obliged to remain in the country. Air and exercise being recommended to her as essential to her recovery, she borrowed a little pony from Miss Watkin, which had been well broke for her/ riding; and Ned Evans had the supreme felicity of attending her, sometimes on foot, and sometimes on his father's horse, in all her little excursions. He fed and dressed the little pony himself, cleaned the silver bit, and took care that all about him should be completely neat, for the charming burthen he was to carry. He did not neglect his own dress, nor the appearance of the horse which he was to ride; being solicitous, in every thing, to appear attentive to the amiable and elegant Cecilia.

Many were the delightful rides they took in that beautiful and romantic country, whose sweetest scenes were studiously selected by Ned to conduct his fair companion to; and their conversation may be supposed to be such as would naturally flow from two virtuous and well-informed minds solicitous to please each other, whose tastes and whose opinions were very nearly alike, although their rank and their education had been so widely different. And indeed so successful had Ned been in finding amusements for/ Lady Cecilia, that time slipped imperceptibly away; and near three weeks had now elapsed before her ladyship discovered that she was restored to the full possession of beauty, health, and strength. Her glass would never have made this discovery; for though she looked in it every day, yet she did not know that she was handsome: but some accidental question about Ireland, one day after dinner, brought it fully to her mind; and her father, her friends, and her country, rushing at once upon her recollection, took full possession of her soul, and absorbed all other desires. She that very

58 *The History of Ned Evans*

evening set about preparing for her journey, and her first care was to send a card to Dr. Jones, requesting his company the next day, and desiring him to bring his bill along with him.

The greatest part of the evening she spent in her own apartment, adjusting her own trunks, and that of her dear departed friend Mrs. Melville. The sight of her clothes, and the ornaments she used to wear, and/ other little circumstances that could not fail to occur, brought the memory of that excellent woman fresh to her mind; she spent hours in the tender and affecting contemplation of the various articles that had once been hers: and when Mrs. Evans came up to summon her to supper, she was under the necessity of entreating to be excused, and to be allowed to dedicate that night to tears, and to the beloved memory of her unfortunate friend.

At length the sources of her sorrow dried; she retired to rest, when a sweet slumber refreshed her wearied spirits, till the morning rose with healing on its wings; and she repaired to breakfast, in all the power of renovated health and beauty. Never did she appear so lovely in the eyes of the Evanses, as at this instant. Whether it was that her returned health, and the complacency of her mind in the agreeable hope of speedily being restored to her friends, did really kindle in her countenance a more than ordinary glow of beauty; or whether, rather, the knowledge/ how soon they were to lose her, did not awaken in the hearts of the Evanses a more lively and impassioned tenderness: certain it is they were all of them more affected with her appearance this morning than ever they had been before; and Ned, in particular, could hardly take his eyes off her, except to conceal a rising moisture, which in spite of all his efforts would sometimes become visible. He was pleased however to hear her propose taking a last ride with him, the day being remarkably fine, and he hastened with his usual alacrity to saddle his own horse and her little pony: neither had he been forgetful of himself on this occasion; for, thinking it might be the last time he should have the happiness to accompany her, and intending to propose a ride, if Lady Cecilia had not herself prevented him, he had taken more than ordinary care that morning of his dress, solicitous (perhaps without knowing it) to appear particularly amiable to her. He had on a peagreen/ frock, quite new, with silver buttons, a casimir[43] waistcoat with a fancied pattern of silk embroidery round the button holes, new doe-skin breeches, and boots; his hat, which was also new, was adorned with a silver loop and band; his hair, which was always beautiful, was this day uncommonly glossy, and disposed in luxuriant curls round his neck; and his whole figure, animated with health, vigour, and activity, was certainly well calculated to make an impression on a female heart.

Lady Cecilia complimented him on the elegance of his dress, which she had not seen before; and he assured her he had made it up wholly with the view of being a more suitable attendant upon her in the excursions which he had the happiness to take with her. Lady Cecilia wore the same elegant travelling habit, in which she had first made her appearance on the unfortunate night of her arrival; and, thus equipped, they rode out together.

They visited in their tour all the places/ to which they had been accustomed to go in their former jaunts, her ladyship having a desire to see them for the last time; when turning her horse to go home, Ned told her he had one sequestered scene yet to shew her, which he had purposely reserved for the last, because he himself thought it the most beautiful, and that, as he was in the custom of often visiting it, he wished it to be endeared to him by her presence and approbation. Lady Cecilia made no objection, and they proceeded, by a narrow road with high hedges, till they came to a valley between two mountains. This valley was not above one hundred yards wide; and the mountains, which rose to a prodigious height on each side, seemed to correspond so in their windings and appearance, as to make it probable that they once were united, but torn asunder by some very remote and violent convulsion of nature. Their sides were clothed almost to the top with thick forests, among which there were so many hollies and other ever-greens as gave them a rich verdure/ even in the depth of winter: here and there a naked rock, loftier than the tallest steeple, stood like a giant baring his breast to the tempest, and bidding defiance both to time and weather. Through the midst of the vale a clear stream ran murmuring over a bed of white pebbles, and brawled among the fragments of rocks, which the revolution of ages had sepa-rated from the lofty summits of the surrounding mountains. The banks on either side were covered with a short thick moss, and a profusion of mountain flowers and alpine plants, which were at once grateful to the eye and easy to the tread. Through this vale they rode by a gently-winding path, till they were stopped by a stupendous cavern, out of which the brook issued, and which was hollowed by nature in an enormous rock, that stretched quite across the valley and united the mountains on either side. Lady Cecilia was prodigiously struck with the beauty and grandeur of the scene, and stood for a long time contemplating the awful entrance of/ the cavern with a mixture of terror and delight. Ned asked her to go into it; but she seemed more than half afraid, intimidated by its frowning horror, and the darkness in which it seemed involved: but Ned assured her there was no kind of danger, and if she could get the better of her apprehension, she would find her curiosity fully gratified.

Encouraged by his persuasion, and relying on his protection, she consented to go in; so, alighting from their horses, Ned fastened them to the stump of an old tree, and led the lovely Cecilia to the mouth of the cavern. The entrance was overgrown with ivy and various kinds of shrubs and bushes, which enriched the nakedness of the rocks, and contracted the mouth of the opening: within, it rose to a vast height, like the aile of a Gothic cathedral, and was adorned with an infinite variety of beautiful petrifactions,[44] which hung like icicles from the

60 *The History of Ned Evans*

roof, and round all the sides assumed a thousand curious and fantastic forms, in/ which a lively imagination could discover a never-ending variety of resemblances to natural objects.

They walked through this wonderful cavern near a hundred yards, when they came to a large hole in the side of the rock, out of which came pouring the stream purer than crystal itself, which watered the valley, and which flowed with an unceasing and unvarying spring.

The terror with which Lady Cecilia entered the cave was now dissipated, for she found it infinitely lighter within than it appeared to be without; and taking advantage of a mossy bank which was near, she sat down to contemplate at leisure the wonderful beauties that surrounded her.

Ned sat down beside her, and, removing a little stone which was at his back, he produced some oranges and dried fruits, which he had before provided for such an occasion as this, and agreeably surprised Lady Cecilia with this elegant refreshment. Out of a deep scollop shell, which he had also brought/ on purpose, he presented her some water, scooped up from the pure and transparent element that issued from the rock; which when she had drunk, and expressed her satisfaction in its delicious and refreshing coolness – 'See,' said he, 'how easily nature is satisfied! and how bountifully and even luxuriously she provides for all who have purity of taste sufficient to relish her simple blessings!'

'Truly, Mr. Evans,' said Lady Cecilia, 'I see it and acknowledge it. This cavern, of Nature's making, surpasses in magnificence the most splendid apartment that wealth and grandeur ever erected; nor can the most laboured cookery produce any flavour so grateful as your fruits, or the most costly wines be so refreshing to a thirsty palate as the living stream which pours from this rock.'

"Twas thus,' said Evans, 'that mankind was intended to fare, by his great Creator, in the days of primeval innocence; when Eve spread her fruits in the bower,/ and Adam and the angel shared them with her. Yet,' said he, 'were this rock and this wilderness mine, and did the lovely Cecilia consent to share them with me, I should not envy Eve her fruits, nor Adam his paradise, though honoured with the company of angels.'[45]

The astonished Cecilia made no reply; a deep blush suffused her radiant countenance, and a universal tremor agitated her whole frame. She cast a look at Ned, in which he thought he saw severity mingled with sweetness; and rising to quit the cave, he hastened to atone for his presumption, and threw himself at her feet. 'Oh! stay,' he said; 'divine Cecilia, stay! and do not quit me in displeasure. Oh! pardon an unguarded word, which, though the genuine sentiment of my heart, shall yet never more offend you.' 'I beg of you to let me go, Mr. Evans,' she replied; 'let me go into the air: I did not expect such a speech from you, and far less that you should betray me into this horrid cavern to make me hear it.'/ 'Oh! best of women,' said Evans, 'say not I have betrayed you. I never did, nor

Volume I 61

never will betray you; I have indeed betrayed myself; betrayed a secret which I ought not to have revealed; which I should have locked up in my heart, till that wretched heart was broke with keeping it.' 'Well, let me pass, Mr. Evans,' said she; 'I did not desire to hear your secret, and wish to God I never had; let me pass, I desire you; I will hear nothing while you detain me in this odious cavern.'

Ned now rising with the most respectful diffidence, led her out of the cave; and then requesting her to sit down for a little, she consented. 'Oh! Miss Cecilia,' said he; 'I entreat you pardon me; on my knees I implore your forgiveness. Pity a heart that cannot live under your displeasure, and which never harboured a thought of you inconsistent with the purest honour and the profoundest reverence. If my unhappy passion has betrayed me into presumption, impute it I beseech you to my/ youth and inexperience, to my country manners, and confined education. That I love you with all the powers of my soul, I have ventured to declare, and never will deny; but this is my misfortune, and not my fault. It is impossible to behold you and not to love you, and surely it can never be criminal to admire excellence wherever it is found. To have dared to hint to you my passion, though in the most distant manner, was, I own, presumption; and for this presumption I entreat your pardon.' 'Mr. Evans,' replied her ladyship, 'you have my pardon; but when I had accompanied you alone in riding round this country, when I came with you to this solitary valley, and even ventured against my inclination into this odious cavern, I thought myself entitled to your protection, and little expected you would insult me with a declaration of love.' 'Cruel, nay unjust Miss Rivers,' said Ned, reassuming some dignity, 'when did I insult you? Know that it is not in my nature to insult the meanest/ woman upon earth, far less the idol of my soul's affection. If to love you with an ardour little short of adoration, with the tenderest and most disinterested passion, inspired indeed at first by your surprising beauty when I saw you in distress, and since confirmed by the surpassing excellence of your heart; if to know no happiness but in your presence, to desire no blessing but your welfare, and to be ready to lay down my life for your sake; if to express these sentiments in the humblest and most respectful terms, be to insult you, then have I mistaken the meaning of that word, and confess myself at a loss in what language to address you.' – 'I am sorry, Mr. Evans,' replied Lady Cecilia, 'that I should have made use of a word which, I confess, is too severe, but which you have taken up in a much stronger manner than I had any intention of giving cause for. I must therefore in my turn sue to you for pardon, for having used so unguarded an expression.' – 'But, oh! lovely Cecilia,' interrupted/ Evans, 'sue not to me for pardon, nor for any thing else – you are formed to command me, and my greatest pride shall be to be able to obey. It is now I fear that I have indeed insulted you, and that I am debtor to your goodness for being forgiven. Oh! pardon me, Miss Rivers, that I have presumed to lift my aspiring thoughts to your perfections. The happiness that I have enjoyed in your company has intoxi-

62 *The History of Ned Evans*

cated me, and made me to forget myself. Your native dignity has awoke me, and brought me to my senses. Who you are I know not, nor what is your rank or situation in life; I believe it, however, to be every thing that is noble and exalted. Pardon therefore, Miss Rivers, a presumption which your own condescension has given birth to. I know I am not worthy of you, and am astonished at my folly that could prompt your poor, forlorn, destitute Evans, without family, without fortune, without friends, and even without hope, to dare to lift his eyes so far above him. Yet believe/ me, Miss Cecilia, no unworthy motive, no sordid view of interest or wealth, has driven me to this madness: it was yourself, your charming self, that was alone the object of my contemplation. Ever since Heaven restored you to our prayers, and that I have had the honour to attend you in these excursions, which were recommended for the re-establishment of your health, I have been dancing on a sea of pleasure too tumultuous for my judgment, and have suffered my imagination to roam into a fanciful elysium, which I now know can never have a real existence; but I am now come home, Miss Cecilia, I will return to reason and myself. Forgive me then, Miss Rivers, this first, and this last transgression; restore me to that place in your esteem which my foolish presumption has too justly forfeited; and though I can never cease to adore you, yet trust me I shall never more insult you with the avowal of my flame, though it should burn in secret till it consumes me.' – 'Why, Mr. Evans,' said Lady Cecilia, 'do you again/ use a word which never should have passed between us? It is ungenerous thus to echo it upon me, when I have already apologized for it, and am sincerely sorry that it ever escaped me. I am abundantly sensible of your merits; infinitely grateful for the protection which your father has afforded me, and for the generous and even heroic part which you yourself have acted towards me. You are therefore in full and secure possession of my esteem, and you may be assured that neither it, nor my gratitude, can ever cease but with my life. But when you talk of love, you talk a language to which it does not become me to listen; and even suppose I could be so weak as to suffer my heart to be surprised, what would be the consequence but misery to us both? I know my duty to my honoured and beloved father too well, ever to dispose of myself without his concurrence; and I know that he would have insuperable objections to our union, though I make no doubt but he will have a just and grateful sense of the obligations/ you have laid us under.' – 'Oh! lovely Cecilia,' replied Evans, 'talk not of obligations, for you owe me none; it is I that am infinitely your debtor, for I owe to you the knowledge of myself. It is enough that you forgive me, that your charming lips have pronounced my pardon, and that you have again reinstated me in your esteem. To-morrow separates us perhaps for ever. I shall never more see you, nor behold you, nor hear the heavenly music of your voice. Your poor forlorn friend will lose the only happiness he has on earth, and you will no more be troubled with his importunities, or his complaints. Grant me then but one request. Grant it me, Miss Rivers, as the seal of my pardon, and I shall never trouble you with any thing more. Say, divine Cecilia, will you grant it me?' 'What am I to grant you, Mr. Evans?' said Lady Cecilia; 'and what request can you make, consistent with honour and prudence, that I can wish to refuse you?' 'O grant me!' he replied, 'one lock of your lovely hair,/ to wear next my bosom, and to remind me in all my troubles, that I have one angel friend to wish me well.' – 'I know not,' said Lady Cecilia, 'whether this request be consistent with prudence or not; but as the seal of your pardon I will give it you: and if you truly regard me as you say, remember, Mr. Evans, that she who gave it you is sincerely your friend; that your happiness and your honour are very near her heart; and let the sight of it remind you never to do anything unworthy either of yourself or her.' So saying, she drew a pair of scissars from her pocket-book, and presented them to Evans to take the lock where he chose. He received them with rapture, and severed one where it could not be missed, but which had played in a curling ringlet down her chaste and snowy bosom.

He returned her the scissars on his knees; and, pressing her lovely hand to his lips; 'What language can I find,' said he, 'in which to thank you for this inestimable gift! I know not what those stupid bigots/ feel who adore the filthy bones which the superstition of Rome has dignified with the name of relics: but I know, that as oft as I look upon this hair, I shall feel my soul expand with every virtue; and I shall pray to him from whom alone come all good gifts, to make me worthy of the friendship of Miss Cecilia Rivers.'

Thus all was cleared, and peace and confidence fully re-established between them. They now mounted their horses to go home, when Lady Cecilia took one lingering and parting look at the spot where they had been sitting – 'Well, really, Mr. Edward,' said she, 'this is a most charming scene, and the cavern the finest union of the sublime and beautiful[46] that I believe nature ever produced: it is a subject for the pencil of Salvator Rosa,[47] and has made such an impression on my fancy that I think I could draw it myself.' – 'May it never be erased then from your memory,' said Evans, 'as I assure you it never will from mine! and may my foolish presumption be buried in/ oblivion, that no circumstance may present itself to your remembrance to make the recollection of this scene unpleasing to you!'

They now rode towards home; but Lady Cecilia proposed calling on Miss Watkin, to take leave, as it was the last time she would have an opportunity of seeing her; and she prevailed on her to accompany them to Mr. Evans's, to spend the evening there. They found Doctor Jones already arrived, according to the invitation that was sent him. He was delighted to see Lady Cecilia so perfectly recovered, and was indeed astonished to behold the blaze of beauty that now surrounded her; which he had no idea of from the transient views he had of her in her sickness, and which received inexpressible addition from her native grace, her unaffected good humour, and from her seeming to be wholly unconscious that she excelled in any thing.

The day was passed with the utmost pleasantness, except that on the part of the Evanses it was a little chastised by the recollection/ that it was the last in which they were to enjoy her company, in all probability for ever; which was in truth to them become a serious misfortune, as her many amiable qualities had so endeared her to the old man and his good woman, that they loved her with the affection of parents, and, next to Ned, considered her as the dearest and the nearest friend they had.

Before Doctor Jones went away, she took occasion to ask him apart for his bill; it amounted to between three and four pounds: she gave him a bank note of ten pounds, which with great difficulty she obliged him to accept; and told him that she still considered herself as greatly his debtor, for his humanity and attention. This piece of generosity he disclosed to Mr. Evans before he left the house, which more and more confirmed his affection and esteem./

CHAP. XII.

THE morning now dawned serene, and the sun faintly gilding the summits of the mountains, shot his tremulous rays into the chamber where the lovely Cecilia was sleeping. A deep blush overspread her glowing cheek; and her dishevelled tresses, curling over her snowy neck, rose and fell respondent to the short and interrupted heavings which marked some inward agitation of her heart. Her heart indeed was the temple of innocence and unsullied purity, and, whether sleeping or waking, knew no thought, nor owned no sentiment, that could ruffle its repose; but fancy at that instant had presented to her sleeping senses a delusive dream, which caused her agitation. She imagined she had been out riding with young Evans, and that they had taken their course to the romantic valley which they had visited the day before. The rocks and the trees glowed/ with an unusual verdure, and all the harmony of the vernal groves was tuned to entertain her. The cavern which had yesterday struck her with awe, was now divested of its terrors, and all its rocks were covered, as she thought, with myrtles and roses, and a variety of other charming flowers, which diffused delicious odours through the whole vault. While all her senses were thus delighted, she beheld the image of Ned prostrate at her feet breathing the ardours of his passion, and pleading his cause with all the energy of native eloquence. She fancied that she heard him with complacency, and that she was even on the point of consenting to an union, when a dreadful tempest rose suddenly in the cavern: the roses and the myrtles died away – the unfortunate Edward vanished, no where to be found – and she was left alone in the cave, in stygian darkness, amidst the roar of waters, the bellowings of thunder, and the continual howl of raging and contending winds.

How charmed was she when she awoke/ and found it all delusion; when the soft beams of a mild and temperate sun, now wholly risen above the horizon, dispelled the horrid vision, and, like herself, beamed with beneficent ray on all around! She rose with joy from her bed; she blessed the new-born day; and poured out on her knees the effusions of grateful adoration to that greatest and best of Beings, who in an instant can break down and make whole again, can draw us from the depth of misery, can illumine even the gloom of death – whose

66   *The History of Ned Evans*

ear is never closed that it cannot hear, nor his hand shortened that it cannot save.

Eased now of her terrors, and her heart restored to its tranquillity, she equipped herself for her journey, and, fresh and fragrant as the moss rose which opens its dewy leaves to the sweet morning of the first of June, she repaired to breakfast to the parlour, where Mr. and Mrs. Evans were already dressed to receive her. A post-chaise had been ordered from Conway the night before for her, by Doctor Jones when he/ returned there, and was newly arrived to carry her to Bangor Ferry; and poor Ned, who had been long risen and dressed to attend his lovely friend for the last time, had gone out to see that all was right, and his own horse ready, that he might accompany her. If Lady Cecilia had had disturbed repose, this affectionate youth had none. In the silence of night, when his thoughts were no longer amused by conversation, or the sight of surrounding objects, they naturally turned inwards on himself, and he imagined the awful darkness of that hour no improper emblem of the gloom of his own situation. Now it was that he revolved in his soul all the transactions of the day; the image of the lovely Cecilia was ever present to his imagination; and her charming voice, enjoining him to love no more, still vibrated in his ear; while the sacred lock, which for the first time had been his nightly companion, reclined upon his breast and instilled into it new fuel to increase his flame. Ah! hapless youth! you are yet a stranger to/ her exalted rank – to her princely fortune – to the elevated sentiments of her family, which, descended from a long line of illustrious ancestors, would shudder at the thoughts of so unequal an alliance. Even she herself, the most virtuous of women and the most dutiful of children, too noble to conceive a passion which should appear below her; too wise to yield to it if she did conceive it; even she herself is leagued against you, and forms the strongest barrier to oppose your wishes. Summon then, ingenuous youth, your firmest resolution. All worthy and all manly as thou art, exert thy noblest courage, subdue yourself – subdue this unhappy passion, whilst yet it can be subdued, and do not cloud the golden morning of your life with hopeless love.

Mr. and Mrs. Evans and Lady Cecilia had begun breakfast before Ned came in. When he entered, her ladyship rose, and wished him a good morning. His eyes thanked her with the warmest gratitude; but his heart was too full to put his looks/ into language, and his tongue would have faltered in expressing it if he had. The truth is, that her ladyship herself was the only unembarrassed person in the company; and nothing but the pleasure she had in the hopes of so soon seeing her father and her friends, could have prevented her from being seized with the same soft infection. The moistened eyes which she beheld around her, were however pleasing testimonies of the sincere affection in which she was held; and the amiable manners of her kind hosts, joined to a just sense of her obligation to them, riveted them in her heart with the strongest attachment: she therefore hastened to cheer both them and herself, by giving a livelier turn to their thoughts – 'My dear and ever beloved friends,' said she, 'my kind and generous protectors, I see by the suffusion in your countenances how much I am indebted to your affection; and if at this instant I appear less moved, trust me it is not owing to any deficiency in the warmth of my gratitude, or in the truth and tenderness/ of my inviolable attachment. – You love me, and it is my joy and my pride to see it. You think you are going to lose me, and that you will never see me more. If I thought so, you would not see me thus unmoved, nor do I know to what lengths I might carry my affliction. No, my beloved friends! be assured your Cecilia can never forget you – far less recollect you with indifference. How then should I apprehend that the narrow channel between Wales and Dublin should for ever separate me from your embraces, or that I should not have many opportunities of seeing my beloved friends, both in their country and my own? I am going to the arms of a beloved parent, who will refuse me nothing; I cannot conceal the pleasure of my soul in the prospect of soon beholding the paternal smile with which he ever meets his children; and I anticipate the rapture with which he will hear of my escape, and the gratitude with which his noble and generous heart will overflow, when I recount to him the tenderness/ and affection I have experienced at your hands. Cease then, my honoured friends, to grieve for my departure; for I foresee many happy days for us all, and many pleasing hours that I trust we shall yet spend together.' – 'Excellent Miss Rivers!' said Mr. Evans, 'I admire the grace and beauty of your sentiments more than of your person; and I beseech the Almighty, who has promised length of days to those who honour their father and their mother, that he will be graciously pleased to make good that promise to you; extending your days to the longest period of human existence, and making them as happy and as prosperous as long. For us, we shall rejoice in every good that can befall you; we trust you will not deny us the pleasure to hear often from you; and, whether we ever meet again, or this is the last time we are to have that happiness, we shall never cease to pray for your prosperity, and to think of you with the tenderest affection and most profound respect.'/

Mrs. Evans joined in all these sentiments of her husband, and poor Ned looked a great deal more than he expressed. The carriage being at last ready, Mr. Evans conducted her to it, while Ned mounted his horse to see her safe over the ferry. As she was stepping into the chaise, she put five guineas into Mr. Evans's hand, requesting him to distribute it to such poor people in his neighbourhood as he knew stood most in need of it; and, waving her hand to Mrs. Evans in a last and tender adieu, she drove off.

Ned rode by the side of the chaise; and the day being fine, he pointed out to her the many beautiful objects with which that road abounds; and Lady Cecilia, wishing to cheer his spirits, which she soon discerned were ebbed into his heart, endeavoured to give their conversation a lively turn, and talked of what she would do when she next visited Wales. In this manner did they pass the time till they came to Bangor Ferry, when a new chaise being to be got/ at the other side, Ned went over in the boat with her to see her safe in it, and that she might have no trouble with her trunks or her postillions. The chaise was soon got, and the trying moment was just arrived when the faithful and affectionate Edward was to take his last adieu – when his heart was to be robbed of its beloved inhabitant, the desire of his eyes to be withdrawn from his view; never, perhaps never to behold her more!

He bore this trial, however, as became a man – as one who knew how to feel, but who would not be overwhelmed. He conducted his adored Cecilia to the carriage, and, taking her hand (which she did not withdraw), two tender tears dropped on it as he placed her in her seat. These he respectfully kissed off; – and as he stood leaning on the door, two others, which appeared in his eyes, fell on a white handkerchief which he then held in his hand. Her ladyship, who beheld his sincere and silent sorrow not without visible emotion, was obliged, for the first time, to put her handkerchief also to her eyes – /'Come,' said she, 'generous Edward!' as she removed it, 'I see the tenderness of your heart, and I respect it. Give me that hand-kerchief, and take you mine: they are embalmed with the tears of friendship, and ought not to be put to any vulgar use.' 'O beloved Cecilia!' replied he, 'how gracious is this gift! Yes, I will retain it as a sacred treasure – and when you see the two initials of my name, O remember your hapless Edward, and pray that I may be enabled to obey your last commands.' The horses now moved – the friends were separated. She waved her hand from the window, and the forlorn Edward remained fixed till the turning of the road withdrew the carriage from his view. When he could no longer see it, he still continued to listen to its lessening sound, till the dying rumbling of the wheels was heard no more. At length he awoke from his trance. He repassed the ferry alone; and, mounting his horse at Jackson's, returned with slow and sorrowing steps to his father's./

CHAP. XIII.

It was almost dark by the time he got home. His first care was to put up his horse in the stable, and to set before him a good feed of oats and a rack full of the best hay: for, though poor Ned himself had not tasted a morsel since the morning, nor did even feel the least appetite, yet he very humanely considered that honest Blackbird, strong as the friendship was between them, might not perhaps sympathize with him in all his feelings. He did not, however, on that account, follow the example of too many, who, when unhappy themselves, wish to make every one connected with them unhappy also; but he followed the natural bent of his inclination, which was to impart pleasure to the utmost of his power to every being around him, rational or irrational; and he justly thought, that if the divine Being had condescended to order/ that the ox which treadeth out the corn should not be muzzled,[48] but should have his share of the corn for his wages, so it became him to provide a comfortable meal and lodging for the faithful beast who had carried him without stumbling for twenty miles. And indeed it were to be wished that those who call themselves good-natured people, would endeavour to manifest that amiable quality in all their actions; for I have often seen instances where those who were esteemed the best-natured people in the world by their superiors, were held in a very different light by their domestics – and he who was the delight of a whole company at a tavern, go home to be the terror of his wife and children. True good nature is the most exalted virtue of the soul. This is that virtue which St. Paul calls charity, and which, to be genuine, must be as extensive as creation. It must not confine its feelings to its friends and benefactors, nor even to its species. It must desire the happiness of universal nature; as far as is in/ its power it must promote it; and it must not behold without commiseration the sufferings of the meanest worm. With this virtue was our Ned possessed, as much as ever it was possessed by any human being; and now having seen all things right in the stable, he went into the house to his father.

The good old man he found cheering himself with a pipe and a mug of ale, while Mrs. Evans was preparing to make tea for herself and Miss Watkin, who had come to spend the evening with her, and to console her friends for the absence of their late guest. And in truth this act of friendship was not unneces-

70 *The History of Ned Evans*

sary; for if one usually finds a want after parting with a common acquaintance, after having been any time together, much more did Evans and his wife regret the loss of Lady Cecilia, whom they truly loved as if she was their own daughter. The whole of the conversation turned upon her many virtues and engaging qualities, and the women would sometimes give scope to fanciful hopes of profit and/ advantage that might arise from her acquaintance. But these Mr. Evans checked, declaring that he desired no profits or advantages further than the consciousness of having done his duty, and the pleasure it gave him to think he had been of any use to her; but as for any change in his worldly situation, he did not know that it could be changed for the better, at least not for any in which he could be more contented. 'Well – but, my dear,' said Mrs. Evans, 'who knows but Miss's father may be some great man, as indeed I am convinced from her appearance that he is? – and who knows but he may get you a living, or perhaps make you an Irish bishop?' Evans looked at her with an eye of pity, not wholly free from contempt. 'My dear,' said he, 'I would advise you not to feed your fancy with such romantic and absurd expectations, which will never produce any thing but disappointment. My head does not ach for a mitre, which I am convinced would neither become it so well, nor sit/ so easy upon it as the worsted night-cap you were so good as to knit for me last week. Miss Rivers's father may, for aught I know, be a great man: but you know nothing of the great, if you think they are disposed to give magnificent rewards for small obligations; they rate the value of their favours at full as much as they are worth, and indeed seldom bestow any thing for nothing except promises.'

Ned sat for the most part silent, wholly wrapped up in the contemplation of Cecilia herself, and altogether indifferent to the titles and mitres either of her father or his own. He longed for the hour of rest, which was to free him from the embarrassment of company; when he might indulge his thoughts without witnesses or interruption – could clasp the sacred ringlet to his bosom, and feed upon that fatal flame which delighted while it consumed him.

Several days now passed over without any remarkable occurrence happening, except/ that both Mr. and Mrs. Evans were alarmed at the visible change in Ned's disposition. He was no longer the gay, the easy, cheerful lad, with joy laughing in his eyes, and health beaming on his cheek. He no longer rose with the sun to help his father in the garden, or follow the hounds with his favourite companions. He sometimes rode out indeed, but it was always alone; and once or twice he was absent from morning till night without any person's knowing where he had been. In company he appeared dull and inattentive, and at all times seemed immersed in some profound contemplation. As his colour began visibly to fade, and his flesh to waste, both Mr. and Mrs. Evans were greatly alarmed, and not without reason, apprehending that he was going fast into a decline. This, however, seemed so opposite to his constitution, that they could hardly imagine it; and the pious Evans began to fear that he might have some secret complaint which he was afraid to own, but which required the aid/ of physic. He determined therefore to watch him close, and, if he found any confirmation of this suspicion, to apply immediately to Doctor Jones. He thought unworthily, however, of his boy, and had the great satisfaction to be soon convinced that he did so; for, going one morning into Ned's room when he was out riding, he there found his escritoir[49] open, which he had forgot to lock; and as several papers were lying on it, he could not resist a father's curiosity (which perhaps in his case was fully justifiable) to examine them.

Here were found several little landscapes of places in the neighbourhood, some of them only sketched, and some nearly finished, in all of which were introduced two figures either riding or sitting, which Mr. Evans imagined bore some resemblance to the forms of Lady Cecilia and his son. There were some attempts to take a likeness of her features; but these were very imperfect, though sufficiently like to indicate for whom they were designed. In one corner/ lay the sacred ringlet, carefully deposited in a small wafer box, and on a loose bit of paper were written the following unfinished lines:

> Why sinks my soul beneath this leaden gloom?
> What woe is this that steals my youth away?
> Why wish I for thy cold embrace, my tomb,
> Ere twenty suns have seen my natal day?
>
> No youth whose gentle heart with mine was twin'd
> In friendship's holy bond, hath prov'd untrue;
> Nor to the grave has cruel death consign'd
> One kindred name whose loss I need to rue.
>
> No foul dishonour stains my youthful fame,
> No secret guilt appalls my conscious soul;
> I never ting'd my parents' cheeks with shame,
> Nor wish'd to wander from their just controul.
>
> Why sink I then beneath this leaden gloom?
> What woe is this that steals my youth away?
> O love! O cruel love! you write my doom,
> You sign my death – and I, content, obey.
>
> But if the angel maid for whom I die,
> Who heard my vows, and yet – /

When Mr. Evans had read these lines, he was no longer at a loss to know the true cause of Ned's distemper; and great was his satisfaction to find his suspicions had been unjust, and that there was not the least reason to be apprehensive of his going into a decline. His being in love gave him no manner of uneasiness, as he

72 *The History of Ned Evans*

thought it nothing but what was natural to his age and constitution, especially as the object of his affections was so supremely amiable. He saw indeed the folly of his passion, and the great improbability of its ever being gratified; but he could not condemn it: he therefore determined to treat it with jocularity, and to find out some employment for Ned that should wean him from it by degrees. As for the escritoir, he left it just as he found it, and hastened to impart his discovery to his wife. That good woman was rejoiced to find it was nothing but love, which she considered in the same light as a fit of the gripes, and almost as easy to be cured: – but it must be remembered that/ she was fifty-six years of age, and that it is much to be doubted whether she ever was possessed of the tender and exquisite sensibility of the gentle and refined Edward.

A little before dinner he came home, and, going into his room, was astonished to see his escritoir open. When he saw, however, the key in it, and all his papers just as he had left them, he was satisfied that nobody had seen them; and, hastily locking them up, he made a secret vow never to be so careless again.

At dinner he could hardly eat any thing, though he had taken a long ride, and though Mrs. Evans had provided something that she knew he liked. However, she did not urge him; but when the cloth was removed, Mr. Evans proposed drinking one of the bottles of wine, which had been left by Lady Cecilia, to her health, and to the hopes of speedily hearing some good account of her. Ned's eyes brightened a little at this proposal; and the wine being brought, he turned over a full bumper to the toast,/ seemingly with great satisfaction. 'Hah, hah! young man,' said Mr. Evans, 'I see what sauce it is that whets your appetite. – Had it been the custom to eat healths, as well as drink them, I fancy the hare we had to-day would not have gone away so whole.' Ned was going to say something in reply, when the old man interrupted him – 'Come, come,' said he, 'I hate these leaden glooms; 'tis time enough for an old fellow like me to be longing for the tomb. Youth is the season of joy, and we should never give up any of it to sorrow, for which we shall find abundant leisure afterwards. So come, my boy, drink another bumper to 'May we have in our arms whom we love in our hearts!'

Poor Ned's face was now one universal glow of crimson – he plainly saw his secret was discovered, and that his father had seen the verses, and the hair, and all the rest of it. He pledged the toast, however, which he drank with no less satisfaction than the first. And Mr. Evans continuing his vein of/ humour, he at length brought Ned almost into the same tune, and they finished their bottle very cordially between them. His spirits being somewhat raised by the wine, and his heart warmed by the engaging openness with which his father treated him, he disclosed to him his whole soul – related all the progress of his love, the adventure of the cave, the attainment of the lock of hair, the exchange of the handkerchiefs, and all the hopes and fears which were preying alternately on his mind.

Happy son! who, when the sorrows of your heart required the comfort of a friend, whose wisdom could advise, and whose gentleness could soothe – found that friend in a father!

Happy father! who uniting the candour and openness of youth to the wisdom and experience of age, who seeking a friend to form to virtue, and to be the honour and the comfort of your declining years, found that friend in a son!/

CHAP. XIV.

NED having thus unbosomed himself to his father, found an infinite load of anxiety moved from his breast, and a secret spring of comfort began to rise in his soul, that seemed to promise the return of peace, though he knew not from what quarter she was to come. Sleep too, who like a false friend had forsaken him the moment he was in adversity, was pleased this night to revisit him, and sealed his eyelids in such profound repose as steeped all his senses in forgetfulness. Not so the worthy curate, who, notwithstanding the pleasantry with which he treated Ned's passion to himself, was yet sincerely alarmed for its consequences. He knew the irresistible fury with which love blazes in some bosoms, and he more than suspected that Ned's was stored/ with whatever is usually supposed to add fuel to that flame.

When therefore he considered the innumerable beauties both of mind and body which centred in Lady Cecilia, he did not wonder at his son's attachment, nor doubt but that it would be lasting; but when he reflected on his humble fortune, and the probable situation of the lady, he trembled for the unhappy youth, and saw nothing before him but sorrow and disappointment. He determined therefore, the very next morning, to set his danger full in his view; and as he wisely considered that idleness was the food of love, so he determined, without longer delay, to engage Ned in some active business, that should fully engross both his time and his attention. But here was the difficulty – what that business was to be, was the great question, and really it was a question that could not easily be determined – Not that it was at all difficult to find out what Ned was fit for; for there was nothing so great but/ what he had both capacity and industry to attain – but, alas! the means were wanting, – for who can attain any thing now a days without money? and where could our poor curate procure it, with a family, and an income of only forty pounds a year! And yet, out of this pittance, he had had the prudence always to have a whole year's income lying by him, in case of any sudden emergency, and he had the great and singular felicity not to owe a shilling in the world.

These advantages however could avail but little in procuring for Ned any reputable employment; and neither his spirit nor his education could brook a situation, however profitable, that should throw him out of the rank in which he had always lived. He had now just completed his nineteenth year, and under the tuition of his father, who was an excellent scholar, had attained as great a stock both of classical and scientifical knowledge as any young man of his years could do in any situation whatsoever./ It was the design of Mr. Evans to send him to the university if possible, and to educate him for his own profession – but the narrowness of his circumstances would not allow it. And why he should think of the church, in which he himself, and even his father before him, had such ill success, can only be accounted for from the extreme reverence in which he held every thing belonging to religion, and that both his father's experience and his own had convinced him that it is possible to be happy in the humblest situation which the church affords – for old Mr. Evans had lived a contented curate to the eighty-fifth year of his age, and now he himself was approaching the sixtieth of his, without ever being able to get a step higher, though possessed of virtues and abilities to adorn the highest. But here let us not blame too hastily the right reverend prelates, to whom the care of the church is entrusted.

Their lordships consider christianity as a glorious edifice, of which they for a time/ have the care, and which it is their duty to transmit to posterity in all its strength and beauty. Men therefore of consummate virtue and abilities, they rightly esteem its strongest support, which, like foundation stones, should always be placed in the lowest part of the building, whilst the more shewy qualifications of courtly manners, splendid names, fine fortunes, great connections, &c. &c. resemble the cornices and corinthian capitals, which, though entirely useless in themselves, and unnecessary, yet always occupy the highest stations, being well calculated to surprise the vulgar and make the people stare.

As the church is now settled in its glory (from which may it never fall!), its learned and most reverend bishops, who boast themselves to be the successors of the apostles, have no manner of resemblance to the ignorant and barefooted fishermen who went by that name in primitive times; their lordships therefore cannot be too much praised for putting into conspicuous stations, those/ whose qualifications resemble their own, because this prevents schism, and because it was truly the apostolic method; whilst those who in their morals and conduct imitate the manners of the first apostles, should, like them, be exposed to hunger and thirst, to cold and nakedness, to fastings and weariness, to journeyings often, and perils from their own countrymen.

This to be sure is the reason why we see so many wise and virtuous characters among the lowest order of inferior clergy, who, like the dogs in the parable, are fed with the crumbs that fall from their master's table; and who may think them-selves very well off that they are not, like other dogs, kicked out of the room.

These anxieties and contemplations kept our venerable curate from closing his eyes this night. In the morning he met Ned, who, refreshed with sleep, to

76 *The History of Ned Evans*

which he had been so long a stranger, and disencumbered of a great part of the load which hung upon his spirits, had recovered a good deal/ of his usual looks, and seemed quite a different man from what he had been for some time past. Mr. Evans led him into the garden, and, seating themselves on that bank which the charming Cecilia had so often pressed, he began seriously to unfold to Ned the probable consequences of his passion if indulged, the absolute necessity he was under of subduing it, and to consult his inclinations on what mode of life he would pursue, that was compatible with their circumstances and situation. I will not tire my readers with a repetition of the arguments and eloquence which he made use of, because I hope that very few of them, if any at all, may be in a similar situation to our unhappy Edward; but I will beg of them to imagine every thing that wisdom, prudence, generosity, friendship, tenderness, and parental affection could suggest, and then perhaps they may form some faint resemblance of Evans's oratory on this occasion, which was not spoken to a dull or unlistening ear, but which sunk deep/ into the mind, and into the heart of his son. Ned saw the precipice on which he stood, as clearly as his father could shew it to him; but he stood in need of his supporting hand to save him from growing giddy, and tumbling headlong down. The arguments therefore of his father had with him the weight of commands, and he declared himself ready instantly to adopt any occupation which he should recommend.

The next point to be considered was what occupation – and here indeed lay the difficulty. The church was out of the question; for, even had it been agreeable to Ned, he was not yet of age to enter into it, and his disorder required an immediate remedy. The army was his passion – and indeed this would have been most eligible, – but, alas! where were the means? The curate had no interest – and, what was worse, no money. This profession therefore was obliged to be relinquished with a sigh. They next turned their thoughts to Doctor Jones. Medicine was honourable, even in/ its inferior departments; and if it is true that apothecaries gain elevenpence half-penny in every shilling's worth they sell, the profession must be allowed to be lucrative. But Jones had two apprentices already; and Ned confessed that though the business was lucrative, yet it did not charm him much; as it subjected the practitioner always to distressing, and often to disgusting scenes; and that for his part he thought a fiddler's life much happier, at least much merrier, than a physician's; and Ned was fond of mirth. – This profession was also laid aside. At length Mr. Evans recollected an old acquaintance of his, who had owed his education to his father, and who, it was said, had made a large fortune by his practice as an attorney. Now, if those who win may laugh, as the proverb says, here was a profession in which Ned might be as merry as he pleased; and Mr. Evans did not make the least doubt but his old friend and play-fellow, Mr. Muckworm,[50] would repay the obligations which he owed to the family, by/ taking Ned as his apprentice without a fee, and by giving him his diet and lodging for the use his pen could be of to him. As Ned made no objection to this scheme, Mr. Evans declared he would set about it that very day, and go and visit his old friend, whom he had not seen for forty years. – He anticipated the joy with which he should renew his acquaintance with the companion of his childhood – the pleasure with which they should talk over their boyish days – and the supreme delight which it must give to Muckworm thus to repay the great obligations which he owed to the family of Evans./

CHAP. XV.

Mr. Josiah Muckworm, the gentleman to whose house Mr. Evans was now going, was the son of Mr. Jeremiah Muckworm, who for forty years had served the office of parish clerk, in the church where Mr. Evans's father was curate. His salary as clerk was about five pounds a year, which never could have maintained his family if he had not also kept a little day school, where children were taught their catechism, and to read and write, for half-a-crown a quarter, which brought him in as much more, kept body and soul together, and put a decent suit of clothes on his back on Sunday; on which day he always got his dinner at old Mr. Evans's after he and his wife had done, and little Josiah used to come often to get a piece of pudding, and play with our worthy curate, who was then a boy much about his own age. As Josiah/ was a shrewd-looking boy, and behaved with great decency and humility, old Mr. Evans was well pleased to have him for a companion to his son; and when the latter was old enough to begin Latin, he thought it would be a good action to give the other some education, of which he seemed extremely susceptible; and that it might be of advantage to his son to have him for a competitor, from that time he took him home to his own house, and treated him in every respect like his own son. The two boys ate together, read together, and slept together, and neither Mr. nor Mrs. Evans made any difference between them; or, if they did, it seemed in favour of Muckworm, who was of a puny and timid disposition, but extremely shrewd and cunning, and so humble and submissive that he would clean any body's shoes for a halfpenny – whilst, on the contrary, young Evans was a sturdy boy, full of life and spirit, and would have knocked any person down, or at least attempted it, who should propose/ such an office to him. He was also full of generosity and good nature; a remarkable instance of which he gave even at those tender years.

There was a little garden at the back of his father's house, and in that garden a standard apple tree of an excellent kind, and a very great bearer. There happened to be a great scarcity of fruit one year, and apples were very dear; but on this tree there was a tolerable crop, and old Evans intended to sell the fruit of it, which in that year would have been worth something, and to have laid out the produce in a new gown for his wife, and a new suit of clothes for little Evans – but, alas!

– 78 –

just as they were ripening, they were all carried off in one night, and sold nobody knows where. Mr. and Mrs. Evans were very much mortified at it, and the old gentleman was determined to find out the thief. He was indeed nearer home than he expected; for it was no other than little Muckworm himself, who could not resist the temptation of the/ price they would fetch, and who, in conjunction with another imp in the parish, who had the charge of selling them in a neighbouring town, stripped them all off one night after the family was gone to bed, and whilst little Evan, his bedfellow, was fast asleep. As Mr. Evans, however, continued his search, Muckworm began to be terribly frightened, and, relying on the goodness and the love which he knew little Evan had for him, he confessed it all to him, and said he would run away, for he was sure his father would whip him to death when it was found out. Poor little Evan, who could not bear to part with his play-fellow, whom he loved much better than he deserved, bade him stay and not be afraid, and that he would take the blame on himself.

The next day, finding his father still busy in his enquiries, and determined to sift the matter, he went to his mother, and, falling on his knees, told her that he had stolen the apples himself with an intent to sell/ them, and had hid them for that purpose, but that somebody else had smelled them where they lay together, and that he had lost them all except a few that he had eaten. Mrs. Evans was very much surprised at this confession, and gave him a long lecture upon honesty; and his father was so inconsiderate as to give him a good whipping, which he received, however, without flinching, horsed upon the back[51] of Muckworm, who laughed in himself at the success of his cunning, and had afterwards the meanness to boast of it.

The two lads lived on together till old Mr. Evans died, when a distant relation had the goodness to finish young Evan's education at the college, and Muckworm got to be clerk to an attorney of eminence, under whom he profited so much as to succeed him in his business; by an indefatigable attention to which, joined to a great appearance of sanctity, and a most rigid œconomy, he in a short time amassed a considerable sum. He then turned methodist,[52] a religion/ which he found extremely well suited to his disposition, as it considers all good works to be like filthy rags, and the purest virtue to be nothing but splendid sin, unpleasing to God, by whom faith only is accepted. As he now became rich, and held all good works in abhorrence, he became a saint with that party, which recommended him to a vast increase of business, and to several executorships, by which his coffers soon became full. He was now the universal banker of the county, and, by timely loans, on good security, with a small premium, &c. &c. he was at this time one of the richest men in it. As it was a matter of twenty miles from his house to that of Mr. Evans, and their line of life was so different, they had never seen one another from their first separation; Mr. Evans not having any estate to

80 *The History of Ned Evans*

give a mortgage on, and Mr. Muckworm being so immersed in business that he had not a single moment to bestow on any other consideration.

As he approached the house he was/ struck with the loneliness of the situation, and a want of neatness in the fences, gates, and offices, which gave it a look of poverty and ruin, rather than the dwelling of a man of opulence. Being arrived at the outer gate, a huge and hungry mastiff attacked the horse, who would certainly have thrown Mr. Evans, if a country fellow who was in the yard had not come to his assistance, and driven the dog away. He then asked if Mr. Muckworm was at home? and the man said he would go and see.

Evans waited near a quarter of an hour with his horse in his hand before the man came back, when telling him he was, he took the horse, and led him away to the stable. A boy with a ragged livery conducted Mr. Evans to his master's room. The room was of a moderate size, but so crowded with book-cases, desks, and a large writing table, that there was but little room to stir in it. The dust lay so thick on the books as made it evident it was never swept; and the windows being secured both/ within and without with iron bars, gave it more the air of a prison than a parlour. Muckworm was sitting in an arm chair, dressed in an old brown damask night-gown, much the worse for the wear, and which seemed to be of the same piece with the covering of the elbow chair; he had a night-cap of the same on his head, with a linen one under it; while his wig, with long grey curls, was suspended on a fire-screen in the corner. He had his spectacles on, and a pen in his mouth; in one hand was a pair of money scales, and on the table was a large green velvet bag, which seemed almost full of guineas, several piles of which, that he had been weighing, were standing round it. When Mr. Evans entered the room, Muckworm made a slight inclination of his head; and the good curate going to shake hands with him, Muckworm begged him to sit down, for he was in the midst of an important calculation, which when he had finished he would hear his business.

Evans was a little disappointed at this/ reception; but concluding, as was indeed true, that Muckworm did not know him, he was not much disconcerted. The other continued counting and weighing and piling up light guineas, which he separated from those that were weight,[53] for near a quarter of an hour without speaking a word, or even once raising his eyes, while Evans surveyed him with a mixture of pity, astonishment, and contempt. He saw with pity the alteration which time had made on that countenance, which in their boyish days he had so often beheld with transport. He saw with astonishment how much deeper the furrows of care were impressed upon his features, than those of time; and he could not behold without contempt, a wretch wasted by avarice to a shadow, and grasping in his feeble hands that gold which he never had spirit to enjoy, and which his wan and meagre aspect seemed to threaten that he soon must leave. At length Muckworm pulled off his spectacles; and wiping his pen, which he carefully laid by, he asked/ Mr. Evans what were his commands with him? 'Is it possible, Mr. Muckworm,' said Mr. Evans, 'that you should forget your old friend?' – 'I protest, Sir,' said Muckworm, 'you have the advantage of me, and I do not recollect ever seeing you before.' 'Did you ever know any one of the name of Evans,' said the curate? 'Evans!' replied Muckworm, 'I know Sir Hugh Evans of Montgomeryshire, and Captain Evans of the navy, his nephew.' 'I thought in the earlier part of your life,' said the parson, 'there were some others of the name to whom you owed some obligation.' 'Obligation!' said Muckworm, 'what obligation? I remember indeed one Evans, an old man, who was curate of the parish where I was born: I believe he might have christened me, if that is an obligation; but he died before I was of age to enter into any legal obligation.' – 'Alas! Mr. Muckworm,' said Evans, 'I find I have mistaken you. I have seen the days when you thought otherwise of my father,/ and when you considered me as the dearest friend you had.' – 'Why, Sir, is your name Evans?' rejoined Muckworm. 'Yes, Sir,' said the other; 'my name is Evan Evans, whom in the days of innocence and childhood you well knew; though now you seem to have forgotten me.' 'Really, Mr. Evans,' replied Muckworm, 'it is so long since I have seen you, I think near forty years, that it is no wonder that I had forgotten you – But how has the world gone with you, Mr. Evans? Have the bishops been as mindful of you as of your father?' 'I have no reason to complain of the world,' said Mr. Evans, 'and I hope it has none to complain of me. I enjoy what is to me a competence, with health and a quiet conscience, without obligations to bishops, or indeed to any except him that made me.' 'I am glad to hear you are so independent,' replied Muckworm; 'I suppose then, by this unexpected visit, you have a purchase to make, or some money to lend on a good mortgage – is it/ so?' 'I am neither a money-lender nor a money-borrower,' replied Evans.' 'You are then a most extraordinary character,' said Muckworm; 'for I have hardly seen a face these twenty years at my house that did not come to borrow – Why now I am just making up a sum of 5000l. to lend to Sir Thomas Spendall my neighbour here; who with an estate of 10,000l. a year is always in want of cash: this is the fourth sum to the same amount I have lent him within these six months.' 'Bless me!' said Evans, '20,000l. in six months! And have you such prodigious sums by you as that, Mr. Muckworm?' 'Why yes, Mr. Evans, I thank God, Heaven has prospered my industry. Whoever comes after me will find I did not hide my talent in a napkin.'[54] 'No. I dare say,' replied Evans; 'I fancy you have made good interest on it.' 'Pretty well, pretty well; the Lord has been favourable to me – he entrusted me with a little, and I have doubled it a hundred fold. Between you/ and me, if I live a few years longer, I shall have all Sir Thomas's estate: he has not been five years in possession of it, and he has spent above 100,000l. Oh! if his father saw how his savings melted away, it would make him fester in his shroud.' 'Pray,' said Mr. Evans, 'how does Sir Thomas spend these monstrous sums? I have not the pleasure to know

82 *The History of Ned Evans*

him, but I have always heard he had a most excellent character, and his tenants say he is the best landlord in the world.' 'Ay, they say – because they eat his beef, and guzzle his ale; but I say he is the worst of landlords, for he does nothing but encourage idleness and profligacy. His house is a palace where the great are entertained like princes, and his servants' hall a rendezvous where all the beggars in the country, and their brats, may fill their bellies every day; and he is such a fool, that if they tell him of their wants and their distresses, he will give them his money into the bargain; nay, he will part with the clothes off his back./ Why there was one of his tenants died last year above 300l. in his debt. He was in possession of a good farm, that was worth a great deal more than he gave for it; and I myself offered fifty pounds a year advance, in order to let it to another for double that sum; when (would you think it?) Sir Thomas would not hear of it, because forsooth the man's widow had been his nurse's daughter, and she had five children to provide for; and so the fool not only continued her in the farm, but also forgave her the debt. Such a man, Mr. Evans, will always be in want of money.' 'God forbid!' said Evans; ''tis a great pity he should want it.' – 'I'll tell you another exploit of his,' said Muckworm. 'You must know, he has lately erected a temple to the devil.' – 'God bless us!' interrupted Evans, 'a temple to the devil! I never heard of such a thing in a christian country.' 'Hav'n't you?' said Muckworm: 'There is not a town in England scarce but has one.' 'What do you mean?'/ said Evans: 'I never heard the like before.' 'Why I mean a play-house,' said Muckworm; 'a private theatre, in imitation of those vile temples of Covent-Garden and Drury-Lane; where he and his company act stage-plays, and all manner of wickedness and profaneness; and where he has even music upon the Lord's day. But now for the exploit. – You must know Sir Thomas is a great lover of music; and some time ago he got one of those Italian fellows from London, one Squallini,[55] to come down to live with him, and to sing upon his theatre; and he had given him a deed for an annuity of no less than 500l. a year for his life.' 'A great sum indeed,' said Mr. Evans, 'for a few songs!' 'Nay, but you shall hear,' said Muckworm; 'he did not get the songs neither. When he came down to the country, Signor Squallini came with him; and a vast deal of company, as usual, came to pay their compliments, and to hear this famous Italian sing. After supper Sir Thomas asked Squallini/ to favour the company with a song. Squallini said he was hoarse, and could not sing; but being pressed hard, he said to Sir Thomas – 'What, Sir Thomas, do you think me come here to be de buffoon? – Me sing for you, Sir Thomas, when alone; and me vil sing upon your theatre: but me will not be made de buffoon for any company in Europe.' In short, nothing could prevail on him to sing. The company, who knew the salary he had, were amazed. Sir Thomas was so chagrined, that in a few days he turned Squallini out of his house; but he could not reverse his deed. The fellow came to me – I gave him 1000l. for it; and Sir Thomas must pay me 500l. a year as long as Squallini lives.' 'And can you think it honourable,' said Evans, 'to be concerned in such an affair?' 'Why not?' replied Muckworm: 'I look upon every thing to be honourable that is lawful.' 'All things that are lawful, however,' said Evans, 'are not expedient; and I should have thought it more honourable,/ if the Italian would sell his annuity, to have let the poor gentleman who gave it to him have had the advantage of it.' 'You think very differently from me,' replied Muckworm; 'and since you have quoted the great apostle, I must also tell you that he says, 'He who doth not provide for his own is worse than an infidel;' in which great truth I fully agree with him. And now, Mr. Evans, give me leave to ask if you have any particular business with me?'

Evans, who was long ere this completely disgusted and disappointed, replied, 'Not very particular. I thought indeed it might have been agreeable to you to meet an old friend whom you had not seen for forty years; and if it had been so, I proposed consulting you about putting my son to your business, who is an exceeding good young man, and has now just completed his nineteenth year.' 'That's rather too old, rather too old,' said Muckworm: 'pray what education has your son got, Mr. Evans?' 'He has got the/ best that I could give him,' replied our curate. 'He is well grounded in Greek and Latin, an excellent English scholar; can read Homer and Virgil ad unguem,[56] and is well versed in history both ancient and modern.' 'A fig for Homer and Virgil,' said Muckworm, 'and all such heathenish nonsense; they fill a man's head with romantic notions about virtue, and honour, and heroism, and stuff which serves no purpose but to mar his fortune.' 'What!' said Mr. Evans, 'are virtue and honour only names, and is there any thing on earth of equal value?' 'I tell you,' said Muckworm, 'I would not give my old shoe for all the virtue and honour upon earth. These are inventions of the devil to disparage the only virtue, which is faith. All human actions are sinful, and whoever relies on good works relies upon rubbish. Your poets, therefore, and your historians, your orators and your philosophers, are all agents of the devil, and enemies to Christ. For my part, I would burn all their books/ together, with those that wrote them, and suffer no books to remain but law-books and the gospel. If I had had the training of your boy myself,' said Muckworm, 'perhaps I might have made something of him; but as it is, I can be of no sort of service to you.' 'God be praised you had not,' said Evans; and so rising up to go away, Mr. Muckworm pulled the bell, and the ragged livery boy, whom we mentioned before, appearing, he desired him to get Mr. Evans's horse. The honest curate hastily mounted him, and turned his back for ever on Muckworm and his inhospitable doors./

CHAP. XVI.

It was near two o'clock in the afternoon, in the middle of December, when Mr. Evans left Mr. Muckworm's. He had rode thither twenty miles from his own house that morning, and the hospitality of Muckworm had not, as we have seen, offered him the refreshment even of a glass of wine. And poor Blackbird had fared no better; for though he was admitted into what they called the stable, yet for any good he got there he might as well have been in a pound. He had not carried his master above five miles in his way home, when the night began to approach, and, what was worse, it brought with it a violent tempest of wind and sleet. Poor Evans, who had not tasted a morsel since he left home, began to droop under the uneasy sensations both of cold and/ hunger. He was a stranger in that part of the country, and long looked out for some friendly roof, that might at least afford him shelter; but nothing appeared before him but a waste and dreary common. – At length, as it was growing almost quite dark, he espied a light which seemed to glimmer through the window of some little cottage; and honest Blackbird making an effort to go down the lane which led to it, the worthy curate took his advice, and in a few minutes arrived at a human dwelling. – Though it was but a cottage, and that too of the meanest kind, yet the finding it was now a comfort; and Evans gently tapping at the door, it was opened by an old woman seemingly about sixty years of age. 'Honest woman,' said Evans, 'can you give shelter to a poor benighted old man, who will heartily thank you for the liberty of your roof and fire?' 'Yes, name of God, can I,' said the old woman, 'and a thousand welcomes; and to your horse too. – Johnny, come here, boy, and take the gentleman's/ horse, and put him up beside the cow, and give him a lock of hay.' 'God bless you, my good woman!' said Evans, 'and you too, my pretty boy!' said he to the child, who was about ten years old. 'I do not know what I should have done if I had not met with you.' 'The night is parlous cold,' said the dame; 'but walk in, sir, and warm yourself at the fire: the cottage is small, but it is clean, and you are kindly welcome to all it can afford.' – Evans gladly accepted this friendly invitation, and, walking in, found a clear fire on a clean hearth; and sitting down in a straw chair which was at hand, he felt himself a thousand times more comfortable than he could have been in the best room in Muckworm's house. The good woman, who now saw by his dress that he was a clergyman, redoubled her attention; for, notwithstanding the poverty of the Welch clergy, which is known even to a proverb, yet there is no country in which the ministerial character meets more respect. 'Lord bless your/ reverence,' said she, 'what brings you out such an evening as this, and where have you dined?' –

'Indeed, my good woman,' said Evans, 'I have hardly tasted food to-day.' 'Name of God,' said she, 'not tasted food! – I'se warrant you've been at Mr. Muckworm's.' 'You have just hit it,' said Evans, 'I have come from there indeed.' 'Aye, name of God! I thought so: he's a parlous rich man, but he would skin a louse for the hide. Well, God forgive him! but if it had not been for him, I need not have been here to-day.' 'Why, did he ever injure you?' said Evans. 'No, name of God, I must not say that – he sought but his own, to be sure; though it killed my poor husband, and brought me to ruin.' 'How is that, my poor woman?' said Evans; 'how is that?' 'I'll tell your reverence all by and by,' said the good woman; 'but first I will get you something to eat, for I am sure you stand in need of it.'

She now spread a clean napkin on a little/ table, and, putting a saucepan on the fire, boiled half a dozen new-laid eggs. She laid down some butter and cheese of her own make, which with new-churned butter-milk, and some fresh oaten bread, afforded Evans the most delicious repast he had ever made; – not that the materials were better than what he had been accustomed to at home, but her generous hospitality, contrasted with the churlishness of Muckworm, touched his heart, and gave an inconceivable relish to his entertainment. Often did he wish for the power of Elijah, that her measure of corn should not waste, nor her cruise of oil be diminished.[57] When he had finished his comfortable meal, and given thanks first to his Maker, and then to his entertainer, he begged of the good woman to sit down, and gratify the curiosity she had excited.

'Alas, sir!' said she, 'my story is very simple, and your reverence will hardly think it worth the hearing; yet for want of better I will tell it you, to amuse you till you go/ to sleep. My maiden name was Jane Williams, and my father was a farmer in Denbighshire; he was well to live, and was said to have plenty of money besides his stock. But it was my misfortune to disoblige him, by marrying without his consent. There was a young man came to live with him whose name was Edward Maurice; as handsome a lad to look to, as you would see in a summer's day – well, rest his soul! – I trust he is with God.

'This lad was not long at the house, before he eyed me with particular regard – and to say the truth, I looked on him with equal affection; but as the poor lad had nothing but his labour to depend on, I knew my father and mother would never consent to our being married: we therefore determined not to ask them; but going once together to a fair, we took advantage of that opportunity, and were married for half-a-crown, by a gentleman who was preaching in a field to a great congregation.[58] Well, we kept all secret for some time, till/ at length it

86 *The History of Ned Evans*

became necessary to tell it, or a little one would do it for us; and then my parents were so enraged, that they turned us both out of doors, and gave me nothing but the clothes on my back; nor would they ever afterwards be reconciled. My poor Edward however did not make the worse husband for that, but carried me to another part of the country, to his mother, who received me kindly; and there I lay in, and lived some years as happy as the day was long. At last the good old woman died; and then my husband, who by his industry had scraped together a little matter of money, resolved to take a farm himself. We rented one of about 20l. a year from the late Lord Squanderfield, and for three-and-twenty years that we were his lordship's tenants, we did very well, and always paid our rent. I had several children in that time; but none of them grew to be men, except my oldest son – and alas! he too is now gone.' 'When did he die?' said Mr. Evans. 'He was killed fighting for his/ country,' said the poor woman. 'Alas! the pity,' said Evans, and wiped a tear from his eyes. 'Come hither, Johnny,' said she; 'go shew yourself to that gentleman. This, sir, is my grandson, my son's son – the only comfort I have left.' 'He is a fine boy,' said Evans, clapping him on the head; 'God bless him, and make him a comfort to you!' 'I thank your reverence,' said she, 'and say amen to that sweet prayer.

'Well, sir, as I was telling you, we did very well all the time my late lord lived; but when my young lord came, the times were altered. – He has a great estate in England, and never comes down to this country as his father did; so that we never saw him: and his agent is always pressing for money, and distraining[59] the moment it is due; for he says it is my lord's order, and he will not suffer any of his tenants to be a farthing in arrear. The lands too are greatly advanced since the young lord's time; and so it happened some years ago,/ after two very bad harvests, that my poor husband was not able to pay at the time appointed; and the agent threatening immediately to distrain, he had recourse to Mr. Muckworm, who, after he signed some papers, advanced him twenty guineas, with which he paid his rent. Well, sir, this did for that time: – but the next year he was again deficient; and Mr. Muckworm came upon him too for his debt, which by some means or other he contrived to make thirty pounds; and when my poor husband could not pay it, he arrested him and sent him to gaol. Meantime the agent ejected us for my lord, and seized on all our things, which were sold to pay his rent, and did not fetch more than would do it, though they cost four times as much. My poor son, who with his wife lived with us, when he saw his father in gaol, and the farm gone, determined to go to sea, and try if he could earn any thing to relieve him. He carried his wife and child home to her father and mother, and entered on board a king's ship,/ where he had not been three months till he was killed in an engagement with the French. His poor wife, who was with child when he left her, took his death so much to heart that it hastened her labour, and she and her infant expired together.

Volume I 87

'My poor husband lay two years in Denbigh gaol: at last some kind-hearted person told Sir Thomas Spendall of our distresses, and that generous and charitable gentleman sent for me; and when he heard the whole account, and enquired into its truth, he not only released my husband out of prison, but promised to set him up in a little farm under himself; and had God spared my poor Edward, he certainly would have done so, for he never breaks his word. But it did not please the Almighty that I should be so happy; for the cold and damps of the prison had so broke my poor husband's health, that he died of the rheumatism in less than half a year.

'However, Sir Thomas did not leave me in my distress; he gave me this little cottage,/ with a garden, and grass plat[60] for my cow, rent free; – and, God bless him! he gave me ten guineas to buy myself necessaries, and said I never should want that sum every year; and indeed he is as good as his word, and better too.'

'Where is Sir Thomas now?' said Mr. Evans. 'Indeed I don't know, sir,' said the poor woman, 'but I believe he is gone to London; it is but last week he went from his house in this neighbourhood.' 'I am sorry he is gone,' said Evans: 'I would walk fifty miles to kiss the hand that could do such noble things.' 'Oh, sir,' replied she, 'he is the best-natured man in the world. There would not be an aching heart in Wales, if he could help it.'

Evans now thanked the good woman for her story, which, he said, was extremely affecting; but he hoped to live to see the day when her little grandson would repay her trouble, and be a new spring of comfort to her. And now expressing/ a desire to sleep, she shewed him into a little inner apartment, where was a bedstead with some fresh straw and clean blankets, and where our worthy curate enjoyed a sweeter and more profound repose than was perhaps experienced on the softest down in any palace in Europe.

CHAP. XVII.

THE morning now glittered through the hedges, on whose naked boughs the night had shed her tears, which the keen air had frozen into gems more pure and transparent than ever adorned the tresses of an Indian queen. Thousands of larks now gathered near the doors, where the sound of the early flail gave them hopes of a breakfast. Now Goody Maurice swept her cleanly cottage, and heaped her hospitable hearth with kindled peats; the smoke of which rose through her humble thatch, till, meeting with the new-risen sun, it ascended in a golden column to the cloudless skies, and, like the pious offering of Abel, seemed to be a sacrifice acceptable to heaven. Now had the sweet-breathed cow yielded her treasure of morning's milk; whilst her new/ companion Blackbird, by the attention of little Johnny, was regaling on some clover hay, collected for her winter's food. And now had little Johnny himself well greased the parson's boots, who was still snoring in his first nap, and then had gone to wash his face and comb his hair against his reverence arose – which probably would not have been for an hour to come, had not the cock, who had been long in vain soliciting the favour of one of his strutting dames, at length succeeded; when mounting on the thatch, exactly over Evan's head, he clapped his wings and proclaimed his triumph aloud.

This clarion waked him; and, surprised to see the day so far advanced, he hastily arose, convinced, by experience, how refreshing is the bed of straw, and how sweet the slumbers of the labouring man. Well was he pleased, as he walked through the outer room, to see the attention of his kind hostess, who had spread her little table as the night before, and prepared new milk and a/ hot oat-cake for his breakfast. Advancing to the door, he saw a bright and cloudless sky, and, clearing his voice, as was his custom in a morning, he made the woods re-echo with a loud hem. 'God bless your reverence!' said goody Maurice, who now came forward from the cow-house; 'I see your reverence has good lungs, and I hope will live this many a year. How did your reverence sleep?' said she; 'I fear you found the straw too hard?' 'Not at all, dame,' said Evans: 'I never slept better in my life, nor ever had more thorough satisfaction in my entertainment.' 'It is your goodness, sir, that says so,' replied the old woman, 'for I am sure it is what your reverence is not accustomed to; but will your reverence walk in and take some breakfast?' 'Yes, my good woman, and thank you heartily.' And now, little Johnny with clean hands and face attending with his boots, he seemed greatly pleased with his neatness and the innocence of his looks. During breakfast he asked him many questions/ in his catechism, and about other such matters as he might be supposed to know; to all which he answered to his satisfaction, which greatly delighted Evans, and did not fail to draw from him much commendation.

And now having finished his meal, and Blackbird being ready, he went to mount; but first he took out half-a-crown to reward the trouble of his kind landlady: but great was his astonishment when she peremptorily refused to take a farthing. – She said the bounty of Sir Thomas had given her plenty, and God forbid she should make a traffic of it, or take such a sum for the pitiful morsel that his reverence had been so good as to accept! 'Good woman,' said Evans, 'I know not which to admire most, your virtue or your good manners: but I know they are both such as may often put the highest stations to the blush.' – Then calling little Johnny, he forced the half-crown into his hand; and telling them both who he was, and where he lived, he/ gave them an invitation to his house, and rode away.

All the way as he went he amused himself with contrasting his reception at Muckworm's and the poor widow's. This led him into many refined speculations on the nature of the human heart; its natural tendency to virtue, and the power of gold to corrupt it: though in the instance of Sir Thomas he had the most satisfactory proof that there were some hearts so pure that riches could not corrupt them. With this pleasing contemplation did he solace himself till he beheld at a distance the delightful prospect of the evening sun glistening on his own windows; and honest Blackbird quickening his pace, and setting up a loud whinny, he soon saw Ned (who had been long expecting him) running to meet him, and with his usual cheerful and rosy countenance welcome him home; where he found a blazing fire, a comfortable meal, and a good-humoured wife ready to receive him.

To those who live in splendid palaces,/ and are occupied in the business of the great world, the soothing transports of domestic happiness are seldom known. Their vitiated appetites, sated by perpetual indulgence, can taste no pleasures but what intoxicate, and therefore cannot relish the simple draught drawn from the pure fountain of connubial bliss, whose unsullied spring flows with ever new delight for those who can enjoy it. – Such therefore cannot conceive the satisfaction which now glowed in the countenances of this happy and united little family on its head's return, nor what an addition of relish the absence even of one day gives to such a meeting. To have viewed the placid face of Evans as he ate his mutton, and the lively eye with which he beheld his amber ale sparkling in the glass, one would have imagined he had returned to his little family full freighted

90 *The History of Ned Evans*

with some news of their advancement, some important success that was to estab-
lish them in future beyond the reach of fortune. Nor, when he told them his
reception with/ Muckworm, did it in the least abate their enjoyment, but rather
added to it: for they made it a subject of much laughter all the evening, and drew
from it besides this comfortable conclusion, that happiness did not lie in wealth;
and that their own situation, humble as it was, was beyond all comparison more
eligible than his. They did not withhold due praise from the behaviour of the
poor widow, to whom Mrs. Evans declared herself infinitely obliged, and that
she would never be at rest till she found out some way of repaying her kindness.

Ned urged his father to take home the little boy, and teach him to read and
write, in doing which he promised to assist him; and that he might be put to
do such work in the garden as was suited to his strength and years, where also
he might learn the whole art of common gardening, which would be a help to
them, and might turn out of the greatest advantage to the boy. Mrs. Evans did
not at all object to this little addition to their household, but seemed/ extremely
desirous to do whatever lay in her power both for the child and the old woman:
and the good curate said he would think of it; but for the present there was no
hurry, as the boy was very young; and besides, he thought it improper to do any
thing without first asking permission of Sir Thomas, who had been extremely
generous to them, and might consider it impertinent in him to interfere with any
body whom he had taken under his protection: – but he declared his resolution
to wait upon Sir Thomas as soon as he returned to the country, for he longed
to be acquainted with a gentleman of whose heart and whose humanity he had
conceived the highest opinion. Mrs. Evans and Ned acquiesced in this determination, the propriety of which struck them now, though in the warmth of their
gratitude they had overlooked it before.

Thus did our good curate conclude his fruitless embassy to Mr. Muckworm. Perhaps it may be thought an argument of his/ simplicity ever to have
undertaken it, and I will not deny but it does look as if he was not thoroughly
acquainted with the manners of the modern world: but that worthy man judged
of other men's hearts by his own; and feeling in himself how infinitely it would
have rejoiced him to have, such an opportunity of obliging an old friend, we may
excuse his error in supposing it would be equally agreeable to Mr. Muckworm.
As it was, though greatly disappointed, yet he was not dejected, but resolved to
trust to Providence and time for some fortunate event in Ned's favour, and in the
meanwhile to divert him at home as much as possible, by engaging him in some
employment that might at once afford amusement to the mind and exercise to
the body.

An accident happened about this time which greatly forwarded this plan. Mr.
Watkin had gone one morning to a fair, nine or ten miles from his own house.
It has been before observed, that he was of a/ morose disposition, and though

in very affluent circumstances, yet so extremely narrow as to allow himself little more than the bare necessaries of life: he was besides excessively proud, and too apt to assume a superiority over his neighbours, who, excepting the article of cash, were in every other respect his equals. This conduct created him many enemies, and prevented his having any friends: and accordingly at this fair he got into a dispute with a young fellow about buying some cattle, in which he gave the young man some harsh language, which provoked him to retaliate: – from words it came to blows; and as he had no body to espouse his cause, or rescue him from his antagonist, he got a most severe beating, without being either pitied or relieved. At last the young fellow quitted him, moved either by returning pity, or fearing he had given a blow too much, for the last stroke had laid him senseless on the ground; and some people more humane than the rest, coming by at that time, laid him in a cart,/ and carried him home to his own house, in a very doubtful situation as to life. His poor wife and daughter, who wanted neither duty nor affection, forgot all that was disagreeable in his manners when they saw him in distress, and, fancying him already dead, vented their sorrow in shrieks and tears. Having washed away the blood and dirt with which his face was clotted, they put him into bed, unable to speak, and seemingly almost senseless; – his eyes were so swelled and black, that they could not tell whether he would ever see again or not; and the only signs of life he gave were, that he still breathed, and now and then drank a little water which they put to his lips. In this distressing situation, they sent for Mr. Evans, who was the usual refuge of all his parishioners when any calamity befel them; and that good man, attended by Ned, went immediately to the house, to give them what comfort and what assistance he could. By his advice they dispatched a messenger for Doctor Jones; and having sat awhile with/ Mrs. Watkin, he returned home, leaving Ned to take care of the women, and to be otherwise assisting as far as was in his power.

This amiable young man never was so happy as when employed in any work of kindness or good nature; he soothed the terrors of Mrs. Watkin, by assuring her that her husband had received no material injury, and that his apparent insensibility probably arose from fatigue, after an unusual exertion of passion, added to his bruises, and perhaps to his having taken a cup of ale too much; for his usual abstinence was so great, that a very small quantity of liquor might affect him. He summoned all his cheerfulness (of which indeed till lately he had a very large stock) to entertain them; and in this he succeeded so well, that Miss Watkin at least thought it one of the pleasantest evenings she had passed for a great while; and indeed an indifferent spectator might have discovered that that poor girl was all the while drinking/ delicious poison from the eyes of Ned, which were intending to beam nothing but good nature, and which were wholly unconscious of the mischief they were doing; for poor Ned's heart was already struck by the divine Cecilia, and was so saturated with love that it was incapable

92 *The History of Ned Evans*

of imbibing more from any object whatsoever. As vanity too had no share in his composition, the gentle Harriet might long have gazed on him, without awakening a suspicion that she viewed him with any other eyes but those of friendship: – the poor girl did not even know it herself; but while she was doting on his beauty, she fancied she was admiring only his wit, his courage, his virtue, and his good nature. 'Tis thus that Love insinuates himself into the heart – the subtle deceiver assumes some flattering disguise to recommend himself to our notice; we admit him into our bosoms under the name of honour, generosity, friendship, or some other splendid appellation, which sooths our vanity, and reconciles us to our/ new guest. But soon do we lament our easy faith – the false intruder sooths no more – he saps our senses, undermines our reason, wrings our heart; he becomes the tyrant, and, alas! too often, the destroyer of our souls. Oh fly then, ye incautious fair! fly, fly whilst yet you may! – listen not to his syren song; shun, shun his first approach, – lest, like the dreadful whirlpool of Maelstrom, you play round him for a time in circles, till, by insensible though sure degrees, you are drawn into his irresistible vortex, and swallowed up for ever.

It now grew very late, and, neither the Doctor nor the messenger returning, Ned was shewn to his apartment, where we will leave him to his repose, and to those happy dreams which sometimes are indulged to innocent and faithful lovers. Mrs. Watkin sat up with her husband, and the poor Harriet retired to her bed, where she slept but little, and began to feel how dangerous a lodger she had admitted into her breast./

CHAP. XVIII.

DOCTOR Jones made his appearance in the morning, and was immediately conducted to Mr. Watkin's apartment. That poor man had recovered his senses and the use of his tongue, but was so sore from his bruises that he was unable to move without great pain. The doctor examined the wounds and cuts he had received; but not finding any fracture or external bruise that was alarming, he quieted the fears of the family in that respect. He observed, however, some feverish symptoms in Mr. Watkin; and in relating the circumstances of what had befallen him, he had been roused anew into so violent a passion that he thought it necessary to warn Mrs. Watkin on that head; and, as there was reason to apprehend he might have a fever, that he should be kept as composed as possible./

When Mr. Watkin was informed that Ned Evans was in the house, he desired to see him; when, thanking him for the kindness of his visit, he requested that he would stay there for a few days, and superintend the management of his business, which Ned promised to do in the best manner he was able; and thus the tyrant Love was contriving to rivet the chains which he had forged for the heart of poor Harriet. That innocent girl was rejoiced when she heard of the invitation, and thought of nothing but the happiness she should enjoy in seeing the beloved of her soul every hour of the day. Mrs. Watkin too was pleased, for she loved Ned with an unaffected friendship; and though she did not dream of her daughter's attachment, yet it is more than probable that, had she known it, she would not have disapproved of it.

The delighted Harriet sat down to breakfast with unusual vivacity; yet before that meal was over did cruel Love introduce a new fiend, his never-failing companion, into/ her gentle heart. This fiend was Jealousy. Who that has ever felt love, is ignorant of this detested name? Doctor Jones seeing Ned at breakfast, very naturally enquired if he had heard from Miss Cecilia? At the name of Cecilia a deep blush suffused the artless youth's cheeks – and, with a sigh that could not be suppressed, he replied, they had received no word as yet. As Eve when she had eaten the forbidden fruit became instantly quick-sighted to discern evil as well as good, so did love open the eyes of the innocent and unsuspecting Harriet, and

– 93 –

94   *The History of Ned Evans*

in one moment discovered to her the fatal truth that Ned's heart was already engaged, and by whom.

The friendship and admiration with which she had so lately and so sincerely beheld the charming Cecilia, were in one moment blasted to the roots; and the baneful passion of envy rising in that bosom which had ever hitherto been serene, resembled those pestilential winds which are said to be formed in the deserts of Arabia, and which,/ passing over the cultivated fields, deface in an instant all the beauties of nature. Oh Love! thou who art called the offspring of heaven – the soother and refiner of the human soul! surely thou returnedst to thy native skies when thy first possessors lost their innocence; and he who now usurps thy name is one of those deceitful fiends to whom their fatal transgression first gave admission – else why should you torment? or why be accompanied with all those pangs and sorrows which flatter first and then destroy?

The fever which the doctor expected soon made its appearance, and Mr. Watkin was for near three weeks closely confined: at one time indeed there were great apprehensions for his life; but the strength of his constitution got the better of his disease, and at the end of the time above mentioned he was able to walk about. During all this time Ned staid at his house, and only went home now and then for an hour or so to see his father and mother. Mrs. Watkin/ had been as attentive to him as if he had been the first personage in the county; and it need not be doubted but that Harriet, who loved him with all her soul, would go hand in hand with her mother in shewing him every kindness. And indeed the indefatigable attention that he bestowed on Mr. Watkin's affairs demanded this respect, exclusive of his native amiableness, which won it irresistibly from all hearts. So that we cannot blame Miss Watkin, nor think her the least deficient in delicacy, if hers felt the impression so natural to her sex and years; but rather lament that there should be any impediment likely to prevent her meeting that return which it is but justice to say she every day deserved. The poor girl herself was not insensible of this impediment; yet would she sometimes indulge the hope that the lovely object of his affections was of a rank too high for him to aspire to with any prospect of success – and in this hope she was not deceived; – and then she flattered herself that the/ fidelity of her own attachment would at last meet its reward, especially as it was more than probable his father and mother would be her friend, since they had always expressed for her the warmest affection, and they well knew how advantageous her alliance would be in point of interest. Indeed this generous girl valued the prospect of her fortune for nothing so much as the use it might be of to Ned, on whom she would gladly confer the Indies if she had them to bestow. She did not doubt either of getting her own father to desire this union, for he had conceived as warm an affection for Ned as it was possible for him to have for any body besides himself; and he was so well satisfied with his care during his illness, that he declared, if Mr. Evans would take a farm for his son, he would immediately advance him money to stock it, and only require common interest; which was a great deal from one of his disposition, who literally loved money better than he did himself./

All these favourable prospects soothed Miss Watkin into some hopes of success, which were the more reasonable, as it was now near six weeks since Lady Cecilia had left Mr. Evans, and in all that time they had not received the least account from her; and indeed the Evanses themselves began to think that, like other great folk, she had forgot her country acquaintance, and that the memory of the Welch cottage was lost in the splendour of her father's palace. But Ned would never give into this suspicion: his terrors were, that she had met with some new disaster, or that she was dead; for he said he would pawn his soul upon it, that she would not live and be well, and neglect them altogether. In this sentiment he was not mistaken; for she was of a mind infinitely too noble to forget her friends because they were her inferiors – of a heart infinitely too just to forget the obligations which she owed to the gallant and the tender Edward. The truth is, that when she arrived in Dublin, she found/ her father in a situation that absorbed all her attention. It has been before observed, that Lord Ravensdale was in the gout when Lady Cecilia left her aunt, Lady Elizabeth Belmont.

The reader is already acquainted with the unfortunate interruption to her journey; and as Lady Elizabeth had written to her brother by her niece, his lordship had not received that letter, and consequently knew nothing of Lady Cecilia's having quitted London. Her ladyship's severe illness in Wales, occasioned by her terror, and her subsequent desire to be unknown, prevented her from writing, thinking every day to go over herself; but Lady Elizabeth Belmont, wondering at not hearing from Ireland, wrote again to Lord Ravensdale by post, and enclosed a letter in it for Lady Cecilia, which was the first intelligence he had received of her having quitted London; and the agony this threw him into, of not knowing what was become of her, threw the gout into his head, and put his life in/ the most imminent danger. Such was his situation when Lady Cecilia arrived; and as at that time he was not capable of seeing her, or of knowing her if he had seen her, the affliction of Lady Cecilia was inexpressible, aggravated as it must be by the reflection how great a share she herself had in his illness. At last it pleased Heaven to abate his disorder, and the sight of Lady Cecilia herself perfected the cure; for no parent ever loved his children better than Lord Ravensdale, and his lovely daughter was his peculiar care. The joy he felt in folding her again to his bosom dissipated all remains of his complaint, and soothed the sorrow with which he heard of the death of his amiable friend Mrs. Melville; and he expressed the utmost gratitude for the Evanses, particularly for Ned, whose gallantry he was determined to reward.

It was a few days after Ned had returned home to his father's, and that Mr. Watkin was entirely restored to his usual health, that our venerable curate was

96   *The History of Ned Evans*

consulting/ with his son on the subject of the farm which Watkin had suggested; and the propriety of being obliged to him for the sum necessary to stock it. Ned expressed a horror of beginning the world with a debt, which he said would encumber his spirits, and be a clog on all his operations. And Mr. Evans highly applauded his prudence, and the delicacy of his feeling on that head. 'He who runs in debt,' said he, 'parts with just so much of his liberty and peace of mind as he borrows, and must for ever feel inferior to his creditor till he is paid: whereas he who owes nothing is always independent, and, though ever so poor, must feel and rejoice in the dignity of his situation. Yet, my dear boy,' continued he, 'there are sometimes occasions upon which a man may contract a debt without any imputation on his prudence, or danger in its consequence; and I think this is one of them: wherefore, if you wish to try your hand in the farming business, you may begin with a small one, which will not require/ much to set it up, and I shall take care that what you may want from Mr. Watkin shall not much encumber you.'

Ned acknowledged with all gratitude the generosity and affection of his father; but absolutely refused his bearing any part of the burthen, or joining in the security. 'God knows,' said he, 'how I might succeed; and if I come to any loss, how much will it be imbittered by involving you!' It is probable indeed, had Ned engaged in farming, and accepted Mr. Watkin's offer, that neither he nor his father would have come to any loss; for his prudence, activity, and skill, were equal to any thing that he should undertake. But fortune had a different scene of life in view for him, which was more adapted to his genius and inclinations; for a day or two after this, as they were sitting at breakfast, Morgan came into the room in a great hurry, and told Mr. Evans that there was a gentleman in a post-chaise at the gate who wanted to speak to him, but that he said he/ had no time to alight. When he went out to the chaise, the gentleman asked him if he was acquainted with the Earl of Ravensdale? He assured him he had never heard of that nobleman. 'Are you then the reverend Mr. Evans of Llanrhwscoedd?' He answered, that was indeed his designation. 'Then, Sir,' said the gentleman, 'I have orders from his lordship to deliver this packet to you (handing a large bundle out of the chaise) and I suppose the contents will explain themselves.' Mr. Evans then pressed the gentleman to alight and take some refreshment; but he said he could not possibly wait, for he must be in London the following day: – so wishing him a good morning he drove off.

Mr. Evans now returned into the house bearing the bundle in his hand; which when Mrs. Evans saw, 'I will lay my mode cloak[61] to a brass pin,' said she, 'that here is some news from Miss Cecilia.' 'I assure you,' replied her husband, 'this packet comes from an Earl; but what the/ contents are I cannot say.' 'Open it and see,' said she. Ned, who was all breathless expectation, cut the string which tied it, when out came – nothing but another bundle within the former. When this was opened, the first things that presented themselves were three letters; one in a man's hand to Mr. Evans; another in a lady's, directed to him also; and a third in the first hand, larger than the two former, directed to Ned.

The lady's letter was first opened, which contained the following words:

Dublin, Feb. 8th, 1780.

My dear and valuable friends,

I fear you will begin to think that your ungrateful Cecilia has been base enough to forget the generous protection and kind hospitality which you afforded her in Wales. Yet can I assure you, that though my heart is not a rock, the impression of your kindness is more durably engraved on it, than it could be on any stone. Inscriptions on/ marble are effaced long before the marble itself is consumed, on which they are engraved; but my heart must perish before it can forget the friendship of my kind protectors.

When I arrived in Dublin, I found my father in such a situation as called for all my care and absorbed all other attention. For many days did I expect the most afflicting stroke with which Providence could have chastened me; but it has pleased Heaven to avert the blow, and to restore my father to his usual health. He writes himself by this conveyance, to express his gratitude to you both, and to Mr. Edward, for all your kindness to me; and I hope his manner of doing it will be agreeable. You will pardon me, my dear friends, if I concealed from you before, the rank which my father holds in this kingdom. Titles oftener embarrass friendships than promote them; and if hiding my own was a deceit, it was the first and the last that I shall ever practise with you./ I beg you will give the inclosed, with my best affection, to Miss Watkin. I hope my dear Mrs. Evans will accept of the few things sent herewith as a token of friendship, and that you will both of you continue to think of me and love me.

It would be unpardonable in me to conclude this letter, without offering my kindest and most grateful compliments to Mr. Edward, and hoping that we may all live to meet again,

I remain
Your much obliged
And sincerely affectionate
CECILIA RIVERS.

The Earl's letter to Mr. Evans, which was next opened, was as follows:

Merrion Square, Feb. 8th, 1780.

Rev. Sir,

I take the first opportunity in my power, of expressing to you the grateful sense I entertain of your extreme civility/ and attention to my daughter, Lady

98 *The History of Ned Evans*

Cecilia Rivers, during her residence at your house; and I congratulate you upon having a son, who, by his conduct to her ladyship in the hour of her distress, is an honour not only to you but to his country. I should not have been so long in making this acknowledgment, had I not been confined by a most severe illness, which had well nigh brought me to the grave; but from which I am now pretty well recovered. The first use I made of my returning health, was to wait upon his Excellency the Lord Lieutenant of this kingdom, who has enabled me to present your son with a pair of colours in a regiment now raising here, and in which my second son is to have a company. I write to the young gentleman himself, and send him his commission enclosed, which I hope will be acceptable to you both.

I take the liberty of enclosing to you a bank bill for one hundred guineas, which I entreat of you to accept, to reimburse/ you any extraordinary expence that you must have been at while my daughter was with you; and I conclude with assuring you that at all times it will give me the highest pleasure if I should be able in any way to promote either your interest or your son's.

I remain, Sir,

With great gratitude and respect,

Your obliged and obedient servant,

RAVENSDALE.

Ned's letter was the next to be opened; when the first thing that presented itself was his commission, written on parchment, and already signed by his Majesty. Lord Ravensdale's words were as follow:

Merrion Square, Feb. 8th, 1780.

Sir,

Your gallant and generous behaviour on the unhappy occasion which first introduced my daughter, Lady Cecilia Rivers, to your acquaintance, has laid me under so great an obligation, that I really want/ words to express my thanks, or the high sense I entertain of your merit. I should have acknowledged this sooner, but for a severe illness from which I have but lately recovered, and that I wished my expressions of gratitude might be accompanied with something more substantial than mere words. I have therefore solicited, and been happy enough to obtain for you, from his Excellency the Lord Lieutenant of this kingdom, a commission which has been signed by his Majesty, and which I send you enclosed, whereby you are appointed eldest ensign[62] in a regiment now raising for his service in this kingdom, and in the company of which my son is to be the captain. I should not have taken this step without consulting you, only that the applications were so numerous that there was no time to be lost; and when I considered your spirit and your youth, I could not doubt but you would as gladly exert your courage in defence of your country, as you have already done in that of my daughter./

'The regiment is expected to be ordered to America in the summer. It will therefore be advisable for you to come over to this kingdom as soon after the receipt of this as may be convenient to you; and while you stay in it, I shall be most happy if you will consider my house as your home.

I have the honour to be, sir,

Your much obliged and obedient servant,

RAVENSDALE.

The surprise and transport of joy which now seized on Edward, kept him silent for some time; yet were extremely visible in his whole frame. His cheeks glowed with a deeper crimson, and his eyes sparkled with unusual fire – not unlike those of the generous steed, when he first hears the sound of the trumpet; when with erected ears he foams upon the bit, and, pawing the ground, devours with his eye the space that separates him from the foe.[63] Such were the first looks of the gallant Edward, when he/ found himself an officer; but soon the soft idea of the lovely Cecilia rose in his imagination, when his corresponding features put on equal softness, and the lightning of his eye melted into the sweet radiance of tenderness and love. His father watched the various turns of his countenance; he saw with pleasure the emotions of his soul; and, clasping him to his bosom with an embrace inexpressibly affectionate, he wished him joy of his promotion. Mrs. Evans too joined in the congratulation; yet she could not suppress a rising tear, which insensibly dropped upon her cheek, when she reflected how soon he was to be torn from her, to what dangers he was to be exposed, and how many dreadful chances there were that she should never behold him more.

We may indulge the mother in these tender anxieties, which are natural to her sex, and suitable to her character: but the generous spirit of the curate disdained these apprehensions, and he heartily and sincerely rejoiced in the new prospect that was opened/ to his son, and in the glory with which his fond imagination already saw him covered. And now their first transports being over, they resumed tranquillity enough to examine the other contents of the bundle: – and these were found to be two pieces of the finest Irish linen; two of damask table linen; twenty-two yards of a rich and grave-coloured silk for a gown and petticoat, and sixteen yards for a gown of the most beautiful Irish tabbinet.[64] These presents gave great satisfaction to Mrs. Evans, who said, when she had done examining them, that she had always been of opinion, from the first view she had had of her, that Lady Cecilia was a woman of the highest distinction. Mr. Evans joined in the eulogium on her ladyship, and in extolling the magnificent manner in which Lord Ravensdale had rewarded them; and Ned took occasion

100 *The History of Ned Evans*

to remind them, that it had been ever his opinion that Lady Cecilia would not forget them.

And now Morgan was dispatched to ask/ Miss Watkin to tea, that she might share in the general joy; and to carry to her the letter which was enclosed for her; and which they afterwards found was a letter of thanks for her attentions from Lady Cecilia, and contained a present of a very rich and valuable diamond pin./

CHAP. XIX.

THE Evanses had hardly done dinner when Miss Watkin made her appearance, so impatient was she to know the particulars of their news from Lady Cecilia. She brought her diamond pin with her, which was extremely rich and elegant, and which had she received a week before, she would have valued ten times more for the sake of the bestower, than for the intrinsic worth of the jewel. Yet she derived some hope from the elevated rank of the lady, which was now ascertained; but when she heard of the commission, and the invitation to Lord Ravensdale's, a sudden paleness overspread her countenance; and if there had not happened to be a glass of water standing on the table, which she drank off, she would probably have fainted. She mustered up resolution enough, however, to wish Ned joy of his commission; but could not suppress/ her tears when she heard of his being ordered to America, and that he intended to go to Ireland in a week or ten days. What passed in her heart it is not easy to describe, nor can be conceived by any but those who have tenderly loved; it may be compared to the sensation of ice freezing all the powers of the soul, whilst hope, which had been lately planted there, died away to the roots, and all its sweet blossoms withered away for ever.

Evans and Ned imputed her agitation to the terrors of friendship for the dangers he was to undergo; but Mrs. Evans was not so deceived – she clearly saw the real cause; she saw and pitied – for nothing could have been more agreeable to her than that alliance, which would not only have been an ample provision for Ned, but would have kept him at home and in safety. And indeed if her wishes were to determine, she would gladly have returned the commission, and kept her son. But this she knew to be impossible – she knew full well the state of/ Ned's heart, which this commission flattered; and were his love out of the question, she knew his passion for glory would never suffer him to forego a profession which it had been the height of his ambition to aspire to; and she knew also that her husband would be of the same sentiments. So that pity was all the consolation she could give to poor Harriet, and this she did give her from the bottom of her soul. Indeed she soon afterwards took her up to her own bed-chamber under some pretence, where she gave her an opportunity to unbosom herself, and where that poor girl had the consolation to find in her all the tenderness of

– 101 –

102 *The History of Ned Evans*

a mother, and all the fidelity of a friend. This soothed her so much as to enable her to return to the parlour, and to pass the evening without in the least awakening the suspicion either of Mr. Evans or his son. And indeed from this evening Mrs. Evans did really look upon her with the affection of a mother, not thinking it at all improbable but that, if Edward lived, she might/ one day become so; for she considered his passion for Lady Cecilia as quite romantic, and that there was not the smallest probability of ever being successful: and Mr. Evans himself coincided with her in this opinion; as he did also in his good wishes for Miss Watkins, when his wife afterwards apprised him of the truth: so that this poor girl found friends and advocates where she most desired them; and was restored, if not to the sweetness of hope, at least to some degree of complacency and tranquillity of mind. Her regret indeed for his absence, and her terrors for the dangers to which he must be exposed, could not be alleviated except by the consciousness how many partners she had in these anxieties; for there was not one of Ned's acquaintance who was not solicitous for his welfare.

And now as the time approached when Ned was to go, Mrs. Evans was hurried in preparing for his departure. The two pieces of Irish linen which Lady Cecilia sent her, she cut up into shirts for him,/ and poor Miss Watkin assisted in the making them: this was a pleasant office to her, and would have recommended them perhaps to Ned, if the consideration of their being Lady Cecilia's present had not already stamped a value on them that could receive no addition. All his friends in the neighbourhood came to congratulate him on his advancement, and to take their leave; and he spent several days in returning these affectionate visits, and in giving and receiving assurances of unalterable friendship.

On the evening before his departure, Mr. Evans had invited a few friends, and, to make it pass off more easily and agreeably, Price was ordered to attend with his harp. Mr. Watkin, who was now quite recovered, with his wife and Harriet, were of the company. They danced from tea till supper; and though some hearts among them were certainly heavy, yet it did not seem to affect their heels, which moved nimbly enough the whole evening. After supper, several jovial songs were sung, and, a large/ bowl of the best punch smoking on the table, all melancholy seemed banished. Some of the company knowing the excellence of Ned's finger on the harp, and how charmingly his voice suited with that instrument, requested him to play, and to accompany it. Though he sung in the most masterly manner, yet, contrary to the common custom of all who do, he seldom required a second bidding, but with the utmost readiness obliged the company. He took the harp, and, having put the strings into complete tune, began the sweet Scots air,

Farewell to Lochaber! and farewell my Jane![65]

Those who have any taste for music, and who have ever heard this charming air well sung, need not be told how powerful the impression is it leaves upon the heart. When he came to that pathetic close,

May be to return to Lochaber no more!/

the aptness of the words to his own situation, and the enchanting sweetness of his voice, overpowered poor Harriet, and she burst into tears. His mother, whose passions were also wound up, wanted only this to set hers a-flowing also, and she very opportunely kept poor Harriet company. Indeed Ned himself was the only person in the room unaffected, except Mr. Watkin, who, in the midst of the sweetest and most affecting part of the tune, was very calmly lighting his pipe at the candle; and hearing his daughter's voice, he thought she was joining in the song, and cried out, 'That's a sweet note, Harriet, do give it us again.' This mistake restored the spirits of the company; for Ned, not being able to resist the impulse of laughter, gave way to it, in which he was joined by the whole table except Mr. Watkin, who could not be prevailed on either to laugh or cry.

The remainder of the evening was spent agreeably on all sides till the hour of separation came. Ned led Miss Watkin to/ her horse; when lifting her into her side-saddle he gave her a parting kiss – the tender and unexpected salute thrilled to her finger's ends, which were resting on his neck as he raised her on the horse, and which, by an involuntary compression, now strained him to her bosom; whilst her faltering voice could hardly articulate the words, 'Dear Edward, fare-well!' The darkness of the night befriended her delicacy, and concealed those tears which now flowed in a torrent from her eyes, and from which they did not cease to flow till sorrow and fatigue at last closed them in sleep.

Ned now went into the stable, to see that the horses were well fed; one of which had been borrowed for him from Mr. Watkin, that Mr. Evans might ride with him to Holy-head. Here he found David Morgan hard at work, preparing all things for the morning's journey. This poor lad, who had a sincere attachment to Ned, had determined in his own mind never to stay behind him after he had once gone away. He had not,/ however, mentioned this resolution to any body; but now finding Ned alone, he embraced this opportunity, and, getting between him and the door, begged of him not to go till he had granted him one request. Ned, not expecting any such matter, was surprised what he could desire, and promised, if it was proper for him to do, he would gratify him. He then asked him to take him as his servant. Ned told him he should be very glad to have him, but that he did not think his income would enable him to keep a servant. Honest David replied, that if that was all his objection, he would make that matter easy; for he would go with him all the world over, and serve him without fee or reward. Ned thanked him for his attachment, but blamed his imprudence; 'for,' said he,' it may very possibly happen that it will not be in my power to support

104 *The History of Ned Evans*

you.' – 'Master,' said David, 'leave that to me; I will not ask any support from you; I desire only the honour to serve you, and the comfort to be/ with you; for by – (Here he swore an oath which I will not presume to write) I never will stay in this country after you are out of it.' – 'Well but,' said Ned, 'what will you do?' – 'I will inlist,' said David, 'in the same regiment with you, and at once serve both you and my king.' – 'I applaud your zeal and your friendship,' said Ned; 'and if you do, I will promise you all the favour that is in my power to shew you; neither will I accept your services for nothing, but recompense you as it may be in my power.' David's joy ran over at his eyes; and this point being settled, he went home to his father's to make known his resolution, and Ned returned into the house./

END OF THE FIRST VOLUME.

THE HISTORY OF NED EVANS.

'O'erstep not the modesty of Nature!'
SHAKESPEARE.

IN FOUR VOLUMES.

VOL. II.

LONDON:

PRINTED FOR G. G. AND J ROBINSON,

PATERNOSTER - ROW.

M.DCC.XCVI./

THE HISTORY OF NED EVANS.

CHAP. XX.

AT length the morning dawned that was to separate Edward from the only home he ever remembered to have had, and from the arms of those tender parents who had hitherto held him in their fond embraces. Though his youthful bosom glowed with delight in the prospect of his new profession, and with the still more transporting hope of soon being in the presence of the beloved of his soul; yet he could not leave his little paternal dwelling, where the/ happy season of childhood was passed, nor the protection of those indulgent parents who had supplied all his wants and soothed all his cares, without being impressed with a tender sorrow, which no prospects of pleasure could entirely dispel, and which would have been a defect in his heart if they could. His father and mother were justly entitled to his most ardent affection, and they fully possessed it. The very stones that formed their habitation, and the trees that sheltered it, were endeared to him by old acquaintance, and by their relation to them. – He rose therefore this morning at the very first peeping of the dawn, and went into the garden to see, for the last time, those scenes where he had so often assisted his father in his delightful task, and which were indebted for most of their beauty to their united labours. Here he came to the seat which he had lately raised and consecrated to the memory of Lady Cecilia; and, cutting two suckers, one from a white and the other from a purple lilac tree, he twisted them/ together,[1] and planted them in a sequestered spot where he thought they would be most likely to thrive.

This was his last labour in the garden: his romantic imagination fancied these two suckers were emblems of Cecilia and himself – and he fondly wished that their affections might be twined together like the twigs he had just planted. He thought, if ever he lived to return, his first visit should be to these shrubs, and that from their situation he would draw an omen of his future love. Poor youth! such are the superstitions to which love bends the strongest understandings, and such the delusions with which it alike flatters the hopes and entangles the hearts both of the simple and the wise! – As he returned to the seat, he was surprised to see at some distance a young woman advancing towards him. This was indeed Molly Price,[2] the daughter of the poor harper; whose blooming cheeks and auburn locks had captivated so many hearts among the neighbouring/ swains (as we formerly mentioned), and who, alas! had been herself enthralled by the many graces of the manly Edward. Sorry am I to record, that this amiable youth was not in all things perfect; and that the passions of nature, which this poor girl's beauty was but too well calculated to enflame, had some months before been too violent for either his reason or religion to restrain, especially when the feebleness of her resistance seemed more like an invitation than a refusal.

This girl was, however, the only person with whom he had ever so transgressed; and never since the matchless charms of Cecilia had inspired his soul with the sublime transports of an honourable and chaste passion, did he suffer his thoughts to wander even for a moment from that pure object, or his heart to form a wish in which the severest virtue could find any thing to condemn. He met Molly therefore without embarrassment, and with that compassionate tenderness to which from him she was/ certainly entitled: her eyes discovered that she had been weeping, and he did not need her information to tell him it was for him. He made her therefore sit down; and in a long and pathetic harangue he lamented the situation in which their mutual indiscretions had involved them, and which, he now learned, could not long be concealed from his father and the public.

During a conversation of near an hour, he said every thing that reason, religion, virtue, and friendship could suggest to afford her consolation: he promised, that though he could not dare to see his father if he should know his guilt, yet he would take care, when he was gone from his presence, to confess it to him by letter, and to recommend her and the unfortunate infant that was to come into the world to his protection and forgiveness. He declared, that though he had made a firm resolution (which he trusted he should be able to keep) never to transgress so again, either with her or with any other woman, yet he should/ ever remember her with the truest kindness, and endeavour to supply her necessities, and those of her child, as far as he should be enabled to do. He then gave her five guineas as an earnest of future favours, which was almost five times as much as ever she had been mistress of before, and which contributed as much as any thing he had said to dry up her tears, and open her heart to consolation; and then, after an affectionate kiss, in which guilt had no share, he led her out of the garden, and he went into the house.[3]

The reader may wonder perhaps how Ned came to have so much money about him, at least to spare: – but he must remember that Lord Ravensdale had sent a bank-note for 100l to Mr. Evans, the whole of which that generous parent would have had him to take; but no entreaty, nor even command, could compel him to accept of more than half, which he said would be abundant for his neces-

108 *The History of Ned Evans*

sities, especially as he had now an income superior to his father's. The good/ curate was therefore obliged to acquiesce (at least for that time), and had given him the day before fifty guineas preparatory to his journey to Ireland.

Mr. and Mrs. Evans were now risen and the breakfast things all laid upon the table, when Ned entered. His baggage had been entrusted to a carrier to take to the Head; and honest David Morgan, with a knapsack on his back and an oaken stick in his hand, was ready with a cheerful heart, and as cheerful a countenance, to follow his young master to the end of the world. Though David had a father and mother and even a mistress to forsake, as well as Edward, all of whom he had taken leave of that morning, yet the glory of being a soldier, and the pleasure of attending Ned, had banished all sorrow from his heart, which indeed was not found to be the residence of much thought or melancholy; and he looked forward to his campaigns in America, with as much eagerness as ever he had done to a fox-chase or a badger-hunt: yet/ he did not want good-nature; but the bustle of war has charms for all young fellows of spirit; and he longed to match old Price the harper, whose glorious achievements had been set to music, and rewarded by a pension of almost five pounds a year.

The good curate had ordered him a tankard of the best ale, and the remains of a piece of cold roast beef, on which he was regaling in the kitchen; and so well was he pleased with him for his attachment to Ned, that he had replenished his pocket with a guinea, which honest David accepted with great pleasure, as an omen of the immense wealth he should acquire by plundering the rebels.

Meanwhile Ned finished his last meal in the parlour, whilst the streaming eyes of Mrs. Evans fed on him with lingering looks, and her trembling hands were hardly able to fill out his tea. The horses were now ready, and the trying moment now came that was to tear him from her arms. I am not able to describe the unutterable/ tenderness with which she folded him to her bosom, nor the devotion with which she raised her trembling eyes to Heaven, when, grasping his hand in hers, and dropping on her knees, she poured out her soul in prayer, beseeching God to bless and to protect him.

If any one who may chance to read these pages shall know what it is to have had an only child – to have reared that child upon her breast, and seen him advance in every grace both of mind and body till he attained the bloom of opening manhood; – if at that season she has lost him, or been obliged to part with him to a remote country, where dangers and difficulties were to surround him, and where a thousand chances might arise to prevent her ever meeting him again – such an one, and such only can conceive what this poor woman felt on this occasion. Her husband was the first to comfort her: he raised her from her knees; he commended her piety and her prayer; he exhorted her to have confidence/ in God, which he said was the way to obtain what we asked; and he ventured to predict, from an unaccountable gleam of comfort which gladdened his own heart, that their prayers were heard, and that they would all meet again.

Poor Ned himself had not a very soldier-like appearance – but, mingling his tears with hers, and joining with his father in his consolations, he gave her a last kiss, and hastened to his horse, to quit a scene which was become more affecting than he could bear. The good curate hastened too; and Morgan assisting him on his horse, they both rode off together. When they had gone about half a quarter of a mile, they came to a turning on the road, which afforded the last view of our parson's little dwelling. Here Ned stopped his horse (whilst his father continued to ride on), to contemplate for a moment the little habitation, and take a last look of scenes so long endeared to him, and which perhaps he should never see again. He was viewing/ the two old oaks that stood before the house, and the window of the parlour which appeared between them, when he saw his poor mother standing near them, and following with her eyes his last footsteps. He could not resist the inclination, which this tenderness inspired, to speak one word of comfort more to her, and throw himself once more upon her bosom. He rode back; he alighted – he hung for a minute on her neck; she strained him once more to her heart; once more he quitted her embrace; he mounted his horse again – and was out of sight in a moment. He soon came up with his father, who was jogging on in a very reverend trot, and so wrapped up in contemplations that he had never missed him. Their conversation now took a livelier turn, which the fineness of the day and the beauty of the country inspired. The fragrance of the air and the exercise of the ride exhilarated their spirits; and still as their distance from home increased, Ned found the weight of parting from it diminish,/ till at last he resumed his usual gaiety. The new prospects which were opening to him in life contributed to this, and to fill his breast with hope, which is the parent of joy; and which the good-natured curate was so far from repressing, that he indulged in it himself, and promoted the sensation of it in his son.

Their journey passed on with pleasure and satisfaction, and in the evening they arrived in safety at the Head, where they learned that the packet was not to sail till about eleven o'clock the next day. This evening therefore they determined to pass with as much cheerfulness as they could, and for that purpose ordered a good supper, and a bottle of the best wine. Over this liquor they sat up till it was pretty late; and their conversation turned upon the entrance of young men into life, and particularly in that profession in which Ned was now engaged. I will not attempt to give a detail of this conversation, though he that had the happiness to hear it made/ a vow never to forget it. But the precepts it inculcated were so opposite to the practice of most of the young officers with whom I have been acquainted, that I am afraid, if I was to relate it, it might bring my friend Evans into contempt with that respectable corps, or at least discredit principles which were known to have resided in the breast of a Welch curate, and which neverthe-

110 *The History of Ned Evans*

less would have done honour to the heart of the ablest veteran in Europe. He did not indeed dwell much upon religion in this conversation, as might perhaps have been expected from one of his cloth. But the reason was not because he thought religion unessential to the military character, but because he knew Ned to be so well grounded in it already, as to prefer his faith even to his commission, and that he had nothing new to learn on the subject; but what he chiefly descanted on to-night was *honour*, which he had often heard called the religion of a soldier, and indeed the only religion which a man of sense should profess. The/ futility of this pernicious sentiment he fully exposed, by shewing that honour was never genuine when separated from religion; and that it was in fact but a beautiful fruit engrafted on that stem. 'Let us part it for a moment,' said he, 'from this great root, whence every thing virtuous must spring, and behold what heterogeneous monsters it will produce! A man of honour, without religion, may ruin himself and his innocent children in an avaricious attempt to bring that same ruin upon another. A man of honour, without religion, may defraud an industrious trades-man of a just demand, and involve his poor family in distress, to pay a debt of honour, as it is emphatically called, to a nobleman who does not want it, or to a sharper who has perhaps won it unfairly – and this he must do, if he is unable to pay both debts, and is desirous of still maintaining the reputation of honour.[4] A man of honour, without religion, may take advantage of the artless simplicity of some unsuspecting girl, to rob her of that/ honour which he prizes so much himself; and afterwards may run her father or her brother through the body, for presuming to call his honour in question. A man of honour, without religion, may traffic for a seat in parliament to keep him out of jail, and may succeed in a bargain with some venal borough; he may then declaim in that parliament against bribery and corruption, and sell the interests of his constituents, to a worthless minister, with as little ceremony as he bought them.'

'These, and a thousand other characters such as these, are the daily product of what the world calls honour. But let not my dear boy mistake me, and think that I am decrying the noblest principle of the soul, or sacrificing honour at the shrine of religion: – if honour without religion is bad, – religion without hon-our is a thousand times worse: '*Corruptio optimi est pessima*.'[5] Now, true religion being the best and most sacred thing on earth, the corruption of it is the worst of all corruptions. Accordingly/ the most flagitious[6] characters that have ever appeared in the world, have been hypocrites; and the most enormous wicked-ness that ever disgraced mankind, or outraged the feelings of humanity, has been perpetrated under the name of religion: – but it was religion divested of honour. Cromwell and his saints may serve for a specimen of the one – The inquisition and the jesuits, the Sicilian vespers, the massacre of St. Bartholomew, nay the whole history of popery abounds with examples of the other.[7] But true honour, and true religion, are not accountable for the corruptions which wicked men

Volume II   111

have introduced in either. These are harmonious principles, wedded together, and which cannot exist asunder. They are sweet concords, whose unison charms the soul, and makes it fit for heaven. As for you, my boy, I have no fear either for your honour or your faith. I have not taught you to place religion in abstract speculations, or in a servile assent to unintelligible creeds – but in those substantial/ duties which the great Author of ours came into the world to preach and to practise, and which, if we would believe himself, is the only thing of worth in any religion. For what does he require of thee, O man! but to abstain from evil; to do justice, and to love mercy, and to walk humbly with thy God? But nothing shews more the necessity of religion to a man of true honour, than the opinion of the world concerning gratitude. Even in this profligate age, no man would be allowed to have honour, who could return an extraordinary kindness with scorn and contempt. Now God is the greatest benefactor that any man ever had, or ever can have. I never can believe therefore, that he who can be false to his God, will ever be true to his king or his country, to his mistress or his friend. And now, Ned, that I have named the word mistress, give me leave to point out to you the only rock on which I think your honour can ever be in danger. I know your attachment to Lady Cecilia Rivers; and I/ think, considering your adventure with her, and some other circumstances that I shall not name, that it is more than possible she may incline to wish you well. You are now going into her presence; and are invited even to dwell with her, by her father. But, Oh remember, Edward, what that father has done for you! and do not abuse his generous friendship, by seducing the affections of his child. You know the immense distance of your rank; and that if she could be weak enough to consent to marry you, the consequence would, to her, be nothing less than ruin. – Let your honour then be triumphant over your passion, let the spirit of a soldier teach you to conquer, and let your first victory be over yourself. Leave fiddlers and dancing-masters to abuse the hospitality of their patrons by robbing them of their daughters; but let my generous Edward scorn such unworthy actions – let him support the honour of an ancient Briton, and shew his noble friend that the barren wilds of Wales, and/ the humble cottages of its curates, may produce spirits worthy of happier climes, and of more exalted fortunes. Let him see that he has not misplaced his friendship, and that the last vice you can be guilty of is ingratitude.'

Here Evans paused for a reply; – but Ned continued wrapped in the profoundest meditation. 'Speak to me, my child!' said Evans again, 'and pass me your word of honour not to attempt to seduce the affections of Lady Cecilia Rivers!' – 'Seduce her affections! No, my father! (replied Ned) by Heaven I would not seduce her to be the monarch of the universe! You say you know my attachment to her: I avow it; and when I cease to be attached to her, I shall be attached to nothing upon earth. But calm your fears, either for her honour or for mine: – her mind is so pure as to resist all corruption, and her understanding so clear

112 *The History of Ned Evans*

that to circumvent it is impossible. – But know that, if it was not so, your son would sooner perish in the dust/ before he would hazard to offend her. You say you think it possible she may incline to wish me well: – I am sure she does so; but in the light you seem to hint, I do not believe she thinks of me at all. Yet, Oh my father! pardon me if I must tell you, that if I thought it possible she should ever bend her thoughts to match herself with your poor Edward, I would embrace my happiness with ecstacy, and aspire to her arms, though she was seated on the throne. And where would be the dishonour in this? or where would be the ruin? It is true I am not rich – and it is true I am not a lord: but it is also true I am a gentleman, and that I have never done any thing to forfeit that character. – In that character therefore I shall ever think I have a right to push my fortune wherever I can find it; and after the charming lesson which you have read me this night on honour and religion, the music of which still tingles in my ears, my dear father! you must excuse my acting so inconsistent with both, as to make/ you a promise which I am sure I shall not be able to perform.' – 'Enough, my son,' said Evans. 'Enough, my dearest child! I will exact no promise, and I am satisfied with your reasons for giving none. Go, my boy – go where fortune leads you! – Court her through the paths of honour, and may glory and success attend you!'

The clock now struck two: – they rang the bell for the waiter. They were shewn to the same apartment; and this being the last night in which perhaps they should ever be together, they resolved not to separate: they quickly undressed, and lay down in the same bed, where their innocent and peaceful minds were soon sealed in the profoundest sleep./

CHAP. XXI.

THE morning was pretty far advanced before either of them awoke; the waiter came to summon them to breakfast, and to inform them that the wind was fair. The captain of the packet had just called at the house, to acquaint the passengers he should sail in an hour. When they had finished their last meal together, Evans took Ned by the hand, and, looking on him with inexpressible tenderness – 'I had something to reveal to you, my dear boy!' said he, 'which may some time or other be of consequence to you, though at present it can be of none. I will therefore suppress it now. But if ever we live to meet again, I will acquaint you with it; and in case it shall please God to take me from you, I shall take care to have it told you. – I know not what fortune may attend you – you may rise to honour and to fame; or/ you may sink under misfortune, and walk in the valley of death. In either case, my darling child! here is your consolation – here is a friend that will never forsake you; that will teach you to use prosperity with moderation, and to support adversity without being overwhelmed. Take it, my child – use it – keep it – consult it upon all occasions, and trust your father when he tells you, it has been his cordial through many afflictions.' He then put into his hand a pocket edition of the Bible. 'I accept your present, my father!' said Ned, 'with thankfulness; and in this case I will make no scruple of passing you my most sacred word of honour, that I will obey your injunctions. And now too, my father, I must tell you in my turn, that I also had a secret to reveal which yet at present I am obliged to suppress. Yet I will acquaint you with it by letter; and I make it my last request to you, that you will comply with my desire.' 'I know nothing, my child,' said Evans, 'that you can demand of me,/ that I shall ever wish to refuse.' – The captain of the packet now came to summon Ned on board, which put a stop to all further explanation: what Evans had to reveal must remain in his own bosom till he chooses to tell it – at this time it could have been of no consequence to Edward, unless perhaps to afflict him, though indeed without reason. What Ned had to reveal to his father, was certainly his affair with Molly Price: but the piety of that ingenuous youth could not bear the presence of his father under the consciousness of guilt.

– 113 –

114 *The History of Ned Evans*

They now walked together to the vessel, and took their last leave upon the beach. They shook hands for the last time with the warmth of sincere affection, but without those tears which are the characteristics of female partings.

Mr. Evans stood upon the beach till the packet got under weigh; he continued to gaze on her till she turned out of the harbour, and the intervening rocks concealed her from his view. He then returned to/ the inn; and having ordered his horse, and paid the bill, he set forward on his way home. He had not gone many miles before the weather began to change. The wind, which had been south-east in the morning, now turned to the south-west, and brought with it heavy squalls of rain. His tears now rose for his son, to whom this wind was adverse, and he was often upon the point of returning to the Head, in hopes the packet would put back, and that he should again fold him in his arms. As he rode on, doubting in his mind, the comfortable little inn of Gwindu[8] appeared, the landlady of which he was long acquainted with, and whose character and hospitality deservedly endear her to all who travel this road. Here therefore he determined to alight, and Mrs. Knowles herself met him at the gate. She received him with the cheerful welcome of genuine friendship, and her house being then full of company going to the Head, she conducted him to her own little parlour behind the bar;/ where he found an excellent fire, a neat room, and every thing else that could contribute to his comfortable entertainment. She now congratulated him on his son's commission, which she had heard of soon after he got it; and when Mr. Evans expressed his anxiety to her for his safety, as he had that morning sailed for Ireland, she allayed his fears, by assuring him there had no accident happened to a packet within any body's recollection. 'They are such excellent vessels,' said she, 'and so well found both in sailors and commanders, that though they sail in all weathers, they always come safe. At present the wind is contrary, to be sure, but it is far from a storm; and it may be fair again before night, for nothing is more common. And so, my dear Sir,' continued she, 'repose yourself here in quiet; the company will soon set forward to the Head, when you can have a room to yourself, and continue your journey in the morning.' Mr Evans thanked her for her kind invitation, but expressed/ his positive determination to go home that night at all events. 'My poor wife,' said he, 'is all alone, and stands in need of my company to relieve her sorrow for parting with her son.' – 'Well then,' said she, 'if you are determined to go, I cannot help it: but I must insist on your obliging me in one thing. I have a chaise here of my sister Jackson's at the Ferry, which I am obliged to send home; and as the evening is still wet, I insist on your going in it at free cost (for it must go at any rate), and your horse may be tied behind it and follow after.' This offer, so obliging and so convenient, was not to be refused: he therefore gladly accepted it; and then asking what was to pay for his dinner, she positively refused to take a farthing. The chaise being now ready, he got into it, after having kindly taken leave of Mrs. Knowles; and fully convinced in his own mind that there were not six such mistresses of an inn in all the world.

When he got to Bangor Ferry, he gave/ the lad who drove him a shilling; and, mounting his own horse, continued his journey home. The evening had cleared up; and the night, which had now set in, seemed much better than there had been any reason to expect some time before. This eased his mind with regard to Edward, and enabled him to meet his wife with more cheerfulness than he otherwise could have done. He found that good woman just sitting down to her solitary meal, which was to serve her both for dinner and supper; for she had long delayed dining, in hopes of the comfort of her husband's return. Were I to relate the tender meeting of this fond and faithful pair, I am afraid most married couples would say it was unnatural – it was so utterly unlike the generality of connubial meetings now-a-days. Yet their happiness was a little allayed, when they saw but two plates upon the table; they missed the third who added so much cheerfulness to their meals, and the thoughts of the absent filled both their eyes with/ tears. Just then Towser, who had been Ned's favourite dog, came wagging his tail to Evans, and put his foot upon his knee. 'Poor fellow!' said Evans, patting his head, and giving him a bone to pick, 'I will be kind to you, Towser, for your master's sake.' Mrs. Evans, whose eye was fixed on a little round hat which Ned used to wear, and which still hung upon the peg, from which she would not suffer it to be removed, said with a sigh which came from the bottom of her soul, 'Alas! my poor boy! – I shall never see you more!' – 'God forbid!' said Evans; 'I trust we shall spend many happy days together yet. Come, wife!' said he, 'uncork a bottle of wine. Sorrow, they say, is dry – let us drink a bumper to Ned's health, and may we live to see him a general officer!' 'God grant that I may live to see him at all!' said she; 'but I will pledge your toast.' So she brought the wine, which her husband well knew her spirits required. He made her drink a/ bumper, and another to the back of it; and affected a cheerfulness which at that time he did not really possess, on purpose to alleviate the load under which he saw she laboured. In part he succeeded; and time, which lessens all sorrows, at length softened hers. And here we shall take leave of this worthy couple for a long season; trusting they will continue to live and to be happy, while we follow the fortunes of their son.

CHAP. XXII.

THE packet had proceeded but a short way on her voyage when the weather changed, as we have seen before; and the wind coming now contrary, and blowing fresh, there was a general discharge among the passengers of all they had eaten the day/ before. Ned was not free from these qualms; yet he was not so taken up with his own sufferings, but that he could feel for those of the ladies who were on board, and whose unavoidable distresses made them real objects of compassion. He endeavoured to relieve them as long as he was able, but the vessel continuing to work violently, he was obliged to retire to his birth. They continued the whole night at sea; but the weather having grown more favourable towards morning, he was able, as soon as it was day, to go upon deck. Here he had the first view of the Irish shore. The sight of any land is pleasant to one who has not been accustomed to the sea, but the bay of Dublin presents objects particularly grand and noble. He saw it this morning in its highest beauty. On one side was the Hill of Hoath, with the romantic rock called Ireland's eye, and the island of Lambay beyond it; on the other were the Wicklow Mountains rising to the skies, and their tops still shrowded with the morning clouds. / In front appeared the lighthouse, white as snow, and looking like Venus rising out of the waves. The spires of the metropolis glimmered at a distance through the mist that always hangs over great cities, while the new risen sun gilded the intermediate country, rich in an infinite variety, where groves and palaces, cottages and cornfields, towns and country seats, masts and trees seemed blended together. Ned, who had a taste for painting, could not fail to be delighted with the beauty of this prospect; but, charming as it was, could he have distinguished among it the dwelling of Lady Cecilia, I believe the other objects would have been but little regarded.

About eight o'clock in the morning they passed the bar; and a wherry always attending the packet, he was in less than an hour after landed on the quay, opposite the Marine Hotel. Here he had a proof of the amazing hospitality and good manners of the Irish; for he had scarcely set his foot upon the ground, when half a dozen ragamuffins/ without coats, and others without shoes, welcomed his honour[9] on shore, and seemed to be almost quarrelling among themselves which should take his honour's trunk to the hotel, which was about twenty yards distance. At last this was effected by agreement; for two carried the trunk, which weighed about three stone, and another carried his boots which weighed about three pounds, and they only demanded three sixpence halfpennies. It had hardly been deposited three minutes in the house, when another very obliging gentleman appeared, who told his honour he was an officer of the customs, and that his trunk must be taken to the custom-house; but, if his honour would give him a shilling, he would dispense with the laws so far as to permit him to take any thing out of it he pleased. Poor Ned complied with the utmost good humour with these extortions, but told the officer he had not less than half-a-guinea about him. The other very politely offered to get it changed;/ whereupon Ned gave it to him directly for that purpose. His sea sickness being now quite gone, and his stomach completely empty, he asked the landlord if he could get any thing for breakfast; who replied, he might have any thing he pleased. He was then shewn into a very handsome and well-furnished parlour, though they had forgot to sweep it for about a week before, and here his breakfast was served; which, to do the landlord justice, was both good and reasonable, and Ned did it ample justice in the eating. Poor Morgan too, who was as hungry as his master, was equally well served without. Ned now wondered the officer did not come back with his change; but those who knew that gentleman better, would have wondered more if he had. The truth is, he was no officer at all; but he thought, by the innocence of Ned's countenance, that he was a fine subject for a cheat; in which he too happily succeeded, and the poor youth was obliged to purchase this first piece of experience at the price of/ half-a-guinea. But now a real officer appeared, whose story, however, was much the same as the other's, and only differed in the authority of the teller. So Ned having taken out some articles of dress, and ten guineas in money, he delivered his trunk to the officer, and ordered David to go with him to the custom-house with the key, and when it was searched to bring it back. Meanwhile he got a hair-dresser to set his head in order; and having put on his best clothes, which were the same we formerly mentioned to be approved of by Lady Cecilia, he only waited for Morgan's return to go to pay his respects to that divine beauty.

His heart was so eager to behold her ladyship, that he thought every minute an hour till he returned; and he was so often at the door of the house looking for him, that the maids took that opportunity of gazing at him till they put him entirely out of countenance. 'He is a charming fellow,' said one, 'and has the finest eyes I/ ever saw.' 'He has the best legs that ever I saw with an Englishman,' says a second, 'but I think he is a little too shame-faced.'[10] 'That's owing to his youth,' said a third; 'but I should like him charmingly for a husband.' Whilst these elegant observations were making, Morgan returned with the trunk, which Ned delivered into the custody of the landlord till he should send for it, and he

118 *The History of Ned Evans*

promised to take care of it. He ordered Morgan to stay there too, and sallied out himself in quest of Lord Ravensdale's.

It was no difficult matter to find his lordship's house. As he went up to the door his heart palpitated at his side, and his breath was as short as if he had run three miles. He had resolution enough, however, to knock at it, when it was opened by a footman in a very elegant livery. Ned asked if Lord Ravensdale was at home? The man answered, that his Lordship and Lady Cecilia had gone down to the country three days before, and that/ they were not expected again soon. This was a grievous disappointment to poor Ned, as the servant, if he had been expert in reading countenances, might easily have perceived. He then asked if any of the family were in town? The man answered, that both Lord Rivers and the Captain were in town, but that his Lordship was not yet risen, and the Captain had gone out several hours ago. Ned was now going away; when the servant asked him if he would not be so good as to leave his name, or that if he would call again in an hour he would probably find Lord Rivers up. 'You may tell his lordship,' said Ned, 'that Mr. Evans from Wales was here, and that I will call again.' He then went away, and the servant shut the door.

As Lord Ravensdale's house was in Merrion Square, he intended to amuse himself with sauntering about the neighbouring streets, and admiring the many beautiful buildings which surrounded him, until it should be time to call again on Lord Rivers./ Passing along Merrion-street, he was infinitely struck with the grandeur of the Duke of Leinster's.[11] The beautiful opening at the back of that noble palace, and the elegant disposition of the ground, with the refreshing verdure of the lawn, and the variety of shrubs that surround it, charmed his fancy, and made him think it a dwelling fit for a sovereign. As he stood admiring it, two stout lads approached him who had each a basket on his head, and a knife with a piece of steel at his side. He asked one of these lads, whose noble palace that was which he was looking at? 'Oh Jesus!' says the other, 'Where were you born, that you don't know who lives there?' 'What's that to you where I was born?' said Ned; 'I ask you whose house that is?' 'What's that to you whose house it is?' said the other: 'Go look, and be damned!' Ned, who was not accustomed to this language, grew a little angry; which the other observing, said, 'By Jesus hur is a Welchman, hur Welch plud is up./ Ah! when did hur cross the ferry, agrah! and how did hur leave St. Taffy, and who milks hur grandmother's goats, now hur is away?' Ned, whose Welch blood was now up in earnest at this disrespectful mention of his country, gave the fellow a stroke with a rattan which he had in his hand; and was preparing to give him another, when the second boy came behind him, and clapped his empty basket downwards over his head, and pulling him back tripped him at the same time, so that he fell backwards on the ground; and the cunning rascal pretending to fall at top of him, wedged his head in the handle of the basket, and left him in that awkward situation, and both of them ran away.

Though Ned was taken unawares, yet he soon recovered himself, and got disengaged from the basket. A chairman who chanced to come by then being informed by him what had happened, went into a gentleman's house; and bringing out a clothes-brush freed him from the dust, and/ assisted to put him to rights. Ned was very thankful for this civility; and putting his hand in his pocket to give him a shilling, he found his purse was gone with the ten guineas he had just put into it; and what he regretted still more, his watch, which was a present from his father, whose companion it had been for thirty years. There was no help for it, however – the thing was so sudden, he would not have known the scoundrels again if he was to see them: like the wind, he could neither tell whence they came, nor whither they went. The chairman however condoled with his misfortune, and thanked him for his intention, as much as if he had got the shilling; and then left him, giving him this good advice, that if in future he should ever be at a loss for information in the streets, never to ask any body but a chairman, who, he could assure him, were all of them men of honour, and would not impose upon a stranger for the world.

Poor Ned being now on his legs again,/ and readjusted as to his dress, though without a penny in his pocket, walked on towards Stephen's Green.[12] The noble grandeur of this magnificent square surprised as much as it delighted him, and he was astonished to see so extensive an open in the midst of a populous city. The trees were already putting forth their leaves, and the grass in the field exhibited the richest verdure, indebted for its early spring to the richness of the ground, the warmth of the city, and the mild openness of the Irish climate, which brings every thing forward a month sooner than in Wales. In the Beauwalk, which he had now entered, were a great number of well-dressed people of both sexes, walking in parties, and enjoying the fineness of the day; whilst the elegant dresses of the ladies, and the freshness of their complexions, made him almost believe he was in the island of Cythera,[13] the native country of beauty and the graces. He might have indulged this imagination for some time longer, if he had not been accosted/ by an old beggar-woman, who with a face of the most abject want, and with hardly a rag to cover her, asked him for a halfpenny. He gave her a look of pity, which unhappily was all he had to give, and told her he was sorry that he had nothing about him, for he had just parted with all the money he had brought out. She gave a sigh, and turned up her eyes to Heaven – 'God bless your sweet face!' said she, 'and may the holy Jesus enlarge your store!' As he walked on he observed the equestrian statue in the centre of the field,[14] though from its distance he could barely distinguish what it was. – He wished to be informed about it; but not seeing any chairman near him, was afraid to ask questions. At last, recollecting that he could not be robbed, and seeing at a distance

120 *The History of Ned Evans*

a gentleman walking alone, whom, by a certain elevation of the head, a sleek countenance, and a coat of the most glossy black, he concluded to be a dignified clergyman, he determined to ask him. Just as he was approaching him,/ he perceived the poor beggar-woman stretching out her hand to him, and beseeching his reverence to bestow something on her for charity. 'Pr'ythee begone, woman!' said the divine, 'I never give any thing to beggars.' – She dropped a curtsy, and retired. Ned's heart was smote: – he suffered him to pass unnoticed. When he was gone out of hearing, he asked the poor woman who he was? 'It is Doctor Porpoise, sir,' said she; 'the greatest preacher in the kingdom, and they say he is to be the first bishop.' 'He may preach as he pleases,' said Ned, 'but his practice is very bad.' 'Oh no,' said the poor woman, 'your honour does not know him – he subscribes to all the charities in the kingdom, and it is thought he will build an hospital himself.' 'He may build ten if he will,' said Ned, 'but he knows nothing of charity, and whenever he dies he will find his charity at the head of his sins.' 'Oh! God forbid!' said the poor woman; 'I wish him well, though he gave me nothing.' 'Good/ woman,' said Ned, 'where do you live?' 'Alas, sir!' said she, 'I am ashamed to tell you – I live in the streets – Where else can such a wretch as I am find a habitation?' 'I will see you here to-morrow,' said Ned, 'and I will give you something to get a better habitation.' He was then going, but the woman held his coat – 'Oh sir, give me leave to ask; but – indeed I am afraid.' 'What are you afraid of?' said Ned; 'ask what you want to know.' 'Are you an angel, sir? for you look so like one, I would kiss the hem of your garment.' The strangeness of the question, for he perceived by her countenance that she was really in doubt, had like to make him laugh. He however kept his gravity, and replied that he was indeed nothing but a man, and a poor one too – 'Nevertheless,' said he, 'I will not deceive you.' The poor woman curtsied to the ground; and while she was praying to the Almighty to reward him, he continued his walk./

CHAP. XXIII.

He made the circuit of the whole green, in which he saw much to admire, and still more to condemn. The magnificence of many of the houses pleased – while the meanness of others, and the want of regularity in the whole, did not fail to offend. But what disgusted him most was the deep ditch which surrounds the fields, with a nasty, stinking, green, unwholesome puddle at the bottom, which can answer no end but to annoy the inhabitants, and which it is astonishing they have so long endured. If that ditch was filled up, over a concealed drain; if the centre field was laid out in walks and shrubbery; if the mean houses were removed, and new ones built on a regular and uniform plan, Stephen's Green would be the most beautiful square in any city in Europe. /

Having now been near two hours on his walk, he returned back to Lord Ravensdale's. When the servant opened the door he informed him that Lord Rivers had been obliged to go out, on business he could not neglect, but that he would be home to dinner, when he hoped to have the honour of Mr. Evans's company. The footman then shewed him up to the drawing-room. – Though Ned was no stranger to the best houses in his own neighbourhood, yet he had never seen any thing like the apartment which he now entered. The room was 44 feet long, 34 wide, and 30 high; – it was hung with silk damask of an azure blue; chairs, sophas, and window curtains of the same; the latter hung in festoons, and ornamented with tassels and a deep fringe of blue and silver. The ceiling and cornices were of the finest stucco, divided into compartments, in the four principal of which were painted, by an exquisite hand, the four seasons: from the centre hung a lustre of cut glass, with branches for six-and-/thirty candles, and which with all its appendages had cost 1000 guineas. The beauty of the chimney piece was inexpressible, which was all of Parian marble, and on the top of which stood the statues of two naked boys, which were worthy to be the work of Phidias.[15] The glasses, the carpets, and every thing else were answerable.[16] – But the richest part of the furniture, and in comparison of which all the rest was nothing, was the pictures. Here were the works of Titian, Guido, Correggio, and Tintoret. A landscape, by Claude,[17] had caught his eye, for this was his favourite kind of painting, when, chancing to turn his head to the glass, he thought he saw Lady

122   *The History of Ned Evans*

Cecilia behind him. He started and looked hastily round, but alas! it was only her resemblance – but then so exquisitely like that it almost made amends for the disappointment. The noble works of the Italian masters were now obliged to yield to the more interesting pencil of Angelica[18] – for she it was who painted this portrait./ Mrs. Kauffman had been some time before in Ireland, and Lord Ravensdale could not miss the opportunity of getting his daughter painted by so excellent an artist. She was drawn in the character of Diana; and never did the goddess herself on the banks of the renowned Eurotas,[19] or in the numbers of the sublimest poet, exhibit a more striking combination of majesty and sweetness, of beauty, chastity and grace. Ned gazed at it with rapture, astonished at the art that could so happily represent the picture in his soul; and here he would still have gazed, had not a thundering rap at the door, which shook the whole house, and which astonished him, who had never in his life heard the like before, announced the arrival of Lord Rivers and the Captain.

The brothers immediately went up stairs; and Lord Rivers advancing to Edward with a sliding bow – 'I am infinitely happy,' said he, 'Captain Evans, to have the honour of seeing you in this house; and I/ can assure you that my father and I, and all the family, have so just a sense of the great obligation you have laid us under, that nothing on our parts shall be wanting to make your stay among us in this kingdom agreeable.' Ned stood blushing to the eyes. – 'Brother soldier,' said the captain, 'I do not make long speeches, but I am glad to see you here with all my heart; and so give me your hand.'

This last address relieved Ned from his embarrassment, being much nearer his own style. He cordially shook hands with the captain; and after expressing his gratitude to his lordship and the family for so infinitely over-rating any little service that he had been so fortunate as to render Lady Cecilia, he sat down. They now enquired about his passage, the weather, the news in England, and, last of all, where he had left his baggage. My Lord told him that he was to consider that house as his home; and, having rung the bell, he immediately dispatched one of his servants/ to the hotel, to bring David and the baggage to the house.

The clock now struck five – when a servant appearing announced that dinner was on the table. The captain said he would shew Ned the way, who followed after, and his lordship went last. In the parlour was a table elegantly covered, and a servant in a laced livery behind every chair. Ned stood some time expecting the grace; but finding it did not arrive, he sat down. He and the captain did justice to a most excellent dinner, as excellently dressed; but his lordship could hardly touch any thing – he piddled[20] a little with a ragout of palates and coxcombs, but was obliged to a glass of Burgundy to make it go down. His constitution indeed seemed wearing apace: – though his countenance was noble, and his figure elegant in the extreme – though he was in the very prime of life, being scarcely twenty-five years of age – yet there was a thoughtful melancholy in his look, which gave him a much older appearance, and/ the perpetual vigils of fashionable dissipation made him much older in constitution even than he appeared. The captain, on the contrary, who loved the sports of the field, and who spent as much time in the country as he possibly could, was as fine a young fellow of twenty-two as you would see in a thousand. When the cloth was removed, and the grace forgot as before, a beautiful dessert in china and cut-glass was placed upon the table, consisting of all the fruits in season, and those that were out of season preserved, whilst the finest wines of France blushed in the decanters. – After a full bumper to the king, and success to his arms by sea and land, Lord Rivers's spirits began to revive: an elegant and spirited conversation took place, which, enriched with claret and enlivened by champagne, abounded both with wit and information. I wish I could repeat it to my readers, but wit at second-hand evaporates; suffice it to say, Ned bore his share, and during a couple of hours that they sat together greatly surprised/ them by his sallies of humour, united with politeness, modesty, and good sense. The captain in particular conceived a warm affection for him, and my lord declared he wanted nothing but a little intercourse with high-life, to rub off his bashfulness, and he would be an absolute *beau garçon*.[21]

His lordship then asked his brother where he was to spend the evening? who answered, that not knowing of Mr. Evans's arrival, he had promised that morning to sup with his poor friend Malone, 'who you know,' says he, 'is inconsolable for the loss of his wife; and nothing but such an engagement as this, which I cannot put off, could make me part with you this evening.' My lord said, he would rather go to a funeral than to such an engagement. 'You will hear of nothing but the graces and virtues of his dear Louisa, and nonsensical whimsies about her employment in heaven. – But come, Captain Evans,' said he, 'you shall go with me; I will carry you to a select set, all of them choice spirits, and fellows/ of the first fashion and fortune in the kingdom. We have a room at a tavern, where such of us as are not otherwise engaged meet every night, and where every thing is cheerful and *sans souci*.'[22]

Ned said, he would be happy to attend his lordship wherever he went. But now being informed that his servant had arrived with his trunk, he was shewn up to his bedchamber, where it was deposited. The splendour of this apartment was suitable to the rest of the house; and now he took out what remained of his money, being somewhat above thirty guineas, not doubting but he should want some where he was going, and not supposing it could be in any danger in the company of Lord Rivers.

The chariot being now at the door, his lordship and Ned stepped into it, and they were driven through streets which surprised Edward by their number and their illuminations, to the place of their destination. They were shewn up-stairs into a large room very well furnished, or rather two/ rooms thrown into one,

124 *The History of Ned Evans*

with a fire-place at each end, and a curtain which could be raised or let down at will in the middle. At one end of the room was a table ready laid for supper, with all things proper for an elegant entertainment; at the other end were four card-tables, at one of which was a party engaged at whist, and two gentlemen standing at the fire. 'Oh Rivers! are you come?' said one of them: 'What the devil kept you so late? Here is Sir George and I have been picking our teeth this hour.' 'Why, how long has the house been up?' said my lord: 'I thought you had been there to-day.' 'Oh, damn the house!' said the other; 'I don't believe 'tis up yet – I expect every minute to be sent for to vote.' 'Why, what are you upon?' 'Damn me if I know! – Flood was making an oration about something or other; but he is so damnably long-winded, I had like to have fallen asleep: so Sir George called me out into the lobby, and we both stole off together.' 'And how will you/ know how to vote then?' said Lord Rivers. 'Oh! damn you, Rivers!' said the other, 'who would think of your asking me that question? When you give your vote, do you always know what is the debate?' – 'Yes, certainly,' said my lord. 'Well, it may be so, *sed credat Judæus*.[23] – But I do not mean to contradict you.' 'Well, come,' said Lord Rivers, 'it makes no difference to be sure, we all of us vote with our party; and if the heads of that know what they are about, it is very well. Here let me introduce this gentleman to you, Trimwell; this is – Captain Evans, from Wales.'

Ned was then introduced to all the gentlemen, who received him with respect; and his lordship proposing to sit down to cards, he was compelled to make one; – but first he declared against playing high, and said he understood so little of cards, that if they could possibly do without him, he would rather not play at all. Lord Rivers said, they played for mere nothing; only for/ half guineas, unless he chose to bet. Ned said he never made any bets; and as he thought it was half-a-guinea a rubber, and that he really understood the game very well, he thought it would be rude to spoil their party: so he was prevailed upon to cut. Lord Rivers and he happened to be partners; and Fortune being in the mood of favouring him he won the rubber. His lordship, who betted on the rubber, and on every odd trick, won also very considerably, and this put him into high good-humour. Ned expected only half-a-guinea; but he received two guineas and a half, it being a rubber of five. This however did not give him much satisfaction, as it shewed him he was playing for a much larger stake than he intended. He was however engaged, and he could not give over without breaking up the party: so he continued to sit on. He played three rubbers more; and Fortune, as if she intended to seduce him to be a gamester, favoured him in every one.

He heard now confused noises behind/ the curtain, which had been let down, among which he distinguished female voices; and one of the waiters announcing supper to be on the table, the card parties broke up, and Ned rose a winner of eight guineas and a half.

Volume II 125

The table was covered to profusion, with every thing rare and elegant, the very names of which Ned never heard before. The ladies, who were four in number, were laughing at the upper end, dressed in the top of the mode; patched, painted, powdered, and perfumed, with plumes of feathers nodding on their heads: he supposed them to be ladies of fashion, by their ease and their forwardness, especially as he remembered Lord Rivers's observation, that he only wanted acquaintance with high life to rub off his bashfulness. He thought however they stared at him more than was consistent with good breeding, and their whispering and tittering did not appear perfectly polite. The company now sat down, Lord Rivers at the upper end. –/'Come, gentlemen,' said he, 'mix with the ladies, and sit as they do in France; let us have no ceremonies here: Captain Evans, as you are the only stranger, and my guest, you will be pleased to sit near me.' All things being now adjusted, they sat down. Every body helped themselves to what they liked, or called to another, if what they liked was not near them. Ned observed the gentlemen scarce tasted anything; but the ladies made amends, for they devoured every thing as if they had fasted during a whole Lent. As soon as one of the ladies could disengage her mouth from the leg of a duck which she had stuffed in it, she asked Ned if he would hob nob. – 'Hob nob, madam!' said Ned, 'what is that? I have not the honour to understand you.' 'O Jesus, sir!' said she, 'did you never hob nob with a woman in all your life?' Ned, who was astonished beyond all conception, could not tell what to answer, but blushed like scarlet. Most of the company laughed – but Lord Rivers said,/ 'Captain Evans, the lady only means to ask you to drink a glass of wine with her; which in this country is called hob nobbing. I believe in Wales you have no such term.' 'I really did not comprehend the lady's meaning,' said Ned; 'but I will drink a glass of wine with her with all my heart.' – She then tossed off a bumper to Love and Friendship; in which Ned pledged her, though he thought in his own mind she was no object of either.

Another of the ladies hearing that Ned came from Wales, asked him if there were not a great many goats in it. He answered, that he believed there might. 'Aye,' says she, 'I thought so; you look so fresh complexioned – I suppose you live upon their whey?' Ned assured her that he never tasted a drop of their whey in all his life. 'By the living jingo, that's very odd,' said she: 'why it is the greatest restorative in nature.' 'O fie, Polly,' said another of the ladies, 'do not swear – you knows I hates swearing, it sounds so wulgar.' –/'God 'Why now!' said the other, 'it is hardly a month since I heard you swear Peg Plunket black in the face.' 'Madam,' said the other, 'I scorn your words; and if I did swear once, it is a profane custom, and I have left it off.' 'Come, come, ladies,' said my lord, 'no quarrelling; all here must have freedom of speech.' 'She is grown so sanctified since she took up with Parson Simper, the methodist,' said the fourth lady, 'that in another month we shall have her preaching sermons!' 'Madam,' said the other,

126 *The History of Ned Evans*

'whatever you say of me, I beg you will spare that holy man, and do not make a jest of religion.' 'Why, what is religion but a jest?' said Sir Thomas Spindle, a worn-out emaciated rake of seven-and-twenty; 'damn me if any thing is so disgusting to me as to hear a woman prate with virtue in her mouth and vice in her heart!' 'Well, Sir Thomas,' said the lady, 'nobody will accuse you of either one or the other – for I defy any body to say they ever heard/ a virtuous sentiment come out of your mouth!' Here the laugh turned against poor Sir Thomas, in which every body joined except Ned, who was now fully apprised of the character of the ladies, and whose disgust and contempt rose to absolute abhorrence.

A reinforcement of gentlemen now coming in from the house, which had just broke up, the conversation took a political turn, much to the satisfaction of Ned, who was thereby relieved from ribaldry and profaneness. Some of the new-comers displayed both genius and sentiment, which a little reconciled him to his situation; and the ladies retiring without any body taking notice, except one or two of the gentlemen going off with them, among whom was Sir Thomas Spindle with the very girl who turned him to ridicule, he resumed his complacency and good-humour.

For some time the conversation was both interesting and instructive, as the subject turned on the war in America,/ in which he was going to be engaged; and he would have listened to it with all his heart: but a difference in sentiment arising, they began to grow warm; when Lord Rivers called them to order, and desired them to remember that that room was dedicated to Concord. A libation of claret being then offered to that deity, cards were again proposed, as those who last came in had not played at all. Ned was again challenged to the field, by the gentlemen whose money he had won, and whom therefore he could not decently refuse. But the game they now played at was not whist, but l00, as taking in a greater number; and Lord Rivers was excused, as presiding over the wine. For some time Fortune continued favourable to Ned; but at last the fickle goddess changed, and, after an hour's run of continual ill-luck, he found he had not only lost all that he had won, but sixteen guineas more. He now determined to give over, which nothing but his *mauvaise honte*[24] had prevented him from doing long before./ He therefore asked Lord Rivers, in a whisper, what time he thought of going home? 'Not these three hours,' said his lordship: 'sure you are not tired – the fun is only beginning.' 'I beg to be excused, for my part,' said Ned, 'for I really am fatigued; I got no rest last night at sea, and I confess I long to get to bed.' 'Oh then, if that is the case,' said his lordship, 'I dare say my carriage is in waiting, which shall carry you home when you please.' As he went out of the room, his lordship followed him; and being alone together on the head of the stairs, he said to Ned, 'Perhaps, my dear fellow, you have been unlucky. If you have lost any money, the only way to retrieve it is to play on; and if you are out of cash, here is my purse for you, which you may always freely command on this or any other occasion.' Ned thanked his lordship, but assured him it was no such thing – he was really tired. But the generosity of the offer, and the noble frankness with which it was made, restored Lord Rivers to his/ esteem, who had begun a little to sink in it before. The carriage being now ready, Lord Rivers returned to the company, and Ned went home to Lord Ravensdale's.

CHAP. XXIV.

WHEN Ned alighted at Lord Ravensdale's, he enquired for Captain Rivers, and was told he had gone to bed three hours before. The servant then shewed him up to his chamber, where a pair of wax candles were burning, and where David Morgan was stirring the fire, and waiting to attend him. When they were by themselves, 'Well, Morgan,' said he, 'what have you been doing, and how do you like Dublin?' 'Oh! master, 'tis the finest place in all the world,' said he. 'Doing! Oh, such rare doing! I never saw the like in all my life. My lord and you had hardly been gone half an hour, when company/ came to Mr. O'Frizzle, my lord's gentleman, and to Mrs. Mulroony, the house-keeper – for you must know they are very great, and always see company together. There was Mrs. Geoghegan, Lady Rumpus's waiting woman, and Miss Flanagan her niece; and there was Monsieur Papillote, a sweetheart of Miss Flanagan's, and Mr. Sideboard my lord's butler – and to be sure they were all dressed like so many lords and ladies. And the ladies came carried by men in leather boxes, but the gentlemen walked – and they were all shewed in to Mrs. Mulroony's room, which she said would be more convenient than the parlour, as Captain Rivers was in town; and there they had tea and cards.' 'Well, and did you play cards too?' said Ned. 'Oh! no,' said Morgan: 'Does your honour think I would be such a fool as to lose my little money among folks so much above me?' 'Hem! hem!' said Ned, 'you were very wise indeed – Go on – what did you do then?' 'Why, Mrs. Mulroony/ desired the cook to have supper by eleven; and she said, 'Yes, to be sure, madam.' So the maids got their tea when the ladies had done, and they invited me and my Lord's footman to drink tea with them; and so we all did, to be sure: and after we had done, then we all went and played blindman's buff in the servants' hall till supper was ready, and then the footmen went to attend upon the ladies; and when they had done, it was brought in to us; and a rare supper it was, and plenty of it, enough to keep a Welch squire for a fortnight: and so we had hardly done when Mr. Sideboard brought a bottle of claret, and gave it to me because I was a stranger; and so I poured it into a large bowl of punch for the good of the company, and we all drank it, and were as happy as so many fiddlers; – and we had hardly finished when your honour came home.' 'Well,' said Ned, 'tis very

– 128 –

fine indeed. But go now to your bed – you need not stay up for me.' So Morgan retired, and left his master to himself./

When he was alone, the events of the day came crowding on his mind. 'What an idiot am I!' said he to himself, 'and how improper to be left to my own guidance! I have not yet been eight-and-forty hours from the protection of my father, and how bitterly do I feel the want of him! Into what distress have my folly and inexperience already led me!' He now took out his purse, and laid it on the table: he surveyed it for a moment in silence, as if afraid to count its contents. At last he emptied them out, and found that of the fifty guineas which his father gave him but two days before, he had but seventeen remaining; and that he had not got one earthly thing, not even pleasure, in exchange. 'This sum,' said he, 'which I have thus lost and squandered in one day, would have maintained my poor father for a whole year. Yet,' said he, 'it shall not be wholly lost; it shall at least purchase me experience: and I have this comfort, that thought I have lost it by folly, I have not squandered it on/ vice. Oh! my loved father,' said he, 'thou art now sleeping in thy bed! Perhaps in the very hour in which thy son was sitting among prostitutes, thy hands were lifted to Heaven in prayer for him. Nor shall they be lifted up in vain,' said he; 'I am not contaminated by the vile society into which I was ignorantly introduced, and into which nothing shall ever betray me again. I will prostrate myself before thy father and mine; and I will commit myself in confidence to his protection.' With these words he retired to his bed-side, and, falling on his knees, spent ten minutes in the most devout prayer. He arose refreshed – the burthen of having done wrong was removed – and a secret gleam of satisfaction, which the consciousness of acting right always inspires, shot through his soul, and restored his spirits to composure. He now undressed to go to bed; but first he determined to put back the remains of his money in his trunk, and never to carry about him more than a guinea/ or two at a time, for fear of accidents. He returned it therefore to the place from whence he took it; and in rummaging about to get a clean night-cap, was surprised to see wedged in a corner his father's tobacco-box. He could not conceive who had put it there; yet he was glad to see it for the sake of him to whom it belonged; for since he had lost the watch, he had no little keep-sake to remember him by. He took it out, and was going to kiss it; but when he felt it, he was at no loss to know who put it there – the good and generous curate had indeed conveyed it there himself, and in it the fifty guineas which he could not prevail on his son to take. Ned stood in no need of this present to endear his father to him; yet the surprise at this unexpected generosity, the delicacy with which it was managed, and the solid comfort which it brought, almost overwhelmed him with gratitude. The fulness of his heart found a vent at his eyes; and now, all burthens being removed, he surrendered himself to/ the sweet blessing of happy and tranquil sleep.

130 *The History of Ned Evans*

It was nine in the morning when he arose, and then he went down to the parlour: there he found Captain Rivers reading the newspapers, and the table laid for breakfast. 'Good-morrow to you, my friend,' said the captain; 'how have you rested all night?' 'Never better,' replied Ned, 'for the time of it that I have been in bed' 'Well, how did you like your company?' said the captain. 'Why, 'faith, to be sincere with you,' said Ned, 'I was a little disappointed there.' 'I was afraid it would be so,' replied the other; 'but when my brother asked you to go, it did not become me to make any objections – Did you play?' 'Why, yes,' said he; 'I could not help it.' 'And you lost too, I dare say?' 'Why, yes,' said Ned, 'you are right there too; but not a great deal.' Ned then recounted to him all the transactions of the evening. 'My dear friend,' said the captain, 'I am glad you have been/ among them once, and I am glad too that you have lost your money – for I did so too; and I dare say you will follow my example, and never hazard it there again. In the company among whom you were last night, were some men both of genius and virtue; and there are many more belonging to the club of the same character, whom you did not see. The ruin of it is, there are others of a different stamp, and unluckily there were too many of these there last night. But what makes it entirely unfit for you or me is, that all the members of it are cursed with great fortunes; which enable them to do whatever they please, and to justify whatever they do. My poor brother is so attached to the freedom and wit that some-times reign there, that I cannot prevail upon him to leave the society, though he by no means approves of every thing that is allowed there, and their late hours have visibly impaired his health. It is hardly two hours since he went to bed. But while we stay in town, I will take the liberty/ of conducting you; and I can assure you, you may keep the very best company in it for a month, and play cards too with them every evening, for the half of the money you have lost last night. And now that I have mentioned money to you, I beg you will not think me impertinent in presuming to offer you some: I know you must want it, and that you will still want it; and I know how dreadful that want is to a gentleman of delicacy and feeling.' He then offered him a bank-bill for fifty pounds. Ned, however, absolutely refused to take it. He frankly told him what money he had by him, and how obtained – and said, he should never forgive himself, if he could not make his pay serve him, which was so much more than he was born to, and which was obliged to serve so many men better than himself.

Captain Rivers applauded his sentiments, and was greatly pleased with the generosity of old Evans. 'As you have so much money by you,' said he, 'I will not hurt/ your feelings by pressing this on you now; but in return I insist upon your making me your banker, and applying to me whenever you are out: – and in this I will not pretend either to friendship or generosity, for I have my father's orders for so doing; and I am sure it is not his intention to leave you to subsist on your commission.' – 'Your father,' replied Ned, 'has already conferred favours upon me infinitely beyond what I was any way entitled to; I cannot think therefore of becoming burdensome to his generosity, or overwhelming myself with obligations which I never can repay but by my gratitude.' – 'And is not that ample payment?' replied the Captain: 'What more precious offering can a generous mind either give or receive? But in your case, my dear friend, the debtor is my father; we are all your debtors – believe me that we think so, and that it is not the paltry gift of your commission that shall acquit us.' – Ned was at some loss to reply. 'You are all of you too good,' said he./ 'But shall I ever see your father? Shall I be permitted to thank him in person for his kindness, and to have the happiness again to see Lady Cecilia?' – 'Doubtless,' said he, 'you shall. We have expected you here some time: – my father has been lately ill, and the physicians thought country air necessary to his recovery – had that not been the case, he would have been in town, for he is very scrupulous in his attendance on parliament. I wrote to him last night that you were come, and I doubt not but the next post will bring us a summons to go down to him.' – This was new life to Ned, whose satisfaction could hardly be increased – unless by the arrival of a mountain of toast and butter, with which the footman now entered the room – for the man was so sagacious, he measured Ned's stomach by the Captain's, and indeed the event shewed he had not been mistaken.

They were in the middle of their breakfast, when a servant came to tell Ned that a chairman wanted to speak to him. 'To/ speak to me!' said Ned: 'What can he want? I know nobody in the town.' 'Bid him come to the door here,' said the Captain, 'and say what he wants. You see Mr. Evans is at breakfast.' 'I am come,' said the chairman, 'please your Honour, to tell you I have discovered the two boys who robbed your Honour yesterday; your watch and your money is found upon them, and they are both in custody.' 'Good God!' said Captain Rivers, 'what is this? Have you been robbed too since you came?' 'I'll tell you all by and by,' said Ned; 'but the adventure was so ridiculous, I was ashamed to mention it before. How did you find them, my friend?' said he to the chairman; 'I see you are indeed a man of honour, as you told me.' 'I hope I am, please your Honour, and worthy of the name which I bear.' 'Why, what is your name?' said Captain Rivers. – 'Phelim O'Shaghnessy, please your Honour,' said the other. 'It is a very fine sounding name indeed,' replied the Captain,/ 'and ought not to be disgraced.' – 'Nor never shall by me,' said the chairman. 'But as I was telling your Honour, after I parted with you yesterday after brushing your Honour's clothes, I thought with myself, now 'tis ten to one but these boys will go into some ale-house near at hand, to drink and to divide their spoil; or perhaps one of them may skulk somewhere about, and come back by and by for his basket. So I sets one of my companions to watch the basket, and I went myself to all the alehouses in the neighbourhood; and sure enough as I fancied, so it fell out; for at Larry Dermot's, the corner of Stable-lane, I sees my two gentlemen set up in

132 *The History of Ned Evans*

a box together, and laughing most heartily over a pot. I made as if I knew nothing, but sat down beside them and called for a pot too. Gentlemen, says I, here's both your healths. Thank you heartily, says they; here is yours. I wonder, says I, what a clock it is; I am engaged to wait upon a gentleman at two. Upon this one of them/ pulled out his watch, Oh! it wants half an hour of two yet. I'm glad of it, says I. Will you be so good, said I, as to keep this pot of ale for me till I go to the corner to speak to my partner? and I'll be back in ten minutes. To this they agreed. So I went and brought Paddy Grogan, and told him what it was to do. Now, gentlemen, said I, you will both go along with us; you are pretty fellows to go and rob a young gentleman in open day, and think to escape – but you shall go along with us to Alderman Ketchup, and he will know best what to do with you. All their laughing was now spoiled, and they looked as lank as shotten herrings;[25] they fell down on their knees, and offered us five guineas to let them escape; but we told them it was affronting our honour to offer us a bribe: so we carried hem away to the Alderman's, but it was eight o'clock at night before we could see his worship, all which time we were kept fasting. At last his worship called us in – At first he began with asking/ us a great many questions that did not seem to be any thing to the purpose, and then he consulted his clerk about law; and then he examined us again, and cross examined us, till I thought he believed that we were the thieves, and not the boys. So I told his worship, to cut the matter short, that I could swear to the robbery, and that your Honour was a great gentleman, and lived at Lord Ravensdale's and that he had better not let the boys escape, for the money and the watch was upon them. At the mention of Lord Ravensdale his tone changed; he ordered the boys to be searched, and sure enough the watch and ten guineas were found; so he committed them to the watch house till further examination. I called here last night, but your Honour was not at home; so I came again this morning to acquaint you.' – 'My good friend,' said Evans, 'I am very much obliged to you, and I will thankfully reward you for your trouble.' 'We will go together to the alderman's,' said Captain/ River, 'by and by; and in the mean time, Mr. O'Shaghnessy, if you will go down to the butler, I will order you something to refresh you.' 'I humbly thank your Honour!' said the chairman, and retired.

'What is this, my dear Evans!' said the Captain; 'not two hours in town, and to be robbed at noon-day? I never heard the like.' Ned then related the whole as the reader has seen; which served as a matter of laughter to them both. They now went out together to the alderman's, where the affair was soon adjusted: Ned got his watch and his money again; and the two boys, who were apprentices to a butcher in Castle Market, were, at the intercession of him and Captain Rivers, delivered to their master again, after having undergone some private correction.

As the Captain had some business of his own to do in the town, Ned begged he would go about it; and said that he would go to Stephen's Green, where he would walk in the mean time, and where he would/ be sure to find him. The two friends then separated; the Captain to go on his errand, and Ned to keep his promise with that poor creature whose heart he had relieved the day before, and to his business with whom he did not wish to have any witness. He had not been long in the walk till he saw her in the same misery as before, and soliciting charity with as little success. Her eyes brightened when she beheld him, and a feeble smile softened for a moment the horrors of her famished countenance. He drew her a little to one side, out of the immediate notice of the passengers. 'I am come,' said he, 'to keep my word with you, and to give you some little relief; tell me then how I can best be of service to you. Have you any friend in this town?' – 'O no, Sir!' said she; 'no, not one.' 'What then brought you to it?' said he. 'I shall tell you, Sir. I was born, Sir, in the county Cork, where my father was a day-labourer, and when I was twenty years of age I was married to a/ man who was also of the same business – by him, Sir, I had four children. He died six years ago come All-Saints.[26] I had three sons, Sir, grown up to be men; two of them went to sea, but whether they be alive or dead I cannot tell, for I have not heard of them for many years. My youngest son, Sir, was groom to Doctor Porpoise, whom you saw yesterday; and while he lived I never wanted for any thing, for he was a loving boy, and, after his sister died, kept me here in a little room, and helped to maintain me out of his little wages. But, Sir, last year, as the doctor and his family were coming up to town, and my son (as was his duty) attending them on horseback, the roads were very bad, and the coach got into a deep rut; it would certainly have been overturned, Sir, had not my son, who was a strong and active young man, jumped off his horse, and supported its whole weight. He saved it from falling till the other servants came up, and got it out of the rut; but he strained something inwardly,/ for he fell sick immediately, and, after languishing four months, died in the hospital, where Doctor Porpoise recommended him. Ever since that time, Sir, I have been in want. I was obliged to pawn my little clothes for support; I could no longer pay the rent of my room; and when I had nothing left to pawn, I should have perished for want, but for the kindness of Doctor Porpoise's servants, who all of them loved my son, and for his sake give me every day through the rails the scraps of broken meat from their table; and sometimes, when the weather is very cold, the coachman lets me lie in the stable, where the warmth of the cattle comforts me.' 'Did you ever represent your case to the doctor, and does he know you are the mother of his groom?' 'O yes, Sir! – he paid me what was due of his wages, which was but a very little; but he never would do any thing more.' 'O merciful Saviour of the world!' said Ned, 'is this man a teacher of thy religion, and does he presume to call himself/ by the name? Have you any friend living in the county Cork?' 'Yes, Sir,' said she, 'I have a brother, who, though a poor man, would, I believe, help me if I could get to him; but alas! Sir, it is so far off, I never could be able to walk it; and all that I can make by begging will not redeem my little clothes and carry me there.' 'How much will redeem your clothes?' said he. 'Ten shillings, Sir,' said she. 'And how much would carry you to Cork?' 'About five more, I believe.' 'Here,' said he, 'are two guineas. Go to your brother, and be happy.' The poor astonished creature would have thrown herself upon her knees; but he left her instantly, to share her emotions, and to hide his own./

CHAP. XXV.

He walked for above an hour in the green before his friend arrived. Captain Rivers then proposed to him to go bespeak his regimentals, and afterwards to take a view of the college. When they came to the end of Grafton-street, he was struck with admiration at the magnificent colonnade which forms the front of the parliament-house, and which surpasses every thing of its kind in being. Yet he thought there was some awkwardness about the roof, and that if a balustrade, with statues, had been added to it, it would have considerably increased its beauty. He was charmed with the noble front of the university, which is built in the finest taste, and every way suited to the dignity of that distinguished seat of learning. He could not help regretting, however, the want of a third building opposite the parliament-/house, which would have completed three sides, and which, if ever such a thing shall be erected, will make College-green surpassingly beautiful. Neither could he conceal his indignation at the vile watch-house shouldering King William's statue, and which he was astonished the inhabitants would suffer to exist an hour. Nor did he much admire the statue itself, which he thought unworthy of the great hero it represented[27] – and the horse in particular such a clumsy brute, that he would have disgraced a brewer's dray.

When he entered the college he was disappointed. The buildings within did not answer the expectation he had formed from those without. But it must be remembered they are not yet finished; and that their effect is hurt by many old buildings being among them, which are intended to be taken down. The old hall and the chapel he condemned, as altogether unworthy of their situation; but the new hall he thought a noble room, as he did also/ the new building opposite, which was then erecting; but he execrated the paltry taste of its internal ornaments, which he pronounced were only proper for a stucco-shop. From hence they went to the library, the vast extent of which first struck his imagination: but when he had leisure to contemplate its just proportion, its excellent contrivance, and the exquisite beauty of its architecture, he was lost in admiration. How did he then lament the sordid parsimony of those who built it – who, to save a few pounds, made use of stone which had nothing to recommend it but its being got upon their own estate, and which, now yielding to the weather, is every where

136 *The History of Ned Evans*

mouldering away; so that in a few years hence its incomparable beauty will be no more! From the library they went to the park, a pleasant and extensive field, ornamented with walks and shaded with full-grown trees, for the recreation of the students: the elegant little building called the printing-house there struck his eye; but/ the press not being at work, he could not get in. The anatomy-house, which is opposite, disgusted by its meanness; and not having much desire to examine its contents, though some of them are very valuable and curious in their kind, he passed it by unnoticed. They continued their walk to the end of the park; when Captain Rivers having a key to the door which opens into Park-street, they passed through it, and in a few minutes afterwards found themselves at home.

When they enquired about Lord Rivers, they were informed he was gone to the house,[28] but that he intended being home to dinner. They now went to dress, it being between three and four o'clock; and when this important business was ended, Ned went down to the drawing room, to contemplate in secret the charming picture with which he had been so much captivated the day before. He had been feasting his eyes for some time, when he was joined by Captain Rivers; and soon after/ his lordship arrived, bringing with him a friend, a member of parliament, whom Ned had never seen before. The first view he had of this gentleman struck him with veneration: his person was of the largest of what is called middle size, but adorned by a just proportion, and a manly grace, which made it perfectly genteel: his countenance was pleasing, though it could not be called handsome; for his complexion was rather of the darkest; but an ineffable benignity beamed from his eyes, which strongly expressed the sentiments of his soul. His mind, which from his earliest youth had been cultivated with the highest care, was a rich treasury of every thing which could adorn or exalt a man – the Muses were all his own – his poems, particularly those of the tender kind, which were written when he was but a youth, were among the best, if not absolutely the best, that ever were composed in any language. His judgment in painting was profound; and his execution in that elegant/ art (taught him only by nature) was almost equal to his judgment. He did not sing, though his voice was melodious; but when he spoke, the power of his eloquence was irresistible: – it did not overbear you like a torrent; but it fell like the dews of heaven; it penetrated to the heart, where it at once convinced the understanding, and captivated the soul. – But, great as were the powers of his mind, the virtues of his heart were still greater. His devotion was warm, without being superstitious – his morals pure, without being austere – his benevolence was bounded only by the creation – and he fell short of being perfect only by being human.

Such was the man to whom Ned was now introduced. To describe the evening which he passed in his society, exceeds all the powers of my pen. The impression which it made on his mind will never be worn out, while memory holds her seat: happy that he once saw him; unhappy only in this, that he never saw him again; for, alas! how shall I relate it? this exalted/ character is no more. Soon after this, whilst yet in the prime of life, he rose to the dignity of a chief judge: but in the very moment of his exaltation he received a wound, which, to a heart like his, was incurable. The partner of his soul was taken from him; and with her perished all his joys. From this moment he declined: not in the powers of his mind, for those were transcendant to the last; and all his conduct as a judge was equal to what the world expected: – but the pillars of his constitution were shaken, and could not long sustain the weight of that affliction with which he was secretly consumed.

Whilst engaged in the discharge of his duty, administering justice in a remote part of the kingdom, he sickened, and in a few days expired. The effusion of heart-felt sorrow which was poured upon his tomb exceeded what was ever shed for man before. His body is in the grave embalmed by the tears of his country! His memory and his fame will live for ever!/

Oh spirit of the immortal Burgh![29] who art not lost, but only translated to thy native heaven; look down from thy empyræan mansion and behold thy weeping country – be still its guardian angel – drop to us thy mantle of impregnable integrity, and impart with it some portion of thy transcendant worth!

CHAP. XXVI.

THE conversation of men of acknowledged virtue usually leaves an impression on every ingenuous mind, that does not speedily wear out; nor would it be possible for the most profligate character, while he retained any sense or judgment at all, to be often in the company of such without improving his morals, and in the end perhaps becoming a proselyte to that virtue which wants only to be known, to be adored. – Lord Rivers was far from being abandoned,/ though deeply immersed in fashionable dissipations: his honour was unimpeached; and though his sentiments on religion were not clear, or determined, yet he never went into the monstrous impiety of blaspheming the object of it, nor, where he had any controul, permitted it to be ridiculed in his presence: his morals too, though not strictly evangelical, were however such as did not disgrace him in the eye of the public; nor would the most orthodox bishop have refused him for a son-in-law, had he done his daughter the honour to address her. The sentiments of the exalted character with whom he spent the last evening sunk deep into his heart, and had already elevated his mind so far that he could not immediately relish the society at his club, and he actually entertained thoughts of withdrawing from it altogether. His constitution too began to feel the good effects of his abstaining from it; for, as he now kept more regular hours, his spirits and his appetite returned. Instead of going to bed at four or five in the morning,/ he now proposed to rise at that hour, and to take Ned with him in his phaeton, and make a little tour through those beautiful parts of the counties of Dublin and Wicklow, which lie in the neighbourhood of the metropolis. Captain Rivers was to accompany them on horseback. They set out for the Dargle at about five o'clock in the morning, and Lord Rivers had the pleasure to see the sun rise for the first time since he was a school-boy. The novelty of this object had a wonderful effect upon his spirits, though the Captain and Ned, to whom it was more familiar, felt nothing extraordinary, except the whetting of their appetite by the keenness of the morning air, in which sensation his lordship also partook, and experienced for the first time in his recollection how excellent a sauce is hunger. They arrived at a little village about eight, for they went purposely a circuitous road; and here his lordship found such tea, butter and bread, as he was astonished the metropolis could not afford;/ but which was indeed indebted for its superior excellence entirely to his ride. – From hence they got to the Dargle about ten: the season was not yet sufficiently advanced to shew this charming dell in its full beauty; though perhaps what it wanted in the richness and variety of its foliage was more than made amends for by the redundance of its water. For the brook which murmurs through it in the summer, was now a torrent, tumbling over the rocks with irresistible rage, and roaring among the caverns, from whence it sent up a foamy mist, which marked its course, and gave a hoary majesty to the awful precipices that frowned above it. Though Ned was accustomed to the grandest views of nature in his own country, yet he could not help being struck with the noble scenery of the Dargle, which, adorned by the elegant taste of its proprietor, unites the beautiful to the sublime.

They passed a couple of hours here with the highest satisfaction, and then proceeded/ through the sweet village of Tinnehinch to Powerscourt. Here a new scene presented itself: – the river, which was swollen by the late rains, tumbled from its lofty bed down a perpendicular rock 300 feet high, and exhibited to the eye a torrent whiter than snow, and crumbled as it were into powder by the resistance of the air, from the great height from which it fell – it precipitated itself with such force from the precipice, that a herd of deer, which were just then roused from the neighbouring forests, passed safe between the torrent and the rock from which it fell. Had Louis the XIVth beheld this scene, he would have been ashamed of those ridiculous water-works which cost him such enormous sums to raise at Versailles, and which none but children and French courtiers can admire; he would have despised the tawdry ornaments of his gardens, and gladly exchanged his palace for this park.

After a charming ride of four hours, during which they were entertained with a/ variety of noble objects, they returned to Tinnehinch to dinner, where they regaled themselves on mountain mutton not inferior to that of Wales. In the evening they set forward for the town. They intended to pass through the Glen of the Downs, but they had sat too long after dinner, for the night came on before they could reach it. And now Fortune contrived one of those malicious accidents, with which she often concludes parties of pleasure. The phaeton in which Lord Rivers and Ned rode, was one of those elevated machines which had been lately introduced into the kingdom by the celebrated Lord Jehu,[30] whose highest ambition was to be thought the best coach man in Dublin – and his sole employment driving up one street and down another, looking into the middle stories of the houses as he passed, and terrifying the peaceable walkers, some of whom got cricks in their necks with gazing at him. Lord Rivers was not without some ambition of this kind also, though he did not carry it to so extravagant/ and ridiculous a length as Lord Jehu, but he prided himself on his skill in driving; which, whether it was not so great as he imagined, or whether the darkness

140 *The History of Ned Evans*

of the night prevented his seeing any impediment that he might have avoided, or from whatever other cause it happened, I know not, but, as he was going on in a full trot, one of the wheels gave way, and the phaeton of course was overturned. If fortune was cruel in contriving this accident, it must be owned she was kind in causing it to happen in the very spot it did; for a poor labouring man, whose cottage was hard by, and whose cabbage garden bordered on the road, had that morning carried out all the dung that was to manure it, and laid it on the side of the road till it was to be used.

Dunghills on the sides of roads are held to be nuisances in almost all countries, and even in Ireland are indictable by law; nor was any body more severe against them than Lord Rivers himself: but on this occasion he found that there is scarce any/ evil but may be productive of some good; for to the hospitable reception which this dunghill gave him, into the midst of which they were pitched, it is more than probable that both his lordship and Ned owed the safety of their limbs, if not of their lives. As the dung was fresh from the cow-house, and they had fallen with their heads foremost, they were a good deal disarranged as to their appearance; but having recovered from their first astonishment, they had the happiness to find nothing injured about them but their clothes. The poor man to whom the cottage belonged now came to their assistance, and they were glad to accept the accommodation even of his humble roof. Captain Rivers enjoyed this scene as soon as he found they were not really hurt, and was extremely officious in helping them to undress, and in procuring tubs of water to pour over them: he told them fresh cow-dung was one of the greatest cosmetics in nature, and would not fail to improve their complexions, as much as it/ did the whiteness of linen when bucked[31] with it.

At length, after much scrubbing and scouring, they were restored to some tolerable decency of appearance, and now it became a question what they were to do. – To go forward to Dublin was impossible, the night being now quite dark, and the phaeton entirely disabled of one of its wheels. There was no smith to be got, nor a public-house nearer than the village of Tinnehinch, which they had left, and from which they were distant near seven miles: but their poor cottager informed them there was one Mr. Grainger in the neighbourhood, who rented a little farm, and was very good to all the poor people near him; but he lived entirely alone, excepting his daughter and one servant, and never visited any company. As necessity has no law, they determined to make trial of his hospitality, and to leave the servants and horses together with the broken phaeton where they were, until they should know/ whether they could be received or not at Mr. Grainger's; and in case they could not; they determined to ride the horses bare-backed to Tinnehinch, and leave the carriage in the road till the morning.

They now set forward to Mr. Grainger's, under the conduct of the poor man who had informed them of him: it was not above a quarter of a mile to the house, but the way was so intricate through the mazes of a thick wood, in which it was embosomed, that they thought, if it even had been day, they never could have found it out without the help of a guide. At last the barking of a dog, and the glimmering of a light through the trees, informed them they approached it. A little Chinese paling stopped their way, and the fragrance of some wall-flowers, and other early blossoms which were exhaling their odours to the nightly dew, refreshed their senses, and gave them no unjust opinion of the neatness and benevolence of the person they were going to visit. They knocked gently at/ the door, which was opened by Mr. Grainger himself, who, hearing their distress, assured them they should be most heartily welcome to whatever his house could afford; which however, he said, he was obliged to confess, was little more than shelter from the night air, and plainer fare than he believed from their appearance they were accustomed to. He ordered the cottager too to bring the horses and servants to the house, but the phaeton was obliged to be left where it was till the morning.

Mr. Grainger now conducted his guests into a little parlour, which was a miniature model of perfect elegance. The walls were papered with a pale blue paper, divided into twelve compartments; on which were painted as many oval landscapes, representing the twelve months of the year, each surrounded with a wreath of fruits and flowers, exquisitely coloured from nature, and adapted to the month to which it belonged; the whole seemed suspended from the cieling by a running festoon. The/ perfect cleanliness of the room, and the cheerful blaze of a wood fire, which had been newly heaped on, gave an air of comfort to the whole that was not to be surpassed: – but the brightest ornament of this elegant little apartment was the artist who contrived and executed it, and who was no other than Mr. Grainger's daughter. She rose up from a settee, whereon she was sitting, when the gentlemen entered; and displayed the most elegant figure, added to the most beautiful countenance, rendered still more charming by an air of deep misfortune that was diffused over it. She was dressed in white cambrick trimmed with black gauze; and at her feet was a little boy with the countenance of a cherubim, about three years old. All the gentlemen were struck with nearly the same feelings when they beheld her: – they saw she was unhappy, and that alone was sufficient to make her venerable in their eyes; but then her grief was impressed upon such lovely features, as interested them deeply in her sorrows,/ and filled them at once with tenderness and respect. As Mr. Grainger however did not introduce her to them, they only bowed to her as they entered, and passed to their places by the fire-side. They were not long seated when the little boy ran to Ned, and, looking up to his face with a smile that might become an angel, asked him to take him on his knee. – Mr. Grainger would have prevented him from being troublesome; but Ned, whose heart was ever open to tender sensations, begged he might be permitted to keep him; and, taking the child in his

142 *The History of Ned Evans*

arms, he pressed him to his bosom and kissed him, which the infant as eagerly returned, clasping his little arms about his neck. The irresistible attraction of artless innocence would have won a far less affectionate heart than Edward's; but in his they sunk so deep as made an impression hardly ever to be erased, and filled him with a passion for the child which could only be exceeded by that of a parent. Mr. Grainger now asked the/ gentlemen if they could like a dish of tea; 'for I frankly confess to you,' said he, 'I never drink wine, and there is not a drop in the house.' They all declared that it would be no disappointment to them, and they should prefer tea though the wine were in their option. 'Then, Nancy, my dear,' said he to his daughter, 'you will be so good as to get us some.' 'Yes, surely, sir,' said she, 'immediately.' She then rose to go about it; when turning to the child, 'Come, Charles,' said she, 'my dear, will you come along with me, and do not trouble the gentleman any longer?' 'No, mamma,' replied the child, 'if you will let me stay on this gentleman's knee, I will promise not to be troublesome.' Ned now joined in the request, which she immediately complied with, and retired. A silence of a few minutes now ensued – when Lord Rivers fixing his eye on Mr. Grainger, 'I am sure,' said he, 'Mr. Grainger, I have had the happiness of knowing you before – though it is so many/ years since, that I must be grown out of your recollection.' 'I protest, sir,' said Mr. Grainger, 'it is very possible; but I do not recollect ever having had that honour.' 'I remember,' said his lordship, 'fourteen years ago, when I was a little boy, to have had the pleasure of seeing you at Mr. Donellan's, when you and I were the only two, except the huntsman, that were in at the death of a hare.' 'Bless me!' said Mr. Grainger, 'are you Lord Rivers, eldest son to the Earl of Ravensdale?' – 'Yes, indeed,' said his lordship; 'I am the very man, and this is my brother, (introducing the captain); and this is Mr. Evans, a gentleman from Wales, whom I love and respect as a brother, though I have but very lately had the pleasure of his acquaintance.' 'Then I assure your lordship,' said Mr. Grainger, 'there are no three gentlemen in the kingdom, that I should be happier to see in this house; for I love and honour your father, and have many personal and great obligations to/ him.' 'But what in the world,' said Lord Rivers, 'has brought you to this sequestered spot? and why do you bury yourself in this solitude, and suffer your lovely daughter to consume her days in a hermitage?'

'*Infandum jubes renovare dolorem*,'[32] said Mr. Grainger; 'but I will tell you all.' – The tea-things now coming in, put an end to the discourse, and here we will also put an end to the chapter./

CHAP. XXVII.

THOUGH the conversation at tea-tables has seldom any thing to recommend it, and is even too often liable to the just censure of being uncharitable as well as stupid, yet we can assure the reader this tea-table was an exception, and that nothing passed at it inconsistent with the purest sentiments of religion, and the most consummate elegance of manners. When the things were removed the lady retired, and gave Mr. Grainger an opportunity of gratifying Lord Rivers's curiosity in the following words.

'The deep misfortune of my life, of which your lordship seems ignorant, though the world has long since been in possession of it, and which has compelled me to bury myself in these shades, was in its own nature so afflicting, and embittered by so many fatal consequences, that if my life had not/ been necessary for the protection of that dear and innocent victim who has just now left the room, I doubt whether philosophy, or even religion itself, would have been able to restrain my hands from doing violence to myself. At the time your lordship remembers to have seen me at Mr. Donellan's, there was not in the kingdom a man more disengaged from sorrow, nor more contented with his situation than myself. Easy in my circumstances, blest in the affection of the best of wives, happy in the prospect of the growing virtues of my children, beloved by my neighbours, at peace with all the world, and with myself; my hours seemed winged with down, and imagination could hardly suggest a wish, the accomplishment of which could really increase my happiness. But in the midst of life we are in death; and it is not given to mortals to drink the cup of joy unmixed. The bitter ingredients with which mine was dashed, derived additional acrimony from my not being accustomed to them. My little estate, which/ had descended to me from many ancestors, was about 300l. of yearly value: it was seated in one of the loveliest spots that nature in these climates can produce; and as we had always farmed it ourselves, it had received from art those gentle assistances which serve to embellish nature without disguising her, and was universally allowed to be a model of rural neatness and simplicity. In this happy abode of peace and of tranquillity I lived supremely blest, with my wife, my daughter, and my son; and oh! might still have lived, if a viper whom I had taken into my bosom had not stung

– 143 –

144 *The History of Ned Evans*

me to death.' 'Who could the wretch be?' interrupted Lord Rivers. 'Your lordship knows him too well,' replied Mr. Grainger; 'or rather you do not know him,
or I am persuaded you would not acknowledge his acquaintance. – It was young
Nettlefield, of Nettlepark,[33] near your lordship's estate.' 'What! Jack Nettlefield?'
said his lordship – 'You surprise me! – I thought him an honest fellow as any
in the/ kingdom, and very much of a gentleman.' 'He has indeed some of the
qualities,' said Mr. Grainger, 'which form part of the composition of a modern
fine gentleman, but which, however they may be thought of in the world, are in
reality the disgrace of human nature, and more pernicious to society by a thousand degrees than many of those crimes for which we daily hang the wretches
who perpetrate them. The petty thief, who steals my sheep, is condemned to the
gallows; – but the villain who has bereaved me of my wife – who has robbed my
daughter of her honour, and my son of his life – who has torn from me all that I
held dear in nature, and repaid my kindness with this base ingratitude – still lives
caressed by the world, and even honoured with a commission from his sovereign.' 'Good God! you amaze me!' said Lord Rivers; 'I never heard of this before.'
'Your lordship was on your travels,' said Mr. Grainger, 'when it happened; and
I am not of consequence/ enough to be the subject of conversation beyond the
circle of my own friends. It is now five years since Mr. Nettlefield, who had just
then got his first commission, came down with a party of his regiment, and was
quartered in a country town in my neighbourhood. I always made a point of
shewing every civility in my power to the gentlemen of the army, and never had
occasion to repent of my hospitality to any stranger but himself. I asked him to
my house, and he was often there, both alone and also with the other gentlemen
of his corps. For a long time I considered him as a very agreeable and amiable
young man; till a nearer acquaintance, brought on by an act of kindness of my
own, developed his whole character, and plunged me into irremediable grief,
which can cease only in the grave.

'He had been one day dining with me, along with some other gentlemen
in the neighbourhood; when returning to his quarters in the evening, he was
arrested/ within a quarter of a mile of my house, for a debt of 30l. at the suit of a
taylor in Dublin. I very soon heard of it; for they carried him to a little ale-house
hard by, by way of spunging-house; and from thence word was immediately
brought to me. I was sorry such an affront should be offered to him so near my
own doors, and from which he had so lately parted, and I waited on him directly;
when I found means to rescue him from the harpies of the law, by paying part of
the debt, and joining with him as a security for the remainder: and this disagreeable business being over, I carried him back to my house, and invited him to stay
there till he wrote to his father, and got some remittances from him to pay his
debts and set him on his legs again.

'In the meantime my son came from the college, to pass the long vacation: he had been there three years, where I intended to educate him for the church; and was then in his twentieth year – not above a year/ younger than Nettlefield himself. The two young men were delighted with each other; and as Nettlefield had all the manners of a man of fashion, and many of their accomplishments too, I was unhappily pleased with the connection, thinking it would polish that rusticity in my son which a country education had caused; and which could hardly be corrected in the learned retirement of the university.

'About three weeks elapsed before Mr. Nettlefield heard from his father. During all this time he behaved with such delicate attention to my wife and daughter, such manly freedom to myself, such openness and attachment to my son, that he established himself in the good graces of all the family. He repaid me the money I had advanced for him, and received in return a cordial and general invitation to my house. As your lordship is acquainted with him, you need not be told that he is handsome in his person, and that among his accomplishments may be reckoned a perfect knowledge in/ music, and a very correct taste for drawing. My poor girl, whom you have seen here this evening, was enthusiastically fond of both these amusements, and never seemed so happy as when Mr. Nettlefield came to the house, that she might benefit by his critical knowledge and indisputable excellence in both of them; nor did he lose so good an opportunity of recommending himself to the favour of a beautiful girl. He spent hours with her, but always in the company of her mother, forming her taste, correcting her drawings, praising her talents, and paying her on every occasion the most assiduous attention and respect. As my wife was constantly present whenever they were together, I had not the smallest apprehension on that account; and if Mr. Nettlefield felt an honourable passion for my daughter, I hardly knew a young man I should have more willingly bestowed her on; as I had the best opinion both of his head and heart, and knew that his fortune, on his father's death, would be equal to any thing that I/ could give with my daughter. I perceived therefore their mutual attachment without uneasiness; and it helped to endear the young man to me still more. My wife too had conceived for him the warmest affection; and so successfully had he paid his court to her, that I believe she would rather have given him her daughter, than to any peer in the three kingdoms.

'At length Mr. Nettlefield broke the affair to me; when I told him, that if his father and mother gave their consent, and would give him a suitable present maintenance, I should have no objection; but unless that was the case, it would be highly imprudent in both parties, and what I could never agree to. He acquiesced in all this, and was from that time received as an intended son in-law. To this time I believe he was sincere; and had his father agreed to the match, perhaps all had been well: – but the old gentleman would not advance a shilling beyond his pay, and moreover bad him aspire to larger fortunes and nobler/ con-

146 *The History of Ned Evans*

nections. When he disclosed this to me, he seemed overwhelmed with affliction; but urged me to consent to his union notwithstanding; declaring his passion to be unalterable, that his love would beget prudence, that he had enough to satisfy present wants, and that his father could not prevent his succeeding to his fortune whenever Heaven should be so indulgent as to take him away. I sharply reprimanded him for this last speech – so undutiful in a son – and so devoid, as I thought, of every feeling of natural affection; and I assured him, that as I never could approve of stealing a man's child myself, so I never would be accessary to it in another, nor suffer my daughter to intrude into any family without the consent and unequivocal desire of the heads of it.

'He submitted in appearance to my determination; but desired to be still received as my friend, if I would not permit him to continue as a lover. To this I very imprudently consented; though, as he had/ never done any thing to offend me, but on the contrary had paid us all the utmost attention, I hardly think yet that I could with propriety have refused him.

'As a friend therefore he continued to visit us; but, oh! how he abused this sacred name you shall hear. His attachment, or rather his pretended attachment, to my daughter still continued; but he had art enough to put on a distance of behaviour before me, to make me suppose he had dropped all thoughts of her, at least for the present; and the more effectually to blind me, his visits became less frequent. But though his open attentions were less, his secret assiduities were doubled; and having completely gained the affections of my daughter, he had the address to gain her mother also to his party; and she, swayed by the entreaties of her poor child, to whom she could refuse nothing, relying upon his honour, and knowing that I myself had a good opinion of him, most imprudently, and most unhappily, consented to/ a private marriage between them; which she sanctioned by her presence, and which was celebrated by a Popish priest since gone abroad. To cut short this unhappy story, which I never think of but it harrows up my soul, and to spare your lordship the fatigue of listening to so melancholy a detail, you must suppose every thing unfortunate to follow. In a few months he went home to his father's, leaving my daughter pregnant of the little boy you saw here this evening. He had there the baseness to deny his marriage; which being solemnized by a Popish priest, is not, I believe, strictly legal by the laws of this country. My son, who could not brook the indignity offered to his sister, flew to revenge the insult, and challenged him to the field. Even in the base soul of Nettlefield courage is not wanting: he accepted the challenge, and skill prevailed over justice; for my generous and gallant boy, the pride of my life, and whom I hoped to be the staff of my age, fell by the first fire./ My daughter went distracted. Such complicated miseries were too much for a parent's heart to bear. My poor wife sunk under them; she blamed herself for all her misfortunes, called herself the murderess of her son; and giving up entirely to an unavailing but too just a sorrow, it brought on a paralytic stroke, which finally relieved her from all afflictions. At the time of my wife's death my daughter was in the delirium of a raging fever, into which she fell upon hearing her poor brother's fate – and it was four months before she recovered the use of her reason. She was then delivered of a son, who, strange to tell, was then as fine an infant, and continues to be so, as is any where to be seen. The maternal feelings, which Nature for the wisest purposes has planted in every female heart, softened the afflictions of my unhappy daughter, by dividing her cares; and when I beheld the little innocent in her arms, the nerves of my heart vibrated, and I could not help pitying the child of misery, though it was/ Nettlefield's. Though it was his, it was yet my daughter's also; and, all unconscious of its father's crimes, was itself doomed to suffer by his villanies. I took it therefore to my bosom; and, as far as his tender age will allow, he repays my kindness with gratitude and affection. As soon as my daughter recovered, I resolved to quit for ever a place which had been the scene of so many afflictions, and which, since the death of my son, had lost the attractions it formerly had for me; neither could I bear the coldness and neglect with which I perceived some of the ladies who had formerly been our friends, began to treat my poor girl.' – 'Good God!' interrupted Lord Rivers, 'was any body cruel enough to neglect your daughter?' 'Yes, indeed,' said Mr. Grainger, 'many – the delicacy of the female character shrinks before the smallest breath of scandal, however undeserved.' 'True,' said Lord Rivers; 'but where the heart has never erred, and where an innocent girl fell a prey to the art of a base/ villain, and neither did nor intended any ill, the women of virtue should have leagued in her defence; and, instead of affecting to shun her, they should have punished, with the most marked contempt, the wretch who took advantage of her inexperience, and not have broken the already bruised reed.' – 'The world, my Lord,' replied Mr. Grainger, 'are in general so selfish, that they commonly rejoice in the calamities of others; because of the favourable comparison it gives them an opportunity of making of themselves in their own exemption. The compassion therefore of most people is more mortifying, and even more malignant, than their hatred; and such indeed my poor daughter and I found it,' – 'I am sorry for it,' replied Lord Rivers; 'sorry for your sake, and sorry there should be so much depravity in the human heart: but I can say this much, Mr. Grainger, that I am so sensible of the worth and innocence of your daughter, and so enraged at the base indignity that has been/ offered her, that I can assure you of the protection of all my family; and that I am certain Lady Cecilia, my sister, will joyfully contribute her endeavours to sooth the sorrows and avenge the cause of injured innocence.' – 'I know the goodness of all your family,' replied Mr. Grainger; 'and I am overwhelmed with gratitude for your Lordship's generous and noble friendship. The world is loud in the praises of Lady Cecilia, and I am sensible that whosoever she honours with her countenance will be every where respected. But I fear it is too

148 *The History of Ned Evans*

late. My poor girl's heart is broke. I know this world has no longer any allurements for her – her affections are now placed where they will never be again disappointed; and hastening, as she thinks, and as I do myself believe, to the mansions of eternity, I cannot wish to deaden her sublime ardour, or call back her desires to objects which she must soon leave, and from which she is already weaned.' – 'Pho, pho!' said Lord Rivers; 'these are the/ melancholy suggestions of your hermitage. Your daughter is an angel, but we will not let her return to her native skies till we see a little more of her. When we get her from these melancholy glooms to the cheerful scenes of Ravensdale, we will make her heart whole again; and I trust you have both of you many years yet before you of health and happiness.' – 'I thank you for your good wishes,' said Mr. Grainger; 'but I can assure your lordship they are ineffectual. I submit indeed, as I ought, with all possible resignation to the chastening of my Maker; but as for happiness, it is not in the power of this world to give it me again.' – 'Well,' said Lord Rivers, 'I hope otherwise; but in the mean time continue your story, for I feel myself interested in whatever befalls you.' – 'I have scarce any thing to add,' replied Mr. Grainger: 'I grew miserable as I told you in the country, and resolved to retire from all scenes which could revive the memory of my misfortunes. I therefore/ sold my estate; and having paid off every debt I owed in the world, I placed the remainder out on government securities. Soon after, in looking for a country retirement, I happened on this little spot; which being to be let, I immediately took it on a twenty one years lease; four of which are now elapsed. I have a few acres of ground, which supply me with milk and butter; and a small garden, the dressing of which is my only business out of doors. My daughter too feels a complacency in adorning it with shrubs and flowers; and whenever the weather permits, we unite our labours, and sooth our sorrows together. Music and drawing, together with the necessary attention to her little boy, employ her hours within, except those she consecrates to devotion; and these are a large portion of her time. Thus, my lord, I have told you my whole story. Few and evil have the days of our years been; but we look forward to the time when all tears shall be wiped from our eyes, and we wait for it/ with patience and with hope. In the mean time the most pleasing circumstance that has ever occurred to me since I came to this retreat, is the honour of seeing your lordship and these gentlemen here; and I beg of you to let my sincerity in this declaration make amends for the indifference of the entertainment I have to give you.'

The gentlemen all expressed the warmest sense of Mr. Grainger's politeness and hospitality; they were glad of the accident which had made them acquainted; they were sincerely interested in the affecting narrative they had just heard; in several passages of which, poor Ned had testified the quickness of his feelings, by that suffusion of countenance which the lively emotions of pity and resentment had alternately and visibly produced. Mr. Grainger had perceived how much he

Volume II 149

was affected; from which circumstance, and his great attention to little Charles, he had already conceived a warm prepossession in his favour. The rest of the evening was spent in a general/ and animated conversation. Mrs. Nettlefield, or Miss Grainger, whichever the reader pleases to call her, did not again make her appearance. She sent in to them, however, a small but elegant repast about ten o'clock; and before twelve they all retired to their repose./

CHAP. XXVIII.

THE affecting narrative, however, which Ned had just heard; the innocence, the beauty, and the misfortunes of the lovely girl who was the subject of it, sunk deep into his mind, and for a long time banished sleep from his eyes. 'Good heavens!' he cried, 'can a merciful Providence preside over this world, and suffer such villany to go unpunished? Shall the virtuous and the meek sink under the rod of the oppressor, and shall there be no after-reckoning to set these errors right? – Impossible! Truth is immutable, and virtue must at last be happy. Verily therefore there is a reward for the righteous – doubtless there is a God that judgeth the earth.' Had the heart of this young man been disengaged, the lovely mourner whose sorrows he bewailed had certainly taken possession of it: as it was, he gave her all he had to bestow./ He gave her pity in an unbounded effusion; but for its sister, love, the purity of his soul could know but one object, and from her he never swerved. To her then he resigned his thoughts; and kissing the locket, which by night and by day was the inseparable companion of his bosom, he gave himself up to the pleasing contemplation of the charming Cecilia, and to the sweet hope that ere long he should actually behold those beauties which were scarce ever absent from his imagination. Sleep, who is in vain invoked by the unhappy, comes unasked to the cheerful and serene. The placid soul of Edward was a residence suited to the tranquil deity; and he took full possession of it till the morning fun, and little Charles tickling him with a straw, dissolved his power.

Ned sprung from the couch on which he had been sleeping (for the house did not afford beds for them all), and took his little favourite into the garden. It was neatness itself, adorned by the elegant taste/ of her who presided over it; and brought to his recollection the little peaceful dwelling where all his days had flown. The heart of Edward was true to duty as well as to love – and, though an officer, he did not disdain to pray. He retired into an arbour, with the cherub Charles in his hand; and bending his knees to Him before whom every knee should bow, he presented a spectacle worthy the eye of Heaven to behold. He remembered his Creator in the days of his youth; and forgot not in his petitions either his father or his mother, his friend or his mistress – the afflicted mourner

– 150 –

for whose sufferings he was grieved, nor the little innocent whom he held in his hand. Smile, ye gay! laugh, ye profligate and profane! ye who know not the sublime and rapturous enjoyment of devotion! Yet when the evil days come, and the years draw nigh which shall have no pleasure in them; then will you feel the want of that friend who alone can sooth the infirmities of age, or make soft the pillow/ of the bed of death: – then will you deplore the folly that never could discern your real interest.

Ned now returned to the house, and little Charles with him. That sweet infant had taken an unaccountable attachment to him, which on his part was sincerely returned; nor was either Mr. Grainger or his daughter unaffected with the tender sensibility he shewed both for them and the child. It was with pain they saw the hour arrive when their amiable visitors were to part: nor did Ned take his farewell kiss of little Charles without mingling a manly tear with those infant drops which plentifully bedewed his little cheeks. He took him in his arms, and deposited him in those of his mother, vowing at the same time never to forget either their kindness or their misfortunes. The phaeton having been repaired by a blacksmith, Lord Rivers and his company took leave of Mr. Grainger, and, without any further accident, they all arrived safe in town./

When Ned went up to his room, he ordered David Morgan to be sent to him; but great was his distress when he was told that poor fellow lay senseless in his bed, unable to move, and very unlikely ever to rise again. Had David been only a common servant, the heart of Edward would have been warmly interested in his fate; but he had been the playfellow of his childhood, and often the companion of his sports since they grew to be men. He was his countryman in a strange land; and he had left his home, and his father's house, from a generous attachment to share the dangers and follow the fortunes of his young master. These were connections that interested Ned more nearly in his behalf, and which made him consider him rather in the light of a friend than of a servant. He hastened therefore to his bedside, to know the cause of his distress, and to pour every balm into his wounds that they would admit of. When he saw him, he found they were indeed wounds, and/ that his illness was the effect of ill usage. Astonished at this discovery, he immediately went to Lord Rivers; and the servants being summoned, the following story came out:

One of the footmen, who it seems liked his pleasures as well as his betters, took advantage of my lord's absence, to spend an evening with some others of his fraternity in company with their girls. They made choice, for this purpose, of one of those infamously convenient houses, which, to the disgrace of all government, are suffered to exist in every capital in Europe. Poor David was asked to be of the party; and his passions being stronger than his discretion, he very readily consented. His friend undertook to provide him with a partner, who was to give him her hand in the dance, and whatever else he might require into the

152 *The History of Ned Evans*

bargain. After passing some hours with the accustomed licentiousness of those places, the whole company sat down to supper, where the flow of their spirits was greatly exhilarated by copious and successive/ bowls of whisky punch. The son of St. David would not be outdone by any of the descendants of St. Patrick, nor did the ladies themselves decline engaging in the contest, being equally the votaries of Bacchus and Venus. It is possible, however, they might have passed the evening without any misunderstanding, had not some new comers joined them when they were pretty far advanced towards general intoxication. One of these, a rough and overbearing fellow, happened to have some previous acquaintance with David's dulcinea,[34] and, with his usual impudence, challenged her as his wife. David was not so simple as to be imposed on by this story, nor so timid as patiently to forego the amusement he was meditating, especially as the girl herself seemed unwilling to part with him, being in truth by far the more agreeable figure of the two: so that after some vollies of oaths and execrations, they came to more destructive weapons; and now discord took full possession of those hearts which so shortly/ before seemed perfectly united; and reason being delivered over to the custody of whisky, passion assumed her place, and a general contest arose without any being very clear upon what account.

If I could possibly imagine that any of my readers could be entertained with a detail of circumstances so brutal and disgusting as now ensued, I might describe a battle of no common kind; but passing by the prowess of the inferior combatants, I shall only take notice of the unfortunate Morgan, who defended his right with astonishing vigour and resolution for a length of time, considering how much liquor he had drunk; till at length the ruffian with whom he was engaged, contrary to all rules of boxing, took up the candlestick, which unhappily stood too near him, and with a violent blow on the head laid poor David senseless at his feet. The woman cried out Murder! and this awful word at once produced silence and the return of their senses. The young fellow who had seduced David/ into this company was sufficiently terrified at its consequences to become perfectly sober. He believed him actually dead; and, from the size of the wound, and the great effusion of blood, there was the greatest reason to believe that he soon would be so, if he was not so already. The villain who had perpetrated the act was of the same opinion, and thought it was full time for him to decamp. The whole company broke up: but Patrick, my lord's footman, who was the original cause of the catastrophe, had generosity enough to remain with the body of David, and swore he would never leave it though it should bring him to the gallows. At length, however, they discovered that David was not dead; and then Patrick conveyed him in a sedan chair to Lord Rivers's, where he was put to bed; and where he attended him with all the anxiety of a brother.

Lord Rivers was exceedingly distressed by this accident. His resentment rose chiefly against Patrick, whom he ordered/ into his presence – 'Thou profligate scoundrel!' said he, 'how dare you presume to go to your odious meetings, and to seduce the servant of my friend to be of your infamous party?' – 'My lord,' replied Patrick, 'I did nothing but what your lordship does yourself every night. If your lordship took the master to your meetings, where the company is not always sober, I saw no great harm in taking the man to mine; neither do I see any great difference between one whore and another, or between being drunk with champagne or whisky punch.' Rage and astonishment were visibly impressed upon his lordship's countenance – but conscience and reason got the better, and his passion immediately subsided – 'Patrick,' said he calmly, 'you are right. You have given me a piece of instruction that I hope I shall be the better for all my days. Here are five guineas for it, which it is well worth; but in the mean time I must tell you, I have no more occasion for your service. Call to-morrow,/ and you shall be paid your wages; but let me never see you afterwards unless I send for you.' Poor Patrick, who loved his lordship, would have apologized, and was very unwilling to take the five guineas; but Lord Rivers was inexorable. He ordered him immediately out of his presence, so that he was forced to go and comfort himself as well as he could with his fee, for the loss of a good place by his indiscretion.

His remark, however, made a deeper impression upon his lordship than the declamation of a hundred sermons. He could not fail to be struck with its force and truth, and sincerely to lament that his example had spread the contagion of vice to an extent that he little thought or was aware of. So circumspect should the great ever be, in whose power it to reform or corrupt a world. In the mean time no trouble or expence were spared to recover poor David, and to secure the villain who had given him the wound. Patrick was very instrumental in this: he did not know/ the man, but he was well acquainted with the girl on whose account the scuffle began. Lord Rivers himself condescended to go to the girl, and, by dint of bribes and promises of protection, obtained from her the principal information, which was, that his name was Reilly, and that he had been a smuggler out of the port of Rush. She could not, or would not, tell where he staid; but, by dint of a promise of a larger sum, she undertook to find him out and to betray him.

David remained in a very doubtful way: his senses were so confused that he had not recollection, and did not even know where he was. The surgeon apprehended his skull was fractured; but his head was so swelled that nothing could be certainly affirmed, except that his life was in danger; and therefore a warrant was procured to apprehend the villain who gave the blow. In a few nights information was given them by the girl, that Reilly was to sup with her that night; when about ten o'clock/ Lord Rivers and the Captain, together with Ned Evans, and some proper officers of justice, made their appearance in her apartment. The astonished Reilly was amazed – yet neither his courage nor his presence of mind forsook him. He did not attempt to make the least opposition, nor even to deny the fact.

154 *The History of Ned Evans*

He said he had no malice upon earth to David, whom he had never seen before; that he was sorry he had been hurt, but that he struck him in his own defence, and that he was ready to go before any court in the world. He added that his character was well known; that he had but lately come to the kingdom, and that he could get many respectable people to vouch for his behaviour. Lord Rivers asked him his name, and where he lived? He said his name was Patrick Reilly; that he dealt in horses, and usually lived in Chester, from whence he had lately come with some to this kingdom. At the name of Chester and of Patrick Reilly the astonishment of Ned Evans was only equalled by his satisfaction./ The trivial accident that happened to David was forgotten, and his transport was complete, when he beheld the detested murderer of Mrs. Melville in his power. Wondering within himself at the hidden mysteries of Providence, and grateful that he should in so surprising a manner be thus twice chosen as the agent to bring this secret villany to light, he was silent for a moment; but soon exclaimed, 'Oh! thou cruel and perfidious villain! God, whom thou hast offended, pursues thee with speedy vengeance, and entangles thee in thine own snares. Thou knowest me not; but know, villain! that I know thee, and all that belongs to thee. Was I not present when thy murderous hand discharged the blunderbuss into the carriage of two defenceless ladies on the road to Bangor, when one of them was killed? Think you that I do not know your master, Mr. Nicholson; and your deluded accomplice, Andrew Collins?' – Had the roof of the chamber cleft in twain, and thunder fallen from heaven into the/ room, the astonishment of Reilly would have been less. When he surveyed Evans, he did not believe that he was human; he took him for some being sent purposely by the Almighty to confound him, and, without answering a word, dropped senseless at his feet. The amazement of the rest of the company was hardly less; and even when they were told the whole, though there was nothing out of the common road of nature in it, yet were they deeply impressed with awful veneration of that Being whose eye can penetrate to the centre of creation, and whose power can over-rule all accidents to the ends of his Providence.

Reilly was now effectually secured, and delivered into the hands of the officers of justice. He was soon after transmitted to Conway, where Collins was allowed to turn King's evidence, and where he expiated on the gallows (as far as the death of such a miscreant could expiate) the various cruelties and crimes of his most wicked life. In the mean time poor David recovered:/ the wound was found only to be a contusion: and, being managed by a skilful hand, he was in a short time able to renew his usual occupations. He was not indeed quite so enamoured with Dublin as he had been at first, but he promised to take better care both of his company and his morals; and consoled himself for his broken head, that it had been the means of discovering the villain Reilly, and that he could now claim some share with his master in the honour of that affair./

CHAP. XXIX.

NED's regimentals were now brought home, and he appeared in them for the first time at the Castle. He had the honour to be introduced to the Lord Lieutenant by Lord Rivers, and to thank his Excellency for the commission which he had bestowed upon him. The Viceroy was struck with the singular beauty of his figure, and the graceful unembarrassed manner in which he spoke; and he paid him a very handsome compliment on the occasion. Several military men too of consequence, who were at the levee, took notice of him, and he found himself at once a conspicuous figure in the first company in the kingdom. Under the auspices of Lord Rivers indeed he had no difficulty in finding admittance into any circle; and being once introduced, his own merits were sure to gain him a hearty welcome/ wherever he was known. It was not only the ladies who admired him, for whom indeed he had irresistible attractions, but the qualities of his mind were found not inferior to those of his person, and gained him the esteem of those on whom beauty could have no impression.

Thus admired and caressed, a young man of less sense and less strictness of education would have been in danger of being over-run with vanity, or overthrown by those seducing pleasures which sprung up every where under his feet: – but Ned carried a guardian in his breast whom he was accustomed to obey. He attended to the whispers of that divine monitor who resides within us, and who never deceives; and he walked secure through all the temptations of the capital blameless. And how indeed could it be otherwise, when his earliest and his latest duty was to solicit the favour and the protection of his Maker, and when his heart was devoted to the loveliest object that ever engaged the affections/ of a man. In vain then did the Dublin beauties display their charms; in vain did pleasure assail him in a thousand forms: a virtuous passion filled his soul, which would not admit of any thing low or sordid coming in contact with it. And now the wished-for letters arrived from Lord Ravensdale, congratulating him on his arrival in Ireland, and containing a most cordial invitation to him to go down to the country: – an affectionate compliment from Lady Cecilia too was not forgotten; which infused new joy into his heart, and new brilliancy into his countenance: so that hardly was there to be found a happier being in the kingdom, or one who more deserved

156 *The History of Ned Evans*

to be so. As the parliament was still sitting, Lord Rivers could not accompany him down but his friend the Captain was ready to escort him, and the next morning was fixed on for their journey. If sorrow is a banisher of sleep, joy is no less so; and never did night seem so tedious to Ned before.

At last it dawned – and, long before the/ sun himself arose, did Ned spring from his bed and prepare for this wished for expedition. The Captain, who was not so eager, would not stir without his breakfast; and though eating was an amusement Ned relished as well as any body, yet he would have fasted a whole Lent rather than not get forward. At last they mounted, and with David and the captain's man bid adieu to Dublin, and left Lord Rivers in his first nap. As the domes and the spires of the metropolis withdrew, the spirits and the satisfaction of Ned increased: every step brought him nearer to the beloved of his soul, and every mile-stone that he counted was a new source of transport to his bosom. Ravensdale however was not to be reached in one day, at least not without relays of horses, which those who travel in Ireland must not always expect to find. The country however was charming, and the alternate objects of splendour and of poverty, of neatness and slovenliness, which seem scattered so promiscuously over the face of it,/ served only to divert his fancy and afford new topics for his philosophy. 'How easily is nature satisfied!' said he, as he beheld six naked children playing on a dung-hill – not naked in rags, but naked as they were born – absolutely divested of all raiment whatsoever. They had however rosy cheeks and mirthful countenances; they laughed incontinently, and seemed to have no want of butter-milk and potatoes. The hovel in which they were born was built in a ditch, the gripe of which formed two sides of it; and the nuptial bed which produced them consisted of one blanket and a bundle of straw. The mother however was singing as she sat spinning on her wheel; and the father was gone to his labour in the demesne of a gentleman whose splendid palace now rose upon the view, whose estate was at least full 20,000l. a year; and who, though married for half a century, had no child to inherit it; and the happiness of whose whole life was poisoned on that account. O equitable Providence!/ who givest riches as seemeth best to thee, although divided in such partial measure; but who bestowest happiness with more equal hand – who hast seated it in the soul, and not made it absolutely to depend on any external circumstance whatsoever!

No accident of any note happened to them on their way: – the second day about eleven, the majestic front of Ravensdale shewed itself through surrounding trees. Embosomed within its turrets lay Edward's cynosure – but no cruel giant, or enchanted dragon, opposed his way. Wealth, honour, hospitality, possessed the dome; and beauty, innocence, and virtue, resided in it. Hail happy hour that conducts young Edward to the mansion of his adored Cecilia! – Behold he sees her! She comes herself, all elegant as she is, to meet him – She is now at home, and therefore frankness has banished form – She takes him by the hand; nay

Volume II   157

she offers him her ambrosial lips, and Edward tastes a bliss which would have overpaid an age of pain!/

The old Lord was confined to his chair by the gout, but far from being a complaint, it was the cure of that disorder which he had in Dublin. He received our hero, as the deliverer of his daughter, with affection, with admiration, with gratitude, and with all that complacency which every man must feel in the presence of an amiable and deserving fellow-creature, whom they have greatly obliged. Ned fancied himself in Elysium; and indeed all that he had ever heard or read of that celebrated abode of happiness, fell short of what he felt. The Captain was but a secondary figure in this group; and though his transports were less, yet his happiness was not little in having Ned for his guest; and the attentions which he paid him did equal honour to his heart, his taste, his rank, and his education. A friendship indeed of the most tender and faithful kind began to take place between them. The Captain considered himself as his guardian and protector, because he was a subaltern in his own company; whilst Ned/ could not fail to love whatever was so near to Cecilia, although he had been less amiable than he really was. The parity of their years too (for there were only three between them) made the same amusements pleasing to both; and the same goodness of heart united to the strongest natural understanding, which in both had received the addition of liberal education, gave taste to these amusements: so that hardly any two could have met more happily formed to please each other, and the circumstances of whose meeting were more likely to bind them in the tender chains of indissoluble friendship.

The rank of Captain Rivers's family might indeed have contributed to keep Edward at a distance; but the nobility of Ireland have nothing of that feudal pride which is so disgusting and contemptible in most other nations. To splendid fortunes they unite the most liberal and condescending manners; and whoever has the education and behaviour of a gentleman, is sure/ to meet from them the frankest hospitality and the most dignified attention.

Ravensdale was a mansion where the splendid and agreeable were happily united, and where every thing that is amiable presided over every thing that is noble. As a beautiful place it could hardly be surpassed in any country; and to describe it would require the powers of the pencil rather than the pen. The house was built by the first lord, in the reign of James the First of England, from a design of the celebrated Inigo Jones; which is enough to let us know that it was at once magnificent and convenient. It was seated on a rising ground, commanding a prospect of many miles over a rich and well-cultivated country, great part of which belonged to the noble earl himself. The celebrated Shannon, whose lordly tide might bear a navy on its bosom, wound round the demesne: when expanding itself into a lake, it formed a sheet of water full thirteen miles in length and half as much in breadth – in full prospect from the/ windows. The banks of this liquid mirror presented the richest and most diversified scenery – sometimes

158 *The History of Ned Evans*

level lawns, the fertile pastured which feed the West-Indies, and all the navies of Europe – sometimes towering rocks, the inaccessible aëries of eagles and of hawks – sometimes groves, who serviceable shades embrowned the rocks, and seemed to grow downwards to the bottom of the lake; whilst the blue tops of the distant mountains melted among the clouds, or poured the golden rays of the setting sun amid the purple shadows of the valleys. Towers were not wanting, the venerable remains of ruined monasteries; nor here and there the rising smokes of cheerful cottages, while the homely meal is preparing for the labourer's supper. The cows low for the pail; the lambs bleat by their dams; the murmur of the village swells in the breeze, and infant voices laughing as they play, proclaim that all is harmony and peace around. Oh happy plains of plenty and of peace! you I no more revisit – yet/ shall the remembrance of you sooth my wanderings; yet shall your prosperity be dearer to me than my own – dearer than the ruddy drops which still warm my heart, that never can cease to love you till it ceases to beat. The gardens of Ravensdale also were suitable to the grandeur of its situation and the opulence of its owner – they were laid out on the most extensive scale of modern improvement, on the models of those delightful farms which have long been the boast and admiration of England; where nature is embellished without being disguised, and all her native beauties called into view by the happy assistance of taste and opulence.[35]

In these delicious groves, the hours of Edward were winged with happiness, whilst the transporting society of Lady Cecilia gave new charms to nature in his eyes, and made Paradise itself sink in them when compared to Ravensdale. Nor was its charming inhabitant less happy in the company of Edward: her chaste and gentle/ bosom loved him with a pure and holy passion; a generous sentiment with which sex had no connection, but which arose from similarity of taste and years – from admiration of the noble and manly qualities of his heart and mind – and from a grateful sense of the protection and essential obligations she received from him. His figure indeed might also be pleasing in her eye, for it was impossible to behold him without feeling that prepossession which beauty inspires; but his mind would have been lovely in any form, and to this and gratitude her present affection was wholly dedicated. Her amiable condescension now repaid the attention which Ned had shewn to her Ladyship when at his father's house; and the sweet walks and rides in which he attended her in Wales were here renewed, with this difference, that now there were always others in company; Captain Rivers or some of the neighbouring gentlemen and ladies usually attending in these excursions: yet sometimes he had the happiness to enjoy/ her company alone. In the gardens were many charming wildernesses of shrubs and evergreens, streams winding through banks of primroses, rustic seats beneath aged oaks and elms, temples and hermitages, where just taste had scattered mottos and poems suited to their situations. Through these walks Lady Cecilia did not scruple to accompany Edward; and here did she often charm his attention by talking of his father and mother, whom she called her dear protectors – and by recalling the recollection of all those simple and peaceful scenes, endeared to Edward from his infancy, and receiving new charms from the happy hours spent in them with her Ladyship, and from being now the themes on which she seemed most delighted to converse. Here could he have been contented to remain for ever! – His heart, which had begun to pant for glory, was every day relapsing into the languors of love; and his commission, which had been the pride and joy of his heart, seemed now almost to be a misfortune, when/ it reminded him that the fatal hour was approaching which was to summon him across the Atlantic – when the soft scenes in which he was now engaged, were to be changed for horrors and for tumults – and when thousands of miles of an inhospitable and tempestuous element were to roll between him and the desire of his soul. The thoughts of this separation were the only thing that detracted from his present transport. Yet how salutary was it for his peace! for what prospect or what probability has he of ever gratifying that passion to which he so incautiously resigns his soul? Poor Ned was not insensible of his delusion – he knew his passion to be hopeless, and a thousand times did he resolve to restrain it within the bounds of reason and inviolable friendship; but one glance of Lady Cecilia's eye was able to overthrow all his resolution, and to rivet him in chains which not even despair itself could unloose. The lovely Cecilia herself perceived his emotions, and pitied what she could not relieve. She/ thought him indeed of all men that she had seen the most amiable and engaging; and sometimes she wished she had been born in Wales, and never known a lot superior to the happy mediocrity of a decent competence. But she was not insensible of the dignity of her station, nor indifferent to the honour of her family. She loved and revered her father with all the powers of her soul, and she would die before she would swerve from the smallest tittle[36] of the duty which she owed him. She knew that of all things on earth he was most tenacious of the dignity of his family; and though he knew how to respect and to reward merit wherever he found it, yet the thought of matching her into a plebeian family was what she was sure he never would endure, and a mortification to which she herself would never expose him. On the other hand she thought every thing short of love was due to Edward. She applauded the sentiment of generous friendship and unbounded gratitude which she felt for him;/ and whilst she confined herself to these sentiments, she thought she might safely indulge them to their utmost latitude. She behaved therefore to him with the utmost openness and frankness, and with that kind of affectionate familiarity with which a sister would behave to a brother – and which the poor youth, who perfectly understood her meaning, received with a timidity and bashfulness wholly unknown to him on any other occasion./

CHAP. XXX.

AMONG the families of distinction in the neighbourhood, who were in habits of intimacy at Ravensdale House, one of its most frequent visitors was that of the Reverend Doctor Burton; a clergyman of large preferment and considerable independent fortune. He had been at college with the Earl, where an intimacy commenced which had never met with the smallest interruption, and which had been of mutual advantage to both on many occasions. The Doctor's unaffected piety being joined to great learning, and adorned with the utmost elegance of manners, contributed greatly to that reverence for religion and cautious regard to moral character which distinguished the Earl, and which in a great measure he imbibed from his early acquaintance with him; and his lordship had in return been extremely serviceable to the Doctor, in/ raising him to the lucrative situation in the church which he then enjoyed.

This gentleman's family consisted of his wife and two daughters; the youngest of whom, Miss Sophia, was a beautiful and accomplished girl, and the bosom friend of Lady Cecilia. The eldest, Miss Henrietta, was also very handsome; but having been educated in the metropolis under the care of a maiden aunt, whose god-daughter she was, she had spent but little time in the country even with her father and mother. She had returned to them, however, lately on the death of her aunt, who lived to finish her education, and, dying, bequeathed to her her whole fortune, amounting to 10,000l. independent of her father and mother. If envy could have harboured in such a breast as Sophia's, the marked attention which was every where paid to Henrietta, even in her father's house, might have given birth to that odious passion: but she looked on the good fortune of her sister with the utmost complacency and/ good nature, and sighed neither for pleasures nor possessions which could not be enjoyed but at the expence of innocence and tranquillity of mind. The society of Lady Cecilia was to her the most delightful of all entertainments; nor did her tender and faithful heart ever wander after gratifications beyond the pale of domestic enjoyments. It is true she had not as yet seen any other; but she had heard her friend talk of them without much regard, and saw her prefer the tranquil pleasures, even when she had the others in her choice, and those too in the highest perfection. But Harriet was of a different opinion. She had been used to the gayest scenes of the metropolis, where her society was courted and her beauty admired – but where her attentions to her mind had not kept pace with those to her person. The country therefore was to her exile; and she felt more horrors in her father's house than Sophy probably would have done in a prison. The Doctor observed this turn in his daughter with regret;/ and thought it ill compensated for, even by her fortune of 10,000l. But her mother viewed her with admiration, and was for ever proposing her as the pattern of elegance to the hundred times more elegant Sophia.

If a fashionable appearance be pronounced to be elegance, she was indeed possessed of this species of it: but fashion itself is not always elegant, and I believe was never less so than at the time I speak of; a certain air of forward freedom and masculine intrepidity having been adopted as the highest ton of fashion among the ladies, utterly subversive of that engaging softness and modest delicacy which used to be considered as essential ornaments of the female character.

Another family, which sometimes used to visit at Ravensdale, though less frequently, was Mr. Nettlefield's, the father of the young man whom we have already heard of in the story of Miss Grainger. The circumstances of that affair, and his base/ behaviour to that amiable and innocent girl, were not generally known, not even to his own nearest connections. He himself was with his regiment in America, where his public conduct as an officer was unimpeachable: his gallantries were considered as natural to his time of life; they were laughed at by the men, and did not discredit him even with the women, doubtless because their malignant circumstances were not fully known; and now that he was absent, it was considered as ungenerous to talk about them. But the knowledge of them in all their blackness prepossessed. Ned even against the father, who came over from his own house on purpose to wait upon him and Captain Rivers, and to ask them there.

Mr. Nettlefield was one of those kind of men who never grow old, but carry along with them to their grand climacteric[37] all the vices and follies of nineteen and twenty. He had once been handsome, and, like his son, had taken advantage of this circumstance/ to engage the affections of a very amiable woman; whom it is very probable he would have served as his son did Miss Grainger, had she not possessed a qualification which of all things he admired, though he was entirely destitute of it himself, and this was an estate of about 600l. a year. Having got the heart, he very soon obtained the hand also of this unfortunate lady, who married him contrary to the advice of all her friends, and who never enjoyed a week of real comfort or satisfaction after. Yet Nettlefield was accounted a mighty good kind of a man, and, except by his wife and daughter, thought to be one of the best-natured fellows in the world. All the young men in the neighbourhood adored him. His house was a rendezvous of pleasure, where every body that had nothing to do was welcome. There were horses, there were

162   *The History of Ned Evans*

hounds, there was claret, there was every thing that could seduce and gratify the passions of youth; whilst poor Mrs. Nettlefield and her daughter, whom sorrow/ had taught wisdom, and who sought for consolations from books and from each other, for the most part sat alone mourning over the impending ruin of their family, and exposed to the brutality of that secret ill nature, which was the more bitter because it was unknown, the more cruel because it was undeserved, and the more insupportable because it came from him who was the last of all persons from whom it ought to have been expected. Such a character, had it been really known, would hardly have been agreeable to any person; but you could discover nothing of this by conversing with Nettlefield, nor even by living with him, unless you were his dependent. He was therefore generally liked, and every where well received: even Lord Ravensdale had a regard for him, and had shewn it by lending him 6000l. to extricate him from the jaws of some pressing creditors, who were ready to devour both him and his estate. His Lordship indeed seldom went to his house, unless to pay a morning-visit,/ and that principally to the ladies, for whom he had a real regard. But the orgies of Nettlefield's table, and the promiscuous company that were sometimes to be found there, deterred him from ever making one at it, as suiting neither his dignity nor his inclination. Mr. Nettlefield, however, was always welcome to his; and the young Lord and Captain Rivers used to pay back the compliment, frequently hunting and sometimes dining with him. Ned therefore and the Captain were under the necessity of returning his visit, and accepting his invitation. His estate lay about five miles from Ravensdale, and the demesne might have been very properly called after the name of its proprietor. The nettles and other weeds which were spread over what they called the lawn, might have furnished specimens to the botanists of all the baneful vegetables that were to be found in these climates; among which a few haggard-looking kine, that started as they rode by, were picking their dangerous and scanty food./

The house stood solitary in the midst, except a few thatched offices at one side; for the timber which once adorned it was long since cut down, and converted into claret and game-cocks. Part of it seemed in ruins; for the rafters appeared through a large hole in the roof, which he wanted either materials or credit to repair. He met them, however, at the door; where a lad with a good livery coat and silver epaulet, but without shoes or stockings, took their horses. The œconomy within doors was nearly answerable to that without. The room into which they were shewn did not seem to have been washed for a twelve-month; and on its floor were many stains of the libations which had been poured out to the God of Revels. Nettlefield called them honourable stains, and swore he preferred them to the finest colours of an Axminster carpet. 'In this house,' said he, 'my jewels, all is freedom! and for fear my friends should not feel perfectly at ease, I take care that there shall/ be nothing that will spoil – even their dogs are welcome to every room in the house.' 'But does Mrs. Nettlefield make them so?' said Ned. 'Oh! I never consult her,' replied he; 'we have long since arranged those matters. She never partakes of my amusements, nor I of hers.' 'What, then, sha'n't we see her and Miss Nettlefield?' said the Captain. 'Aye,' said the other; 'if you prefer a sermon to a bottle of claret. The truth is, there was a mad parson here some time ago, and I believe he bit them both; for they seem so utterly devoted to the other world, that they are no longer fit for this. I never can get either of them down when any body is with me; and (egod!) I would as soon go to church as sit with either of them alone. So Liberty being my motto, I let them take their way, and I take mine.' 'Very right, Sir,' said Counsellor Grogan (who was one of the company invited to dinner) – 'the Irish make the best husbands in the world, and know best how to deal with their wives./ I remember a gentleman, a friend of mine, who did not live with his wife upon those happy terms which you and Mrs. Nettlefield have adopted. The lady indeed would not suffer her husband either to share her pleasures, or have any of his own. He bore it longer than a man of his sense and his fortune might be supposed to do. At length he took the opportunity of an altercation that happened one morning at breakfast, and he told his wife, 'My dear Mrs. Clappertongue,' said he, 'for what purpose is it for you and I to sit and torment one another this way any longer? I have come to a resolution,' said he, 'that shall at once give us quiet, and make us live upon the best terms possible.' 'And pray what is your resolution, Mr. Clappertongue?' said she. 'Why, my dear, I am come to a resolution to divide the house with you,' replied he. 'Nothing can be more agreeable to me,' replied Mrs. Clappertongue. 'But do you know how I intend to divide it?' said he. 'No!' replied/ she, 'how should I know?' 'Then, by J – –, my dear, I will tell you. I will take the inside, and you shall take the out: and so set about packing up your things, for by G – it shall be divided before dinner!' My friend was as good as his word, and has been as happy a married man as most in the kingdom ever since.'

Dinner coming in put an end to this ingenious conversation, and interrupted the reflections which were rising in Ned's mind. He was glad indeed to be relieved from the necessity of making any reply to sentiments without wit, and wit without sentiment: but if his intellectual entertainment was barren, his corporeal one was profuse – and the attentions of Nettlefield, together with the excellence of the fare, contributed to restore him to good humour, and to make him endure a man of whom his first impressions were not favourable, and who had not risen in his esteem by any thing he had heard or seen.

When the cloth was taken away, and/ the deck cleared, as Nettlefield termed it, he called for ammunition; by which my unenlightened readers are to understand wine, and any other liquors that the adepts choose in the great mystery of drinking. The church, the king, the mother of saints, and various other ingenious and patriotic toasts were drunk with all the honours, and in such copious

164 *The History of Ned Evans*

bumpers that Ned began to feel himself elevating. He soon made an attempt to withdraw; but now he found how little some men's mottos and professions agree with their sentiments and practice. The door was locked; and this house, where liberty was the motto, was converted into a bacchanalian bastile. It is true they were for the most part willing prisoners, but this was not the case of Ned or the Captain. They begged, they implored, they remonstrated – but all in vain; so finding what brutes they had to deal with, they submitted to their chains, but determined never to be taken in them again. For the rest, all was conviviality – the wine was excellent,/ and it was not spared: they laughed, they roared, they danced, they sung, all except our two gentlemen and a fat farmer, a Mr. Shamrock, who luckily sat between them. This gentleman very soon fell fast asleep; and happening to have on a very wide pair of boots, Ned wickedly took the advantage of emptying the greatest part of his glass into them unobserved; an example which the Captain followed on the other side, and thus happily preserved themselves in a state of tolerable sobriety. They were at last released; not, however, before the dawn had begun to dapple the eastern clouds; and were glad when they got to Ravensdale, to find themselves once more in the realms of real liberty and pleasure./

CHAP. XXXI.

But whatever dislike these gentlemen had to the noisy orgies of Nettlefield's table, they had none at all to his company in the field; in all the sports of which he was a complete adept. They accordingly often accompanied him a hunting; and Lord Ravensdale, though he never shared in that diversion himself, and disliked the trouble of a pack of hounds, and the society to which they unavoidably led, yet took care to be always amply provided with excellent horses, for the accommodation of such of his friends or visitors as loved the sport, but were unprovided with the means of enjoying it. To his choice of these Mr. Evans was always welcome; and indeed, to him, there could not be a higher gratification; for the love of horses, as it was one of his earliest, so it continued to be one of his strongest passions./

It was one day after they had had a severe chace of many hours, when reynard[38] succeeded in foiling all his adversaries, and the company were dispersed over the fields, that Ned took the opportunity of their dispersion to return home without taking leave of Nettlefield, and hoping that Captain Rivers, who was not immediately in sight, would follow him. He was somewhat fatigued with the length of the chace, and had no mind to engage in the still severer toil that he knew he must undergo had he accompanied Mr. Nettlefield to his house. Wrapped up then in pleasing meditations on his present happiness, and the new and busy scenes that were opening to him, he gave his horse the bridle, permitting him to take his own choice of the way he would go home; and not doubting but he would lead him the nearest, if not the easiest road. In this, however, he was mistaken; for the horse had been purchased from Nettlefield, who bred him; and being now seized with a desire to visit his native fields,/ he was actually conducting Edward to the very spot in which he was foaled. In their way was a deep glen, through which ran a stream of water, and beside it stood a lonely cottage, whose ruinous appearance and deserted situation pronounced it to be the abode of neglected misery. Ned stopped a moment to contemplate this sequestered spot, and to slake his thirst with the cool and limpid stream that was gliding by; when a poor and feeble, but venerable and decent old woman came out of the cottage; supporting with a stick in one hand her tottering steps, and bearing in the other

166 *The History of Ned Evans*

an empty pitcher, which when filled with water, she would scarcely be able to carry back again. When she saw Edward, she would have retired; but he immediately alighted from his horse, and, with all that good nature which was ever an instinctive movement of his soul, relieved her from the burthen of her pitcher, which he filled for her with water, and insisted upon carrying it for her into the house. This little/ act of kindness, however inconsiderable in itself, yet afforded a dawn of consolation to the afflicted object for whom it was performed; for it was the first act of pity or attention that she had experienced for a long while, though no person could be more in need of both, nor better deserve them. The good old woman surveyed Ned for a minute in silent gratitude, and then burst out into tears. 'Alas! dame,' said the sympathizing youth,' 'surely some deep misfortune has befallen you, that you live thus lonely in this ruinous cottage, so far from any neighbour or assistance.' 'Oh! Sir,' replied she, 'I am not quite alone, for God is with me; and he perhaps has sent you here this day to witness the distress I am in, and may be to save the life of my poor child. Pray, Sir, have the goodness to look in here, and see if you can do any thing for her.' She then conducted Ned into a little space partitioned off the cottage by a few wattles, where, on a pallet of straw, lay a beautiful girl of about eighteen, in/ the highest paroxysm of a pleuretic fever. The slush that was on her countenance gave a transient illumination to her beauty; but the fixed stare of her eyes, and the burning heat of her body, joined to the short pantings of her breath, seemed to indicate that a very short period would place her beyond the reach of all worldly calamity.

Ned was not a physician, but he was able to bleed; a part of the art which he had first learned for the benefit of his horse, but which he had found useful to know how to do upon many occasions before the present, and had skill enough to be convinced was the first thing to be done in the case before him. He took a lancet therefore, which he always carried in his pocket-book, and, with the assistance of the mother, soon performed the operation, to the visible and almost immediate relief of the patient; and as soon as he had bound up her arm, he hastened to gratify his curiosity respecting their situation. The poor old woman prefaced her narration with another burst of/ tears, in which those of sorrow were mingled with those of gratitude.

'My name, Sir,' said she, 'is Alice Doran, and it is only a fortnight comes tomorrow since my poor husband died upon that bed on which you have now seen my daughter laid, and who, if it shall be the Almighty's will, is I hope prepared to follow him.' 'Did your husband die of the same fever that your daughter has?' interrupted Ned. 'No, Sir,' replied the dame, 'he died of a broken heart, and my poor child has caught her present illness by cold and fatigue in her attendance upon him: for, alas! Sir, we have not been always so destitute; we never knew what it was to want the decent necessaries of life till our cruel landlord first took from us the staff of our age, and then abandoned us to want and misery.'

– 'Who is this tyrant?' asked Ned. 'Mayhap your Honour knows him,' replied the old woman; 'it is Squire Nettlefield.' – 'O yes, I know him,' said the youth, 'and can believe all that you say./ Pray let me hear your story out.' 'Why, Sir, as I was saying, we always had the decent necessaries of life, for we rented a small farm, which enabled us to live as long as we were able to manage it; which we might have done yet if the Squire had left us our son, and it had pleased God to have continued my dear husband to me; but indeed it was the loss of our boy that was the beginning of all our misfortunes.' 'What became of him?' interrupted Ned. 'He was listed for a soldier, Sir,' replied the old woman. 'About two years ago there was a regiment raised here to go all the way to America to fight; and the officers got their commissions according to the number of men they could raise. Mr. Nettlefield's son got advanced in that regiment by his father's forcing all the tenants and cotters[39] to part with their sons, or be turned out of their farms; and I would to God we had been turned out at first, and then I should not have been bereaved of my husband and my child! And had we kept together,/ we might have still been well to live; but they wheedled my son away, and promised him twenty guineas, and he never got more than five; and God knows whether he is living this day or not, for I never heard but once from him when he first got to America, and they say they never will be able to beat them, and perhaps my poor boy has been killed.' 'Oh! never despond,' interrupted Ned. 'I myself am going to America, and they who told you we should not beat them know nothing of the matter. I'll warrant we'll give a good account of them, and bring home your son in triumph too.' 'I ask no triumph,' replied the poor old woman; 'I ask only for peace. Would to God I had been suffered to have lived with my family in peace, and I would not have moved a mile, far less four thousand, to have disturbed that of any creature upon earth.' 'Pooh,' said Ned, 'now you speak like an old woman.' 'I speak like what I am then, Sir,' replied she; 'but I speak also like a/ christian.' – 'I acknowledge it,' said Ned. 'I beg your pardon. I did not mean to offend you.' – 'Oh! Sir, you cannot offend me,' said she. 'But, to resume my unhappy story. When my son was gone, the work was too heavy for his father; and though the poor dear girl who now lies on that sick pallet, as well as myself, exerted ourselves to the utmost to assist him, yet we were all unequal to the task, so that my poor man lost all heart, and with it his health; and when he was unable to pay his rent, the squire seized all, even the very beds from under us, and turned us out of house and home; and had it not been for the friendship of a neighbouring farmer, who gave us this cottage, we should not have had a shelter for our house-less heads. We have now been here, Sir, about nine months. My poor husband, as long as he was able, used to do a little work for the good man that befriended us, and who still continues to assist us; but his heart was quite broke, and, as I said, it is a fortnight tomorrow/ since God was pleased to deliver him from all his sorrows.' 'My good woman,' said Mr. Evans, 'I heartily feel for your afflictions;

168 *The History of Ned Evans*

but if you will allow a young officer to preach to you, I would desire you not to despond. I am one of those who are not ashamed to confess that they believe in God; and that his providence is over all his works. Perhaps it is he who has directed my steps hither this day, for certainly I had no thoughts of coming here myself; and if he has been pleased to make me an humble instrument of bringing any good to you, I shall gratefully accept the charge, and be thankful that he has made my duty suit so exactly with my inclination. Your daughter is relieved by the bleeding, and I will call again to see both you and her. In the mean time you know all that is necessary for her in her present state; which that you may be able to provide for her with more comfort, you will please to accept this small matter till I am able to see you again.' With these words he/ slipped two guineas into her hand; and without waiting to hear the fervent ejaculations of piety and gratitude which the good old woman was devoutly offering up to Heaven in his favour, he mounted his horse, and was out of her sight in a moment.

When he got to Ravensdale, he found Captain Rivers had got home before him, and that Lord Rivers also had come down from Dublin, and brought with him an English nobleman, who had never been in Ireland before, and to whom the reader shall be introduced in the next chapter./

CHAP. XXXII.

THE nobleman who had arrived so unexpectedly at Ravensdale, was the Viscount Squanderfield, the very Lord who had been so assiduous in his attentions upon Lady Cecilia when she was with her aunt in London, and with whose attentions her ladyship did not seem to be at all flattered. He was, however, very high in the graces of Lady Elizabeth Belmont, by whom a title and the manners of a man of fashion were considered as first-rate accomplishments, and sufficient to atone for the want of most others. Her ladyship had observed with pleasure that her niece seemed to have made an impression on this noble lord when she had been in London, and did not conceive it possible but his addresses must be highly agreeable, not only to Lady Cecilia, but also to her father and the rest of the family; she had therefore furnished his/ lordship with the warmest recommendations to her brother, the Earl of Ravensdale, magnifying, or rather creating his virtues and endowments, among which she reckoned as not the least an estate of near 20,000l. a year; and indeed if she could have made good this last character she had given of his lordship, I doubt not but many others would have acquiesced in the opinion that it was a qualification and endowment of a most exalted kind. But whatever his lordship's estate might have been when he took possession of it, which was hardly four years before this time, it is certain that it was now diminished pretty nearly in the same proportion, and that hardly a fourth part of it remained. We must not therefore give his lordship entire credit for that discerning eye with which he so soon discovered the uncommon merits of the charming Cecilia, nor for that ardour of affection which had now borne him across the sea in pursuit of this beloved object. The truth is, the supreme object of his lordship's regard/ he wisely chose to keep so near himself, that he need never quit his own room to pursue it any where; and it is a question whether all the mental or corporeal perfections of Lady Cecilia would have been able to raise him out of his arm chair, had they not been connected with other endowments of a more solid and weighty nature, and which were of the highest value in his lordship's eyes. We are therefore so far from admiring his lordship's discernment in his selection of Lady Cecilia, that we are rather disposed to wonder at his want of it, did not the experience of every day convince us that self-love is able to absorb all other passions, and to shed so dark a

170 *The History of Ned Evans*

mist upon the understanding as to render it impervious to the rays of even truth itself. Had this lord contemplated himself in any other glass than that of pride, he never could have presumed to lift his thoughts to such a character as Lady Cecilia. Nursed up under the doting care of a fond and foolish mother, to whom he was an only child, he/ was ten years old before he knew his letters; and all the learning he had since acquired was little more than to spell them and put them together. He was an adept, however, at cards; which did him this service, that it was his desire to study Hoyle[40] that prevailed upon him ever to read at all. But for this knowledge he had paid most dearly, and with a greater sum than probably educated and maintained Sir Isaac Newton through the whole course of his long and glorious life. Nor was the person of this nobleman more apt to inspire affection than his abilities were to create esteem. Tall and wan, he resembled those exotic plants which spindle up in our hot-houses, where they put forth some sickly blossoms, but which wither and drop off the instant they are exposed to the natural atmosphere. Weak as his constitution was by nature, it was rendered still more so by an early initiation into all the vices of the metropolis, and by that wearisome pursuit of dissipated pleasure which is the epidemic fever of the/ times, and the consequences of which are so fatally visible from the highest even to the lowest orders of society. His rank, however, entitled him to a polite reception any where; and at Ravensdale he would have been sure of this, even though he had no such pretensions to it.

Lord Rivers had been acquainted with this nobleman in London, where he often met him at his aunt's, and had contracted with him that kind of friendship which now-a-days subsists between young men of rank, whose chief occupation is the pursuit of pleasure, and who in that pursuit are willing to take as a partner whoever is disencumbered with principle, but sufficiently laden with cash; from which burthen too they commonly have a charitable view of relieving each other. His lordship was rejoiced therefore at the arrival of his English friend on the territory of St. Patrick, and resolved to shew him all that genuine hospitality which the sons of that renowned saint are acknowledged to possess. Neither/ was he at all displeased with the motive which Lord Squanderfield avowed to have induced him to cross the sea, and promised him in the pursuit of it all the influence which he could exert both with his father and his sister. With this view he recommended to him to set off as soon as possible to Ravensdale, without sending any warning of his approach, to shew that the ardour of his passion would not suffer him to be amused by any of the novelties that Dublin or its neighbourhood was able to present; and he promised to conduct him himself in his own phaeton and four, although parliament was still sitting; so that Lord Squanderfield had every reason to be highly pleased with his first reception on the Irish shore.

The two noble lords set out accordingly the next morning, and performed their journey without meeting any disagreeable adventure, except that Lord

Squanderfield damned all the inns, the waiters, and the chambermaids; and that Monsieur Papillote,/ his lordship's gentleman, got a black eye from one of the latter, as he was presuming to grin love to her through his French lantern jaws. When they reached the gate that enters into the park at Ravensdale, the view of that venerable mansion, and the noble sheet of water which the Shannon there exhibits, forms a very striking and majestic scene; but Lord Squanderfield was so taken up with a little French lap dog he had with him, that he had no leisure to observe any of the surrounding objects. He had indeed nearly overlooked Lady Cecilia herself, who, seeing the carriage at a distance, and knowing it to be her brother's, had come out to meet him. Her surprise was only exceeded by her mortification, when she saw who accompanied him. But Lord Squanderfield, awakened by Lord Rivers, got out of the phaeton, and, with his little dog under one arm, had the presumption to offer the other to Lady Cecilia, who he swore by G – was the finest woman he had ever seen out/ of England, which made him desirous to transplant her thither; and this with another oath he affirmed was the sole business that had brought him over. Her ladyship was so surprised at seeing him, and so confounded by this sally of impertinence, that she was fairly at a loss what to reply. She blushed, however, into a deep crimson, which his lordship fondly interpreted into an evident expression of the most favourable sentiments for him; a mistake into which nothing but the blindest and most partial self-love could have led him. The only passion he was capable of exciting in the bosom of Cecilia was either that of pity or contempt. Her placid temper and her excellent understanding preserved her from anger; and the consideration that she stood upon her father's ground induced her to suppress every emotion of resentment, and to suffer his lordship to lead her into the house.

After some cold enquiries about his voyage and other uninteresting matters, she left him to the care of her father and/ her brothers, and retired to her dressing-room, more discomposed than those who were best acquainted with her had ever seen her before. From this embarrassment she was, however, somewhat relieved by the arrival of Dr. Burton and his two daughters, who we before said were in habits of intimacy at Ravensdale, and who came over with the intention to spend the day there. Miss Harriet was delighted when she heard of the arrival of the English lord, which she rightly considered would make some bustle in the neighbourhood; but Sophia, whose disposition led her to the calm enjoyments of domestic life, felt more in unison with Lady Cecilia on the occasion, and regretted any interruption to those pleasing moments which she used to pass with her among the tranquil and deep embowering shades of Ravensdale. When the necessary preliminaries of adjusting their dress were over, and the hour of dinner approached, the ladies went to the drawing-room, and were accompanied by Captain/ Rivers and Mr. Evans. They were all introduced to the newly-arrived lord, who proportioned his bows exactly to the rank of each, passing over Evans with a careless air, as if his lordly

172　*The History of Ned Evans*

dignity had no attentions to bestow on any man, however amiable, that was not at least in some remote connection allied to the peerage. The youth was not, however, disconcerted by this neglect; indeed amends were made him in the warm attachment of Lord Rivers to him, and the visible preference which Miss Sophia gave him, who was well acquainted with the whole of his spirited and generous conduct to Lady Cecilia, and who beheld in his person all those graces and prepossessing elegancies which few would exchange for the long shanks and sounding titles of Squanderfield. Doctor Burton too had conceived a very high opinion of Ned – for he had discovered in him a just and dignified sense of religion united to classic knowledge and taste; so that though in point of rank he was the humblest of the/ company, yet he was very far from being the lowest in private estimation.

Dinner being announced, Lord Squanderfield led Lady Cecilia to the head of the table, and immediately seated himself beside her – unmindful that Lord Ravensdale had not yet got to his chair – unmindful that Dr. Burton had still a ceremony to perform, which at Ravensdale was never neglected, but which he himself had so long disused, that he hardly knew the respect that was due to it. When the cloth was removed, a very interesting conversation took place relative to the situation of public affairs, which at that time was very critical; but in this Lord Squanderfield took no warmer part than he usually did in the debates of his house – simply answering yes or no, when any question was addressed to him. His lordship's attention seemed indeed to be wholly employed in rummaging among some nuts that lay with other fruit on the table. Having at last discovered among the shells a couple of maggots, he/ seemed as if new waked, and immediately making two circles on the table with some wine that was in his glass, he placed a maggot in the centre of each, and offered to lay a hundred guineas upon the head of either jumping over the circumference, if any person at the table would take up the bet, and lay upon the other. Lord Ravensdale stared; and Dr. Burton cast up his eyes to heaven: a deep blush suffused the cheek of the lovely Cecilia, arising probably from a mingled emotion of pity and contempt – to which possibly might be added some small portion of indignation, that such a character should ever be thought of as a fit object of her affections. The penetrating eye of Evans saw these several emotions clearly working in her mind; it was fixed fast upon her, which her ladyship soon perceived, and was as alert in reading Edward's mind as he had been her ladyship's. She relieved herself and the company soon after from the awkward embarrassment of this silly adventure, by rising with the two Miss/ Burtons from table; and his lordship not finding any one disposed to gamble with him, not long after fell asleep in his chair, unable to contribute any thing to the fund of rational conversation, or to derive any amusement or advantage from it himself./

CHAP. XXXIII.

THE insipidity of Lord Squanderfield's character was a great mortification to Lord Rivers, and no small disappointment to Lord Ravensdale himself – He had been led, by his sister Lady Elizabeth Belmont, to form a very different expectation of his noble guest; and as the wish nearest his heart was to see Lady Cecilia happily and suitably settled, he was sensibly touched by his failure in the present instance. To Lord Squanderfield's family or situation there could not be any objection; but to unite one of the most sensible and amiable, as well as noble and beautiful of her sex, to a man who did not know the value of such perfections, seemed to his lordship to be like Jephtha sacrificing his daughter,[41] and little less impious than the immolation of virtue upon the altar of Mammon. – To this cruelty no worldly views could ever persuade him; and upon/ consulting with Lady Cecilia herself, he had the happiness to find her sentiments entirely coinciding with his own, and that in this instance her duty went hand in hand with her inclination. Indeed this ecclaircissement[42] with her father had a happy effect upon her ladyship; for, now that she was relieved from the apprehension that Lord Squanderfield's addresses would be supported by her father's recommendation, she recovered her usual gaiety, and appeared much more willing to entertain him, and to make his stay at Ravensdale agreeable. But in proportion as Lady Cecilia recovered her gaiety, poor Ned lost his: – he could not be long insensible to the alteration in her conduct towards Lord Squanderfield; nor was he able to account for this alteration from any other motive than that of her acquiescence to the will of her father to receive his addresses – 'Good God!' he would say to himself, 'she cannot love him! – A mind like hers, fraught with every virtuous, wise, and noble sentiment, can never love a man who/ (whatever may be his fortune) has a soul inferior to the hind that plows his fields, or the footman that wipes his shoes – She cannot love him – and where she cannot give her heart, honour will never let her give her hand – But, alas! why do I rave? Unhappy Edward, what is it to thee whom Cecilia loves? – Canst thou forget the difference of your stations, or overlook the mighty gulph which nature and fortune have placed between you?'

174 *The History of Ned Evans*

This poor youth had indeed drunk large draughts of love's intoxicating potion since his arrival at Ravensdale – The intimacy in which he dwelt there (being considered as one of the family), and the daily and unreserved intercourse he had with Lady Cecilia, had put him off his guard; so that he swallowed the delicious poison, almost without knowing it, till the alarm of a rival let him into the knowledge of his real situation – It was then his eyes opened on the gulph into which he was ready to fall. The misery this gave him was inexpressible – He recalled/ to his mind the scene in the cavern in Wales, and the agitation of Lady Cecilia on the most distant and respectful hint of his attachment, at a time when she was his guest, and he unacquainted with her rank. To renew any solicitation of that kind would be now presumptuous in the highest degree: it would be to break the sacred promise he had made to Lady Cecilia – it would be to abuse the confidence of Lord Ravensdale, and the hospitality of his house – it would be to lose that friendship which had already done so much for him, and which was ready to do more – and, what was worse than all, it would be to lessen him in the eyes of Cecilia herself, and probably be the means of banishing him from her presence, and perhaps from her heart for ever. But to forego the sweet hope, to quench in his soul that cordial drop which he had so long cherished as the precious panacea of all his cares and afflictions, this was like parting with life itself, and which, when once lost, could leave nothing behind to interest or/ engage his affections. The necessity of this sacrifice however was obvious: and here he made the first trial of his resolution, for from this moment he determined to depart from Ravensdale; not to give up the idea of the adored Cecilia, but to make himself worthy of her, if fortune, who is said to favour the brave, should at any future period smile upon him. His regiment was soon to embark at Cork for America: he determined to make this a pretence for quitting Ravensdale, that he might be with them some time before they failed; and resolved to take an early opportunity of communicating this resolution to Lord Ravensdale and Captain Rivers.

This victory over himself was a source of much consolation to him: – however tender the fibres of his heart were, however powerful the passion that rent those fibres almost to breaking; yet the inward approbation of his mind, the joyful consciousness that he was going to sacrifice passion on the altar of virtue, supported him in the conflict, and/ enabled him to be more than conqueror. And here fortune did for once reward his resolution; for an accident happened which at once displayed his vigour, courage, and address in the highest point of view, and made Lady Cecilia a second time indebted to him for her preservation.

There was upon Lord Ravensdale's estate, a few miles from the house, a mountain of a singular form, and which commanded one of the noblest prospects that is any where to be seen: the top of this mountain is a level plain, containing about fifteen acres of ground, and which is as smooth and as richly covered with a short pile of velvet grass, as if it had been formed for a bowling green, and kept by constant care in the highest order.[43] One side of this plain is bounded by forest trees, which connect it with other mountains higher and more craggy; the other side forms a natural terrace, descending in a sleep slope, equally smooth and velvet-like with the top, which continues for several hundred yards to the bottom;/ which is washed by a deep bend of the river Shannon, which there forms an extensive lake, over which the eye ranges for several miles, and discovers beyond a variegated scenery of woods and lawns, mountains and valleys, streams and villages.

The morning was fine, and particularly favourable for viewing this resplendent scenery. It was proposed to carry Lord Squanderfield thither, and Lady Cecilia agreed to be of the party. It was the fashion for men of quality at this time to wear the dress and assume the manners of grooms and coachmen – indeed to drive a phaeton was by some of them considered as the acmé of human ingenuity: among his other follies, this was one with which Lord Squanderfield was strongly tinctured, and from which, as we have seen, Lord Rivers was not wholly free. To display his skill before Lady Cecilia was an ambition worthy of the English peer, and her ladyship with more good nature than prudence consented to accompany him in her brother's phaeton./ Ned Evans was mounted on a very fine hunter belonging to Lord Squanderfield, which he brought with him from England, and Lord Rivers and the Captain accompanied on horses of their own. Every thing was pleasant and agreeable, and they arrived at the plain on the mountain in perfect safety. Lord Squanderfield was standing in the phaeton with the reins carelessly lying at his side, and admiring or pretending to admire those beauties which Lady Cecilia was pointing out to him, when a loud holloa, as if they were just in at the death of a fox, was very suddenly and unexpectedly vociferated almost in their ears. This proceeded from Nettlefield, who by chance had been out riding that way, and, seeing them, chose to surprise them by this mode of salutation. The horses in the phaeton, which were very high mettled, took fright, and instantly set off like arrows out of a bow. Lord Squanderfield, who was standing at the time they set off, was slung out by the suddenness of the jerk, and narrowly/ escaped being killed by the wheel going over him. Poor Lady Cecilia held fast by the phaeton, but in a situation of terror that hardly left her the power of knowing what to do. The first emotion of Nettlefield was to laugh when he saw Lord Squanderfield tumbling from his seat. Lord Rivers and the Captain stood petrified with apprehension. Evans alone retained any presence of mind – he watched the course the horses were taking – he saw them skirting round by the wood, and that they would soon inevitably make towards the slope, in which case certain destruction must be the consequence: – he spurred his hunter therefore full speed towards the slope, so as to get between it and them, and then facing round he resolutely placed himself directly in their way:

176 *The History of Ned Evans*

they were now coming, as he foresaw, still at full speed; the noble animal on which he was mounted stood firm, and died on the spot, for the pole of the phaeton entered above two feet into his breast – there he stuck impaled with Ned still firm/ in his seat: the shock threw Lady Cecilia forwards, and he was fortunate enough to catch her in his arms, which prevented her receiving any material injury. The horses in the phaeton stood trembling in a lather of sweat; they were soon disengaged by Lord Rivers and the Captain, who now came up, and nothing was really hurt but the generous beast which had so well seconded his rider's views.[44]

As for Ned Evans, his conduct was above all praise – nothing upon earth could have saved Lady Cecilia's life, but the very step he took; a step which required the utmost unconcern for his own, and also a presence of mind which, if it had been deferred but three minutes, would have rendered all assistance fruitless. Their first care was for Lady Cecilia, whose terror was greater as she had leisure to contemplate the danger from which she had been rescued – but whose gratitude was still greater than her terror, when she considered the means by which she had been saved: she even resumed courage enough to/ mount again into the phaeton, but under the guidance of Ned Evans, who drove her safely home to Ravensdale House. As for Lord Squanderfield, he chose to remain at a cottage in the neighbourhood till a carriage could be sent for him; where he damned Nettlefield and Evans, and Ireland, and the prospects, and every thing about him. Nettlefield thought the best apology he could make was to ride off. Captain Rivers followed the phaeton with his sister and Ned; and Lord Rivers, out of respect to the peerage, waited to accompany Lord Squanderfield./

CHAP. XXXIV.

SUCH was the issue of this day's adventure, which seemed to open new prospects to the aspiring views of Edward – for certain it is, the service he had now rendered to Lady Cecilia was greater than that which first introduced him to her notice, and his personal courage and prowess were more advantageously displayed. Her ladyship no sooner alighted than she waited upon her father, where Captain Rivers soon joined her, and related to his lordship all the circumstances of her wonderful escape. The terror of the recital where the horses approached the precipice in full speed, made him tremble so that the chair in which he was sitting shook under him; but when he heard of the gallant action by which his daughter was rescued from instant death, he folded her to his bosom, and burst into tears. The agitation of his mind indeed/ was so great that it overpowered his body, and he was obliged to lie down; – not, however, without sending, by Captain Rivers, the warmest acknowledgments to Ned Evans, with an assurance of an indelible remembrance of this new and signal favour which his noble and gallant conduct had conferred upon him.

Ned had walked out into the garden to compose a little that tumultuous agitation which the fearful event of the morning had naturally raised. He sought the deepest solitude and the inmost recesses of the grove. He revolved in his mind the imminent peril in which Lady Cecilia was, and the happy presence of thought which had enabled him to rescue her from it; and when he considered the great danger to which he himself was exposed, and the almost miraculous preservation they had both experienced, he could not help believing that an omnipotent arm had interfered; and thinking himself alone, he poured out upon his knees a grateful effusion of praise and thanks-/giving to that Being whose providence he verily believed was over all his works – whose ear was never shut that it could not hear, nor his arm shortened that it could not save. Ned fancied himself alone; but chance conducted Captain Rivers to the very spot. He saw him through the trees upon his knees, and his wicked imagination first suggested to him some amorous assignation – but when he discovered how he really was employed, his disposition to laugh was instantly checked. The overpowering sense of virtue awed him in his presence, and the character of this young

178   *The History of Ned Evans*

man blazed upon him at once in all the radiance of personal courage, and all the sacred awfulness of personal virtue. If he loved him before, he now added veneration to affection; he checked his unhallowed steps that were going to interrupt him, and waited with respectful silence till he saw he had finished. He then met him as if by accident, and, taking no notice for the present of what he had seen, Ned still supposed himself to have/ been unobserved. Captain Rivers then congratulated Evans on the magnanimity he had displayed – informed him by his father's order of the high sense he retained of this new obligation, and added such enthusiastic encomiums of his own, that Ned was determining in his own mind to reveal to him the situation of his heart, and make him the confidant of his love for his sister. Twice he was on the point of opening all his mind to him, and as often did his voice falter so as to refuse the power of utterance. Captain Rivers thought something was the matter with him; but he assured him he was perfectly well. Lord Rivers and Lord Squanderfield just then appearing in a distant walk of the garden, the Captain went to join them, and Evans struck again into the recesses of the grove. 'Good God!' said he when alone, 'was ever any thing so unaccountable? Wherefore did Nature give me a tongue but to express myself? Who hindered me to speak? Why could I not reveal my sentiments to/ Captain Rivers two minutes ago with as much ease as I have done a thousand times before, and as I am persuaded I could now do if he was here again? Is love dishonourable, that a man should be ashamed of it? – Perish the thought! Say rather, is it not the most sacred and exalted of all passions? Is it not the soul of every thing that exists? God is love – and a pure and chaste passion is an emanation from heaven. Yes! adorable Cecilia! I will cherish the holy flame you have kindled in my bosom. It shall warm, it shall comfort, it shall illuminate my heart; it shall consume, by the ardour of its concentred[45] rays, every sordid wish or ignoble desire, and purify my thoughts with greater effect than ever the refiner's fire was able to exert on gold.' With such reflections did Ned justify his passion, and resolve to cherish it however hopeless it might seem: – and indeed I must so far confess myself to be of his mind, that I believe love, when it is fixed upon a chaste and virtuous woman, far from debasing or enervating/ the mind, on the contrary fortifies and exalts it – expands the heart from a mean and solicitous attention to self, and inspires it with a desire to attain those qualities which may render it most estimable in the opinion of the beloved object.

He now returned into the house, and joined the noble company who inhabited it; but neither Lord Ravensdale nor Lady Cecilia were composed enough to come down to dinner, so that the two younger lords, with Captain Rivers and Ned, had the whole of the entertainment to themselves. I know not whether Lord Squanderfield had conceived any jealousy of Ned Evans, or whether he fancied Lady Cecilia looked upon him with any more favourable eye than she did on himself; but it is certain that from the first he shewed no great disposition of regard towards him, of which, if envy was the cause, the event of this morning did not contribute much to the soothing of that passion. The glass circulated freely after dinner, and Lord/ Rivers did Ned the honour to fill a bumper to his health, as the gallant deliverer of Lady Cecilia. The Captain filled his glass to the brim: but Lord Squanderfield said he could not possibly pledge the toast, at least under that title; for he could not see any thing in the action but perfect madness, the effects of which had fallen upon him; but 'he expected Mr. Evans would make good to him the loss of his horse, which he had so unnecessarily and so cruelly destroyed; and for which he had given fifty guineas a few weeks before.' Ned Evans replied, 'that it was a matter of perfect indifference to him whether his lordship drank his health or not: – that what he had done was the impulse of the moment, which appeared to him to be the only possible chance for saving Lady Cecilia's life, and which perhaps his lordship's inattention to the reins, notwithstanding his having so precious a charge under his care, was the primary cause of bringing into danger: – that for his own part, he would gladly have laid/ down his own life to save her; and therefore could not hesitate a moment to sacrifice that of a horse, though it were the most valuable of the race: – that fifty guineas, which he demanded as the price of him, was but a paltry consideration even to him who was but an ensign, in comparison with the satisfaction it gave him to think he had been serviceable to Lady Cecilia – a satisfaction which he could assure his lordship (poor as he was) he would not forego for fifty thousand.' So saying he rose up and left the room. 'The gentleman is in a pet,' said Lord Squanderfield, as soon as he was out; 'but by G – I will not be choused[46] out of my horse.' Lord Rivers replied, that he was surprised to hear his lordship make use of such an expression: – that since he thought proper to demand a compensation for his loss, he was certain Mr. Evans would make it, for a spirit like his was incapable of any sordid affection. At the same time he must inform his lordship, that Lord Ravensdale and himself,/ and the whole family, considered themselves so much indebted to Mr. Evans upon this occasion, that they would never suffer him to be at any loss by it; nor could any comment on his conduct diminish the glory of it in their eyes, nor their gratitude to its author.

Mr. Evans now returned into the room, and brought with him a draft for fifty guineas on the agent of the regiment, which he handed to Lord Squanderfield without speaking a word, and which his lordship with equal silence put up in his pocket-book. Indeed the party was likely to become very disagreeable; for nothing but that inviolable respect to the laws of hospitality, which is above all other laws sacred in Ireland, could have prevented both Lord Rivers and the Captain from shewing that contempt and disgust which they had conceived for this right honourable character, nor suppressed their resentment for any unworthy slight offered in their presence to their young friend, whom they justly held in/ the highest estimation. They soon after separated – the brothers to enquire

180 *The History of Ned Evans*

after their father and sister – and Ned to revolve in his mind what course he should pursue.

The evening was serene: – a soft shower, which had fallen an hour or two before, had refreshed the buds, which were almost ready to burst their crimson folds: – an odoriferous fragrance exhaled from the surrounding shrubs which every where profusely adorned the sequestered walks of Ravensdale: – the groves rung with the melodious notes of thousands of the feathered songsters, whom the return of spring had waked to joy, and who were now tuning their little throats to sing the raptures of new-born love: – all nature seemed to smile, and to bear in her benign bosom that peace and tranquillity which was the richest endowment of the bowers of Eden. Ned felt the beauty of the scene in all its power; and, oh! thought he, what dæmon is it from hell that envies man these blissful abodes, tears them from the endearments of/ nature, and drags them five thousand miles over an inhospitable ocean, to blast the peace of other men like themselves, and worry one another to death! 'How soon must I myself engage in the dreadful conflict! How soon must I, who have no animosity to any human being, exert all the energy of my mind and all the power of my arm, to plunge those who never injured me into the dust of death! O war! offspring of hell! I detest thee! Yet will I pursue thee: for thou only canst array me with that glory that can encourage me to raise my aspiring hope to the divine Cecilia. O my adored Cecilia! – ' Just as the words were pronounced, Cecilia herself appeared – they vibrated on her ear: – the sweetness of the evening had tempted her out also, and, like Eve in her days of innocence, she had been visiting her shrubs.[47] Intent among them, and concealed among their boughs, she had neither seen nor been seen by Edward, till the sound of her own name so passionately breathed forth, aroused her, and the next instant discovered to her/ preserver. Both stood – both gazed! A deep blush suffused the lovely cheek of Cecilia, while a quick vibration of the heart almost suspended in Edward the power of breath. At length his voice found utterance – 'Yes, my adored Cecilia!' said he, taking her hand and pressing it gently to his bosom – 'feel here the throbbings of a heart which beats only for your service, and which, if you refuse your love, shall soon cease to beat for ever.' – 'Oh! Mr. Evans,' said Lady Cecilia, 'why do you oppress me? Is this the promise – ' 'Talk not of promises,' said Evans, 'I have vowed to love you for ever, and I shall be perjured if I break it. Oh! my Cecilia, blessed be this day, which has given me some claim to an interest in you! And blessed be Fortune, who has so well seconded her favours as to give me this opportunity of declaring to you how I adore you!' The hand of the lovely Cecilia was still locked in his, from which she did not attempt to withdraw it. A tear, chaste as/ the dew of the morning, trickled on her crimson cheek, which the enamoured Edward kissed off, whilst the unresisting Cecilia leaned on his bosom. A few moments of this tender rapture passed between them, sufficient to tell Edward he was beloved – sufficient to spare Lady Cecilia the pain of confessing it. Yet her generous and noble mind did not wish to conceal longer an affection which she thought so justly placed. The soul of Edward now felt a transport which he had never experienced before. To say this was the happiest moment he had ever known, is but a feeble expression for that ecstacy of joy which thrilled through every fibre of his heart. He again pressed the lovely Cecilia to his bosom, and sealed upon her willing lips the vow of everlasting love. Nor was the heart of Cecilia less moved with pleasure than that of her generous Edward. He had long been amiable in her eyes, and certainly possessed a considerable share of her affections: – but the adventure of this morning, which made her/ absolute debtor to him for her life, seemed to her to demand every return she could possibly make with honour; and what could be more just, and therefore more honourable, than that she should repay with her love the gallant youth whose love for her made him encounter the most imminent peril, and rate his own life as nothing provided he could rescue hers? Oh! amiable and faithful pair! may every guardian power, to whom fortitude and generosity in man – to whom modesty and truth in woman are dear and estimable, watch round your fortunes, and direct the events of your lives! that the barriers which now seem to separate you for ever, may be removed; and that your hearts, which seem formed only for each other, may at last be united in the indissoluble bonds of wedded love. But, alas! Fortune seems for ever to continue the unrelenting foe to Love. Not relying on those almost insurmountable impediments she has already placed between you, she calls in the/ aid of war – she lifts up the trumpet of Bellona, [48] and, with its horrid blast, dissipates those gentle prayers I would waft to heaven in your behalf./

CHAP. XXXV.

There are moments of rapture scattered thinly in almost every lot, the happiness of which is too intense to last, and which perhaps, if much prolonged, would, by the agitation they produce in the mind, degenerate into pain. Providence therefore has wisely ordered, that the brightest objects shall have a shadowed side, and that the most fortunate and favourable events shall still be mixed with some alloy inseparable from this state of trial. The present moments were such to Ned Evans: – the most lovely and most beloved of women was leaning on his bosom: he adored her with all the powers of his soul; and he had now for the first time the supreme delight to hear her own a similar affection, and candidly confess a mutual flame – 'But, oh! my Edward,' said the charming Cecilia, 'though truth and gratitude/ compel me to acknowledge to you the sentiments of my heart, yet think not that I ever can be yours; whatever may be my wishes in your favour, yet I am not at my own disposal. My father loves you, esteems you – and I have his commands to tell you, that his gratitude to you will not cease but with his life. Yet, oh! my Edward, did he suspect there was any attachment of love between us, I know how soon his pride would eradicate all these sentiments – I know he would rather see us both dead at his feet, than that we should be united. My brother too, with pride still greater, and a heart far less tender and affectionate, would become your fiercest enemy; whilst in the storms that would ensue your poor Cecilia's peace would suffer shipwreck.' – 'Rather let mine be destroyed for ever!' replied the enraptured Edward: 'but say, my Cecilia (for I must claim the privilege to call you by that tender name), Will you not allow me to hope? Can you have the goodness to acknowledge to me a sentiment in my favour, and the cruelty with/ the same breath to bid me despair?' – 'No, Mr. Evans!' said Cecilia: 'I do not bid you despair; but, for both our sakes, I beg of you to act with the utmost caution and circumspection. You must consider your own situation as well as mine; your country calls you now, and I know my gallant Edward will not let her voice be drowned by the lamentations of a silly woman; for, alas, I must and will lament you! But while my sincerity confesses this, the same sincerity obliges me to declare, that I would not suffer you to remain, though it were in my power. The call of honour must be obeyed; and I will not scruple to say to you, that your honour is dearer to me even than your life.'

'O matchless Cecilia!' said Mr. Evans, 'how glorious is my lot when such a heart as yours deigns to unite itself with mine! Yes, I will obey you, you shall be my guardian angel; I will implicitly follow your commands, I will go where honour calls, I will court glory in the fields of death – and if in those fields to die shall/ be my fate, the same breath that carries away my soul shall waft a prayer to heaven for my Cecilia.' – 'And mine shall not be wanting,' replied Lady Cecilia, 'to avert that fate from you – but should it happen, my Edward shall find a tomb in the heart of his Cecilia.' 'No – let me live there,' said Edward, passionately folding her in his arms – 'Love and Fortune, which have already done such wonders for me, will not desert me – they will shield me in the day of battle, and bring me back to lay my trophies at Cecilia's feet.' – 'I hope they will,' replied her ladyship, 'and that you will be restored safe to me. But if you wish our hands should ever be united, the most distant thought of such a hope must not now escape you. We are both young enough – we have neither of us yet seen twenty years. Let us then, by a little timely prudence, lay a foundation for future happiness, and not, as is too often the case, blast the comforts of a whole life by some momentary act of indiscretion.' – 'I submit,/ Lady Cecilia,' replied Ned; 'I have told you already I implicitly submit. I see and acknowledge your wisdom, and whatever you command I will obey.' – 'Then, Mr. Evans, all I have to request is, that you will keep your attachment to me a profound secret from all the world, and above all from my own family. I have dealt with you with that candour to which I think you entitled. I have scorned the silly affectation of my sex; and feeling as I do for you the utmost gratitude, and even more than gratitude, I have not been ashamed to own it to you. Rely therefore on my constancy and truth; but know at the same time, that I will never disobey my father, and that I would rather die this night than ever give him cause to shed a tear for my misconduct, or to accuse me of undutifulness by disposing of myself without his consent.' – 'Lovely Cecilia!' replied Evans, 'equally gracious in what you grant and what you refuse, how shall I express my gratitude to you for your noble/ and generous confidence? Accept then the solemn vow I here make upon my knees before you – and do thou, O my Creator, witness it! – that from this hour I dedicate my life to virtue and Cecilia. I will go, my Cecilia – I will serve my country and my king; but, for the reward, it is to you, thou empress of my soul, that I look up!' 'Rise, Mr. Evans!' said Lady Cecilia, 'and do not hazard the being seen in this posture. Go, my Edward! serve your king and your country; act worthy of yourself, and rest secure of your Cecilia's love.' The charming promise was sealed with a transporting kiss, through which their souls seemed breathed into each other. When the rapture of their mutual explanation had a little subsided, they returned into their usual habits of conduct to each other. The consciousness of being beloved

184 *The History of Ned Evans*

by Lady Cecilia was a never-failing banquet for the soul of Edward to feast upon; but, like a voluptuous epicure, he was compelled to feast on it by himself – for Cecilia, though/ she had owned her love, lost none of her dignity, which she well knew how to preserve, and to which indeed Ned, to do him justice, was not a bit less disposed to pay all due respect. But though all the outward forms of ceremony were strictly preserved between them, yet their private conversations were considerably changed, and became much more interesting – for Ned now took no step without consulting Lady Cecilia; and her ladyship, feeling herself deeply interested in his welfare, frankly entered into his interests, and gave him such advice as her excellent judgment deemed most likely to promote them. She approved highly of his intention of immediately joining his regiment, which was now lying at Cork, and shortly to embark – 'What though I lose you a few days sooner?' said she, 'yet I know this step will be approved of by my father, and will certainly prevent his forming the slightest suspicion of any attachment between us – for who knows what that odious lord might suggest to him?/ The wretch knows I hate him as much as I can hate any thing; and the envy of your gallant conduct to me this day has, I perceive, already rankled his base soul into hatred against you; I dread therefore the effects of his resentment.' – 'Dread nothing for me, my Cecilia!' replied Edward: 'he dare not for the life of him attempt any thing against me.' – 'Not against your person, I am convinced, my Edward,' replied her ladyship; 'but the baseness of his envious heart may strike a blow which you can neither see nor parry, and nothing more likely than to endeavour to injure you with my father.'

Just as she was speaking, Lord Squanderfield himself appeared at the end of the walk: he was alone, and was turning to approach Lady Cecilia; but, viewing Ned with her through his opera glass, he passed off through another path that led into the wilderness of shrubs. 'There he goes!' said Ned; 'and there let him meditate what/ mischief he may! I despise his malice, and defy it; nor do I believe that your noble father would receive an unworthy impression of me from any insinuation of his. But, my ever beloved and ever adored Cecilia! I have promised to obey you; and though to part with you is, I am persuaded, more painful than to part with life, yet I will begin my duty by making this sacrifice; in the certain hope that this your first command will be the severest you will ever lay upon me – and that when I have been able to surmount that difficulty, you may reasonably expect I shall not be deficient in any future duty to you.'

They were now within sight of the house; and the hour of tea being nearly arrived, they walked towards it in their usual manner, and with as little embarrassment as if nothing interesting had passed between them.

END OF THE SECOND VOLUME.

THE HISTORY OF NED EVANS.

THE HISTORY OF NED EVANS.

'O'erstep not the modesty of Nature!'
Shakespeare

IN FOUR VOLUMES.

VOL. III.

LONDON:

PRINTED FOR G. G. AND J. ROBINSON,
PATERNOSTER-ROW.
M.DCC.XCVI.

THE HISTORY OF NED EVANS.

Chap. XXXVI.

Lord Ravensdale was not yet composed enough to join the company in the parlour; but when tea was over, he sent down his compliments to Mr. Evans, and desired to see him in his library: he advanced to receive that youth with the most engaging condescension; and after paying him the justest compliments on his spirit, and expressing the warmest sense of the obligation/ it had laid him under, he adverted to the strange conduct of Lord Squanderfield to Ned, after dinner, the whole of which had been related to him by Lord Rivers and the captain. Ned was going to offer something or another in excuse for Lord Squanderfield, and to express that for his own part he did not feel the smallest uneasiness, and far less any resentment for any neglect that might be shewn him by that nobleman. 'I know,' says Lord Ravensdale, 'that great minds are not moved by trifling causes; and an author, whom I know you revere, has told us, that it is the glory of a man to pass over a transgression: – but though his lordship's ill manners have made no impression on your temper, yet his meanness, as I am informed, has made a very deep one on your purse, which however it is my duty to repair, and therefore I request your acceptance of these notes.' Ned Evans, somewhat embarrassed, would have declined this present, assuring his lordship that he had already/ done so much for him as to prevent his being distressed by Lord Squanderfield's demand. 'That is of no consequence,' said his lordship; 'this is a matter of justice, and not of favour, so put up the fifty guineas as your right; but know, my young friend, that nothing I have yet done for you does at all acquit me in my own mind of the debt I owe you, which the adventure of this day has so much increased. I do therefore from this day take you under my particular patronage, which, if it pleases God to spare both our lives, will, I hope, be able to push you up in your profession. Amid the scenes in which you will shortly be involved, you will find many demands for necessaries, more I fear than your pay, however wisely managed, will be able to furnish. I will therefore add to it two hundred guineas a-year, which will be paid quarterly to the agent of the regiment, along with the allowance which I give my son, and which you may draw for as you find occasion. And that you may not lose/ an opportunity of rising when it offers,[1] for want of a little money on the spot, you may consider yourself as possessed of one thousand guineas in my hands, for which I will order a bond to be made out and given you, bearing interest at five per cent. and which may lie and accumulate till you can lay it out to advantage.'

'My lord,' replied Ned, 'your lordship's generosity, as it is altogether unbounded, so does it so far surpass whatever I could have thought of or conceived, that I hope your lordship will not think me ungrateful, because I can find no words to express my feelings for so much goodness; but if a heart entirely devoted to your lordship and your family, and a life the business of which shall be to deserve that patronage which you have so generously bestowed upon me, can be an offering any way acceptable to you; I beg leave to lay both at your feet, and to kiss that hand which has raised me from the dust, and placed me on an eminence commanding so many extensive/ views.' With these words he raised Lord Ravensdale's hand to his lips, whilst the old nobleman enjoyed the exquisite delight of filling a most virtuous and deserving heart with joy and gladness.

Oh! what luxurious enjoyments could riches purchase, if rightly applied! How excellent a friend might we make of mammon, did we but place our esteem upon its real merits! Far from being a delusive possession, which makes unto itself wings and flies away, or which, even while it stays, mocks its owner with unreal joys, that it may the easier plunge him into real sorrows, it might, if wisely managed, be rendered a source of unceasing delight in this world, and at the same time be laid up in the treasury of heaven, to bear an interest of ten thousand fold to all eternity.

Ned now acquainted Lord Ravensdale with his intention of shortly taking leave of his lordship, and joining his regiment, which was in a few weeks to fail for America. His lordship approved of this resolution;/ but hoped that this disastrous war would soon be brought to a conclusion, and that they should both live to meet again at Ravensdale, where, as long as he was master, Mr. Evans should always find a cordial and sincere welcome.

Ned made his bow, and retired. Inclination would have led him immediately to have sought Lady Cecilia, and communicate to her the generosity of her noble father; but he remembered the caution her ladyship had given him, and resolved to wait till fortune should grant him another precious opportunity of meeting her unperceived, and laying open to her the inmost recesses of his heart. He went up therefore to his own room, to indulge a while in silent meditation on the transactions of that day, which had brought forth so many extraordinary events, and produced so fortunate and so unlooked for a change in his own circumstances. He had not been long there when the post arrived from Dublin; and David Morgan,/ whom we had almost lost sight of among the higher characters

188 *The History of Ned Evans*

at Ravensdale, came up with much joy in his countenance, and brought him a letter from Wales. Ned kissed the seal, which he knew to be his father's, and dismissed David, telling him he would inform him of any news respecting him before he went to bed.

It is so long since we have had any intercourse with the honest curate, that with Ned's leave we will take the liberty of reading his letter ourselves, as we are confident there are no secrets in it, which he might wish to conceal from us.

Ti-gwin, April 17, 1780.

My dear Ned,

I received your last letter with singular satisfaction, because I know no quality in the human mind more estimable, nor any in which it is more apt to be deficient, than the forming a just estimate of its own misconduct. You seem so fully sensible of this, and speak so feelingly on the subject/ of the great error you have revealed to me, that it would be ungenerous in me, and I think needless, to add to your affliction on that account: what I shall offer therefore shall be consolation, and to assure you that the poor creature shall receive from me all the compassionate assistance that her situation will require.

I should have satisfied you in this point sooner, but that it was some time before I could recover the surprise of the circumstance; and since then I have been much hurried, and perhaps agitated about an event that happened soon after you left us, and the conclusion of which I have not been able to inform you of till this time.

You must know, then, that my old rector Doctor Ellis has paid the great debt of nature: and as I have been a curate thirty-six years, eighteen of which I have served this parish without ever being absent but two Sundays, this was thought by my good friends Sir Edwin Thomas and Mr. Rowland, the principal landowners/ residing in it, a good foundation for them to make application for me to my Lord Bishop; and this application was backed by all the congregation who were thought considerable enough to sign it. I own I did give way to the pleasing hope that I should have been successful, especially as the bishop has always behaved to me with much kindness and condescension. Your poor mother too was delighted with the affluence which was to cheer our old days, and was projecting some comfortable additions to the house, and a number of kind things for some of our poorest neighbours, which, to say the truth, it is a thousand pities will never take place. I endeavoured to repress, without quenching her expectations; for I thought it barbarous to interrupt the first pleasing moments I have seen her enjoy since she lost your society; and I therefore joined in her amiable reveries, always however qualifying them by adverting to the comforts we might have, even though we should not get the living./

At length the bishop wrote to Sir Edwin and Mr. Rowland, lamenting, in terms which I believe sincere, his inability to comply with their request, he being under the engagement of a promise to the nobleman who made him a bishop, for a gentleman, a near friend of the member for the county.

Thus, my dear boy, unless you get into parliament, I shall never have a living in my days. But, alas! even this is not the worst of it. Our new rector is come down, and officiated for the first time last Sunday. He is a young man, hardly five-and-twenty; and having lived mostly in England, is not very perfect in his Welch. When I mentioned the time I had served as curate, he seemed surprised, and lamented that I had not been provided for, especially as he, being so young a man, could not think of having any person to do his duty for him, and therefore in future he would dispense with my assistance; – so that, instead of getting the living, I have/ lost the curacy. I confess to you, my dear Ned, that the first emotion this intelligence caused in me was like an electric shock, for it was wholly unexpected: and as it lops off at one blow half of my income, I may be excused if it staggered me a little. Yet I declare, the bitterest pang I felt was for the effect I feared it would have upon your poor mother. Yet in this I was happily mistaken. Whether the first disappointment was so great that this made less impression, or whether she had framed her mind to meet all the disappointments that can arise to her, I cannot tell. But when I communicated the intelligence to her, and expected her to be violently affected, it was no such thing. She turned to me with a look of benevolence and love, her eye moistened with a tear, and, like Andromache, δαχρυεν γελἀσασα,[2] she threw her arms about my neck, and said, 'Whilst they leave me my husband, and I know that my Edward lives, I shall never be unhappy.' Though I have been/ six-and-thirty years the happy husband of this excellent woman, yet did I never know the full powers of her mind, nor the strength of her confidence in God, till this occasion. I had never indeed before seen her so much tried. All that she laments in the diminution of our income is the inability it lays her under of continuing many little comforts and kindnesses which those about us used to share in. It has also in some respect reconciled her better to your absence. The little round hat you used to wear, and which hung over the sideboard, she has never suffered to be removed, nor the cane switch you used generally to carry out with you, and which still stands in the corner where you left it. Last night, after supper, she took down the hat, and held it some minutes on her knee. 'I used to like to see thee hang yonder!' said she, 'for thou remindedst me of the dear head thou usedst to cover, and it looked as if he still was near. But now, my dear!' said she, turning to me, 'I am glad he is from/ us, and that it hath pleased God to open a way to him in which he may earn a subsistence, and escape the many mortifications he could not avoid feeling had he remained with us.' – 'My best beloved!' said I, 'the whole of our dear Ned's success is the Lord's doing, and it is marvellous in our eyes: and let this give

190 *The History of Ned Evans*

you confidence, as it really does me, that he will never leave us nor forsake us.' – 'God forbid,' replied she, 'that I should ever want this confidence! I rest fully satisfied in it – and believe from my soul that whatever he ordains for us, will at last be found to have been the best.' Thus has this seemingly most unfortunate circumstance been productive of some immediate good. We are now as low as we can fall; but let not my dear Edward think that we are unhappy on that account. It is the very reverse, I assure you; for this perhaps was the only event that could at this time have reconciled your poor mother to your absence: and having now no deeper blow to fear/ from Fortune, we bid defiance to that capricious dame, nor envy any the possession of her gifts, the tenure of which is so precarious.

I have extended this letter to an unusual length, because I know you will get it free, and because I wished you to be fully apprised of the alteration in our affairs, and how little we are discomposed by it.

As for the news of this place, there is little that can be interesting to you beyond the precincts of this humble roof. Our neighbour Watkins is labouring assiduously, and I dare say successfully, in amassing the treasures of this world. His daughter was very frequently with us after you went away, and, if I mistake not, mingled her tears with your mother's: but time is a remedy for all sores; and rumour says that young Colebrook of Ashfield is shortly to obliterate the traces of any former attachment she might have conceived. I saw our friend Doctor Jones lately: he and/ his family are well, and desire to be affectionately remembered to you. Your dog Towser is in excellent keeping, being taken under the immediate protection of your mother ever since your departure. Tell Morgan, his father and mother are both well, and desire their blessing to him, which I hope he will deserve. And thus having dispatched the domestic occurrences, I have nothing farther to add, than to beg you to present our most respectful, yet most affectionate compliments to Lady Cecilia; and that you will yourself receive the benefits of those fervent prayers which we do not fail to offer up to the Throne of Grace for your well-being and happiness both here and hereafter, and that you may be in due time restored to the embrace of
Your ever affectionate father and friend,
EVAN EVANS./

CHAP. XXXVII.

Had Ned received this letter a few days or even a few hours sooner, it would not have failed to have cast a deep gloom upon his spirits, and to have rent his heart with dutiful and tender sympathy for those accumulated distresses that seemed to be gathering round the head of his virtuous and venerable parent. But the first thought that struck him was his own power to relieve them, which the great and good Lord Ravensdale had that evening so beneficently enabled him to do. Full of this idea, he returned immediately to his lordship, and told him he took the liberty to request him to read the letter which he had just received. When his lordship had finished, and looked towards Ned, in whose eye a tear stood glistening, though pleasure glowed upon his countenance, he instantly discovered the sentiments that filled his soul; which/ fully approving and participating in, he prevented any embarrassment by thus breaking the matter himself – 'I read in your countenance, my amiable young friend, the virtuous desire of your heart; you wish to make an offering of the first fruits of your fortune upon the altar of filial duty and affection. I applaud your piety, and shall rejoice to assist in this sacrifice.'

'Your lordship,' replied Ned, 'has truly divined my wishes, and your generous participation in them overpowers me with pleasure.' – 'There is no need for your being overpowered,' said his lordship, 'for I will take a share of this pleasure with you. I have told you that you might consider yourself as possessed of one thousand guineas in my hands, and that it should bear interest at five per cent. from this day. Now what is it that you wish to do?'

'I should wish,' replied Ned, 'that your lordship would have the goodness to remit that interest regularly to my father.' 'Then my lordship will have that goodness,' replied/ the earl, 'and you may inform him of it as soon as you please; and I would give it to him myself, but that it would be depriving you of the heartfelt satisfaction that I know it will give you to be the means of making the remainder of your father's days easy, and him of the delight of owing that comfort to your gratitude; and believe me, Mr. Evans, no money I ever laid out in all my life, gave me so much pleasure, or brought me so rich an interest as this thousand pound has already repaid me, which makes me hope that it will be attended through-

192 *The History of Ned Evans*

out with a peculiar blessing. So I would have you acquaint your father with this pleasing circumstance the very first post; and you shall have a bill for twenty five guineas to make him his first remittance of his annuity.' Ned, all rapture, was going to throw himself at his lordship's feet; but he took him by the hand, and, giving him a cordial shake, insisted upon his not speaking a single word more upon the subject. His lordship was shortly after/ as good as his word; and Ned had the heartfelt pleasure to reply to his father's letter in the following words.

Ravensdale, April 27, 1780.

My Dear Sir,

Your letter of the 17th now lies before me, and if you will believe me, I am actually at this instant shedding tears over it; not however of sorrow for your unexpected removal from the curacy, nor (I will confess to you) of contrition for the great error in my conduct which I have revealed to you, but of gratitude for the gentle manner in which you reprove that error, and the generosity with which you promise to protect the unfortunate partner of my guilt, in the expected hour of her distress.

Oh! my father, if every parent would be thus gentle and friendly, I do not believe there could be an undutiful child in the world.

The account you give me of the loss/ of your curacy, if I had received it a few days ago, would have afflicted me extremely; but, my father, there is a power who never forsakes the righteous, nor suffers his seed to beg their bread. Surely that power has led me hither, and directed the events, by which I am enabled to prevent your being distressed by this circumstance. A terrible accident had like to have happened to our lovely friend Lady Cecilia, and, under God, she owes her life to these hands. Her generous father has rewarded me in a princely manner, and desires me to remit you the enclosed bill for twenty-five guineas, and to inform you that a like sum will be sent you every six months, the interest of one thousand pounds, which he allows me to call my own, and for which I have his bond. He moreover adds to my pay two hundred pounds a-year. I am not vain enough to ascribe all this to any merit of my own – No, my father, it is the provision of Heaven for your virtue, and I am graciously/ made an instrument in it, that the blessing might come heightened to you with every circumstance that can endear it.

I anticipate my dear mother's delight, when you read to her this letter, particularly as she will now be able to put some of her benevolent plans in execution, and to increase the little circle of her domestic comforts; and tell her, that let her contemplate the round hat, and reflect ever so often upon the head it covered, yet she will not think oftener nor more tenderly of me than I do of her; for though I have no external remembrancer of her, yet she is the constant inmate of my heart, and the object of my dearest recollection.

Volume III 193

You have already been informed by me, how we spend our time in this noble mansion. I have nothing to regret, but the rapidity with which it wings its flight, and the short remnant that is left me of the happiest hours that ever were indulged to a human being. Ah! my father, can you not discover the source of this felicity? –/ Yes – Cecilia loves me – the most amiable, and one of the most elevated of women deigns to think kindly of your humble Edward. But hush! I tell you this in the confidence of duty and affection; and though I place no bounds to my aspiring hopes, yet you may rest assured that I shall never forget for a moment the honour of a soldier, nor the delicacy of the situation in which I am placed. A few days therefore will tear me from this paradise, perhaps never more to behold either it or its lovely inhabitant: – but then I know I shall live in her memory and her affection; and I should be unworthy of so much excellence, if any private passion, though dear to me as life, should outweigh the duty which I owe to my king and to my country. I expect therefore, the day after to-morrow, to leave Ravensdale, and proceed to Cork, where the regiment is shortly to embark for Charlestown; and in quitting Ravensdale, I quit a place become as dear to me even as Ti-gwin – a place/ where I have experienced the tenderness of a father, the kindness of a brother, the fidelity of a friend, and, above all, the generous attachment of disinterested love.

Forgive me then, my father, if I can no longer offer you the whole of my heart; half of it I am constrained to leave behind me – but so ennobled by its sympathetic union with that of the divine Cecilia, that the part which remains, and which you will never cease to possess, is much more valuable than the whole used to be, before it was animated by the promethean fire[3] of her eyes.

Were I disposed to be vain, I might brag of the preference given me by her ladyship over a rival you would think formidable indeed – no less than an English viscount, with twenty thousand pounds a year; but he is so wretched a sample of a man, whatever he may be of a lord, that I do not feel disposed to plume myself much upon this victory. By the by, he has an estate in our country,[4] and is landlord, or/ rather was landlord to the good old woman who so hospitably lodged you the night you left old Muckworm's. It is the viscount Squanderfield I talk of, who has been here some time. The knowledge of his conduct towards those poor people gave me an unfavourable prejudice against him, which a little longer acquaintance has not contributed to remove.

I rejoice in the health and happiness of all my old friends in Wales, and particularly in the probability you mention of Harriet Watkin being speedily married to her own and her friends' satisfaction. I beg you will remember me in the kindest manner to her and the family, and in general to all those who are obliging enough to enquire after me. David Morgan desires his duty to you, and to his father and mother; he is a stout, strapping fellow, and accords vastly well with the land of potatoes, where the lasses seem to be very fond of him: nevertheless,

194 *The History of Ned Evans*

like his master, he will sacrifice love on the altar of duty,/ and, I am persuaded, acquit himself like a man, in whatever warfare he may be engaged.

And now, my father, I know not when I shall address you again, nor when I can hope to have the happiness of hearing from you; if the thoughts of the few miles of sea that divide Wales from Ireland filled me with regret when I parted from you, what must be my feelings when I contemplate those thousands of miles of ocean which are soon to roll their inhospitable billows between us! I confess to you, this thought, if I was to dwell much upon it, would overwhelm me with melancholy. I will banish it therefore from my mind, and yield to that more just as well as more pleasing contemplation, that though I take the wings of the morning, and remain in the uttermost parts of the sea, yet I shall still be under that eye which regards us both, and in the protection of him to whom all distance is as nothing, and who I confidently trust will grant us the blessing/ to meet again. In this sweet hope, with every tender and grateful sentiment for my mother, I remain,

dear sir,

Your very affectionate and dutiful son,

EDWARD EVANS.

No opportunity occurred to Ned, this evening, of meeting Lady Cecilia again. Her ladyship complained of a head-ach, and absented herself from supper; but it was probably more on account of her dislike to Lord Squanderfield than for any real indisposition. Indeed that nobleman began to perceive that his design would be totally fruitless; and, notwithstanding his high opinion of himself, even to suspect that the humble son of the Welch curate had an influence on that noble and spotless heart, which all his dignity and fortune could never attain. This made him determine upon shortening his visit at Ravensdale, but not without hinting his suspicion of Lady Cecilia's attachment, both to the/ old and young lord. They imputed this suspicion entirely to malice, which they were but too sensible his lordship was mean enough to let rankle in his breast; and as they knew of Ned's determination to join his regiment immediately, they did not give either themselves or Lady Cecilia any uneasiness about the matter.

CHAP. XXXVIII.

THE stealing hours of time had now brought round the last day in which Edward was to enjoy the hospitality of Ravensdale, and the society of his adored Cecilia.

His friend Captain Rivers had agreed to accompany him to Cork, to introduce him to the regiment some little time previous to their sailing. This last morning they employed in making some farewell visits in the neighbourhood, and among others to the Nettlefields. On this occasion Ned/ was introduced to the ladies of the family, and could not help lamenting, that so much gentleness and good sense as they discovered, should be grafted on such a rough and austere stock as had fallen to their lot. Ned did not fail on his return to revisit that house of mourning, on which his accidental presence had some time before shed the first beams of comfort and consolation. Here he had the satisfaction to receive the fervent blessing of that widowed heart which he had made to sing for joy; and to hear the prayer of gratitude for recovered health uttered by the loveliest lips, and witnessed by the most radiant eyes that perhaps ever beamed from under the humble thatch of an Irish cottage.

Ned indeed could not have recognised his patient in any other place; and the captain was all amazement, having never heard of the adventure, nor ever before beheld so much elegance in rustic beauty. 'I am come, my good dame,' said Ned, 'to take my leave of you, and to tell you I/ am going to the same wars with your son. If I see him, I shall be kind to him for your sake. In the mean time I am happy to see your daughter looking so well, and hope, when I return, to see you both better and happier in every respect.'

'May the Lord be your shield by day, and your pillow by night!' replied the old woman; 'and may he bring you back in safety, and my son with you! for, had it not been for you, neither my daughter nor myself would have been alive this day.'

Something Ned said in return, for he alighted, and spoke to both the women; but what it was Captain Rivers could not hear, for indeed on some occasions he was so secret that his left hand hardly knew what his right hand did.

– 195 –

196 *The History of Ned Evans*

When they returned to Ravensdale, they found Doctor Burton and his family come to dinner. The doctor had a high opinion of Ned, and wished exceedingly to cultivate his acquaintance. Neither was this liking less on the part of Mr. Evans, who/ was highly pleased with the graceful and dignified manner in which he performed the service of the church, and who could not be insensible either to the classic elegance of his learning, or far less to the high character be maintained for uniting the most rigid and circumspect morality with the utmost sweetness and gentleness of manners. The youngest of his daughters, too, was a most interesting character to those who could be pleased with native beauty, unsophisticated with any of those artificial airs which those who are bred in towns mistake for grace, but which all lovers of true nature consider as the meretricious trappings of deceitful art. She was besides the bosom friend of Cecilia, which alone was sufficient to make her dear to Edward. And indeed, had Lady Cecilia not been, she seemed of all others the most likely to love and be loved by him. An infant attachment was perhaps formed in her gentle bosom towards him; but in her unreserved intercourse with Lady Cecilia, she early discovered/ in her ladyship traces of a similar sentiment, and therefore wisely suppressed the embryo passion in her own breast, before it could shoot forth those blossoms which would probably be blasted before their prime, or produce only thorns to sting and corrode her heart. Her attachment then, though it stopped short of love, yet reached to the fullest extent of friendship, and was answered by a similar and sincere affection on the part of Edward.

On this day Lord Ravensdale came down to dinner, and in the evening Lord Squanderfield accepted an invitation from Doctor Burton to pass a few days with them, to the great joy of the eldest Miss Burton and her mother, and to the regret of nobody, if we except the gentle and elegant Sophia.

When his lordship stepped into the coach, he took a formal leave of the family of Ravensdale, but passed by Mr. Evans with as little regard as he did the footman who closed the step after him. Ned answered/ scorn with scorn, and thought himself fully as much honoured by his lordship's neglect as he could have been by any attention he could have shewn him.

In the evening Lord Ravensdale sent for him to his library, when, taking him by the hand, he thus addressed him:

'I am happy, Mr. Evans, to find the first impressions I received of your character, from the account Lady Cecilia gave me of your conduct and that of your worthy father to her when under your protection in Wales, greatly heightened and improved by the present observation I have made of you, since I have had the pleasure of seeing you at Ravensdale. Next to my own sons there is no young man whose interest I have so much at heart as yours, nor any indeed who has so just a claim to whatever little patronage or protection it may be in my power to bestow. Of these, therefore, and of whatever else the most disinterested friendship can do for you, you may always rest assured. I am sorry that the necessity/ of the times calls you away from me so soon; but my son William has, I know, the affection of a brother for you; and as he has some little more experience of the world than it is possible you can yet have acquired, I think he will be a faithful, and I am sure he will be a willing adviser to you, in case any difficulties should occur to you either in the line of your duty, or in any other event of your life. It will give me pleasure therefore to hear that the friendship which has so happily commenced between you, may continue to improve through life, to the mutual comfort and advantage of you both. As for your moral conduct, you have been so well tutored by your excellent father, and you seem to have profited so well by that tuition, that I have nothing to add on that score, unless to forewarn you, that in the scenes in which you will shortly be engaged, there is no possible temptation by which you will not be assailed, nor any corruption in which you will not be countenanced and supported/ by numbers. You will have need then to put on the whole armour of God;[5] and as I have reason to think you are well supplied with this armour, and know perfectly how to wield it, I shall thank you to endeavour to arm my son with some of it, for the misfortune of the age is, that it is too often laid by to rust. – Of sordid or disgraceful vices I cannot think it possible that either of you should be ever guilty; but the army is a school of refined vice, where the most pernicious errors are set off and adorned with every thing that is most engaging and alluring. There, malice and revenge are called honour; prodigality, generosity; adultery and lasciviousness, gallantry and spirit; profaneness, wit; and so on. But the vice that is most common in camps, and most ruinous, is gambling; and I am sorry to hear that this prevails in the most deplorable degree throughout the whole of our army in America. This vice you will see practised and countenanced by the first characters there, and therefore I would particularly/ warn you against it, that you might not be misled by great examples.

'For the rest, I have nothing to add, but to commit you to the care of Heaven, which I trust will send you back safe to your country and your friends, among whom I desire you will rank me as one of the most sincere; and as I hope often to hear from you, so I shall have still greater pleasure in seeing you, whenever it shall please God to still the madness of the people, and restore to us the blessings of peace.'

His lordship then took down a sword, which had belonged to his nephew, the late Lord Rivers, and which was very richly ornamented with cut steel and precious stones, and, presenting it to Ned, desired him to wear it in remembrance of him, as well as of its former owner, whom he really thought he much resembled, and who, had he not been cut off in the flower of his age, would have done as much honour to the name of Rivers as any person who ever bore it. Ned received the present with/ the most profound respect; and after thanking his

198 *The History of Ned Evans*

lordship with the most lively gratitude for all his princely beneficence to him, and assuring him of his constant regard and unceasing remembrance of his wise and affectionate advice, he took his leave visibly affected with emotions, which could not but be pleasing to Lord Ravensdale, as they unequivocally expressed the sentiments of his heart.

From his lordship's library Ned retired to the garden, the usual scene where, among its charming solitudes, he indulged his silent meditations when any event called him to particular reflection. It was night: a faint crimson streaked the extreme verge of the western horizon, and marked the departing footsteps of the golden lord of day; whilst, on the opposite side, the silver queen of night was already mounted in her radiant orb, cheering with her shadowy light the silent groves. Close in their feathery nests the woodland songsters hid their heads beneath their wing. Silence/ reigned around, whilst odours worthy paradise exhaled with the dew from sleeping roses mixed with woodbine and sweet brier, which were every where profusely scattered around. The sweet spirits of innocence and happy love had tranquillised Ned's soul into an harmonious concord with surrounding nature, when lo! a soft and heavenly voice seemed to ascend upon the wing of night, and charm the listening stars: the warbled notes, accompanied with soft touches of the lute, could come from a no less skilful musician than Cecilia herself. Ned gently approached the bower in which she was sitting. All ear, he drank in strains able to soothe pain itself into delight. With what rapture did he hear those heavenly lips warble these few words:

> Go, gallant youth! – Go, reap applause
> Where Britain's sons her standards rear:
> Go, guard thy injur'd country's cause,
> Nor heed a hapless maiden's tear.
> And may the powers who love the brave
> Protect thee on the ensanguin'd plain,/
> Guard thy dear life through wind and wave,
> And bless me with thy sight again!

Ned could no longer refrain: he cast himself at Cecilia's feet. She was not alarmed. What had she to fear? Where love and honour are present, what evil dare approach? The happy – yet the cruel moment was arrived, which favoured him with a last interview with his soul's idol. How imperfectly could words describe the feelings of these tender and faithful lovers! For half an hour their souls enjoyed that intercourse which might have passed between two angels in heaven, and to the chaste raptures of which nothing on earth could bear so near a resemblance. But such moments are too precious to be often bestowed, or to be allowed to continue even when they are indulged. The felicity of this half-hour was to be a sustaining cordial, which was to support Ned's spirits through many perils, and for a length of time, perhaps for the remainder of his days: it had/

need therefore to be strong; and it was such as enabled him to support the cruel separation which the next morning was to doom them to, with all the fortitude that became a soldier. The remainder of the evening passed with that tender and chastised cheerfulness which might be expected to take place among dear friends who had met together perhaps for the last time. Lord Ravensdale had retired to rest, and only Lord Rivers and the Captain, with Lady Cecilia and Ned, sat down to supper. The most cordial harmony subsisted in this united family, and every member of it felt for Ned the attachment of the sincerest friendship. When therefore the hour of their separation came, with so many chances against their ever meeting again, it is not to be wondered at if their last lingering look was dwelt on with moistened eyes, and that the door as it closed seemed like a barrier betwixt time and eternity./

CHAP. XXXIX.

THE morning had hardly begun to dapple the east, before the horses were at the door which were to convey Captain Rivers and Ned upon their journey. Ned envied every peasant he saw, nay even the trees whose rooted habitation detained them in the neighbourhood of Cecilia. He cast his eyes up to the windows of her chamber, which were still closed, and breathed forth an ardent prayer for the beloved inhabitant, whose sleeping fancy was perhaps just then occupied with the visionary repetition of their last night's conversation. Oft did he turn his head as the groves of Ravensdale receded from his view; and at the last spot from whence its friendly turrets could be seen, he stopped his horse, and gazed a long farewell – 'Adieu, sweet shades! and ye, beloved and revered inhabitants! May Heaven shed its selectest/ blessings on your heads, and grant us once again to meet in joy!'

As the day now advanced, the country became more interesting: the fields had every where put on the vivid livery of spring, and soaring larks were singing their aërial songs up to the very gates of heaven: the genial air flung[6] health and fragrance, to which the blossoming haw-thorn gave a liberal share. Ned's spirits began to revive, and by the time he joined the Captain had recovered their usual tone. On the second day they reached Cork to dinner, and were not a little pleased to find an excellent one prepared for their mess, and a very agreeable company to partake of it. Here Ned was introduced to such of his brother officers as he had never seen before; and, during the conversation after dinner, he had displayed so much gaiety and good humour as gave them a very favourable impression of him, particularly as the events which led to his commission, and his recent prowess at Ravensdale, were not/ unknown to them. In the evening he accepted an invitation from Captain Fanshaw, one of the officers of the regiment, to drink tea with him at his lodgings, where he was introduced to Mrs. Fanshaw, a beautiful woman, with two sweet infants, who could not be prevailed upon to stay behind her husband, but was determined to undergo all the fatigues and dangers of a campaign with him. Here they spent a charming evening; for Mrs. Fanshaw was an excellent performer on the piano forte, and had a very fine voice: her husband played well on the bass viol: both Captain Rivers and Ned

– 200 –

could play on the violin and the German flute: and Edward's voice was hardly to be surpassed, even by the most admired performers. A little concert, in which some other ladies, friends of Mrs. Fanshaw, also assisted, contributed to give Ned a most flattering specimen of his companions, and the new mode of life into which he was entering. An elegant little supper refreshed them/ after their performance, from which they were prevailed on not to rise till a pretty late, or rather early hour reminded them that they were not all eyes or ears, and that Nature required pauses even in her most agreeable sensations. The Captain and Ned had taken private lodgings together in one house, to which they retired highly pleased with their evening's entertainment.

The next morning they dedicated to the amusement of walking about the town, and observing whatever was curious in it. In the course of their perambulation they came to the mall, or public walk, which is very extensive and well sheltered with trees, and at times the resort of much elegance and beauty. They had not been long here when they were met by a fresh-looking little man, who, by his rosy gills and capacious paunch, seemed to live upon the fat of the land. This gentleman accosted them with the utmost frankness, although/ he had never seen them before; but, perceiving they were strangers and officers, the laws of Irish hospitality required that he should pay them attention, which indeed his own disposition would have prompted him to do, although custom had not made it necessary. He conducted them to several of the public buildings, and also to a private museum, rich in curiosities both of art and nature: and after having attended them for more than a couple of hours, he brought them to his own house. He then told them they were in the house of Alderman Suet, who would give them as good a dinner and a skinful of as good claret as could be found in the city of Cork, and a hearty welcome into the bargain. The offer was worth accepting: the good humour and frankness of the Alderman had won their good opinion, and they saw that his house, as well as himself, had the face of opulence and contentment: so begging leave to go home just to adjust/ themselves, and enquire if any calls had been made for them, they promised to return at four o'clock.

In their way home they passed by a fruit-stall, where, amidst a variety of garden-stuff of all kinds, there were some very fine-looking strawberries, quite ripe, and neatly set out in small baskets, and a clean and decent-looking elderly woman sitting by them, and knitting a stocking. Captain Rivers had a mind to taste some of the strawberries; so they both went to enquire the price of them. As the captain and the good woman were bargaining about them, she happened to cast her eyes upon Ned; when instantly flying from her seat, she threw herself upon her knees at his feet, and devoured his hand with kisses. He, as well as the captain, was all astonishment, and thought she must be disordered in her senses; but she was actuated by the spirit of gratitude. Perceiving Ned's embarrassment

202 *The History of Ned Evans*

and surprise, she said, 'I see you do not recollect me; but the features/ of your angel's face will never be out of my mind while I can remember any thing. It is to you I owe all the comfort I have in the world, and to you I am indebted for being perhaps alive this day. Do you not remember the miserable object you so nobly relieved in Stephen's Green, when Doctor Porpoise, in whose service my son died, would not give me a farthing?' 'I do recollect you now,' said Ned, 'and I assure you, I am very happy to see so favourable a change in your situation.' 'May the blessing of her that was ready to perish, be ever with you!' said she, 'for you have been a blessing to me: the money you gave me that day, enabled me to redeem my clothes, and to come here to my native place. I found my brother still living and in comfortable circumstances; he rents a garden near the town, and I live with him, and attend this stall all the day. My two sons too, that were sailors, are both living; one is serving his majesty aboard a man of war, and the other is even now in this harbour,/ on board one of the transports which are going to America; and now, if it had not been for you, I should never have seen one of them again: wherefore night and day I put up prayers for you, although I do not know your name; but he that knoweth all things will reward you.' – She then pressed Ned to take a basket of her strawberries, and begged to know where he stayed, that she might bring him them every day, and whatever else her brother's garden afforded. He told her his direction, and perhaps never reaped so much satisfaction from any money he had ever expended, as he did from the reflection how much happiness had flowed from those two guineas which had thus restored that poor and grateful creature to her dearest connections.

At the appointed hour they returned to Alderman Suet's, and were agreeably surprised to find the company no strangers to them. It consisted mostly of those with whom they had passed the evening before; for Mrs. Fanshaw was daughter to/ the alderman, a circumstance which our gentlemen did not know before; and now they were introduced to her sister, an unmarried girl of about twenty, who did the honours of her father's table, for he was a widower. But the beauty of her person did not seem to promise that she would long continue her services in that way; for she was a figure that any man in the kingdom might contemplate with delight, and who could sit down at few tables, of which she would not be the brightest ornament.

'T was well for Ned that every corner of his heart was pre-occupied; the lovely image of Cecilia opposed itself to every new impression, and kept him faithful to his first passion. But the captain's bosom was not so well defended, but certainly received a shot from those bright eyes, which the music of her voice, and the lively turn of her conversation, did not contribute to cure.

The dinner was excellent, as indeed you may always expect it to be in Cork; and as for the claret, the alderman recommended/ it, by swearing by St. Patrick that there was not a headach in a ton[7] of it; for which we must give him due credit, as, if any such thing was in it, he certainly must have found it long before that day. Indeed the frankness and good humour of the alderman made this day very agreeable to our gentlemen, although he was no friend to the cause in which they were embarked – for he condemned the American war in every instance, both the principle and the conduct of it; and in this he was very disinterested, for he made a great deal by it, as he dealt very largely in the victualling line, which is never so profitable as in time of war. But he was a man who loved liberty and humanity better than money, and he considered both as outraged in this contest. 'I love my country,' said he – 'I love the king – I revere the constitution – and therefore I deeply lament that there should be men about the throne so short-sighted as to involve their sovereign in a contest that may very possibly in the end shake the/ kingdom to its foundations.' 'Why in the world should you think so?' said Captain Rivers. 'I have always thought so, Captain,' replied the alderman; 'I consider the principle of this war as unjust from the beginning, for England can have no right to tax America without her consent. If it was just, it is yet impolitic; for America would liberally give to your request what she never will yield to your sword. We were told in the beginning of this contest, that it would be a dispute of a few months only, and that two thousand disciplined troops would scour the continent from one end to the other. We are now entering upon the sixth campaign, every one of which has been more unfortunate than that which preceded it; and after having lost above forty thousand lives, and incurred one hundred millions of additional debt, we are farther from the point than when we commenced. But this is not the worst of it: we have, by our perfidious politics, goaded those into implacable enemies who were/ disposed to be our friends; and we have moreover roused them to consider their natural rights – an enquiry which those who wish to govern should above all others have hushed into silence – an enquiry which I promise you will not be confined to America, and which I will venture to predict will plant thorns, never to be eradicated, in every crown in Europe.'

'My dear Alderman,' said Captain Rivers, 'let us go to the ladies. – Here is a bumper to the unity and prosperity of the British empire! May your prophecy prove false! but if it should not, may I never live to see it completed!'

The alderman in vain pleaded for the other bottle; the gentlemen were unanimous in preferring the charming harmony of the ladies' voices to the din of politics, of whose discussion there was no end; and retired by common consent to the drawing-room. Here Miss Lucy shone to new advantage in the eyes of Captain Rivers, who had the pleasure to fit next her at the tea-table, and/ who ventured to whisper to her some soft compliments, which she received with such lively raillery as convinced him the brilliancy of her eyes was a faithful index of her mind. Cards were proposed after tea, but over-ruled by the gentlemen, who preferred music, and particularly by Captain Rivers, who longed to hear the powers of Miss Lucy's voice. She sung, and accompanied herself upon a lute, an instrument which she touched with great delicacy. Rivers was in Elysium, and drank so deep of Love's delicious poison that all the waters of Lethe were never afterwards able to cure him.

CHAP. XL.

MANY a pleasant evening passed away in the elegant and enlivened society of Mrs. Fanshaw and her sister, and of other families to whom they had the kindness to introduce our gentlemen; and to many a noble libation did the alderman/ invite them, though he did not entirely approve of their deserting his claret for the squalling of his girl: however, as he had always friends enough that were willing to sit as long as they could retain their seats, he was the more indulgent to our gentlemen, and permitted them to do as they pleased.

Captain Rivers, indeed, was so charmed with Miss Lucy, that all company began to grow insipid when she was not of the party; and he no longer looked forward with that impatient ardour to the glory of the campaign, which seemed before to engross all his desire. She, too, was not insensible either to the figure or the merits of the captain, and began for the first time in her life to lose that disengaged and lively cheerfulness which had hitherto been an invariable trait in her character. She had no longer any entertainment in those parties of pleasure which are so much the fashion among the Irish ladies, and which are really/ so very agreeable. Solitude was now her delight. She would rather sit in her chamber looking at the moon when all the family were gone to rest, or sit leaning on her arm, and listen to the warbles of an Eolian harp, than be the most admired in the gayest assembly or most splendid ball in Cork. So powerful is love in either sex, to change all the inclinations of the heart, and engross every faculty of the soul!

Rivers also was a stricken deer, and wandered from the herd to seek the deepest recesses of the groves, and listen to the murmurs of the water-falls. But this sweet delirium could not last. The first favourable gale was to dispel this delusion, and the dæmon of war required the sacrifice of these two hearts, as he had before done of those of Edward and Lady Cecilia.

It was a consolation however to Rivers to know that Mrs. Fanshaw was to be in the ship with him; in her he could behold somewhat of the features of his beloved,/ and could at all times dwell upon that theme, which was now the constant subject of his thoughts.

– 205 –

206 *The History of Ned Evans*

Ned was not so happy, for Lady Cecilia had enjoined him not to reveal any thing of their loves to her brother: but he fed the more upon it in secret; and in the many tedious and uninteresting hours of an Atlantic voyage, he used to contemplate the locket that held the sacred pledge of her affection, which she allowed him to sever from her lovely neck in Wales, and which ever since had hung around his own, and occupied the station next his heart.

At length the day arrived, in which all the soft and amiable passions of the heart were to yield to the stern commands of duty, and when glory was to extinguish with his ardent rays the milder beams of love and hope.

The fleet is ready, and the wind fair; and Lucy and her father, with many other friends, stand on the beach, and wave with their handkerchiefs the last farewell as the boat rows from shore. They return to/ the city, where Lucy from her window follows the vessel with streaming eyes, and Rivers from the deck contemplates the habitation of Lucy till it is lost in the obscurity of distance. The old head of Kinsale, which has braved the ocean ever since the birth of time, now presented his aged and majestic front; a grey mist sat brooding on its summit, which, as the evening advanced, rolled down its venerable sides in hoary wreaths, which added greatly to the dignity and antiquity of its appearance: at length it was wholly enveloped, and, the shades of night soon after descending, they lost sight of it and of the land together.

To a person who has never been at sea before, there is something unspeakably awful in launching out into the great deep; and the last sight of land, and the cheerful habitations of men, cannot but impress a temporary gloom even on the most cheerful disposition. The most of our voyagers were in this predicament, for we can hardly reckon the passage between England and/ Ireland any thing more than a pleasurable excursion. But now there were to be thousands of miles of ocean to roll between them and their dearest relatives. Captain Fanshaw indeed had his wife and his children with him; and Captain Rivers found in Mrs. Fanshaw some consolation for the absence of her sister. But poor Ned felt entirely forlorn, and betook himself to his birth at an early hour, to ruminate in silence on the mountains of Wales, the groves of Ravensdale, and all the dear connexions who remained embowered in those happy residences. The dangers he was to meet, when he next approached the habitations of men, occupied but a small share in his contemplations; yet, whenever they presented themselves to his imagination, their impression was agreeable, for they roused the natural ardour of his mind, and renewed that activity without which no sensation can be happy. Their destination was Charlestown, which had lately surrendered to the British arms, and where/ they expected to share in those memorable exploits, which, though finally unfortunate, yet reflected much glory on the courage, perseverance, and ability both of the commanders and the troops.

The weather was fine, and the wind favourable; yet it was some days before every body could recover that tone of health and spirits, which the parting with their friends and the usual squeamishness of sea sickness had interrupted. By degrees, however, both these wore off, and, as they advanced to the warm latitudes, enabled them to enjoy the fresh air upon deck, and amuse themselves with the novel sight of flying fish, and the beautiful colours of the dolphin. In the cool of the evening they used often to amuse themselves with music; and had Neptune and the Naiads[8] frequented the seas now, as the poets tell us they did of old, no doubt they would have risen from their deep abodes to regale their ears with such unusual and delightful sounds.

But several weeks had now elapsed without/ their beholding any thing but the sun rising in the east, and setting in the west. The world of waters rolled around them, blue and uniform, presenting the idea of a boundless waste, till at last a butterfly happening to come on board, seemed to announce the vicinity of land. It was one Saturday evening, the last which they expected to spend on board, that the gentlemen, according to the sea custom, were drinking with the captain in the cabin, to the health of their wives and sweet-hearts,[9] when they were suddenly alarmed by a shriek from Mrs. Fanshaw, who was sitting with the children upon deck. It was a fine evening, and the eldest little boy, about four years old, was diverting himself running fore and aft, as he had often done before; when, either by climbing or some unlucky trip, he fell overboard and plumped into the sea. Mrs. Fanshaw saw the accident, shrieked, and instantly fainted. The gentlemen immediately went up, when the consternation and despair of her husband/ were beyond the power of language to express.

David Morgan, who happened to be forward at the time, influenced by the first impulse of a generous nature, jumped instantly into the sea. The ship was going on at an easy rate, and had passed to a considerable distance before she could be wore into stays,[10] and the boat launched out. From the deck neither David nor the child was visible; but from the round tops they could discover David buffeting with the waves, though unable to say whether he had got the child or not. Mrs. Fanshaw continued wholly senseless; and the agony of her husband, between fears for her and anxiety about the child, almost bereaved him of all recollection. Captain Rivers stayed with him, as much to assist him as the lady; but Evans went in the boat, to have the earliest knowledge of the event. When they approached Morgan, they saw he had indeed the child, but whether dead or alive they could not tell: both were/ however taken into the boat, and they had soon the unspeakable pleasure to see the little fellow open his eyes, and by degrees recover his senses. When he was thoroughly come to himself, he had no recollection whatever of the event, further than he knew he got a fall. But the sudden revulsion of nature in the mother when she got him again into her arms, had nearly proved fatal to her, and was attended with feelings more affecting and

208 *The History of Ned Evans*

more alarming even than when she thought him lost. A day or two, however, restored her to tranquillity; and now the dogs were observed to run frequently forward to the bowsprit, and to snuff the air with uncommon pleasure; for these sagacious creatures were sensible of the smell of land, though no person on board could perceive it. At length, during the calmness of the night, a light air springing from the shore, wafted an aromatic gale distinctly perceived by every one on deck. Those who were below came up to enjoy this new pleasure,/ and experienced how truly Milton observed nature in his beautiful poem of Paradise Lost, where he records this very circumstance:

> – As to those who sail
> Mosambique off at East, North-west winds blow
> Sabæan odours from the spicy shore
> Of Araby the blest.
> Pleas'd with the grateful smell, old Ocean smiles
> For many a league.[11]

The next morning indeed brought them in view of the shore, the first appearance of which was like a vast fleet of ships; for the coast being entirely flat, the pine-trees appeared rising out of the water long before they could see the soil which supported them. A pilot-boat soon appearing to conduct them in, they got safely over the bar, and were landed on the quay of Charlestown about four o'clock in the afternoon.

As soon as Mrs. Fanshaw and the children were settled at an inn, and had got some refreshment, the gentlemen dressed, and waited on the Commander in Chief, who received them with all the politeness due/ to their stations, and that might be expected from his own. After some general conversation on affairs in Europe, and the recent events in America, his Excellency enquired about the circumstances of their voyage. He was much affected by the accident of little Fanshaw, and so much pleased with the conduct of David Morgan on that occasion, that he promoted him to an halbert[12] on the spot.

CHAP. XLI.

CHARLESTOWN, the capital of South Carolina, was before the war esteemed among the most elegant, though not the largest of the cities of British America. It is situated in the 32d degree of latitude, at the confluence of the rivers Ashley and Cooper, which are navigable for between twenty and thirty miles farther up; and/ though they are inconsiderable when compared with other rivers in America, yet in Europe they would make a very respectable appearance. The entrance to the harbour is however rendered difficult by reason of a bar, which often shifts, and never admits ships of very large burthen. The city used to contain about ten thousand white inhabitants, and perhaps three times as many black and mixed. The inhabitants were for the most part opulent, some of them extremely so: and as they were not soured by any morose sentiments about religion, being mostly of the church of England, public places were more numerous, and had a gayer appearance than in any other part of the Continent. It had been usual too, in the happy æra of peace, for the wealthier inhabitants to send their children to England for education; so that the manners and mode of thinking upon all subjects, of the higher orders in this city, were little different from those of similar rank in Europe; which contributed much/ to make Charlestown the most agreeable place to strangers of any on the Continent. But, alas! the infatuation of Britain in exasperating, by the most wanton outrages, all the feelings of the human heart, to procure by force, and by the violation of the very first principles of English liberty, that revenue which they had only to ask for to obtain, had so estranged the affections, and altered the disposition of men from one end of America to the other, that, when our voyagers arrived there, it bore no resemblance to the happy, fertile, and luxuriant country which it had been but a few years before. About nine miles above Charlestown the two rivers approach one another so as to be separated only by a narrow neck of land about half a mile over: after that they widen again to a considerable distance before they unite their streams below the city, and fall into the Atlantic. This peninsula was in a state of the highest cultivation, covered with the villas of the richer/ inhabitants of the colony, most of whom having been educated in England, had transferred to this paradise the taste and elegance of the parent country; with this great

210 *The History of Ned Evans*

advantage, that the whole country being covered with timber of various kinds, and with an inconceivable variety of the most beautiful and odoriferous shrubs, they were not under the necessity of waiting half an age to create a place; but, by a judicious clearing and pruning, found it ready formed to their hands. Nothing then could have been more charming than these residences were when possessed by their owners – the happy abodes of prosperous industry, of public and private worth; of peace, opulence, innocence, and beauty. But Satan, envious of the felicity of this second Eden, hissed for the dæmon of destruction, who heard the call, though at five thousand miles distance, and swept over the Atlantic to obey it.[13] Alas! that any voice should arm kindred souls against each other. But so/ it was: and no sooner were the British in possession of the town, than this beautiful peninsula went to ruin.

I do not by this account mean to lay any thing improper to the charge of the commanders, or the troops. I take for granted they did nothing contrary to the rules of war. But when I see women and children of the first condition burned out of their habitations, and turned naked into the wilderness; the precious productions of art and science mutilated and destroyed by brutal ignorance and barbarity; the face of nature blasted and deformed, I cannot help cursing from my soul the art of war, and every one who has a share in kindling its flames. That a spirit of implacable hatred should be raised in the Americans, can never be wondered at by any who know how much they endured, and with what injustice they were attacked. But, like all other dispensations of infinite wisdom, this injustice will probably be its own punishment; and America, at no very distant period,/ be gratified (if her generosity should not forbid it to be a gratification) with the most ample revenge. The effect, however, of this alienation of sentiment was necessarily felt severely by those who were obliged now to reside in the colony.

Though many of the inhabitants remained in the city after it surrendered to the British arms, yet they were mostly of the lower classes: and even these, unless in a very few instances, had imbibed all the hatred and animosity against England, which invariably burned in the breasts of the higher ranks: so that no intercourse of friendship or regard could any longer subsist between them. On the part of the troops, was a haughty and suspicious controul: on the part of the people, a sullen and indignant repose. The power of the British, however, extended but a very little way beyond that neck before mentioned, which they had strongly fortified for the security of the metropolis: but the colony at large was still in the hands of the Americans,/ between whom and the British were many very severe engagements, in which both parties profusely spilled their blood, without reaping any advantage by it.

In these engagements our young heroes soon expected to take an active part; and that enthusiasm which is so natural to youthful minds, and which they pos-

Volume III   211

sessed to a very considerable degree, made them impatient to be in action, that they also might come in for their share of renown, and have their names transmitted home with approbation. They pleased themselves with the imagination how anxiously certain gentle spirits would peruse the newspapers, what dewy pearls would drop from radiant eyes when any danger was imminent, and how brilliantly they would clear up when the names they loved were mentioned with applause. Thus do these imaginary pleasures support the spirits under the pressure of real calamities: and wise and happy is the mind that habituates itself to contemplate only the bright and pleasing sides of/ such objects as are presented by necessity to its observation. But it was thought necessary to let the new troops repose a little after their voyage, and be somewhat inured to the climate, before they were called into the field: so that the high and aspiring hopes of our young men were for the present obliged to wait: and indeed, if prudence had not dictated this measure, necessity would have enforced it; for before they were a fortnight in the country half of them were attacked with fevers and agues, and the remainder were so sore and swelled by the bites of bugs and musquitoes, that they were hardly able to move. Our gentlemen, indeed, by a liberal use of bark[14] and Madeira, escaped the first of these evils; but for the bugs and musquitoes the fresh blood they brought from Europe was too delicious a repast for them to hope by any means to escape; and therefore for a considerable time they suffered extremely, which is invariably the case with all people coming from Europe; for after they have/ been in the country some time, though these insects continue to bite, yet the wound is not attended with that pain and inflammation which at first is universally experienced.

But though they had not as yet been called out into the field of Mars, yet in that of Bacchus they were obliged often to contend; in which, it must be confessed, they neither of them supported the character of their respective countries, being always flinchers, and often deserters, from that noble contest: neither did they reap much glory in the field of fortune,[15] which capricious deity had a temple in every tent, and an idol in almost every heart throughout the whole army. This made them be considered by some as rather queer fellows, who had got some whimsical notions of propriety and morality, and who would have cut a better figure as chaplains than captains. Among those who had imbibed this opinion was young Nettlefield, whose regiment was at this time at Charlestown,/ and whose letters from his father in Ireland had made him well acquainted with Ned's history before his arrival. Perhaps he envied him the applause he had got in the Ravensdale family, and the important services he performed to Lady Cecilia; for this Bobadil[16] had a high opinion of himself, and did not despair of rendering himself amiable in any eyes which he should take the trouble to please. His conduct to Miss Grainger, he flattered himself, was not known; and though it should, his gallantry, in killing her brother, he supposed, would go far in justify-

212 *The History of Ned Evans*

ing it. Whatever was the cause, he certainly from the beginning had a jealousy of Ned Evans, who, on his part, had conceived a just detestation of him long before he had any idea of ever being acquainted with him.

It happened one evening that a number of officers had agreed to sup together at a public house; among whom were Ned Evans, Captains Rivers and Fanshaw. Another party had dined at the same house,/ among whom was Nettlefield; and in the evening they had, as usual, sat down to cards, at which Nettlefield had been unsuccessful. At the hour of supper the two parties agreed to join, and they all sat down together. The supper passed off very well, and several bottles of wine were drunk, without any appearance of ill humour on any side, notwithstanding that the policy and justice of the American war were very freely discussed, and with very opposite opinions, though they were all engaged on one side. At length religion came on the tapis;[17] when Ned happened to lament how that must suffer on the Continent, from the overthrow of all establishment, and the departure of most of the regular clergy. 'That's like the canting son of a Welch curate,' said Nettlefield, 'sighing for his leeks and his toasted cheese, which the superstition of his countrymen supplies him with. Damn all religion, I say, and all priests, and all their posterity! Let men be governed by honour, which is what we/ all can understand, and then we shall have no need of hypocrites and enthusiasts.' It was impossible for the serenest temper at the age of nineteen, and in the habit of a soldier, to sit silent under so unmerited an attack. 'Sir', said Mr. Evans, 'the folly of your blasphemous sentiment can only be equalled by its falsehood and ill-manners. With respect to myself, I am neither ashamed of my country, nor my father, nor his profession; and when next you venture to talk of honour, take care that nobody in the room has ever heard of Miss Grainger.'

Nettlefield, at the sound of this name, turned first as red as fire, and then as pale as death. He rose from his chair, and went round towards Ned Evans, who supposed he was going to speak to him, perhaps indeed to call him out. Nettlefield leaned down towards him, and Evans turned round to hear what he had to say; when, to his infinite surprise, he discharged all the spittle he could collect in his mouth,/ full in his face. The astonished youth instantly drew his sword, and the other as quickly did the same. In the second pass Evans wounded Nettlefield in the arm, who, stepping back, by some accident tripped, and fell. Ned's resentment instantly subsided; and leaning forward over Nettlefield, he said, 'I hope you are not materially hurt?' The other made no reply, but, shortening his sword, which he still held fast in his hand, gave a home-thrust at poor Ned, who was all unguarded, and ran him quite through the body.

CHAP. XLII.

THE whole of this unfortunate rencontre having passed in less time than it has taken to relate it, there was no opportunity, nor perhaps any possibility, for any person present preventing it. The company were all sensible of the great impropriety of Nettlefield's/ behaviour in the commencement; but when they saw his base conduct in stabbing the unsuspecting Evans, whilst he was anxiously and kindly fearing he had been materially hurt, they were shocked to the soul, and with one voice cried out, 'Oh, for shame, Nettlefield!' The sword passed under the short ribs of Evans's right side, and, glancing upwards, came out below his shoulder blade.

'My dear Rivers, support me!' was all he said. He had indeed caught him in his arms, and with the help of Captain Fanshaw and the other gentlemen laid him on a sofa.

The commander in chief being informed of this affair, and all its circumstances, ordered Nettlefield immediately into arrest: he did Evans the honour to send his own surgeon to attend him, and saw him himself as soon as he was removed to his lodgings.

When the surgeon had examined and dressed the wound, he told Captain Rivers, that though he could not pronounce it to/ be absolutely mortal, yet it was dangerous in the highest degree; particularly as the season of the year (which was August) was extremely unfavourable, from the intense heat of the climate, and the epidemic fevers which constantly rage at that time.

Nothing could exceed the affectionate attention of Rivers, but the patience and fortitude of Evans, who bore the excruciating torments of his wound without a murmur, and without either conceiving or expressing any resentment against his murderer; for surely the unfair and ungenerous manner in which he gave the stab justifies that name. On the third day of his confinement, the fever made its appearance, with every alarming circumstance of aggravation. Those roses of health which blushed so deep upon his manly cheek, were now all withered; that vigour which could curb the fiercest steed, and against which few arms could be raised with impunity, was now laid prostrate, unable to turn itself on the bed. Those eyes which so lately/ shot forth rays both of sweetness and intelligence,

– 213 –

214 *The History of Ned Evans*

now languished in their sockets; and even that intelligence itself, but a few days before so brilliant and so lively, was now obscured with delirium, and lost the functions both of perception and of memory.

Rivers never left him, but watched over him with all the attention of a nurse, and all the affection of a brother. He had languished in this way for a considerable time, the doctor supposing every night would be his last; when, after he had just gone, and Rivers was sitting by his bed-side, Evans suddenly lifted his eyes, and seemed to recover his senses –

'My God!' he cried, 'I thank thee that in a foreign country, far from the help and endearments of my parents, thou grantest to my last hours the consolation of a friend. – Oh, Rivers! I am going from thee; but bear me witness that my last sigh was vented in prayers for you and for your family.'/

'My dear fellow,' cried Rivers, 'I rejoice to hear your voice again! I trust you have many years yet to live, and that this return of intellect is the turn of your complaint.'

'Alas, no!' replied Evans; 'I feel the approach of death, but it is a calm approach; and believe me I dread it not – for, oh, Rivers! I am a Christian. – And now, my friend, there is a duty incumbent upon every Christian, before he leaves the world, which is to forgive his enemies. Indeed I did not know that I had any enemies; why Nettlefield became so, I cannot tell – but tell him, Rivers, I forgive him, from my soul I forgive him; and if he should be called to account for my death, tell the gentlemen who try him that I hope they will acquit him.

'Oh, Rivers! look at my bosom – behold this locket, it contains your sister's hair – I will not leave the world without imparting to you a secret, which I long wished to disclose to you, but never before could find/ courage to reveal. I have dared to love your sister – Yes! my aspiring heart dared to love Lady Cecilia – I believe she pitied my presumption without hating it. This locket which you see, she had the goodness to give me herself – it has ever since hung on my heart, and shall remain there while that heart continues to bear. But, oh! my friend! when I am dead, take you the sacred pledge – perhaps a lock of my hair may then be acceptable to her – cut one off, and present both to her as the last offering from a man who felt in death no agony like parting from her.'

'And do you think, my dear friend!' said Rivers, 'that this secret was never known to me before? – You surely must suppose I have had no observation. But now, in my turn, I will tell you another secret; and that is, that I know Cecilia loves you: and so let me hear no more of dying, for I am persuaded you are growing better; and if you will not live for me, I hope from my soul you will for Cecilia, for I know nobody/ so well intitled to her. What would you give to see her?' said Rivers. – A transient smile dimpled the cheek of Evans: 'More than I have in the world,' said he. 'Then behold what I have never shewn you before.' He then presented him with a most exquisite miniature picture of her, painted when she was in London, which Evans had still life enough left to gaze at with unspeakable pleasure. 'I lend you that,' said Rivers, 'till you get the original; and let that hope be a cordial to you, to recall the ebbing tide of life, and rally the spirits about your heart.' Whether it had this effect or not, I cannot tell; but certainly from this hour Ned's fever abated, and the alarming symptoms of his wound disappearing, he was soon after pronounced out of danger.

The important victory at Camden, gained in this month by Lord Cornwallis over General Gates,[18] had so depressed the spirits of the Americans, and exhausted them of resources, that the whole province of South/ Carolina was considered by the British as subdued; and as they had neither the means nor apparently the inclination to make any further stand against the conquerors, several months intervened before there was any probability of the new troops being brought into action. This repose gave time to Ned to recruit his strength, and to become familiarized to the climate. Nothing can be more charming nor salubrious than a Carolina winter, and its genial influence soon restored the roses to his cheeks, and its vigour to his arm. The base attack that had been made upon him, and his spirit in the contest, had interested all parties in his recovery, and particularly the ladies, to whom Mrs. Fanshaw had with the warmest eulogiums related his history; so that he was a particular favourite in all their parties of pleasure. Even the American ladies, who in general receded from any sort of communication with the British officers, relaxed in favour of him; and often lamented that they were compelled to/ consider as an enemy, one whom they so much desired to love as a friend. He was indebted for this partiality to an accidental favour which he had in his power to bestow on one of the most distinguished of those ladies, who, with her daughter, about twelve years of age, had happened to wander beyond those boundaries which the commandant had prescribed for their liberty to walk in. In this situation they were very rudely accosted by a sentinel, who took the child by the arm, and frightened her so that she fainted, whilst he insulted the mother with all possible insolence and indecency. Ned happened to be a witness of the scene. He severely rebuked the sentinel, who, though he had a right to stop them, had none to abuse or insult them, and assured him that he should receive an adequate punishment. He then took the young lady in his arms, and, by soothing her with the gentlest language, soon dispelled her fears, and conducted both her mother and her to their/ own house. The sentinel received two hundred lashes for his cruelty and insolence.

This lady had been of the first rank and opulence in the country; her husband was a member of the congress, and his father had been president of it. None were more distinguished for integrity in private life, nor for zeal and ability in their public stations. Attached to their country by nature, and to its cause by principle, they had from the beginning been active agents in the revolution, which had

216 *The History of Ned Evans*

raised in the royal commanders a spirit of peculiar resentment against them, and, I wish I could not add, of unmanly revenge.

A beautiful seat, the residence of the husband of the lady, situated upon Ashley river, about sixteen miles from town, was unnecessarily and purposely made a barrack for soldiers. A noble collection of pictures, which the proprietor had made himself in Italy, were by these barbarians wantonly defaced: a capital library of books, of the/ best authors, in all languages, had been torn to pieces to light their pipes, or to serve even meaner purposes: a magnificent philosophical apparatus was destroyed: the walks in the gardens, which were laid out in the highest style of European taste, and which one would have thought might have served them for recreation, were by their implacable spirit grubbed up and defaced. Even the tomb, in which the ashes of their unoffending ancestors peacefully reposed, and which among all the American families of distinction is seated in some hallowed and sequestered part of their garden – even this sacred deposit could not escape the illiberal malice of these blood-hounds, but was broken to pieces; the mouldering remains dug up and scattered to the air, and the venerable trees which shaded the sacred repository cut down and burned. If the dead were treated with this indignity, it is not probable the living would be spared. Accordingly these gentlemen, who by the capitulation of Charlestown were allowed/ to reside there on their parole[19] with their families, were afterwards notwithstanding forced from them in the dead of night, without any pretence of their having broke their parole, and with many others in similar circumstances sent off to Augustine;[20] no attention whatever being paid to the means of their subsistence, nor to any of those necessary accommodations which people of their rank and time of life must stand in need of. It cannot be wondered at, then, if the deepest resentments for such unnecessary and cruel treatment should be fixed in the breasts of all those dear relatives from whom they were torn. The miseries and distresses which at this time seemed the unavoidable portion of every one who adhered to the independence of America, would in many instances have subdued the spirit of the men, had not the noble fortitude of the women exhorted them to persevere; those who had been in the highest ranks, and therefore most sensible of their present afflictions, repeatedly entreating/ their sons, their husbands, and their brothers, never to suffer family attachments, and much less private inconveniences, to interfere with the duty which they owed their country. Among the most distinguished of those heroines was Mrs. Middleham, the lady to whom Edward recommended himself by his humane interference; and who to great family opulence added the dignity of a fine person, and all the graces of a European education. The coldness, not to say aversion, which she felt towards the British officers in general, was softened with regard to him; and her gratitude, for his civility, procured him more attention from the American ladies than was paid to any other officer in the garrison./

CHAP. XLIII.

THE repose in which the army was suffered to remain in Charlestown during the winter, and which the British fondly supposed was likely to continue, was soon interrupted in the following year, when Green succeeded Gates in the command of the continental troops. That spirit which they supposed was entirely quenched, was now rekindling in its ashes; and the execution of Colonel Haynes, attended with circumstances peculiarly affecting, and which does not appear to have been justified by the proceedings of the court which tried him, raised these sparks into a flame, and reanimated every breast with fury and indignation. The corps in which Captain Rivers and Ned served were now sent upon duty, and the hour was approaching, which they had both long earnestly desired,/ of sharing the dangers and the glories of their countrymen.

The first service they were sent on, was to surprise an American out-post at a few miles distance from the main army. This unhappy party had been severely harassed, the day before, by a long march, without provisions, and with but very scanty clothing; and now hungry and fatigued were laid down to get a little sleep. It was the dead of night; and though they had taken every precaution to prevent surprise, yet their videttes[21] were taken unawares, and put to death by the bayonet without being able to give the alarm. The British party went undiscovered to the camp, where all was silence and repose: the slaughter was dreadful, for most were murdered in their sleep; a poor youth about sixteen clung round the knees of Ned, and implored for mercy. No voice ever sued to him for that in vain; but whilst he was yet on his knee, and Edward was raising him by the hand, Nettlefield, who was by, cried out,/ 'Damn you! will you spare a rebel?' and instantly plunged his pike into his heart. Hardly a soul escaped, whilst on the British side not a single man was either killed or wounded. This was called a glorious action, and they received the thanks of the commander for their spirit and alacrity. I pass over several engagements in which both our young gentlemen displayed the highest courage and address, because the relation of these dreadful scenes can only be pleasing to a military ear: but I must observe, that in all these engagements, though the victory was commonly claimed by the British, yet the real advantage lay wholly on the side

– 217 –

218 *The History of Ned Evans*

of the Americans, who rapidly recovered, one after another, those places which they had lost the preceding year. At last, on the eighth of September, they were attacked by General Green in person at the head of the whole American force destined for the support of South Carolina.[22] The engagement began about four o'clock in the morning. The/ charge was brisk on the side of the Americans: and as they had outnumbered the British, who were only advanced parties, they were obliged to fall back, till the main body of the army came to their support. The action now became general, and great execution was done on both sides. Two men made an attempt to wrest the colours from Ned's hands, but they paid for their temerity by their lives. Victory seemed to decide in favour of the English, and the Americans were giving way, when a reinforcement of Maryland and Virginia Continentals coming opportunely to their aid, restored the fortune of the day. The British were then routed in all quarters, and a corps of cavalry, commanded by a relation of General Washington, charged them so briskly as allowed them no time to rally or form. Rivers did all he could to call back his flying men, and induce them again to face the foe. Whilst he loudly called them to return, and bravely shewed them the example, he received a/ bullet in his breast, which brought him to the ground. The enemy's horse were driving on full speed; but no love of life, nor any fear of death, could prevail on Evans to desert his friend. He took him on his back, and carried him through the hottest of the fire, till he himself received a shot upon his hip, which brought him also down, and entirely disabled him from moving a step farther. The enemy, regardless of them, continued the pursuit; and it is wonderful they were not trampled to death: but Heaven spared Ned just to manifest his zeal for his friend, and to receive his last breath. The noble and the generous Rivers, exhausted by the loss of blood, but still sensible to the last, just squeezed him by the hand, and, whilst endeavouring to thank him for his care, expired in his arms. When the soul was fled, and those eyes were closed for ever; when the voice was lost which he should hear no more, and which he had never heard but with emotions of pleasure, it is/ impossible to express the agony of grief with which the heart of Edward was oppressed. He contemplated the body as it lay over his lap with mute sorrow, till at last a flood of tears relieved the throbbings of his bosom – 'Oh Rivers, my beloved friend! would to God I had died with thee!' The situation indeed in which poor Edward lay made it highly probable that this would very speedily be the event. The enemy were now off the field in pursuit of the flying British, and very possibly might not return to it again. Numbers of bodies lay around him, in some of whom were still some quivering signs of life, but not any that appeared capable of the least sensation. His own wound was not in itself mortal, nor even dangerous had help been at hand; but then it was such as deprived him of all power of motion on his feet. The night was coming down apace, and solitude and silence replaced the din of arms, and the shouts which accompanied the dreadful business of the day before./ The body of his friend lay still beside him, and with his clay-cold hand still locked in his he determined to await that fate which he supposed inevitable: but even in this situation he was not without comfort. He believed himself to be still in the sight of his Creator: and, relying upon his mercy whenever he should think fit to call him, he prepared with resignation to follow his dear friend, and determined that their bodies should be found together. An affecting remembrance of his dear relatives in Wales, and of the idol of his heart in Ravensdale, did indeed rise in his mind, but it was only to recommend them to Heaven; and his principal thoughts were entirely occupied on that almighty and eternal Being before whom he expected shortly to stand. Several hours had he passed in these melancholy contemplations, still lying by the body of his friend. No sound interrupted the silence of the night, which was remarkably still, unless sometimes that he thought an expiring groan, faintly uttered,/ issued from some of the bodies with which the field was strewed. At length his listening ear thought it heard the sound of steps; and shortly after the figure of a man seemed to approach, and busily to examine the bodies as they lay. It was of little moment to poor Ned whether he was friend or foe, but nature compelled him to ask for assistance. What transport rose in his bosom, what gratitude to the Almighty, when he found himself supported by David Morgan! That brave and faithful fellow, when the pursuit was at an end, and that his master and Captain Rivers were missing, determined at all hazards to return to the field of battle, for the mere chance of finding them alive; and Providence directed his steps to the spot where Evans was still lying, and at an hour when the darkness would enable them to pass undiscovered from the fatal scene of action. The transport of David Morgan was not less than that of Evans; and their first business was to return thanks to God for this singular instance/ of mercy. Poor Ned embraced the body of his dear friend for the last time, embalming it with the precious tears of genuine friendship; and faithful Morgan taking him on his back, moved on at a venture towards the thickest woods, hoping to be concealed until Ned should recover strength to endeavour to join some party of their scattered forces.

In America thick woods are never very distant, and to these our unfortunate friends had made their way long before the morning dawn could discover to the enemy the dreadful execution of the day before. The return of light served them indeed for little purpose, but to shew them more clearly the dangers and calamities to which they were exposed. The anguish of Ned's wound, which struck just upon his hip-bone, made it impossible for him to move a step, or even to support himself on his feet. No article of food was within their reach, nor even a drop of water to cool that intolerable thirst which the heat of the climate, added to/ pain and fatigue created. Morgan indeed had a musket; but to fire it was not advisable, lest the report should discover the place of their

220 *The History of Ned Evans*

retreat. This faithful fellow, who, being unhurt, could easily provide for his own safety, scorned the selfish idea, and swore to live and die with his beloved master. Indeed, had he had less generosity, Ned must have perished, for he was at this time almost as unable to assist himself as the day on which he was born. Morgan raised him again upon his shoulders, and carried him further into the depths of the forest; he there laid him at the foot of a tree, whilst he went to discover if possible some spring of water. Whilst Edward still lay reflecting more on the dear friend he had lost than on the misery of his own situation, his attention was roused to an object of a very extraordinary nature within a few yards of the spot on which he was lying. A large grey squirrel, not much less than an ordinary rabbit, was running up and down a tree which was/ opposite to him, seemingly in great distress. It appeared as if it endeavoured to get away from some object to which it was continually drawn back by some irresistible attraction. Sometimes it would endeavour to climb up the tree – but before it had got a yard, its hind legs seemed to fail it, when it would utter a feeble cry, and then come down again. Sometimes it would endeavour to escape along an horizontal branch; but its efforts here were equally ineffectual, attended with the same feebleness, and the same unwilling return. Every time it came back it descended lower and lower, whilst its agonies and terrors seemed greater and greater. So extraordinary a circumstance seemed to Ned wholly unaccountable, till at last he discovered among the thicket at the bottom of the tree, the head of an enormous rattle-snake, whose vivid eyes were fixed constantly and invariably on the poor creature destined to be its prey. Its huge mouth stood gaping wide open, which at last received the unfortunate animal./ The monster swallowed it whole, yet not without difficulty, for its gullet stood distended to a considerable size larger than the rest of its body.

By what means these dreadful creatures are enabled to fascinate the smaller animals destined by nature for their prey, is I believe as yet unknown, but the fact is incontestable: the same power extends to birds within a certain distance, and seems to be placed in the eye; for if any noise or other accident disturbs the snake, the creature feels instantly relieved, and makes its escape.

Whilst Ned was contemplating this singular phænomenon, and perhaps moralizing on the melancholy truth, that no part of the animal creation is exempt from misery, David returned with the welcome news that he had discovered a spring, and brought some water in his cap, which, though perhaps not the most inviting of vessels at any other time, was yet at this most acceptable, for it was now near thirty hours since the poor wounded youth had/ tasted liquid. He had been fortunate enough too to fall in with some wild grapes, which at this season happened to be in their most eatable state; and though they are but a harsh and austere fruit, yet were they cooling and refreshing. This mouthful of food, scanty as it was, was sufficient to revive the sinking spirits of poor Edward: it renewed his confidence in that Power who was able to spread a table for him in the wilderness; who had sent to his relief the person in the world who at that time was most able to afford it; and who fed him by a miracle little less striking than if the materials of his support had been brought to him by the ravens.[23]

CHAP. XLIV.

EDWARD had no sooner related the adventure of the rattle-snake and the squirrel, than David went to search for that/ formidable reptile, whom he found basking among the underwood[24] at the bottom of the great tree where he had devoured his prey. His voraciousness indeed proved his ruin; for, as but a few minutes had elapsed since he had swallowed the squirrel, it had not yet reached his stomach: so that the size of it in his gullet incommoded him, and prevented his being able to make his escape, and David cut his head off with one stroke of his sword. All danger from the poison of the animal (the most subtle perhaps with which any animal is endued) was by this means removed, and the poor squirrel became David's prize; and at this time not a bad one; for a squirrel is just as good eating as a rabbit, and it was not a bit the worse for being swallowed by the snake, who might himself be eaten with all possible safety, the poison fangs being first removed: but of this at the present time they made no advantage.

Morgan, however, stripped the squirrel of his skin, and gutted him; and having kindled/ a fire with a little gunpowder and some wadding, he could be at no loss for fuel in the midst of the forests of America; so that in a short time he made a funeral pile for him, on which when he was pretty well broiled, Edward and he did him the honour to convert him into a part of themselves, much to their comfort and refreshment; and there being no want of squirrels in the American forests, this was a feast they might hope to renew at pleasure, provided they could catch them without firing their guns, which nothing but absolute necessity should in their present circumstances compel them to do.

When they had finished their repast, Morgan proposed to Edward once more to reascend his back, that he might carry him to the spring which he had discovered, where he hoped to be able to make some kind of accommodation for him, until he should be able to move a little again upon his own legs; and indeed this indefatigable friend, whose ingenuity was not less than/ his attachment, did immediately lay about him with his sword among the shrubs and underwood, with the twigs of which he very soon formed a sort of cradle, of size and strength sufficient to bear Edward at full length. This he half filled with moss, a singular production which hangs in long wreaths from the branches of the old and full-grown trees in America, and which being of a grey colour gives them an appearance of amazing dignity and age. This moss is soft, light and elastic; and, stretched upon it, our poor Edward enjoyed more ease and repose than, at the time he received his wound, there was any probability he would ever do again.

When David had finished his cradle and put the moss in it, as before related, he suspended it by the roots of some trailing plants twisted together, from the branches of a thick oak which grew near the spring, and raised it about four feet from the ground; so that there Ned might swing at ease, and be removed from the apprehension/ of snakes or any other venomous reptile approaching to annoy him. He then lifted his beloved master into it, who found unspeakable comfort in the situation; and Morgan perched himself among some of the neighbouring branches, where he watched the cradle and its suffering inhabitant with as much care and anxiety as the stock-dove[25] does her nest.

Three weeks had nearly elapsed, during which they had met with no interruption, and the pain and swelling of Edward's wound had so far abated, that he was able to get out of his hammock and walk a little about for refreshment. But the care of providing for support still rested solely upon Morgan, who had invented many traps and gins,[26] in which he seldom failed to ensnare some or other of the wild inhabitants of the desert, so as to banish all fear of perishing by famine. It was one day when he was absent on this necessary employment, and that poor Edward, reclined upon a bank, was ruminating on the memory of his dear/ friend Rivers, and on all the tender ideas associated with that name, that he was suddenly alarmed with the report of a musquet very near him, the ball from which went through his hat, and lodged in the tree just at his back. He had scarce time to start up, when he was still more alarmed by the hideous yells of the war-whoop, and saw before him a party of Indians advancing with tomahawks and scalping-knives, and with all those ferocious menaces which with these savages are the preludes to destruction. He saw at once that he was lost.

Utterly unable either to resist or to fly, he remained fixed in his attitude, determined to meet whatever death they might put him to, with the firmness of a man, and with the resignation of a Christian. The Indians have a respect for courage; and perceiving that Ned was young, and no wise deficient in this admired quality, they changed their first intention of scalping him, and determined to carry him with them as a prisoner. These Indians were/ of the Agigua tribe, a branch of the Cherokees,[27] and were settled along the banks of a river from which they derived their name. In the beginning of the American contest, they were unfortunately induced, by the mistaken policy of the British agents, to take up arms with the expectation of assisting them; but it being a matter of entire indifference to them which party prevailed, they determined to study no interest but their own, and plundered and put to death both parties whenever they had an opportunity of doing it with impunity. No object could be more defenceless

224 *The History of Ned Evans*

than the unfortunate youth who stood before them: wounded, and alone, his situation would have excited compassion in any breast capable of entertaining that godlike sentiment; but compassion is not numbered among the list of Indian virtues, and he who sought it, or he who bestowed it, would be alike despised. Ned was not unacquainted with this part of their character and therefore determined, let them do/ what they would, to suffer without flinching. They began with stripping him to the skin, and dividing his raiment among them. A piece of an old blanket which one of them had about his loins, he generously exchanged with Edward for his breeches; but he had not gone far in his new acquisition, till he found them an incumbrance, and threw them away with all they contained, without however demanding his blanket again. As Ned conceived himself just going to be murdered, the loss of his clothing gave him no uneasiness; he was anxious only to preserve, as long as he should live, the locket with Lady Cecilia's hair, which hung about his neck: and this indeed was the only thing they left him; for they considered this to be his Manitow or Toutam, that is, his tutelar deity; and the piety of an Indian, however he may torment you himself, never wishes you to forfeit the favour or protection of your God. The whole party who had thus got our poor youth into their power were about/ twelve, and they had with them two other white prisoners, one of whom was known to Edward, being indeed a soldier in Nettlefield's regiment, and the very man whom his father had compelled to quit his fields for the army, and whose mother Ned had relieved in his way to Ravensdale. This meeting was affecting, for poor Doran did not want for gratitude: but now their common misfortunes had thrown down all distinctions; and their inhuman masters tied them all together, loading them with whatever plunder they had to carry, and driving them, naked as they were, before them.[28]

Doran had been near a fortnight in their hands, being taken after another skirmish subsequent to that in which Edward was wounded; and the other man was an American, one of the Carolina militia, whom they had picked up as he was endeavouring to return home to the back country. But it was all one to the Indians in what service they were engaged; scalps and plunder were all they wanted, and those two poor/ creatures were preserved only to load their backs with what they obtained, and in the end perhaps to be rewarded with more refined tortures.

To these unhappy victims poor Ned was now added; and as he was driven bound from the old tree, which for three weeks had been his shelter, he could not help reflecting on the endless gradation of human woe. How soon a calamity, which we now think the deepest that can befal us, may be exchanged for another, in comparison of which the first which we so lamented may seem like heaven! Certainly the old tree, with its suspended hurdles, and the affectionate attention of David Morgan, miserable and forlorn as it first appeared, was paradise

Volume III 225

in comparison of the toil and affliction he was now to suffer; and in the midst of all his own sorrows, he could not help lamenting the agony which he knew his poor friend would undergo, when he should return and find him irretrievably lost. But notwithstanding the depth of wretchedness/ to which Edward was now reduced, his soul, supported by religion, rose superior to it. The world he considered as lost to him for ever; but he did not on that account think himself entitled to quit it before his time. He supposed, indeed, that if he lived to get to the country of the Indians, he should then be sacrificed, as was their custom, by lingering and cruel tortures; but still he conceived it to be the appointment of his Maker, and that he had no right to desert his post by a voluntary death, or to elude whatever dispensation the Almighty might think fit to lay him under. Firmly depending upon the ultimate mercy of his Creator, he fortified his mind with that confidence, till the vigour of his soul actually braced that of his body up to its own tone. The anguish of his hip was now become to him a trifling consideration, and really diminished the more he used exercise, till at length it went totally away. Whenever any soft idea stole upon his mind, he endeavoured to banish it directly,/ and turned his thoughts to those sufferings he was to undergo, and which he determined to endure with all the firmness of an Indian. A foretaste of what he was to expect he saw the second day of his journey; for the poor Carolinian, not having the strength of mind even of Doran, and far less of Edward, began to bemoan himself with many tears; nor could all that either of the companions of his misery could say to him prevent his sinking down and giving vent to his sorrow. The Indians beheld him with ineffable contempt; and one of them coming up as he sat on the ground, said in his own language, that he had the soul of a Stinkbingsem (a timid animal, whose only defence is its nauseous smell), and not a man, and instantly split his skull with his tomahawk. He scalped him on the spot, and held the bloody flesh in his teeth till he untied the fetters by which he was fastened to poor Ned and Doran, and then they were driven on as before./

CHAP. XLV.

A MURDER so sudden and so atrocious could not fail to fill Edward and his unfortunate fellow sufferer with the utmost horror, and with no ill-founded apprehensions that one of themselves would go next; and Ned at this time happening to stumble, he fell under the load that was heaped upon him, and was unable to help himself by reason of the fetters with which his hand was fastened to John Doran's. The young savage, who had just killed the unfortunate Carolinian, came up to him immediately, with his bloody scalping-knife drawn in his hand. Poor Edward supposed his last moment was arrived, and meekly laid his head to receive the blow: but the Indian cut the cords by which he was tied, and helped him to rise; he even eased him of part of the burthen which he carried, and/ took it on himself, at the same time offering him his pipe which he had in his mouth to smoke. A kindness so unexpected astonished Ned, and made him believe that the heart of this savage was still formed in a human mould. His face, though wild, was expressive of good-nature: he took therefore his pipe, which he knew to be an emblem of peace among Indians, and, after smoking a whiff or two, returned it, offering him at the same time his right hand, which the Indian accepted, and from this time attached himself to Edward as his friend.

This young warrior, whose name was Awattahowee, that is, the deer killer, was induced to shew kindness to Ned, not from any sentiments of compassion, but from his observation of the firmness with which he bore his misfortune.

Every night when they encamped (if we may give that term to a halt where they had no covering but the heavens and the trees, which indeed spread wide their/ branches covered with the thickest foliage), our unfortunate prisoners Edward and Doran were relieved from the burthens which they carried, only to suffer greater hardships: their hands were tied together with cords made of vine-twigs twisted together, and drawn so tight as to force the blood out of their fingers ends; with these cords they were fastened round a great tree, against which they could lean, but could not lie down. The Indians then kindled a fire, on which they dressed whatever animal provisions they had, such as pole-cats, or racoons; and when they had finished, they condescended to give what remained to their unhappy prisoners, sometimes untying their hands, and sometimes not;

but always watching them with the most jealous eye. If they happened to have no animal food with them, then the Etussu Zargetoon, that is, the beloved waiter, a kind of commissary who attends every expedition; deals out to every man an equal quantity of parched corn, always very sparingly;/ which corn is consecrated, and the blessing of the Supreme Being solemnly invoked upon it before they set out, and committed to the trust of this officer, who distributes it in exact proportion to the whole party, prisoners and all, because they suppose it to be the property of the Almighty, who deals his blessings impartially to all; and therefore no distress could tempt an Indian to steal a particle of it, nor to withhold the share which the Divine Being wills to be given to all his creatures. In the present instance, indeed, they had no necessity to recur to this holy deposit; for they were not in a country of hostile Indians, but on the borders of the back settlements of the Whites, whom they spared not to plunder, and whose plantations abounded with all the essential necessaries of life. A memorable instance of this plundering disposition happened on this night. They were now amongst the remotest of the white settlements on the confines of the great wilderness, through/ which they had a distance of near 500 miles to march before they reached their own nation. As soon as the sun was down, therefore, the warriors held a council round the fire, at which it was determined that four of the party should set out at midnight, and proceed till they should fall in with some plantation, which they were to pillage and destroy, bringing away as much as they could that was eatable. Nothing can exceed the caution with which the Indians attack an enemy; for the glory of their warfare is to do the greatest possible mischief with the least loss. It is all therefore carried on by stratagem and surprise, not without a considerable degree of superstition. As soon as the moon was down, and darkness covered the face of nature, the four warriors, of whom Awattahowee was one, received from the etussu a consecrated drink, made of certain roots and herbs infused for three days and nights in water. This is to induce the Deity to guard and prosper them; and on no account whatever are/ they to drink again, until the object of the expedition is either attained or lost. He likewise gives at the same time to the leader of the expedition a certain quantity of the holy parched corn, according to the number of the warriors, and the days which they intend to be absent. This he puts into a deer-skin bag, or any other convenient carriage, never however omitting to rub it three times against the holy war-chest, which contains the consecrated corn; and by this operation it is also rendered holy. If any person was to presume to touch these sacred repositories with a design to plunder them, they believe that Ishtooboolo, or the great master of life, that is the Supreme Being, would plague him with all his curses, and that the offending hand would rot off. Having received these necessaries for their expedition, the warriors departed, the leader singing the first stave of the solemn war song, which is taken up by the one immediately behind him, and so on, as long as they are in hearing/

228 *The History of Ned Evans*

of their friends; but as soon as they are out of that they are all silent, and never speak more except by preconcerted signals, lest they should give notice to their enemies of their approach. These signals consist in imitating the voices of all the creatures which inhabit the deserts, whether birds or beasts, and which all expert warriors are able to do with astonishing exactness, so as often to deceive even the creatures themselves. They follow one another in an exact line at the distance of three or four steps, and endeavour to tread exactly in each other's marks, that, if they should be tracked, the enemy may not be able to discover their number. In this way the four warriors proceeded all that night without lighting on a plantation; but at the dawn of day they saw, from the top of a hill, a dwelling at about two miles distance; and this they resolved to attack, but not till the following night. Having received, therefore, their allowance of consecrated corn, they lay down among some/ logs of fallen timber, pulling some branches over them, so that they were in no danger of being discovered.

Poor Edward and Doran in the mean time suffered by the absence of Awattahowee. They remained fast bound to the tree; the rest of the party sleeping around them, and sanctifying themselves with a most rigid fast to ensure success to the expedition. They therefore continued without any species of refreshment, and not without horror to think what cruelties would be perpetrated on poor defenceless unsuspecting people, nor how they themselves might be involved in them. All that night and all the next day they remained in that miserable situation, till nature was almost exhausted; but on the morning of the second day the signal of their return was heard, and soon after the party themselves appeared, driving before them an old man and a young one loaden[29] with the wrecks of their own goods: but one of their own number was missing; it/ was not however Awattahowee. Had the party returned in perfect safety, their arrival would have been announced with shouts and every gesture of joy, and singing the song of triumph. But one of their party being lost, they simply gave the signal of return, and then advanced as they went one after the other in profound silence. Their first care was to appease the ghost of the deceased warrior, which they did by singing a solemn dirge to his memory, and threatening the old man (who indeed had shot him from his window) with the most dreadful vengeance. Their next was to refresh themselves and their brethren, which was indeed now become highly necessary to all; and on this occasion Awattahowee had the goodness to release both Edward and Doran from the tree, but not from each other, lest they should attempt their escape. The two unfortunate prisoners they had brought with them were tied up in their room. Nevertheless they gave them share of the repast/ which they prepared, and which they were well entitled to, since it was formed from their own provisions. This short-lived kindness was, however, but the prelude to the greatest barbarity, on which indeed they knew too well how to refine.

The old man's name was Joseph Atkins; and, at the time when these blood-hounds assaulted his house, his family consisted of his wife, two daughters (one of them a married woman with an infant at her breast), and his son a youth about sixteen. Two other sons, and the husband of his daughter, were absent on service, fighting the battles of their country. It was the dead of night when this unhappy family (long before retired to their repose) were awoke out of their sleep by the dismal sound of the war-whoop, which is always the signal of attack with the savages. The unfortunate old man knowing their merciless disposition, and perceiving that there were but four of them, was in hopes that he might be able to repel them before they/ should break open the door. He fired therefore from the window two or three shot, by which one of the Indians fell. This only exasperated the others, and roused their anger into tenfold rage. The door was at length broke open: and here I hope my readers will excuse my entering into the particulars of those atrocious barbarities, in the commission of which the miserable women, with the innocent infant, lost their lives in presence of the wretched father, who, with his son fast bound, were made to be spectators of the scene. Having scalped these victims of their fury (a ceremony which they never neglect to perform) they proceeded to rifle the house of whatever drink or provisions they could get; and having found a little horse in the stable, they loaded him, and their prisoners, and themselves, with all that they could carry, and set fire to the rest, dancing round the miserable owner, who envied the lot of those lost objects of his affection, who were insensible of those flames/ in which they were consumed. Their next care was for the Indian that was killed: him they interred with all his war ornaments about him; and doubtless they would then have sacrificed the old man to his manes,[30] but that they reserved him for a more public spectacle. Those captives who are far advanced in life are certain to alone for the blood they have shed, by the tortures of fire. The younger prisoners are generally offered to families who have lost relations, to be adopted in their room: and if they are fortunate enough to be accepted, they succeed to the rights and even to the affections of the deceased: but old age meets no compassion; and it is not uncommon for parents, when very decrepid, to be knocked on the head by their own children, and that at their own desire. When their feast was ended, and they had regaled themselves with some of the liquor which they had taken from poor Atkins's habitation, they rose up to divert themselves with the barbarous amusement/ of torturing the old man. They began by stripping him naked, and painting him all over with various colours, which they always carry about them for their own use. Then they would pluck the white hairs from his venerable head, and tauntingly tell him that he was a fool for living so long, and that they would shew him kindness in putting him out of the world. Afterwards they would hold lighted torches of pitch pine so near his skin as to raise it in blis-ters, and then let the burning pitch drop upon it. When he was so wearied with

230 *The History of Ned Evans*

these tortures as to be in danger of fainting, they would pour cold water on him to revive him, and give him food and some of his own liquors to enable him to undergo them again. His unhappy son was all the time spectator of his agonies, bound to a neighbouring tree, whilst all the anxiety of the suffering father was directed to him, to prevent his betraying any weakness, lest that might provoke his merciless tormentors to treat him in the/ same way. Poor Edward and Doran were obliged also to behold the sad tragedy in silence, and to suppress those emotions either of pity or resentment which alternately rose in their breasts.

CHAP. XLVI.

THE Indians having, by this barbarous massacre and robbery, obtained a sufficiency of provisions to last them the remainder of their journey; and having now no enemy between them and home, set forward on their return with the utmost spirits and alacrity. However cruel and irreconcileable they are to their enemies, they do yet possess many great virtues, among which truth and hospitality are not the least. An Indian will never deceive you, unless he has been himself first deceived: and indeed,/ excepting in the instance of cruelty to enemies, and the insatiable desire of revenge, whatever other vices now deform their character are chiefly owing to the corruptions introduced among them by their intercourse with the Whites, and by no means to their natural disposition, which is open, generous, friendly, and sincere. Poor Edward derived much advantage from this temper in Awattahowee, who having once conceived and expressed a friendship for him, was incapable of being moved from it, unless by some unworthiness on Edward's part – a defect which we need not apprehend. The age of this young Indian was much the same as Edward's; and, bating that ferocity in war which the prejudices of their education make them esteem a virtue, he had a heart no ways unworthy even of a Christian bosom. From his first observation of Edward's firmness he had conceived a good opinion of him, and thought he would not be unworthy of becoming an Indian/ warrior – a character which, in his estimation, was the highest to which human nature could attain. To exalt Edward into this, if possible, was the intention of Awattahowee, and even to ingraft him into his own family. He had a sister, one year older than himself, who in her native town was generally esteemed a beauty, and who had been married to a young warrior of a very distinguished family: but he, like Adonis of old, had unfortunately lost his life in hunting a few months before, and left his widow big with her first child. The wish of Awattahowee was, that Edward might be pleasing in her sight, and that she would adopt him in the room of her beloved lord Onondoga, in which case he would succeed to all his rights, and even to his name. And indeed, considering Edward's figure, and the alternative on his part of being burned to death, if no head of a family should adopt him, there were good hopes of his not being disappointed./

– 231 –

232 *The History of Ned Evans*

With these friendly dispositions therefore towards Edward, and with the outward testimonies of them which he shewed him, often easing him of his burthen, and sharing with him his beloved brandy, it would have been unnatural, as well as ungenerous, if no return of sympathy could be excited in his breast, notwithstanding his abhorrence of shedding innocent blood, with which he knew Awattahowee was deeply stained. But the guilt of an action depends upon the knowledge and intentions of him who commits it: and when we consider Awattahowee's education and national prejudices, notwithstanding what we have seen, we cannot pronounce him unworthy of Edward's gratitude. Be that as it may, he certainly obtained it; and Ned now felt comfort from that very presence which but a few days before chilled him with horror. Poor Doran too, and the young American, partook of Indian bounty; but the venerable head that stood most in need of it was the only one to/ whom it was denied. He had killed an Indian, and was besides guilty of the unpardonable crime of being old. He was therefore devoted to vengeance: and if they did not torture him to death upon the spot, it was only that they might feast the eyes of their nation with his sacrifice when they got home. Seventeen days did they march through the wilderness, before the lake of Agigua made its appearance; on the borders of which, and of the river which runs from it, the towns of their tribe are situated. This joyful prospect was soon announced with singing and dancing, not forgetting a double portion of brandy, and some new indignity to the unhappy Joseph Atkins.

On the eastern point of this lake stands a very high rock, projecting from the surrounding cliffs with majestic grandeur, whose summit was crowned with a forest of aged evergreens, which at no season of the year lost their verdure. At the base were a number of romantic caverns dark and/ gloomy, the unmolested retreat of various species of aquatic fowls, as well as of amphibious monsters which frequent the lakes of America. To this rock the Indians had, from immemorial tradition, annexed some idea of sanctity. They called it Ashemic Manitoo, that is, the dwelling of the Spirit. The air passing through the caverns they supposed to be the breathings of the spirits who inhabited them, and the most courageous Indian would not dare to approach them without awe, nor on any account to pass into them beyond the precincts of clear day-light. As they approached this rock they all bent their bodies to the ground, and threw into the lake various articles they had about them, particularly some of the consecrated corn, as an acknowledgement to the Deity for having supported them with food while away, and now brought them back again in safety to their own country. When they approached the village, instead of hastening to see their friends or relatives,/ or being impatient to tell the story of their adventures, they followed their leader, one by one, the prisoners being in the centre, and all maintaining a profound silence. They do not enter the village on the day they approach it, but encamp near it all night in a place marked out for the purpose. In the centre of this place is fixed a high war-pole, painted black and red, to which the prisoners are secured. Poor Joseph Atkins, who had not been able to walk for some days, was tied upon his horse, and both fastened to the pole. Ned, with his other fellow-sufferer, shared the same fate; but they were all refreshed with as much Indian corn pounded and stewed with bear's grease as they could eat, which they call sagamity; and Ned, through the favour of his friend Awattahowee, got some rum mixed with his water to wash it down.

On the following day they were all conducted in the same regular and silent order into the town, and the prisoners were secured/ in the head warrior's war-house, till it was determined by the council what should be done with them. This war-house is nothing but an oblong room, secured however strongly enough; it stands by itself, and is lighted from the top. There are loop-holes also all round it, through which muskets may be fired, or arrows shot. It is entered by a low door, not above a yard high, and in the centre is a war-pole fixed, to which the prisoners are tied. The wall on the inside is painted red, with black streaks, and sometimes with coarse representations of some of the warrior's exploits. The scalps that he has either taken or inherited, are also hung round or fastened to his war-pole, and these are the most valuable articles of furniture any Indian can possess; they are cured into a consistence like glove-leather, with the hair on, and are stretched on a small hoop, and the bare side painted red, and sometimes adorned with shells or beads.

Such was the room into which our unfortunate/ prisoners were conducted, and from which few ever remove but to torture.

The coolness of Indians does not allow them to determine any thing in a hurry, and therefore these unhappy sufferers remained ignorant of their lot all that day and the following night. Edward employed this time in fortifying his own mind, and endeavouring to strengthen those of the companions of his misfortune, to sustain with firmness whatever trials were prepared for them. He represented to them various instances of the most glorious fortitude related in profane authors; of heroes who despised death, although not supported by any certain hopes of any thing beyond it; but, above all, the noble army of martyrs furnished him with the most copious as well as most brilliant examples of patient virtue, bearing and surmounting, nay willingly and gladly undergoing whatever the most barbarous inventions of cruel tyrants could inflict, whose names on that account were/ handed down to posterity full of honour, and whose sufferings of a moment were now rewarded with an eternal weight of glory. By such discourses the sullen hours of this night of darkness and of doubt were cheered. The terrors of his companions were appeased; and Joseph Atkins in particular resigned to death, which indeed could alone stop the issues of his grief, and put an end to sorrows which nothing in time could ever heal.

234 *The History of Ned Evans*

In the morning the sound of the war-song announced the approach of the Indians, and all the prisoners were led forth in Indian file, that is, one after the other, to the great square in the middle of the town. Here every inhabitant, male and female, young and old, was assembled. In the centre of this square was erected a black pole, from the top of which was suspended a burning firebrand; and three other poles painted red, were placed at some distance from it. Poor Ned, with Doran, and the young American, were stripped as naked as/ they were born, and bound to their respective poles. The venerable Atkins was next fast pinioned, and a strong rope of twisted vine-twigs being tied to the top of the black pole, the other end was fastened round his neck, not so as to hurt him, but to secure him, and so long as to allow him a space of some yards to course round the pole. A pair of moccassins, or Indian shoes, made of the skin of a black bear, with the hairy side outwards, was put on his feet, and this is the death warrant. The chiefs then retire to the circle, and the punishment is left to the women and children. – Oh Nature! how were thy sacred laws then outraged! Surely the dæmons from hell must have usurped thy power, and torn from thy tenderest works the hearts which thou hadst given them, to make them residences for themselves. Each of these furies, armed with a brand of flaming pitch-pine, attacked the naked and the feeble Atkins, whilst the young fiends shot arrows at him, tipped with flints, to which burning bits of lightwood/[31] were fastened, and which stuck in every part of his body. One of them scooped his eye out with a scalping-knife, and instantly placed a burning cinder in its room, whilst another offered him brandy to revive him. Not a soul of whatever age or sex shewed the least pity to his sufferings; the women sung with frantic joy, and shouts of laughter echoed through the surrounding circle of the men. At last his white head bowed to the ground, and a merciful stroke of a tomahawk put an end to his tortures. The unfortunate son, who witnessed these afflictions, might learn indeed from his venerable father how to bear them, but could not have the comfort even of one parting word. Fast bound himself to the stake, he expected his own turn would be next, or that of Edward or of Doran, who, alike prepared for the event, longed only for the moment that should place them beyond the fear of what man could do unto them.

But now the Indians, satisfied for the/ present with blood, raised up the body from the ground, and, fastening it in an erect posture to the pole, surrounded it with dry canes and pitch-pine, and set the whole on fire, whilst they danced round it rejoicing and singing the war-song.

When the whole was consumed, an elderly matron, who had borne no part in the tragedy but as a spectator, advanced towards Ned, and stood for a few minutes just before him. She repeated some words which he could not understand, but supposed to be the prelude to his death; for, immediately when they were finished, she clasped her arms about his neck, round which she fastened a

Volume III 235

large belt of wampum. His friend Awattahowee, whom he had not seen since his imprisonment in the war-house, now immediately sprang forward and cut asunder the bands by which he was fastened to the war-pole. Naked as he was born, the old lady did not seem at all disconcerted at his appearance, but took him by the hand, and frequently repeated the/ words Ashemic Janis, that is, Home my son, whilst Awattahowee endeavoured to make him understand that he had found a mother.

Poor Ned did indeed perceive that he was rescued from immediate death, but was at a loss to know in what relation he stood towards the female who had conferred on him this favour, or by what duties she expected him to shew his gratitude.

CHAP. XLVII.

Poor Edward, clad only in the suit which Nature gave him on his birth-day, walked off in naked majesty between Awattahowee and the old lady, accompanied however with the songs and acclamations of the surrounding multitude; and turning about to view what became of his companions, he had the satisfaction to see they also/ had found deliverers, and that the spectacle of misery was at an end. Weenacoba (or the Turkey Hen), the name of his kind protectress, led him directly to her wigwawm, a habitation far from being uncomfortable. Her first care was to anoint his whole body with bear's-grease; an operation which, though entirely new to him, and perhaps not the most agreeable, he yet soon found to be highly beneficial, as it effectually protected his skin from the bites of musquitoes and other insects, and also from the heat of the sun. She next threw over his shoulders a grand war-belt, from which was suspended the spotted skin of a panther, dressed in a manner that rendered it as soft as velvet, and which relieved his modesty from any of those awkward sensations from which the more liberal manners of the lady seemed to be entirely exempted. She then powdered his hair with vermilion, and, setting herself down on a kind of sofa, cut (not without art) out of a solid block of timber, she contemplated his figure with the utmost/ satisfaction. Lastly, fastening on his feet a pair of moccassins, which are so contrived as to adjust themselves to almost any measure, he was completely dressed.

Having thus liberally provided for his outside, she rightly judged that he stood in need of some internal comfort, and immediately set about preparing it. Awattahowee, who was present all the while, pointed to another seat, on which Ned sat down; and then shaking him by the hand, he left the wigwawm.

It is natural to suppose that the being relieved from the instant expectation of a cruel death must have raised Ned's spirits in a considerable degree; yet the awkwardness of his situation, not being able to understand a word that was said to him, nor to guess at what was intended to be done with him, held him in disagreeable suspense; though he could not help perceiving that in his present residence he had nothing to expect but kindness, seeing the old lady was busily employed in cooking him/ some Indian broth, and only interrupted her work to cast on him every now and then looks of complacency and affection. But he was soon relieved from this anxiety by the return of Awattahowee, who brought with him another young man, an Indian of the half breed, that is, the son of an Indian woman by an English trader. This young man had often been at the White settlements with his father, and, during the time he lived with his mother, had picked up as much English as enabled him to be tolerably well understood. His name was Quanshebo, or the Pack-carrier, because he was sometimes so employed by his father. After the first salutation (which Ned was equally surprised and rejoiced to hear uttered in English), he informed him that the woman who had adopted him was the widow of Ostaboa, a sachem of the first distinction in the nation, and the mother of Onondoga, who had married the sister of Awattahowee, and who was unhappily killed by a bear as he was hunting. That Awattahowee/ had done every thing he could to make his sister Sheerasta, or the White Lily, transplant him into her bosom in the room of her husband that she had lost; but she declared she had no room in her heart for any other warrior, and that she would breed up her son, who was then sucking her breast, to inherit the name and glory of his father. 'Awattahowee (said he) loves you ever since he smoked the pipe of peace with you; and when he found his sister was resolved never to receive another man, he determined to try his influence with Weenacoba to adopt you as her son, in the room of Onondoga. She said she would do it, if your behaviour at the war-pole was like that of a warrior; but if you shewed the heart of a cat, she would leave you to your fate. The event has proved how well she was pleased with you; and now, brother, she expects from you the duty and attentions of a son, and you will receive from her the tenderness and affection of a mother. In a few days she will adopt you before the holy and beloved/ men, and from that moment you will become a warrior of the illustrious Agigua nation.'

While Quanshebo was explaining his situation to Edward, the eyes of Weenacoba were often directed towards the youth, who, whatever might be his real sensations, certainly owed to her and to Awattahowee a considerable debt of gratitude. He thought himself happy that the exemplary fidelity of Sheerasta to the memory of Onondoga had exempted him from a trial which he dreaded more than death, and therefore willingly took Weenacoba's hand and raised it to his lips, as an expression of those grateful sentiments which he really felt for her. The venerable squaw returned his compliment with a warm embrace, which, though at another time he perhaps would have excused, yet in his present circumstances he might well consider as the most enlivening kiss he had ever received.

The broth being now ready, which consisted of the fat paw of a bear, stewed down/ with two young puppies, and some Indian corn, a clean matt was spread upon the floor, and the kettle placed in the middle; a bowl of a coarse earthenware, made by themselves, and a wooden spoon was given to each, and the hospitable Weenacoba divided the treat. Poor Edward, who had not tasted food

238 *The History of Ned Evans*

for four-and-twenty hours, and indeed who had not made a meal for six weeks but in peril of his life, now found a young puppy an excellent morsel, and that nothing more is necessary to make any dish palatable than health and a good appetite. When they had eaten to suffice, but not to burthen nature, their kind hostess presented them with other bowls filled with a liquor made by throwing warm water on the pounded kernels of hiccory-nuts, which being allowed to stand for a few days, ferments, and when it subsides becomes a kind of clear whey of a gentle subacid taste: the addition of a little of the sweet juice of the maple-tree, which abounds every where through the country, makes this a most/ wholesome, nourishing, and pleasant beverage, which may be drunk in any quantity without danger. The calumet[32] of peace concluded the entertainment; and though Ned was no smoker, yet he could not refuse to take a friendly whiff with those to whom he was indebted for his life, and who desired nothing more than to live with him on brotherly terms of love and concord.

When the hour of rest arrived, Weenacoba shewed him to a recess partitioned off from the wall of the house, and large enough for him to lie at full length with ease. On the ground were placed four logs about a foot high, which supported several slender poles, on which a large quantity of moss was laid, and over that the thick and shaggy skin of a bear; another skin of the same kind, thrown over him, served him for bed-clothes; and stretched upon this his weary limbs at last found secure repose, and his mind a temporary suspension of those sorrows and regrets which the expectation/ of immediate death had in some degree overpowered, but which, since the removal of that apprehension, had returned with redoubled force.

On this couch then we will leave him for the present to recruit his fatigues both of body and mind, whilst we enquire what became of the affectionate and faithful David Morgan.

We have before related, that David had gone into the woods to search the snares, in which he hoped to find some of the wild inhabitants of the desert entangled, on which they principally depended for subsistence; and that he had left Edward, who was beginning to be able to walk a little about, reposing on the bank at the bottom of the tree, from which his hurdled[33] cot was suspended. He had been absent some time, and was returning with high satisfaction, having been fortunate enough to catch a racoon and two squirrels, when he heard the shot which the Indians fired, and the ball from which so narrowly failed to put/ an end to all poor Edward's sufferings at once. No gun that he had ever before heard fired, though in the midst of battle, appalled him with half the terror of this report; he dropped the creatures he had taken in the spot where he was, and immediately sprang forward to assist his master, or to share his fate. When he came to the tree, and found all silent, and no Edward there, words cannot describe his agony of grief and consternation. The hurdle cradle he found rummaged and overturned; but not seeing any marks of blood, he hoped that Edward might be still alive. As he was musing in sorrow, the distant found of the war-whoop struck his ear; on which immediately he got up into the great tree, and ascended to its highest top, from whence he got a glimpse of the Indian party with their prisoners passing through the woods; and the dismal cry of the war-whoop sounding fainter and fainter on his ears, he discerned the full extent of Edward's misfortune. Had it been possible/ for any exertion of his to be of the smallest use to him, he would have flown to his assistance, although at the almost certain cost of his life: but he rightly reflected, that the most essential benefit he could now render him, would be to relate his situation to the regiment, if indeed he could by any means rejoin it, or happily fall in with any other party of the English forces. Coming down from the tree, therefore, he took a final leave of its friendly shade, not without tears when he reflected on his dear master, and the little probability there was that he should ever see him again; knowing well the barbarous hands into which he had fallen, and fully sensible to how many dangerous hazards his own life was exposed. To preserve that life, however, was the first dictate both of nature and duty; and as it was plain that parties of Indians were abroad, he determined for the present to go no further than to recover the provisions he had dropped, and to continue his journey only by night./

He found the racoon and the squirrels just where he had left them, and then mounted the thickest tree he could find, until the friendly shade of night should lend him her protecting mantle. In the mean time he flayed his racoon and the squirrels, and stretched the skins in the manner of scalps upon small hoops made from the boughs of the tree in which he was perched. The racoon's skin served him for a knapsack, in which he could stow his squirrels, or what other food he should be lucky enough to fall in with; and with this employment he beguiled the hours till the sun went down. As soon as it was dark, he descended from his aerial situation, and walked the whole night as nearly in one direction as he could. The myriads of fire-flies, which at this season of the year swarm through all the American forests, were like so many vivid sparks quickly glancing in all directions, and, by the gleams of light they diffused, served to cheer his way, and in a small degree to illumine it. No accident/ worthy of commemoration happened to him on this first night of his journey, nor yet on the next, which he performed in the same manner, after passing the day in a tree as before. But on the third night, about midnight, the noise he made rustling among the leaves alarmed a party of Indians, who were lying round a small fire, which he did not perceive; they suddenly started from the ground, and, seizing their fire-arms, ran into the woods. Poor David was fixed to the spot in terror and consternation, and one of the Indians passed very near him. At that instant a deer, which is always attracted by the light, approached the fire: the Indians perceived it, and shot it; when, supposing it was that which created their alarm, they very cheerfully returned to their station; and while they were all busily engaged with their prize, David with more cautious and silent tread pursued his course, till he had got to such a distance from them as put him out of the way of immediate danger./

CHAP. XLVIII.

As soon as the dawn arose, David perceived he was approaching the cleared country, and therefore ascended a high hill which he saw before him, in order to reconnoitre. At the distance (as he supposed) of about five or six miles, he descried some habitations of white men on the left, and a good way further off, others on the right: his wish was to avoid all these, if possible, supposing them to belong to the friends of the American cause. He continued however his route, although it was light, and endeavoured to steer his way between them. All day he kept in the deepest covert of the woods, notwithstanding the excessive difficulty of penetrating through them; but in the evening he adventured nearer the path. He had not been long there, when he met two little boys with satchels on their/ backs, and these he ventured to address. They told him they were the sons of one M'Farlane, a Scotch planter, and that their father was absent with the army; but that their mother was at home, whither they were returning from a little school which another Scotchman kept in the neighbourhood. The innocence of the children could not inform him in which army their father served; but finding that the woman only was at home, he determined to accompany the children, and trust to her humanity for some refreshment; which if she should be so barbarous as to refuse, he thought, armed as he was, he could always secure his retreat. It is a remark pretty universally made, that hospitality is a virtue which they who live in lonely and desolate situations seldom want. David found this exemplified in the present instance; for the good woman, with her husband, had formerly emigrated from the Highlands – a country famous for hospitality; and with many of their neighbours, who,/ like them, had fled from feudal oppressions[34] and inclement skies, had transplanted their national virtues and attachments to the back woods of Carolina, where, had they been permitted to remain in peace, they would doubtless have much amended their situation. But though they were little indebted to the soil which gave them birth, yet their affection for it could not be shaken; and therefore these honest people had most of them joined with the rest of their countrymen in adhering to the interests of the parent state; and the good man of the house was at this time actually serving in a corps of Loyalists. Nothing could then be more fortunate for poor Morgan than falling in with

– 241 –

242 *The History of Ned Evans*

the boys, who, in the innocence of their hearts, conducted him to their mother, from whom it is needless to add he met a kind reception. Having refreshed himself here for a few days, until he recovered the extreme fatigue he had undergone ever since the unfortunate day of the engagement, he set forward/ again, but under the conduct of some other young men whose fathers had also emigrated from Scotland, and who remained attached to the royal cause. Every where as they went they had the mortification to find that cause declining. The French had now joined the Americans effectually, and the British forces were obliged to retreat before them, till at last the surrender of the army under Lord Cornwallis may be said to be entirely decisive of the war. Morgan had, however, before this event, rejoined his regiment, in which every officer rejoiced to hear that there was a chance for Edward's being still alive; but above all Captain Fanshaw, who, thinking both he and Captain Rivers slain, mourned for them with the affection of a brother, but now rejoiced that one was still alive, and a possibility yet remaining that he might be restored to his friends and to his country.

In the mean time Edward continued to receive from Weenacoba every mark of tenderness/ and affection which her open and untutored nature could shew, the highest demonstration of which was her public adoption of him as her son, in the presence of the nation, and his consequent enrolment in the list of Agigua warriors.

The ceremony of adoption being somewhat singular, it may not be unentertaining to relate it –

Weenacoba first intimated her intention to two principal warriors, and to the old beloved man, who she intended should preside at the ceremony. She next proclaimed a feast, to which she invited as many chiefs as she could possibly find provisions for, and to which as many more were welcome as would bring provisions for themselves. The chief dish is broth made of bears' flesh, dogs, and huckleberries. Of this all are expected heartily to partake, and especially the young warrior elect; for on the strength of this meat he must subsist three days, that his body may be pure, and his dreams favourable; for/ no important business is ever undertaken by an Indian without fasting and dreaming. Poor Edward, on the third day, being questioned as to his dreams, declared that he thought himself standing beside the great lake, when he saw three bears come out of the woods, and attempt to wash themselves in the water: but a large swan, who was swimming on the lake, attacked them all, and swallowed them down one after the other. – Whether Ned really dreamed of this mighty feast in consequence of his long fast, or whether he only invented it for the present occasion, is not necessary to enquire. The old beloved man declared the dream favourable, and Warbish-condar, or the White Swan, the name that he should assume. A sweating-house was now prepared, that no remains of impurity might be left about him, into which Ned was put quite naked as he was born. This house consists of three poles set into the earth at convenient distances, and made to meet at top, over which are thrown blankets/ or skins, to keep it quite close. A hole is dug in the ground within, into which some stones made red-hot are placed; and on these water is sprinkled from time to time, the steam from which throws the person enclosed in the house into a profuse perspiration. Ned endured this operation as long as the old beloved man thought necessary, and then was carried between the arms of the two Indian warriors, and, reeking as he was, plunged over head and heels into the river. It is amazing that any person can survive this treatment, yet no one seems ever to be injured by it. On his coming out, he was laid down on his back on a place built to receive him; and the old beloved man proceeded to inflict on his skin the marks of his adoption in the following manner: He drew on each breast certain figures with a pointed stick dipped in gunpowder and water; and then, with ten needles, made of bone and fastened to a bit of wood, he pricked the delineated parts, marking them with vermilion. A/ deeper line surrounding the whole was cut with a gun-flint, and the wounds washed with water in which an herb resembling box is steeped, which soon heals them, and prevents their festering. These marks have their variety of red and blue from the materials with which they are stained: they are indelible by any washing, but may be removed by a blister. During the whole of this painful and fantastical operation, Ned never moved hand or foot, for he knew patience to be esteemed among the principal of Indian virtues. When the beloved man had finished, he raised him by the hand; and, a beaver robe being thrown over his shoulders, and a belt of wampum put round his neck, he was led forward to the Assembly. Then the head warrior pronounced, 'We receive a brother warrior, who appears to have sense; shews strength with his arm; and does not refuse his body to the enemy.' The old beloved man concluded the ceremony by imposing his name in the following address to the/ Deity: 'Ishtooboolo, master of life! view us well – we present unto thee our brother Warbishcondar, beseeching thee to grant him many days, and those happy.' – All the chiefs then took him by the hand in order; and, being seated on another beaver robe, a grand war-pipe was presented to him to smoke, which was afterwards handed round to all the other chiefs; and thus Edward became incorporated into their illustrious fraternity.

Another feast of dog's-flesh, bear's-grease, and huckleberries, concluded the solemnity, in which Warbishcondar bore his part with considerable applause; for it is certain that a three days fast, when the body is in perfect health, will reconcile the appetite to almost any digestible thing that can appease it.

It is a sure sign of a great mind, when a man can accommodate his temper to endure those misfortunes which Providence or unavoidable necessity appoints in his lot. Ned possessed this excellence both by nature/ and education: the sweetness of his disposition, supported by constitutional cheerfulness, prompted him always to contemplate the favourable side of any event that hap-

244 *The History of Ned Evans*

pened to him; whilst his deep veneration for the wisdom of God, and his entire confidence in his goodness and mercy, rendered him solicitous only to approve himself to him in the first instance, and then to submit, without repining, to whatever crosses he should lay upon him, from the hope and conviction that their ultimate effects would somehow or another turn out to his advantage. This sentiment, as much the dictate of reason as it is of religion, was able to preserve him from any approach of despondency even in his most hopeless situations; and though it is not to be doubted but the mode of life into which he was thrown was exceedingly disagreeable to him, and that he would gladly have embraced any favourable opportunity of getting rid of it, yet the difficulty and danger of the attempt, which, if it failed, would expose him to certain/ death by the most excruciating tortures, without any hopes of a new respite, deterred him for the present from undertaking it. He conformed therefore cheerfully to the necessity of his situation, which he held it to be his duty to do, however irksome that situation might be; and though his lot was cast among savages, yet he resolved, as long as he should live among them, to live respected; and, if it should be his fate to die, to die regretted. He entered therefore into the full spirit of the Indian life, and encountered all its dangers and fatigues with as much bravery and hardiness as those who had been accustomed to it from their birth. As the adopted son of Weenacoba, his first duty was to supply to her the place of Onondoga, whom she had lost; and it may well be questioned whether she was any loser by the exchange.

It is the universal fault of savages to consider women as inferior beings, born only for the use and convenience of men; rarely therefore do they pay to them any of those/ tender and endearing attentions which constitute the most amiable features of European manners, and form the firmest basis of the happiness of civilized life.

The love of an Indian is little else than that coarse passion which we call desire; and which when gratified loses its charm, and leaves the unhappy object of it to all that coldness and neglect into which sometimes even love itself degenerates, except when it is founded upon sentiment: and if this be the case with love, the strongest of all our passions, it can hardly be expected that it will fare better with duty, or that the attachment of a young Indian to his mother would be greater than that to his mistress. In Edward, therefore, Weenacoba found far more attention than ever she had received from Onondoga, for the generosity of his nature could not suffer him to be unkind to any woman whatsoever; but the great obligation which he owed to her, and the continued marks of affection which he daily received from her,/ inspired him with a regard for her truly tender and sincere, and which he manifested towards her on every occasion which put it in his power to shew it.

Her little plantation of Indian corn, which surrounded her wigwawm, and the care and labour of which are generally left entirely to the women, whilst the lazy Indian smokes his pipe in indolence, was by Edward's management put into much better condition than ever it had been before; and enriched with the addition of several kinds of peas and beans, which he had observed wild in the woods, and became a very comfortable addition to their subsistence; – whilst his skill and activity in hunting, the great business of the men, was not surpassed by any Indian in the nation; nor was Weenacoba's stock of winter's provision ever so plentiful or so various, nor her wardrobe of skins ever so rich, as when they were provided by the skilful and vigorous arm of her grateful and accomplished Warbishcondar./

CHAP. XLIX.

THE friendship of Awattahowee continued unalterably faithful to Edward; and he, with the assistance of Quanshebo's interpretation, began not only to comprehend a great part of what was said to him in the Agiguan language, but also to express himself so as to be tolerably well understood. His knowledge of civilized life enabled him to add many comforts to Weenacoba's wigwawm with which she had not before been acquainted, among which a sort of candles that he invented was not the least; and as he had been remarkably successful in his hunting, there was no dwelling in the tribe so well prepared against the winter, which was now set in.

Among Indians in general, there are no fixed meals; but every one eats when the cravings of nature require it. But Edward introduced the custom of a social meal at/ night, of which Awattahowee frequently partook, as did also poor Doran and the American, together with Quanshebo, and not seldom several of the chiefs. As vast quantities of wild honey were to be found in hollows of the old trees, Ned procured plenty of this, some of which he preserved in the comb, and of the rest made metheglin,[35] which he had often seen in Wales, and which, added to the milk of the hiccorynut, made a very palatable liquor.

Weenacoba was delighted with him, and felt an attachment to him fully equal to what she had ever shewn for Onondoga; and if Ned could have extinguished memory, perhaps his life might have glided on with as much happiness, or at least with as little care, as usually falls to the lot of any man. But the passion of his soul was no way abated, nor the dear remembrance of his first connections any way effaced. Every morning and every evening were his fervent prayers put up for their welfare, and some favourite trees were selected in/ the most retired recesses, on which he carved the name of Cecilia, and under whose shade he devoted many hours to the tender recollection of her features, and to the memory of her dear brother. The locket with her hair was still around his neck, and, according to his Indian creed, became his Manitoo. But the picture which he had from Captain Rivers he fortunately left at Charlestown, along with several other things of value, which he hoped to regain if ever he should have the good fortune to escape; at present, however, there was no feasible opportunity for attempting it, and therefore he wisely determined to endure his situation with patience, and to make the most of it, by accustoming himself to the fatigues, and learning the resources of the Indian life.

For this purpose he was an unwearied hunter, which is the most important occupation of an Indian, as all his domestic comfort and convenience depend upon it; besides which, it is the school of war, and they who excel in it, justly attain the respect/ and confidence of the whole nation. An accident which happened in one of his excursions, raised him to the highest estimation of the warriors, and gratified all the generous feelings of his heart.

His friend Awattahowee was almost a constant partner with him in the toils of the chase; and one day as they were coming home after a long and fatiguing range, in which they had met hardly any thing, Awattahowee discovered a deer at some distance, and immediately discharged his musket at it. Whether he wounded the creature or not was never known; for a large panther, who was lurking in a thicket near at hand, and who very probably was himself watching the deer, alarmed at the report, instantly sprung from his covert, and with one bound fastened his claws in Awattahowee's breast. The force with which he struck him knocked the Indian fairly on his back; and poor Awattahowee would infallibly have been torn to pieces, had not Edward (or if you please Warbish-condar)/ instantly sprung to his relief with that undaunted courage and ready presence of mind which never failed him on any emergency. To fire his musket was to endanger Awattahowee's life in the most imminent degree, for the beast was fastened on his breast, where he uttered a most hideous growl; but Ned sprung on him in his turn, and grasped his throat with both his hands so firmly that the ferocious creature could not breathe: this made him disengage his claws from poor Awattahowee's breast, which however was miserably torn; and then with his scalping knife, which always hangs at a warrior's belt, he pierced his heart, while Ned still held him by the throat till he expired.

Awattahowee, thus rescued from death, embraced his friend with every demonstration of lively affection, and Ned exulted in the opportunity of returning to Awattahowee a service not inferior to what he had received from him. Some herbs of a salubrious nature, with which all Indians are/ well acquainted, were now sought for; Awattahowee chewed them, and Ned spread them on the wounds, which in a few days were healed. The panther they flayed upon the spot; and Awattahowee dressed his beautiful spotted skin in the Indian manner, adorned it with a rich fringe of wampum-shells, and then presented it to his friend, to be worn by him on all occasions of ceremony or festivity.

The fame of this adventure endeared Edward to the whole tribe; and Awattahowee made a grand entertainment, to which the whole village was invited, where the panther was stewed down into soup, and became himself the prey of his once prostrate foe.

248 *The History of Ned Evans*

It was not long after this that the last party of the warriors came home, and brought with them some unfortunate prisoners, among whom were two children. It seems that these warriors had lost some of their brethren in the engagement in which these prisoners were taken, and in their/ rage they had solemnly devoted them to the stake: not even the children could be spared. Ned was grieved to the heart, and applied to Awattahowee; but he assured him, that as they had been solemnly devoted to the torture, the sentence could not be retracted, else the Matchu Manitoo, that is, the evil spirit, would bring all manner of plagues upon the nation.

Ned, however, endeavoured still to exert himself with the other chiefs, and entreated of them only to spare the children; but he received the same answer from them all: he told them that Ishtoboolo, or the good spirit, was the protector of innocence, and would not fail to be the avenger of it, if they destroyed the children; but still they were inexorable. No circumstance he ever met with afflicted him so much, nor filled him with such inexpressible horror. The day was appointed for this dreadful sacrifice, which to the Indians was a day of rejoicing; but Edward shut himself up in his wigwawm, where he took no food, but/ spent all the intermediate time in fasting and prayer, deeply affected with the lamentable tragedy they were going to act, as well as with gratitude to God, who had exempted him from the same fate. He prevailed on Weenacoba not to assist at such a spectacle; but Awattahowee would not stay from so high an entertainment. The shouts and acclamations, which he could not help hearing as he lay on his bed, whilst this bloody scene was transacting, pierced his soul, and made him almost curse the whole nation.

My readers will spare me the recital of the atrocious barbarities which were committed. The two unhappy infants, who were ill before, were the first who perished, in the sight of their parents, who, however, were in a short time insensible to all sufferings. Awattahowee came to give Ned an account of this massacre; but he would not listen to it, and begged of him to leave him to himself for some days: – even Weenacoba's attentions were vain, and she for the/ first time saw displeasure painted on his countenance.

But now the prediction that Edward declared to the chiefs, that the good spirit would avenge the shedding of innocent blood, was fully and severely fulfilled. The children, before they were massacred, had been seized with the small-pox, and some of the perpetrators of that inhuman action had caught the infection. As the disease was in a manner new to them, they had no knowledge how to treat it, and the devastation it soon made was dreadful. Among other victims that fell, was little Onondoga, the only child of Sheerasta, Awattahowee's sister; and the afflicted mother herself was seized with it.

When Ned discovered what the disease really was, he called an assembly of all the old beloved men and chief warriors, in the mountain house, that is, what one may call the town-hall, which no Indian village is without; and there, by the help of Quanshebo as an interpreter, declared to them,/ that this plague was sent to them by Ishtoboolo, as he had predicted, in vengeance for the innocent blood that they had shed, and because they would not listen to the entreaties that he had made to them in favour of the children: that, nevertheless, Ishtoboolo was merciful, and had revealed to him a way to prevent the fatal consequences of the distemper, provided they would swear never to torture prisoners again, but especially children, and provided they would implicitly submit to follow his directions during the distemper.

A few of the warriors consented to this; but the greater part, and especially the old beloved men, who were priests, physicians, and enchanters, treated it with derision, and had recourse to their consecrated physic-pots, and incantations. In the mean time the ravages of the distemper increased, and threatened the whole nation with extirpation.

Awattahowee's confidence in Edward prevailed on him to be of his party, and he/ submitted to be inoculated.[36] Several other young warriors were led by this example, who all had the disorder in the usual slight manner, and even Sheerasta recovered under his treatment; but hardly one escaped who relied on the priests.

At last poor Weenacoba herself was seized; for she, having a brother among the beloved old men, had adhered to her ancient superstitions, and would not be inoculated. Ned attended her with as much care and affection as if she had really been his mother; and when her disorder was so violent that she could not lie down, he supported her for whole days in his arms. She was fully sensible of all his grateful attention to her; but it was in vain – on the seventh day the eruption went in, and her spirits totally failed. He was sitting behind her on her bed, while her head lay upon his bosom, in which posture only she could get breath – her understanding still remained, though her sight and hearing were gone; but on the evening of that day she/ pressed his hand with hers, saying, 'Janis, Janis, Neepan!' that is, 'My son, my son, I die!' – and with these words she expired.

Ned's grief for the loss of this benevolent woman, whose whole conduct towards him had been truly maternal, was as sincere as it was well-placed. He buried her with every ceremony that the Indians held to be honourable, and moistened her grave with tears of true affection. The alarming progress of the distemper, by which upwards of two hundred had already fallen, filled the warriors and the old beloved men with consternation; and they determined, in a solemn council, to send for Warbishcondar, and adhere faithfully to his directions. The youth appeared among them in their great house, and there repeated the necessity of appeasing the wrath of Ishtoboolo for shedding innocent blood, by proclaiming a day of solemn fast and purification, and for ever renouncing putting prisoners, but especially children, to death. The first, he thought wisely,

250 *The History of Ned Evans*

might be a proper preparative/ for inoculation, and there was a possibility that the other might, for a time at least, restrain the ferocious custom of torturing men to death.

Almost all the surviving children of the nation, as well as the warriors, and several of the beloved old men, consented to be inoculated; the happy effects of which were soon visible by the complete recovery of upwards of seven hundred patients, with the loss only of three or four, and those advanced in years.

CHAP. L.

A SERVICE so essential raised Edward to the very summit of honour and esteem with the whole nation; they considered him as in the confidence of the good spirit, because he declared to them beforehand the punishment that was to be inflicted on/ them, and afterwards was himself the means of averting it; and accordingly they reverenced him even above all the old beloved men. Had Edward been so disposed, he might have erected himself not only into a sovereign, but perhaps even into a deity over the Agiguans; but, like the last character, he contented himself with doing them good, without looking to any personal reward to himself. His thoughts, indeed, were now wholly bent on withdrawing himself from the country; but to do this with safety was a matter of extreme difficulty, because the Indians would never forgive his deserting them, and would probably pursue him, even for a thousand miles. The opinion of his communication with the good spirit, however, was favourable to him on this occasion; and I think we may acquit him of want of integrity, although he availed himself of that opinion to deceive them. He told his friend Awattahowee that Weenacoba had appeared to him, and that Ishtoboolo had sent her to acquaint/ him that he should shortly require his presence. Awattahowee was inconsolable at the news; but superstition is deeply implanted in every Indian bosom, and the commands of the spirits suggested to them in dreams are never known to be disobeyed. To give the greater appearance of truth to this story, Ned rigidly conformed to all the Indian ritual of purification, and frequently passed the whole night at the grave of Weenacoba. It was upon a solemn occasion of this sort one night, when the moon had newly risen, and his thoughts were wholly intent on the great business he was meditating, that he was surprised to see, at some distance from him, a female figure kneeling on the ground, upon which she was almost prostrate, and seemingly intent on some act of devotion. The place she had chosen was exceedingly retired; but the gleams of the moon shone strong upon her, and discovered her, notwithstanding the trees which surrounded her. A sight so uncommon excited his curiosity, for he/ never saw any serious expression of devotion among the Indians before, and he determined to be more assured if it was really such he now saw. She was so intent upon her employment, that he

– 251 –

252   *The History of Ned Evans*

approached her unperceived, and then, from behind a tree, beheld the faithful and afflicted Sheerasta, a widow of only nineteen, weeping at the grave of her husband, and milking her breast on the new-made grave beside it, of her little son, whom likewise she had lately lost.

An expression of grief so tender and affecting did not fail to touch Edward's sympathizing heart. He reverenced that truth and intense affection which filled the faithful, though untutored heart of this gentle savage.[37] He called, Sheerasta! She knew his voice, and, rising with dignity and without surprise, replied in words that may be thus translated: 'Warbishcondar, the master of life has taken from me the apple of my eye, and the core of my heart, and hid them in these graves; I will water the one/ with my tears, and the other with the sap of my breast, till I find them again in the country where the sun never sets.' – She then retired towards her own home, leaving Edward touched with the tenderest sensibility, and filled with admiration of that constancy and virtue, which, if it had been found in civilized life, would be equally honoured and applauded.

The season being now so far advanced that he might expect to find berries and other fruits in the woods during his long and perilous expedition, Ned determined to put it in execution let the event be what it would; but first he told Doran his real intention, recommending it to him to remain some time longer, and to divert the Indians from making any search after him if they should be so inclined.

He then called a meeting of the warriors and the old beloved men, and informed them, that Ishtoboolo had sent to him the spirit of his ever loved and lamented Weenacoba to order him to meet him on/ the first day of the new moon, in the sacred caverns of the holy rock; that he should remain there thirty days and thirty nights; but that whether Ishtoboolo would permit him to return to them, or order him to attend on Weenacoba in the world of spirits, he could not tell. In either case he would never cease to pray the Father of days to send them plenty of beavers, and make their enemies turn their back in battle.

The speech was received with every demonstration of implicit faith and affectionate esteem; and a deputation of beloved old men and head warriors were appointed to attend him to the lake, and see him embark for the sacred caves. On the last evening previous to his departure he invited Awattahowee to his wigwawm, where he entertained him with the best fare he had. He could not help pitying the concern which that young man expressed, and endeavoured to sooth him with the hopes of seeing him again. He committed to his/ trust all the valuable scalps and rich furs which composed the furniture, telling him that if he did not return on the thirty-first day, that he might be sure he was gone to the world of spirits, in which he would not fail to pray Ishtoboolo to protect him; and, in that case, to take all to himself: – that he would carry nothing away but his arms, the wampum belt which Weenacoba had given him, and the panther's skin which he himself had dressed for him. Poor Awattahowee, though heir to all these possessions, left the wigwawm with a sorrowing heart, and Warbishcondar stretched himself for the last time on his bear-skin couch.

When he was left entirely alone, and all was silent about him, the importance of the expedition he was about to enter upon occupied all his mind. The greatest danger and difficulty he hoped he had already overcome by the pious fraud he practised on Indian credulity, whereby he left their country not only with their consent, but/ even with their applause: – but still much was before him; a journey of upwards of seven hundred miles, through an uninhabited desert, infested by serpents and wild beasts, and (if he should get through this) four hundred more through an enemy's country, to be undertaken singly and alone, without any chance for refreshment or succour in case of sickness or accident, was surely a formidable prospect, and sufficient to damp the ardour of any less steady and fortified mind than Edward's. But his resolution was equal to any trial; and the habitual recollection that, in whatsoever point of space he could be placed, he should still be in the sight and within the embrace of his Creator, was a consolation, which, as he never let it out of his mind for a moment, gave him confidence and firm support in every possible situation, though it should be death itself. Fear therefore he delivered to the guilty, as not becoming him who had put on the whole armour of/ God; and placing hope in his view, he trusted to a successful issue of his undertaking, and gave up his mind to the contemplation of the happy hours, when perhaps he might again behold the soft eyes of Lady Cecilia smiling in tears, while he related to her the heroic death of her gallant brother, and his own perilous adventures.

Here the tender recollection of his beloved friend rose in his mind, and claimed the generous tribute of manly sorrow: – the glimmering light of his taper now dying in its socket, shone by starts on the empty couch of poor Weenacoba. His soul was tuned to tenderness, and in that instant the tear of gratitude mingled its precious stream with those of friendship and of love. At length he slept. – Oh ye virtuous! ye who confide in God, and love your brethren of mankind! ye whose every action springs from duty and from sentiment! it is yours alone to sleep alike sweetly and secure in/ the wigwawm of the savage, the moss of the desert, or the downy bed and splendid chamber of the great.

Poor Awattahowee, whose repose had been less tranquil, arose with the first dawning of the day, to take his last leave of his beloved Warbishcondar. The chiefs and the old beloved men attended as they had agreed; and Ned walked forth, clad only with the panther's skin around his loins, the wampum belt around his neck, and a pair of new moccassins on his feet. At his back hung an Indian bow, with a quiver full of arrows; at his side a tomahawk and scalping-knife, not for their usual ferocious purposes, but as being really useful instruments on many

254 *The History of Ned Evans*

occasions. In his hand he carried his musket, and from his belt was suspended a small bag with about two pounds of powder, balls, and flints.

Thus accoutred, he came to the banks of the lake, where Awattahowee had provided him a small bark canoe, with two paddles,/ and a bag of parched corn as an offering to the great spirit.

As he stood on the bank, all the warriors and beloved men shook him by the hand; and the great beloved man, that is the oldest, desired him to remember them to Ishtoboolo, and to entreat him to send them good hunting seasons. This on his part he promised faithfully to do, and to represent to him how kindly they had behaved to him, for which he now thanked them. When he took Doran's hand, he bade him 'remember!' which single word was sufficient to direct his conduct. The last he spoke to was Awattahowee – as he held him by the hand his eye dwelt long upon him, for he knew it would be his last sight. – Awattahowee wept – the savage wept – for nature formed him of her richest clay – He hung upon Ned's neck, and his parting words were, 'May Ishtoboolo preserve bright the chain that binds fast the heart of Awattahowee to Warbishcondar!' – Edward's heart was full; he gave him a last/ embrace, and paddled off in his canoe. As he went off from the shore towards the holy rock, which we before mentioned the Indians held in such veneration, and which was at the distance of somewhat better than a quarter of a mile, they all set up the solemn song which they sing annually on their great festival of general expiration. Ned heard their voices softer and softer as he receded; they continued on the bank still gazing and still singing, and he continued still looking and still listening, till he approached the sacred caves. As he entered the awful arch, he fired his musket for a last salute: the Indians answered it from the shore, and, amidst the roar of echoes, he lost sight of them for ever./

CHAP. LI.

No situation, in which immediate danger does not form a part, could well be more awful than that in which he now found himself. The human countenance even in its most savage state has something in it divine; and to lose sight of it for ever, would perhaps be a melting consideration even to the hardest heart. But Edward, during a year and a half that he had resided with the Agiguans, had experienced all the tenderness and affection which nature planted in her genuine offspring, and in a degree more intense and faithful than perhaps the disguised manners of polished life can either attain or express. When, therefore, he could see them no more, he almost felt himself forlorn; and this moment, which he had long panted for with all the fervency of desire, he found, when it arrived,/ damped with regret. He cast his eyes upwards to the awful and sublime cavern, into the recesses of which he was perhaps the first human being that had ever dared to enter; and, adopting the Indian idea, that it was the temple of the great spirit, he resolved that the first words he uttered should be dedicated to his praise 'O thou Almighty Being (said he) who inhabitest eternity, and from whose eye the profoundest caverns of the deep cannot be hid! deign to behold with mercy the humblest and least worthy of thy creatures, who hath no strength but in thy arm, no confidence but in thy help, and who, in all the trials which thou hast appointed him, beseeches the aid of thy grace to enable him to persevere!' – A deep and hollow voice resounded from the inmost recesses of the cave, 'Persevere!' Ned knew it to be but the echo of the last word which he pronounced; but, seizing it as a favourable response, he determined to trust the omen, and, after doing all that he could for himself, to leave the issue to God./

With this intent he resolved to penetrate as far as possible to the bottom of the cavern, where he intended to remain till night, lest any of the Indians might be induced to watch his motions, and should see him come out again. A multitude of water-fowl built their nests in the sides of this cave; and this being their laying season, he might have freighted his canoe with eggs if he had had a mind. He took as many as he needed for present use, and spared the lives of the birds that layed them, as a satisfaction for the robbery. The parched corn, which the piety of Awattahowee had sent as an offering to the good spirit, he

256 *The History of Ned Evans*

reserved for his own use, without thinking he did that spirit any injury, or that he would deprive his friend of any blessing in return; and thus he proceeded in his canoe as far as the water would carry it. In this spot he might have remained in perfect security as long as he pleased: but as he perceived the cavern extended much farther, though without water, his/ curiosity prompted him to explore it: for this, however, a light was necessary, as that of day could serve him no farther than the next turning. But here was a difficulty which, however, he in part surmounted, by twisting the fibres of some withered vegetables, which, as far as the influence of the external air and light extended, grew from among the crevices of the rocks; and, by rubbing them with pounded gun-powder a little damped, he formed a kind of spunk,[38] which kindled like a squib, and yielded for a time a dull light. Having provided a parcel of these, and swallowed half a dozen raw eggs, with some parched corn, and put the remainder in his pouch, he set forward on his investigation. The way was long and dismal, like that which the poets feign to lead down to Tartarus, and little less dangerous in reality, since there were many pits and slippery places, in which a false step might be death. Poor Ned, when he undertook the task, did no know the danger, and began to wish he/ had not attempted it; but as, by the glimmering light he had, the way seemed rather to widen and grow more easy, he continued to go on, till all on a sudden he fell down, and rolled along a slippery rock for the length of many yards. During the time he was falling he expected nothing but to be dashed to pieces: he, however, found himself at the bottom, unhurt, but in total darkness, and, what was worse, all his spunks lost in the fall. His situation was now dreadful, as he could not move a step without the apprehension of breaking his neck; but his musquet was still in his hand; and all his other accoutrements, which were fastened about him, still safe. His first resource was to fire his musquet. By the light of the flash, and the dismal resounding of the echoes, he perceived he was at the bottom of a great vault; and the ground being smooth under his feet, and composed of small sand, he was not in danger of breaking his neck: but, alas! he was immured as it were in the grave, since to/ ascend to where he fell from, was impossible without assistance, and his most diligent search did not discover any other outlet. While life remained, he determined to exert himself to preserve it, and, when he could do that no longer, to die contented. His first exertion was to procure light; and this he effected by wetting some gun-powder with spittle, kneading it into a paste in his hands, and then setting fire to it with dry powder in the pan of his musket: by the light of this he was fortunate enough to recover his spunks, which had rolled from him in his fall, and were lying at the bottom of the rock; he discovered too that the cavern he was in was large, but though he went round it and round it a hundred times, he saw no possible exit. Exhausted by his fruitless fatigue, and conceiving himself to be irretrievably lost, he resigned himself quietly to his fate, and laid himself down upon the ground. How he employed himself there we may judge from what we know of him/ already; he attained however to that submission of will and composure of spirits, that lulled his sorrows to oblivion, and actually suffered him to sleep. How long he lay in this state of suspended sensibility he never knew; all that he could tell was, that he dreamed he was in the cavern where he actually lay, and that on a sudden it opened at the top, and that his dear friend Captain Rivers called to him from thence, and taking him by the hand he found no difficulty in mounting from the ground and going away with him. The passionate eagerness to escape instantly woke him: but his surprise was great, when he actually found some creature licking his hand: of what species it was his feeling could not discover, but his presence of mind dictated to him to light his spunk, which he did in his usual manner. The flash frightened the beast, which instantly fled to a part of the rock that jutted out, and disappeared behind it. The discovery revived hope: he immediately hastened to the same spot,/ where he perceived a hole which with some difficulty admitted his body; he found it sloped upwards, and through this he continued to creep for near an hour as he supposes, till at last he had the comfort to discover light, and, in a few minutes afterwards, the inexpressible joy to gain the open air. The creature to whom under God he owed his deliverance was of the badger kind, which, though of great strength of body, and considerable size, is yet perfectly harmless and inoffensive, industrious only in seeking out the deepest and most lonely recesses for its habitation, and perhaps was now directed to make that cavern its retreat by the express providence of God to deliver his servant. In this light it is certain Edward took it, and derived from it proportionable trust and confidence.

At the time of his emerging from this frightful cave, the morning seemed but little advanced, so that he concluded he had passed a whole night in it, and a great part/ of the day before. He found himself within half a mile of the spot where he entered the sacred rock, and thought (perhaps not without reason) that as it was the first time, so should it be the last that he should be so venturous.

The desert was now before him; but no danger it could present could be in any degree so terrible as that which he had escaped, especially as, being now so used to the woods, and so accustomed to the Indian life, he was not inferior to any native either in hardiness or in resources. His intention was to return if possible to Charlestown, and for this purpose to endeavour to shape his course so as to fall in with the back settlements of Carolina. But they who conceive no difficulty in this, must be told, that the forests of America, to a person not accustomed to them, are fully as trackless, and greatly more intricate than the Atlantic Ocean. You may wander for ages in this boundless desert, incumbered with briers, stopped with swamps, exposed to wild/ beasts and noxious reptiles, without ever being able to see twenty yards around you. Compass – Ned had none, though highly necessary to the safety of those who should only venture

258 *The History of Ned Evans*

for a mile beyond the settled plantations; and as for the face of any of the celestial luminaries, it was rarely that the thickness of the trees would ever let him discover one of them. One observation he had however made, that the branches are always larger and the foliage more luxuriant on the south side of a tree than on the north, and this was the guide he steered by; sometimes indeed he got a glimpse of the sun himself, or mounted to the top of one of the tallest pines to observe him, and by this corrected his course. Seventeen days had he passed in this laborious journey, without ever descrying human face or vestige of human foot. At last he observed some blazes on the trees, that is, part of the bark chopped off on certain trees within fight of each other: this he knew to be a path, and accordingly found/ his road somewhat less incumbered. Five days more he journeyed in this path, with more ease, but equal solitude, always reposing at night among the branches of the thickest tree he could find. On the evening of the fifth day, about sunset, he heard the sound of Indian voices singing some of their cheerful songs, and soon after discovered the party preparing for their evening's encampment. In former days this would have been a sight of terror, but was now a circumstance of the highest satisfaction. According to the etiquette of Indian politeness, which admits of no intrusion, he gave notice of his approach, by the peculiar holloa used on such occasions, and then stood still in his place. Two of the party were immediately deputed to bring him to the circle, where he was received by the rest with all their usual respect and hospitality. They soon perceived he was a white man, but saw by his marks that he was an adopted warrior of a nation with which they were in alliance. It is not the/ custom, however, to trouble any stranger with questions, until he is rested, and they have entertained him. It was with much pleasure that poor Ned beheld a good fire kindled, and preparation for a plentiful supper, there being no want of provisions nor yet of good liquor in the company; and even the sight of human faces, after so long a solitude, was a circumstance of considerable satisfaction. The party he had fallen in with belonged to the Chickesaw nation,[39] who were in friendship with the Agiguans, and were now returning from Charlestown, where they had been to purchase various articles according to the now constant practice of the Indian nations; and by these warriors Ned was informed that the great king beyond the salt lake was not able to bring back his rebellious children to their duty, and had therefore given them up altogether, and ordered all his red warriors home; or, in other words, that there was peace between England and America, and that Charlestown was evacuated by the/ British troops. Though Edward was too good a patriot not to mourn for the disgraces of his country, yet he was also too good a christian not to rejoice in the return of peace, and that a period was put to the desolating miseries of civil war.

As he had no personal enmity against the Americans, their establishing their independence gave him little concern; but the country being in peace was a mat-

Volume III 259

ter of the utmost moment, and seemed to smooth all his difficulties at once. He entertained the chiefs with just so much of his history as he thought proper; informing them, that he was an English officer, but had been adopted by a friendly nation, for whom he felt the sincerest affection; and that he was on his road to Charlestown, to serve their interests as well as his own. The grog and the pipe went merrily round; and after a dance hand in hand about the fire, in which Ned heartily joined, they all lay down to sleep, with their feet towards it, according to the Indian fashion, and some horses that/ they had with them tied to the trees without them. In the morning they gave Edward another repast, and presented him with some necessaries, particularly a powder-horn fully replenished, and some rice biscuits that they had brought with them; and then took leave, according to custom, with shaking of hands and another song.

Four days more he travelled alone before he arrived at the back settlements, which at last he reached on the twenty-ninth day from his quitting the cavern; and had the comfort to sleep that night in a christian habitation. The good man of the house was an Irishman, and with his three sons had served by turns in the American army; for his countrymen had adhered to the American cause, almost as universally as the Scotch did to the British. When Paddy first saw Ned, he took him for an Indian, and even in that character was willing enough to shew him hospitality; but when he discovered him to be/ a British officer, and that he had been in his own dear country, there were no bounds to his kindness; and all that he had, and every thing in and out of his house was at his service./

CHAP. LII.

THE impatience of Edward to hear something of his friends, to join his regiment, and to regain the comforts of civilized life, did not permit him to accept of the honest Irishman's hospitable invitation, to repose himself for a few days with him; but as he had still nothing on him but his wampum belt, and panther's skin, he was obliged to one of the young men for something of a more decent dress, and got from him a shirt, a short jacket, and a pair of trowsers; he likewise furnished him with a horse, and undertook to conduct him to Doctor Denton's, about thirty miles from where they were, but which was the nearest settlement belonging to any gentleman of fortune in that part of the country. This was highly acceptable to Edward, for he had some little knowledge of the doctor, having seen/ him once or twice at Mrs. Middleham's, to the sister of whose husband he was married; and he knew him to be a gentleman of such liberal manners, and unbounded benignity of heart, that his having been compelled in the line of his duty to appear once as his enemy would have no weight in diminishing, whatever it might have in adding to, the number and the delicacy of those attentions which he never failed to pay to every person who required them from him. The doctor, indeed, was of a character somewhat singular, but then it was an amiable and a virtuous singularity. He was a younger son of one of the wealthiest planters in the province, who at the same time had the character of being one of the most rigid and severe. The cruelties which he exercised over his negroes had drawn on him the animadversions even of those who seldom pitied them; but had almost broke his son's heart, which being filled with the sweetest milk of human kindness, could not endure to witness those barbarities which/ no intercession of his could soften, and which at last obliged him to estrange himself wholly from his father's house.[40] He sought therefore and obtained his leave to go over to Europe, where he applied himself to the study of physic, as well as to several other branches of polite literature, in all of which he attained to a considerable degree of eminence. On his return to his native country, he commenced practitioner of physic, and such was his skill and success that he must soon have made a considerable fortune: but here the extreme delicacy of his feelings again interposed, and he was perhaps the only professional man in any country who

– 260 –

felt wounded by the number and the greatness of his fees: but so it was; he could not bear to receive money for his assistance; and as few were either entitled or would choose to ask it for nothing, his practice became confined either to his immediate relatives, or to those on whom he bestowed it as a charity; and of these, indeed, the number was/ far from inconsiderable. On his father's death, he became intitled to a considerable fortune, which was increased by his happy union with the amiable daughter of the elder Mr. Middleham, and sister to the husband of the lady whom Edward rescued from the impertinence of a sentinel. Having now an income fully equal to the moderateness of his desires, the doctor retired to the back country, where he had a very extensive plantation, and where his first care was to compile a short and plain code of laws, formed on the most manifest utility, for the government of his negroes, who amounted to about four hundred. Impressed with a deep sense of religion himself, which was also a striking feature in Mrs. Denton's character, he endeavoured to communicate this enlivening principle to all over whom he had any influence, and therefore made it his constant practice, as there was no clergyman within two hundred miles of him, to perform divine service himself every Sunday in one of his outhouses/ fitted up for the purpose, to which all were welcome to come that were in the neighbourhood, and where he required the presence of all his negroes who were of an age to understand the business they were about.

In this affecting duty the doctor was engaged when Edward arrived at his house. He had been so long among the heathens, that he really had forgot the days of the week, and did not know that this was Sunday till he heard how the doctor was employed. He instantly hastened to the house of prayer, and rejoiced in the opportunity of pouring out the effusions of his grateful heart to the merciful Being who had conducted him through so many perils, and brought him at last into a christian land. When the service was ended, he advanced to the doctor and Mrs. Denton, who did not at first recollect him, but, upon his explaining to them his situation, received him with the most cordial hospitality, and with the offer of every accommodation they had/ to bestow. Among the rest, the doctor insisted upon Ned's receiving a supply of money, which indeed was now become necessary to him, and which he did not refuse taking, as he knew a very considerable sum was now due to him from the agent of the regiment.

In a remote situation like the doctor's, every gentleman is under the necessity of having large supplies of all the usual accommodations of life, and all the ordinary trades most in use were carried on by some or other of his negroes: from these magazines, therefore, Edward got a temporary supply of all the articles of which he stood most in need, and was in a few days thoroughly equipped to proceed on his journey to Charlestown, from whence he hoped to find an easy passage to Europe. But he had so ingratiated himself with the doctor and his amiable wife, that they could not bring themselves to part with him; and at last

262 *The History of Ned Evans*

when they found him bent upon going, they determined to accompany him as far/ as Mr. Middleham's plantation, which indeed might be said to be the whole way, as it lay within sixteen miles of the city.

Ned dismissed his back-woods man with a handsome present for his trouble in attending him to the doctor's, and with much satisfaction accepted of a seat in their chaise, accompanied both by the doctor and his lady. The journey was still a length of some hundred miles, which shewed the extreme kindness of his new friends in undertaking it, purely to accommodate him; for it was but a few weeks since they had been at Mr. Middleham's in their way down to their own house. Every night they were entertained by private families, there being no public-houses at so remote a distance; but their fare was excellent, and as freely given as it was thankfully received. The contrast between this part of his journey and that which he had so lately passed, gave Ned an unusual flow of spirits, and made him wonder at the strange paradox which some modern/ philosophers have advanced, 'That the savage life was upon the whole more desirable, and more productive of real happiness, than the civilized.'[41] – Edward had tried both; and though he acknowledged a contented mind could make to itself happiness in the savage state, yet there was no comparison in the degree to which the same mind could attain in civilized society.

At last they approached the domains of Mr. Middleham. The quantity of cleared ground with cattle of all kinds grazing, interspersed with trees that seemed coeval with the creation, and between which might be discovered the windings of Ashley river, on the banks of which, on a high terrace, stood the noble mansion belonging to this accomplished and virtuous patriot, recalled to Edward's mind the groves of Ravensdale, or at least some European seat the habitation of taste and opulence. If the approach to this charming residence filled Edward's mind with a tranquil pleasure, how much was it increased, and how joyful was his/ surprise, when, upon entering the gate that led up to it, he saw David Morgan in the avenue! His astonishment would hardly let him trust his own eyes; but making an apology to the doctor and Mrs. Denton, and telling them the occasion, he jumped out of the chaise, and filled Morgan with still greater amaze and still greater raptures than he had himself experienced. The time would not allow them to enter into minute details of their mutual adventures; only Morgan informed Ned, that after the cessation of arms he had attached himself to Captain Fanshaw, and had returned with him from the northward to Charlestown, to see Mrs. Fanshaw, who being very near her time could not travel when the British evacuated that place, but remained in her own lodgings, and received many civilities from several American ladies, and particularly from Mrs. Middleham, who had the kindness to ask her out with her to this seat; that both she and the captain were there, and that he had come with them./ 'But, my dear master,' added David, 'I hope nothing will ever separate us again! I am

Volume III 263

yours to the end of my days, and to the farthest corner of the world.' Ned shook him by the hand in confirmation of the bargain; and now Captain Fanshaw's two little boys advanced jumping and overjoyed to see Edward again, who, as he came near the house, met Mr. and Mrs. Middleham, with all the rest of their company, coming out to welcome him to their house. Ned had never seen Mr. Middleham before; but the good report of Mrs. Middleham had secured him a most cordial reception, not diminished by the details of those noble parts of his character with which Mr. and Mrs. Fanshaw were well acquainted, and which they had related to Mr. and Mrs. Middleham even when they almost despaired of ever seeing him again. Upon the whole, it was hard to meet with any group more worthy in themselves, or more entirely agreeable to each other. If there was any thing to/ damp the satisfaction which Captain Fanshaw and Edward felt in their situation, it was to behold the marks of that brutal and ungenerous mischief which the British soldiers had committed in every part of the house, and through all the ornamented grounds, while they held it in possession. This they felt as an everlasting reproach to them whenever they opened their eyes, or to whatsoever object they turned them: but a syllable on the subject never escaped from the generous proprietors, nor yet an expression of exultation on account of the glorious issue of the contest in which they were so long engaged; a delicacy inseparable from elevated minds prevented them from touching upon subjects that could have the remotest tendency to wound the feelings of any individual under the protection of their roof; but they took the noble revenge of subduing the hearts as well as the arms of their enemies, and of obliterating the remembrance of injuries/ by the more pleasing recollection of kindnesses.

In the mutual intercourse of friendship, and in a round of amusements equally elegant and various, in which both the Middlehams and the Dentons were well able to excel, did Ned spend three weeks of the happiest hours he had experienced since he left Ravensdale. And now Captain Fanshaw having received advice from Charlestown, that a fleet was shortly to sail for Europe, the first that were going to English ports since the peace, he and Edward determined to take their passage together, and once more to cross the Atlantic, perhaps for the last time; being both of them thoroughly awakened from their dream of glory, and deeming the ploughshare and the pruning-hook far more pleasing, as well as more useful instruments, than the sword and the bayonet.

Their good friends, Mr. and Mrs. Middleham, with Doctor and Mrs. Denton,/ felt sincere regret in parting with them; they accommodated them with their own coach and a post-chaise, with a horse for David Morgan; and after a thousand vows of unalterable gratitude and regard, they set off together for Charlestown.

END OF THE THIRD VOLUME.

THE HISTORY OF NED EVANS.

THE HISTORY OF NED EVANS.

'O'erstep not the modesty of Nature!'
SHAKESPEARE.

IN FOUR VOLUMES.

VOL. IV.

LONDON:

PRINTED FOR G. G. AND J. ROBINSON,
PATERNOSTER-ROW.
M.DCC.XCVI.

THE HISTORY OF NED EVANS.

CHAP. LIII.

As they approached the peninsula, on which Charlestown is seated, every object became interesting. Ned could not help observing how the benign influence of peace was already become visible. The Quarter-house,[1] which is situated near the neck which connects this peninsula with the interior country, and which during the war had been converted into a fortified station, now returned to its original destination, and was again a house of public entertainment and rural resort. The charming/ villas which had been profusely scattered through the surrounding natural garden, which had been either consumed by fire, or suffered to moulder in neglect, were now everywhere re-erecting their ornamented fronts, whilst the redoubts and the palisadoes[2] were in their turn condemned to the consuming element. The cheerful songs of new-born liberty succeeded to the shrill scream-ing of the fife or the deep thunder of the hollow drum. The pale phantoms of hatred[3] and terror were removed from every brow, and in their place sat confi-dence and contentment. Even the birds, which the perpetual roar of musquetry and cannon had banished from the groves, were now resuming their native seats, and pouring forth their liquid lays to listening nature. A sympathetic cheerful-ness won upon our travellers, who, as they felt the comforts of their situation, and reflected by whose civility and kindness they enjoyed it, were tempted to rejoice in the miscarriage/ of their expedition, which secured to their amiable friends the enjoyment of those unalienable rights which a brave man would rather perish than surrender. At length they arrived safe in town, and were set down at those lodgings which Mrs. Fanshaw had occupied ever since her first arrival. The good landlady, who was an American, but who lived unmolested while the British were in possession, was rejoiced to see Ned return, whom she had long supposed to have been killed, and often lamented as an amiable youth whom it was a pity Fate had not spared to his friends; and she manifested her joy in a manner that entitled her to Ned's gratitude and best opinion. But the richest cordial she could have brought, she now presented, which was a packet from the commander in chief, containing several letters from Europe, among which were two for Edward, sent at a venture by the two persons dearest to him on earth, Lady Cecilia and his father./ On opening this packet, Captain Fanshaw perceived it was written by the general's aide-du-camp, to the following purport:

New-York, August 17, 1783.

Sir,

I am ordered by the commander in chief to inform you, that in consequence of preliminary articles for a general peace having been signed at Paris, the British forces are ordered home, and that your regiment is already embarked. His excellency desires me to forward to you the enclosed letters, which have lately been sent from Europe under cover to him; particularly requesting to know if there is any account of Mr. Evans, who we understand was surprised when wounded by a marauding party of Indians, and taken prisoner. We deeply lament the fate of this young and gallant officer, but are still not without hopes of his being yet living, and shall rejoice to/ find those hopes verified. I remain, with respect, Sir, Your obedient servant,
CHA. PHILMORE.

When Ned received his letters, the contest between love and duty did not let him for some time determine which to open first. He went into a room by himself, and first broke the seal of that from Wales: – but before he read two lines he opened that from Lady Cecilia; and when he saw her signature, he pressed it to his lips, whilst the palpitation of his heart set his whole frame trembling, and hardly permitted him to breathe. At length he recovered calmness to read the following words:

Ravensdale, April 15, 1783.

My ever dear friend!

With what pleasure should I sit down to execute my father's orders in writing to you this letter, if I could be certain it/ would ever reach you, or, alas! if I could even be assured that you were yet living to receive it; but when I reflect on the murderous hands into which you are fallen, my heart dies within me, and my frighted imagination presents you in a situation too horrible to relate. Ever since we have heard of your unhappy captivity, I have not ceased to weary Heaven with prayers to shut the lions' mouths, and deliver you from the fangs of those ferocious tigers.[4] I trust they will be heard; and in the hope of that event, and of the possibility that this may find you, I unite with my dear father in expressing our cordial thanks to you for your kind attention to my ever lamented brother, who, we know, breathed out his gallant soul in your arms. Oh, Edward! what a loss was there! – My father, with all his resignation, feels it

268 *The History of Ned Evans*

through every fibre of his heart, and contemplates in tears for hours together his picture which hangs in the library. Nor is this the only loss/ which I fear he will have to mourn: – my poor brother Rivers is now at the Hot-Wells of Bristol,[5] in a very declining state, worn out in the very prime of his life, by that laborious pursuit of pleasure which seems to be the madness of the age. The weight of these misfortunes hangs heavy on my father, and will, I fear, bring down his grey hairs with sorrow to the grave. He has lost all his spirits, sees no company but Doctor Burton, whose soothing manners and truly apostolic piety are well suited to the present melancholy turn of his thoughts. Oh, Edward! were you here, you might see the inefficacy of worldly pomp to bestow happiness. But I know you have not this lesson to learn – your good father's humble roof shewed me the mansions in which true happiness loves to dwell, and which I often contemplate with the most grateful recollection. I had a letter from the dear good man lately, and have the pleasure to tell you, both he and/ your mother are well. Captain Nettlefield, who since the peace has lately come home, called here the other day. My poor brother George let us know enough of his affair with you to make me hate him, as far as I can hate any thing – he did not rise in my favour by his visit. He talked so long of your imprudence in suffering yourself to be surprised – the impossibility of your escaping, if you should be alive – and the far greater probability of your being scalped and roasted to death, that I verily believe the wretch wished it might be so: it threw my father into violent agitation, and I begged of him not to dwell on a subject which nobody that knew you could hear without the deepest affliction, and which my father's spirits could not at that time bear. He bowed submission; but a self-complacent smile sufficiently shewed how glad he was to have that theme to torment me with. Now I talk of torments, I have happily got rid of one, which is my odious Lord Squanderfield:/ he has actually married Harriet Burton, much against her father's inclination; but her mother countenanced it, and she was independent. She expects to come back here soon lady lieutenant, and his lordship is actually talked of for the office; but if he should be appointed, I shall have a strange opinion of our rulers. I, for my part, would not trust him with the government of my lap-dog; and surely I shall think the nation sunk indeed that is put under his subjection.[6]

Adieu, my dear Edward! May God grant you a safe deliverance from the hands of your enemies, and restore you to the prayers of the most faithful and affectionate of your friends,
CECILIA RIVERS!

'Blessed name!' cried Edward as he kissed the signature: 'lie there next my heart till I see what my dear father says.' With which words he hurried the letter/ into his bosom, and then read that from Wales:

Ti-gwin, April 12, 1783.

My dear Edward!

It is not easy for me to express with what emotions of heart I sit down to write to you at this time, not knowing whether you are any longer to be numbered among the living. Hoping the best, yet tortured with the apprehension that those fell tigers in human shape, to whom the inscrutable decrees of Providence have delivered you, may have long ere this imbrued their murderous hands in your heart's blood. Yet if the unceasing prayers of a heart humbly devoted to the will of its Creator; if the torrents of tears shed by your poor mother in the agonies of her soul, can avail any thing at the throne of mercy, you may yet be safe, and we again be blessed with folding you to our hearts. The very idea cheers/ my soul, and something seems to whisper to me, 'Be of good comfort!' Many indeed are the comforts which the good providence of God has indulged to me in every stage of my being; among which none of the least is that disinterested friendship with which the noble and excellent Lady Cecilia Rivers condescends to honour us. Oh my Edward! it is to you (under Heaven) that I am indebted for this blessing, and that our declining years are placed by the generous Lord Ravensdale beyond the pressure or apprehensions of distress. His bounty is secured to us for life, and as regularly paid as the day comes round on which it is due. What pity is it that his noble lineage is in danger of being extinct in the male line! We know in whose arms the gallant Captain breathed his last; and it is with extreme grief we hear his Lordship's eldest, and now only son, Lord Rivers, is too likely soon to follow, being at this time in the last stage of a rapid and/ deep decline. Amidst this gloomy intelligence it will be some comfort to inform you (if, alas! you can yet be informed of any thing) that your mother and I continue to enjoy the blessing of uninterrupted health, and that we have no wish unaccomplished but to see you, and know that you are happy.

Were I sure that this letter would ever reach you, I might perhaps extend it, and tell you some anecdotes that would amuse you; but I must keep them till I have the great felicity to see you, if indeed so happy an hour is still reserved for me upon earth. I must not, however, omit acquainting you that Miss Watkin is married to Mr. Colebrook of Ashfield, and that she is likely soon to be a mother. Another female you were interested in is the mother of a very thriving boy, who shall not want the protection of him who remains

Your ever affectionate father and friend,

EVAN EVANS./

P. S. David Morgan's friends are well. It was from his letter we were first acquainted with your disaster, which he very feelingly lamented; and we are all well pleased with his attachment to you.

270 *The History of Ned Evans*

It was some time before Ned could calm the transports which these letters conveyed to his soul. Happiness flowed in upon him with so full a tide, that he was in danger of forgetting it could ever ebb again, if the recollection that there were still five thousand miles of ocean to be passed before he could behold the dear objects of his affection had not occurred to his mind, and a little damped that ardour with which he fancied himself just going to throw himself into their arms. A serene joy, however, glowed in his heart, and diffused itself over his countenance; which was instantly taken notice of by the Captain and Mrs. Fanshaw, as soon as he returned to them. They too had received pleasing intelligence from/ their friends in Ireland, particularly from the good alderman in Cork, who was highly delighted with the termination of the war, however lucrative it had been to him; but lamented the change in his daughter Lucy's disposition, who seemed to have lost all the usual gaiety and cheerfulness of her temper, and to give herself wholly to thought and retirement. They were no strangers to the cause of this change, which never was reflected on by one of them without the tenderest emotions: but this day was not a time to indulge in melancholy, the recollection of which they banished by introducing hope, and eagerly looking forward to the hour (not far distant, as they imagined) when the green hills of Ireland, or the white cliffs of Albion, should delight their eyes, rising out of the deep, and inviting them to the enjoyment of love, liberty, and peace. – To the speedy arrival of this happy hour! the Captain and Edward poured a libation of/ excellent Madeira; and Ned having recovered all those things he left in his old lodgings, particularly the picture of Lady Cecilia, given him by poor Captain Rivers, he returned in the evening to Captain Fanshaw's, and lodged in the same house with him until the fleet of merchantmen which were bound for Europe, and ready to sail with the first fair wind, should put to sea./

CHAP. LIV.

It was not many days before this wished-for breeze sprung up; and on Wednesday the third of September, about eleven in the forenoon, they embarked on board the good ship Columbus, Captain William Hatter, bound for London: but the harbour of Cork being nothing out of the way, the captain, who was also part owner of the vessel, promised to touch there, and land them at the Cove. The vessel was laden chiefly with rice and indigo; and about three o'clock the pilot left them, having seen them safe over the bar. The day was fine, and the wind fair; and they continued upon deck gazing at the receding land, till the spire of St. Michael's, the last object visible, sunk in the waves. As the evening advanced they retired to the cabin, where Captain/ Hatter had tea and coffee ready for them; and his son, who was his mate, and had a good voice, sung several sea songs; and the evening passed agreeably, till, the motion of the ship increasing, they perceived they had reached the gulph stream,[7] when Mrs. Fanshaw and the children retired to their births; but the gentlemen, not being affected with any sickness, ate a good supper, and joined with the captain and his son in drinking a bowl of punch to a happy sight of the Cove, and the further success of the voyage! Before morning they were clear of the gulph, and, with a fair wind and smooth sea, proceeded as prosperously as hearts could wish. Every day at noon, when their observation was made, they traced their course upon the map, and saw with pleasure every hour bringing them nearer to the object of their hopes. Oh! happy ignorance! which hides with an impenetrable veil the events of futurity, and suffers not the hour of distress/ to afflict us before our time! They had now been twenty-seven days at sea, during which time they had for the most part favourable winds, which allowed them continually to stand their course: so that, according to their reckoning, they had run down above 40 degrees of longitude, and were rejoicing in the comfortable prospect of seeing their friends in about two weeks more. But on the evening of the last day of September the wind shifted to the south-east, and the sun set in such a dark and troubled bank as intimated an approaching storm. The vigilance of the captain and the crew was not wanting to prepare for it: the top-gallant masts were taken down; the topmasts lowered; the sails reefed, and every thing put in the best trim possible.[8] Mean

– 271 –

272 *The History of Ned Evans*

time it grew profoundly dark – the wind whistled through the shrouds – and the rumbling of the distant thunder, every peal growing louder and louder, announced the arrival of the/ tempest. The sea now rolled like mountains, the summits of which, brightened by the vivid flashes of the lightning, shone luminous on the black horizon, and threatened to overwhelm the struggling vessel in the profound abyss beneath them. The captain himself was at the helm; our passengers all closed in their births, where sleep was the least of their thoughts, and where poor Mrs. Fanshaw and her infants lay terrified almost to death. Her affectionate husband was tenderly leaning over her, and endeavouring to allay her terrors, when, about midnight, a tremendous crash, accompanied with a dreadful peal of thunder, was heard upon deck. The dreadful cry of 'All hands aloft!' intermixed with the prayer of 'Lord, save us, or we perish!' chilled even the stoutest hearts, and bade them prepare for death. Ned instantly went upon deck, but prevailed on Captain Fanshaw to stay below with his family, nothing that they could do being of any use even to their personal/ safety. When he got upon deck, he saw the danger imminent indeed. The mainmast had been shivered with lightning, and two of the sailors struck dead. The poor captain was still at the helm endeavouring to keep the vessel's head to the waves, whilst his son and the surviving crew were cutting away the remains of the mast and clearing them from the shrouds. The poor fellows who were struck were stowed away by themselves; and their messmates almost envied them that they had been so speedily relieved from all their terrors. Towards morning the gale abated; but the sea continuing to run mountains high, the ship laboured[9] dreadfully, and made so much water that they feared the lightning had done her some material damage. The crew was now reduced to six mariners, with the captain and his son; three male passengers, Captain Fanshaw, Edward, and David Morgan; Mrs. Fanshaw and her maid, with three children: in all sixteen souls, eleven of whom only could be of/ any use. The weather continued rough and squally; and the leak, notwithstanding that all hands relieved each other constantly at the pumps, considerably increased upon them. Five days did they struggle with these disastrous circumstances, when, finding that notwithstanding all their labour there were now seven feet water in the hold, they gave it over, and a melancholy council was called to see what they should do. They computed that they were somewhat above 500 miles from Cape Clear in Ireland, and about 400 from the Azores. There were two long boats in the vessel, one considerably larger than the other, but either of them capable to carry all that remained of the company: – but then the hazard of being exposed in the Atlantic ocean at a stormy time of the year, in an open boat, scarcely gave them a chance for life; whilst, on the other hand, the ship seemed to afford them still less, for she was filling fast with water, and could not, in/ their opinion, float for four-and-twenty hours longer. Their only chance in her was some vessel heaving in sight that might discover their distress, and take them on board. As long as this faint hope held out any possible prospect, they determined to wait upon the deck, which alone was now habitable, for the water was two feet deep in the cabin; but a thick fog coming on in the afternoon, this last hope was taken away, and nothing remained but to trust themselves to the boat. Poor Captain Hatter was advanced in years; and almost all that he had in the world being embarked on board this vessel, he determined never to quit her while she remained above water, and at last, if no relief came, to go down with her. His son did all he could to make him change this resolution, but in vain; and when he found him immovably determined, he piously and affectionately resolved to share his fate, let it be what it would, and never to abandon his dear/ parent in the hour of distress. All the seamen, however, determined for the boat; and the largest of them was accordingly launched into the water. The good captain gave them free liberty to take whatever stores they could find either in the cabin or from the cargo. The latter was almost wholly overwhelmed with water; but from the cabin they got some biscuit[10] and rice, as also a case of spirits and some wine. Ned carried with him his musket and Indian belt, with powder and ammunition: a hogshead[11] of fresh water was also put on board, and a compass. The evening was dark and gloomy; and night coming down apace. It was the fifth of October, between four and five in the afternoon, when they departed from the ship. Poor Captain Hatter and his son stood on the quarter-deck, and, with a magnanimity truly heroic, gave them three parting cheers. They were answered from the boat with that heartfelt affection which/ the melancholy presage that they should never meet again in this world would naturally inspire. As long as light permitted them to see, their eyes were mutually turned towards each other; but the increasing thickness of the fog, added to the coming down of night, soon closed this sad interview, and separated them for ever. The night, though gloomy, was not boisterous,[12] and the wind was fair; yet the consciousness of their forlorn condition, and utter inability to weather any future gale, forbade them to build any strong hope on this favourable circumstance. Poor Mrs. Fanshaw, unused to difficulties of any kind, and with an infant at her breast, was an object of the most affecting consideration. Every attention that was possible to be paid to her, she received, not only from her husband and from Edward, but also from the whole crew. Her terror, however, was extreme, and the first consequence of it was her milk going away./ The little innocent, who had as yet known no other food, and who in this situation could get no substitute, fell a sacrifice to this loss, and expired in its mother's arms on the second evening of their melancholy voyage.

Though few women possessed greater strength of mind than Mrs. Fanshaw, nor any perhaps more perfect resignation of spirit, yet she could hardly be brought to believe that her dear infant was really dead, and would not part with it till its countenance became shocking even to herself to look on. She at last committed it to the deep, but with it all her strength and resolution. They

274 *The History of Ned Evans*

had been now four days and nights in the midst of the ocean, in an open boat; and the weather being tolerably favourable, they had not felt any extraordinary inconvenience: but now it turned squally again, with heavy showers of rain, which drenched them all to the skin. Poor Mrs. Fanshaw's constitution could not stand out against all these/ accumulated hardships; all that her husband and Edward could do was not able to sooth her, nor even induce her to take the refreshment of a little biscuit soaked in wine. Her thoughts ran entirely on her little daughter whom she had lost, and she followed her to Paradise on the third evening after.

It is not possible to express the agony of grief with which poor Captain Fanshaw beheld the body of this justly beloved woman launched into the abyss, whither he himself would certainly have followed, if Edward had not forcibly held him down, and presented to his arms his two yet surviving children. Indeed it was to Edward only these poor boys clung now for protection. The youngest remembered how he had before saved his life, and always since looked up to him as a benefactor. But now their unhappy father was so overpowered with his affliction, that his reason seemed affected, and, except when he lay in a state/ of stupid insensibility, he kept continually calling for his wife. At last he grew outrageous,[13] and it was with infinite difficulty he was secured so as that he should not throw himself overboard.

Hitherto the wind had been pretty favourable; and as they had now run before it for eleven days, the boatswain,[14] who was considered as commander, cheered them with the hope of soon seeing land. In fact, the next morning they fancied they descried it, and began to give a loose to hope; but thick rain and heavy squalls from the southwest coming on about noon, these hopes were again dashed, and the greatest apprehensions conceived that they should not be able to live through the night. The evening, indeed, set in with all the horrors of tempestuous darkness, in which their only care was to preserve, if possible, the boat from being filled. Poor Captain Fanshaw lay bound in her bottom, there being no safety for him in any other state; and his/ two poor boys clung round Edward's knees, in an agony of terror and of affection not to be described. In this perilous situation they ran before the wind for some hours, in the midst of a darkness which would not permit them to behold any thing. At last one of the men forward cried out, Land! – and presently the thundering of the breakers appalled every heart – To tack[15] was impossible – to go forward almost certain death – A huge billow at this instant lifted the boat as it were to the skies, and, thundering down, split it to pieces on a rock, sweeping with irresistible force every thing before it./

CHAP. LV.

SELF-preservation is certainly the first principle implanted in every thing that has life. Under the influence of this principle Ned supported himself amid the waves as soon as he emerged from that which had overwhelmed him. A second soon came thundering on in like manner as the former, and bore him forward towards the shore: – as it receded back, he felt his feet touch ground, and at the same time caught a firm grip of sea-weed which grew upon a rock; to this he clung, and established himself upon it before the next wave broke over him, which receding in its turn gave him time to breathe. For two hours he clung fast to this rock, whilst every wave overwhelmed him with a deluge of spray, but left him time to get breath in the intervals/ of its approach. At last, as the tide ebbed out, he became in some measure relieved from this inundation. Though still wet with the spray, the body of the wave did not reach him, and he maintained his position on the rock without being in danger of being washed off from it. The morning at length dawned, and discovered to him an iron coast of lofty preci-pices, round whose bases the Atlantic thundered for ever, though in vain. His station was on a rock detached from the cliff by an interval of about thirty feet, and which had probably at some remote period tumbled from the top: at high water it was covered with the tide, which luckily proved his preservation, as the quantity of sea-weed with which it was covered at once enabled him to catch a grip of it, and prevented his being much bruised when he was thrown upon it. With a sorrowing yet a thankful heart he cast a melancholy look around him, but could discover no particle of the/ boat, nor yet a vestige of any human being; but as the day advanced, he was himself discovered from the summit of the preci-pice by some fishermen who were taking their early rounds along the coast, and passing to the creeks in which their boats lay. The sea was still too tempestuous for any boat to venture on it; but these humane people determined to use every exertion to save their fellow-creature, taught by their own hazards and misfor-tunes to succour the distressed. With this charitable intention, some of them were let down from the summit of the cliff by ropes fastened round their middle, and secured at top by their comrades, till they found a pretty firm footing nearly on a level with the rock on which Edward lay. He soon perceived them; but

276 *The History of Ned Evans*

how to avail himself of their humanity was a matter of considerable difficulty, as the rock was insulated by a streight of about thirty feet wide, through which a tempestuous sea was still foaming. After many ineffectual struggles,/ in which his strength and hope were nearly exhausted (as the tide was now again coming in), he was at last fortunate enough to catch the end of a rope, which he made fast to a part of the rock on which he lay, whilst they secured it on the other side where they stood; and having fastened another rope round his body for security, the other end of which they held, he warped along the first over the chasm, and was received with joyful huzzas[16] by his generous preservers. He was, however, so exhausted as to be hardly able to stand, and was obliged to be hoisted up to the top of the cliff without any exertions of his own. A humane lady, who dwelt about half a mile off, in a sweet situation by the sea-side, and who had been early informed of his condition, had sent a horse to convey him to her house, not knowing but he was a common seaman; and had also sent some biscuit and warm wine for a present refreshment. To this hospitable lady's he was/ conveyed, and had the pleasure to hear by the way that two more of the crew had been saved in a creek, and were taken to some of the fishermen's houses, but they did not know their names. When he arrived at the house, he was received by an old and faithful man-servant of the lady's, who conducted him to a comfortable chamber, in which a warm bed and clean linen were provided for him, the things in the world he stood most in need of, and where he was suffered to repose without being as yet troubled with any questions; his fatigued and exhausted spirits evidently pointing out the necessity of quiet.

Providence, however, in bringing him to this house, had committed him to the protection of one who would be more interested in his welfare, than either he expected, or she herself at present knew. The benevolent inhabitant of this pleasant and retired mansion was Mrs. Mary Waldron, the relict of Doctor Richard Waldron, a/ most worthy and respectable clergyman of the diocese of Cork, and mother to that beautiful but unfortunate lady who was married to the late Lord Rivers contrary to the wish and approbation of his father, who therefore would never see him more. We have before related, that this young and amiable lord had died without having had the happiness to be reconciled to his parent, leaving his wife big with child; and the lovely widow herself lived only to be delivered of a son, whom his grandmother Mrs. Waldron never saw, happening to be absent, in the very house she then inhabited when her dear daughter Lady Rivers died; and receiving intelligence soon after from the present Lord Ravensdale, that the infant had died also at nurse, by which he himself became heir to the honours and estate of Ravensdale.

The present lord, who was then only Colonel Rivers, but possessed of a very good fortune, had never approved of the/ severity of his brother to his only son and the heir of his estate; particularly as the beauty and amiable virtues of the lady he had married were such as justified any young man, let his quality be ever so great, in exalting her to his own rank. He tried therefore, sincerely, every effort to induce his brother to be reconciled; and when this proved in vain, and that his lordship was so inexorable as to withdraw also his pecuniary allowance, leaving his son to subsist only upon his pay as a captain of dragoons, the colonel had generously interfered, and allowed his nephew, out of his own pocket, an annuity of five hundred a year, two of which was secured to Lady Rivers, in case she should survive her lord; but in case Lord Rivers should succeed his father in his titles and estate, it was then agreed that he should repay to the colonel or his heirs the amount of the annuity with which he accommodated him. When both Lord Rivers and his amiable/ lady died, the whole annuity reverted to Colonel Rivers; but in the same letter with which he acquainted Mrs. Waldron with the melancholy account of the sudden death of her infant grandson, by which all impediments were removed between himself and the succession, he endeavoured to mitigate her affliction by the assurance that the two hundred a year which he had settled upon her daughter, should be secured to herself during her life, as a token of the great respect he had for her memory, and well knowing that her circumstances were in no respect equal to her merits, nor to the situation which she had hitherto enjoyed. What the colonel thus generously offered he punctually made good, adding a very handsome present when he himself assumed the title of Ravensdale; and Mrs. Waldron had now for two-and-twenty years constantly received her annuity of two hundred pounds, and was secured in it by his lordship for her life. It is no wonder then/ if her grateful heart should be deeply attached to his lordship and to every person he regarded, though as yet she did not know the young man she had then in her house was of the number; for indeed she was ignorant of his name, though, had she heard it, she would have been struck with it, for she had passed part of this very summer at Ravensdale, whither she often went, and was no stranger to the gallant conduct of Evans, nor to the high estimation in which he was justly held by her noble friends.

The good lady was herself a model of every thing amiable, gentle, and humane. Somewhat past her grand climacteric,[17] her eyes still beamed with good nature, which spread a soft lustre and prepossessing character over her mild and venerable countenance. Her person was rather full, but not inelegantly so. Blessed with a strong constitution, which a contented mind preserved still unimpaired, she felt but little of the infirmities of age; and her whole/ appearance seemed to justify the hope that she might still continue for many years to be the delight of her opulent neighbours, and the refuge of those who were distressed.

The house in which she resided was pleasantly situated at the bottom of a bay which opened to the south, and was defended on each side by lofty precipices, whose aged bases were washed by the ocean, and where nature appeared in some of her most august forms. To the north was a hill, the summit of which

278 *The History of Ned Evans*

was crowned with a thriving plantation; and along the sides were stretched the gardens sheltered on all sides from the winds, but open to the sun, whose genial influence matured the fruits and flowers of the climate to uncommon perfection. Between the house and the sea was a pebbly strand, and through all the neighbourhood a multitude of little sheltered bays, bounded with rocks and promontories, and adorned with a vast/ variety of shells and corals, and marine plants. The naturalist here might have found an inexhaustible mine of knowledge and amusement. To this study her husband Doctor Waldron had been addicted, which induced him to rent this place from a great proprietor who lived in England, and to make it his favourite residence. His widow felt a similar attachment to it, and her life being in the lease, she held it for that term.[18] A maiden lady of the name of Walker, somewhat younger than Mrs. Waldron, but with similar dispositions, usually spent a great part of the year with her, and was in the house at this time. They were both warmly interested for the young man who had been so surprisingly rescued from death, and longed to know the particulars of his situation; but they would not suffer Edward to be disturbed till he woke of himself, though William the servant had orders to stay constantly in/ the chamber, and to get for him whatever he required.

Several hours elapsed before Edward awoke from that deep repose into which the great fatigue both of his body and his mind had thrown him. At length he opened his eyes, and at first could hardly recollect where he was. Seeing the servant, however, he enquired of him to whom he was obliged for his humane and comfortable reception; and when he was informed, he gratified William's curiosity with respect to himself, who immediately conveyed the tidings to his mistress. Mrs. Waldron was no sooner acquainted that it was Mr. Evans she had in her house, than she immediately went to his chamber, and seated herself by his bedside, where she was satisfied, from his own mouth, that he was the identical Evans she had heard so much of at Ravensdale. 'Oh,' says she, 'what blessed tidings these will be for my good old Lord and my dear Lady/ Cecilia!' Ned would have asked her a thousand questions relating to them, but she would not satisfy him in any. She was afraid of his being taken ill in consequence of the dreadful hardships he had undergone; and it was in vain that Ned assured her he was as well as ever he was in his life. She knew, she said, it was impossible, and therefore insisted upon his lying still and taking his repose. She ordered William to get some wine whey[19] made, and a piece of dry toast. Ned pleaded for a beef steak and some potatoes; but this the good lady, who was a notable physician, positively interdicted, and compelled him to submit to her regimen, which indeed Ned saw he could not oppose without danger of offending her. He determined, therefore, to obey her for this day, and, in gratitude for her care and attention, to lie still till the morning; but he prevailed on Mrs. Waldron to enquire the names of two others of his unfortunate shipmates, who,/ he understood, had been saved. It was with true joy he learned that David Morgan was one; the other was the boatswain: but they were both so bruised among the rocks, that it would be some days before they could be able to move. Poor Captain Fanshaw, with his two boys, were never heard of more: the maid and five mariners shared the same fate. Some of the bodies were afterwards thrown ashore on different parts of the coast, and were decently interred: but of all the crew who failed from Charlestown, Ned, David Morgan, and the boatswain, alone got safe to shore./

CHAP. LVI.

THE next morning proved fine, and Ned (resolved not to be again compelled to an unnecessary indolence) rose at an early hour, and prevailed upon William to conduct him to the cottages where Morgan and the boatswain were lodged. He found the poor fellows still very sore from their bruises, but in a fair way to get better; and Morgan in particular, deeply impressed with a grateful sense of the mercy of his deliverance, and hardly less thankful for that of his master than his own. He returned by the coast side, and, as he viewed the rock on which he had been thrown, admired by what miraculous providence he had been enabled to retain his station on it. A tender recollection of the Fanshaws, with whom he had lately been so/ happy, and over whose cold and scattered remains the ocean he was now contemplating rolled its billows, drew from his breast a sympathetic sigh, not unaccompanied with a friendly tear, the last and only tribute he could pay to their memory. The living now claimed his attention; and therefore he bent his way back to Mrs. Waldron's whom he found waiting for him to break-fast, and under some uneasiness that he had ventured so soon abroad. The good lady, however, soon banished her apprehensions, when she beheld the demoli-tion he caused in her hot loaf and butter, the ruddy colour of his cheek, and the animated lustre of his eye. Indeed, the activity of his Indian life had strung all his nerves with vigour, and given to every muscle its most perfect contour; so that no statuary, even of antiquity, ever produced a more finished model of male beauty, nor any painter a richer glow of apparent health. His dress indeed was/ nothing but the jacket and trowsers which he had on when he left the ship, for to this his whole wardrobe was reduced; but his person did not stand in need of ornaments to set it off, and never looked more engaging than in the simplest attire.

Mrs. Waldron could hardly take her eyes off him all the time he sat at break-fast: not that she had any pleasure in gazing on handsome young men, but she fancied she discovered in his countenance a strong resemblance of her dear daughter,[20] whose picture she had hanging at her watch. The same idea struck Miss Walker too; and however fanciful it might be, it still had the effect to con-ciliate, in a very high degree, Mrs. Waldron's affection, and to interest her heart in Edward's welfare much more powerfully than perhaps any other circumstance could have done. After breakfast the ladies invited Ned into the gardens, which, though more laid out for use than ornament, were yet/ charmingly disposed, and abounded, even to profusion, with every fruit that the climate could bring to perfection. The season was not yet entirely over for some of these luxuries; and therefore Mrs. Waldron had ordered some of the best kinds that remained to be carried to a rural seat in the garden, whither she and Miss Walker conducted Edward, and where, after he had regaled himself with some nectarines, they requested he would entertain them with an account of his adventures.

My indulgent readers, who are already acquainted with the most interesting parts of them, will excuse me from entering into any new detail of them, and content themselves with knowing that for upwards of two hours the ladies listened with unwearied attention, and seemed to take as deep an interest in the relation as if they themselves were sharers in the events. Mrs. Waldron was particularly pleased with the faithful attachment of David Morgan; and/ when she learned that he also had survived the shipwreck, and was in her neighbourhood, she determined to have him up to her house that very night, and to afford him every comfortable accommodation that was in her power to bestow. The more she saw of Edward, the more deeply did she feel interested in whatever befel him; and saw, or fancied she saw, new likenesses to the deceased Lady Rivers, who had been the idol of her heart, and every feature of whose face, and even the tones of her voice, were still fresh in her recollection. A guitar happening to lie in the parlour-window, Ned chanced to take it up; and turning over a book of old Scotch songs which lay beside it, he lighted on 'Will you gang to the ewe-bughts, Marion?'[21] and played it, accompanying it at the same time with his voice. It had been a favourite air with Lady Rivers, and the very instrument on which he played it had once been hers. Mrs. Waldron at first listened/ with delight; but, over powered with the recollection, she burst into tears, and was obliged to leave the room. Poor Edward was extremely disconcerted till Miss Walker explained the cause, and then he resolved to touch no more upon such tender strings whilst he remained at Glendemus, the name of Mrs. Waldron's house. But the sensation which Ned's voice excited in that good lady's bosom had more of pleasure in it than of pain; at least it possessed that tender melancholy which a gentle and affectionate heart loves to cherish. When therefore she returned into the room, she insisted on his taking up the instrument again, and made him play a variety of tunes, and sing a number of songs, that awoke all her tenderest recollections, and gratified every feeling of her soul. At night, when Edward retired to his chamber, Mrs. Waldron went to that of Miss Walker. 'Well!' said she, 'my dear Miss Walker, what do you think of this/ young man we have got?' 'Think of him?' said she, 'I think him beyond all comparison the most engaging young fellow I ever saw. If I were not secured by the hoary wisdom of sixty winters, I don't know but my heart would play me a trick.' 'I can assure you, my dear Jenny,' said

282 *The History of Ned Evans*

Mrs. Waldron, 'he has won mine, yet not in the way of love. O Jenny, he is so like my Lætitia! – His eye, his manner, nay his voice brings her so strongly to mind, that if the dear infant to whom she imparted life in the moment that she lost her own, had not so soon followed its blessed mother, I could almost be persuaded this youth was he. He too is Edward, and his age exactly corresponds.' – 'I confess to you, my dear Mrs. Waldron,' replied Miss Walker,' that there are certain turns in Mr. Evans's countenance that do very much remind me of poor Lady Rivers; but that he should be her son appears to me so romantic, that I am amazed you could/ give way to such a supposition even for a moment. This young man was born in Wales, and never from under his father's eye till about three years ago; and how then can you reconcile such a contradiction?' 'My dear Jenny,' said Mrs. Waldron, 'I do not attempt to reconcile it, nor know nothing about it. I never saw my grandson; but this young man is so like my daughter, that my heart yearns to him. There is also something very extraordinary in his history. An accident the most uncommon introduced him to Lady Cecilia Rivers, who, I am convinced, loves him, and is determined to marry him. Should this take place, and Lord Rivers die, whose life is not worth a week's purchase, then this young man will heir[22] Ravensdale, and (except the title) stand in my grandson's place.' – 'The case,' replied Miss Walker, 'is extraordinary, but still I cannot possibly conceive him to be your grandson. The/ character of Lord Ravensdale, who is honour and integrity itself, makes it impossible; and therefore, my dear Mrs. Waldron, I would not mention such a thing for the world, nor even indulge such a hope; but granting the possibility of the circumstance, then Providence seems to be in the train to disclose this mystery; and on this account also I would leave it to him, and never hint to human being that I had such a conception, unless something much more convincing than the mere circumstance of resemblance and co-incidence of name should arise.' – 'Your advice, my dear Jenny,' said Mrs. Waldron, 'is what I perfectly approve, and what indeed my own thoughts suggested to me. I have the highest opinion of Lord Ravensdale, and certainly owe him an immense debt of gratitude. If I feel interested in Mr. Evans, as I confess I do, his lordship does so likewise; and I well know Lady Cecilia does still more;/ so that on this head there will be no difference. The events of this young man's life are so extraordinary, and the last not the least, which has thrown him under the protection of my roof, that I feel my heart entirely at ease about him, and that I may safely confide him to the guidance of that Almighty Being, who seems in an especial manner to protect him, and to direct his outgoings and his comings-in; and who no doubt will order all things concerning him with strictest justice and unerring wisdom.' With this pious sentiment Mrs. Waldron retired to her room, but not to rest. Her spirits had received an impulse that would not suffer them immediately to subside, and through far the greater part of the night agitated her imagination with a thousand conceptions for and against the strange impression she had received. At last, wearied with the perplexing contradictions which presented themselves whatever side of the question she contemplated,/ she sunk to rest, and enjoyed that balmy repose which Heaven reserves for virtuous minds alone, and which frequents the cottage and the truss of clean straw fully as often as the marble palace and the bed of down./

CHAP. LVII.

It was not till a late hour that Mrs. Waldron came down to breakfast; but Edward, whose spirits were now buoyant as the air, rose with the lark, and had amused himself with wandering among the rocks, and exploring the various bays, with which the shores about Glendemus were indented. In one of these was a huge cavern, not unaptly termed the cathedral,[23] to the noblest of which in the Gothic style it bore a strong resemblance. Edward had a horror of caverns ever since his adventure in the sacred cave of Agigua; nevertheless, he was tempted to peep in, and was rewarded with a spectacle of grandeur, which a lover of the sublime in nature would have thought ample recompense for a long journey. At high water the tide/ flowed in to the end of this cavern upwards of five hundred feet, and at all times left a pool of the most crystalline transparency for nearly its whole length, and deep enough to float a ship. The bottom was formed of shells, which through the water appeared of the most resplendent beauty; and all the sides were lined with mosses and sea-plants in boundless variety. A bath so inviting tempted Edward to strip and plunge in; and being an excellent diver, he got up several handfuls of the most beautiful shells, as well as specimens of various mosses which, he observed, Mrs. Waldron had a taste for; and combined into several beautiful pieces of shell-work, so as to resemble, in the most lively manner, grottos, obelisks, groves, and ruins; as also flowers so correct as to deceive even upon a near inspection. He had observed somewhat of a similar taste in Lady Cecilia Rivers, and therefore was determined to make use of his present opportunity to collect/ a quantity of these rarities for her. He intended, indeed, to surprise her ladyship, and throw himself at her feet, as soon as he was in a condition to travel; and only waited the answer to his letter to the agent of his regiment in Dublin, and the cash which he expected from him, to equip himself with immediate necessaries, for the ship-wreck had left him nothing but the clothes on his back, and poor Weenacoba's wampum belt, which happened to be about his neck. In the mean time he was in the happiest quarters in which he could be placed; and every hour endeared him more and more to Mrs. Waldron, whose affection could hardly be greater if he really was her grandson. When he came into the parlour, and shewed her his shells and mosses, she knew by his

– 284 –

dripping curls where he had been, and gently chid him for venturing alone to swim in those deep pools, and among slippery rocks. He smiled, and asked her if she would have/ one of the maids to attend him, since she thought he could not take care of himself. She said, 'No:' she did not know whether she would trust him even with one of the maids; but she would attend him herself, unless he promised not to run any more hazard of being drowned while he was under her protection. 'You are so kind to me, my dear Mrs. Waldron,' said he, 'that I should be unpardonably guilty, if I should willingly give you any uneasiness: therefore, whatever commands you lay upon me I shall obey.' – 'It is dutifully spoken,' said she (and she looked at Miss Walker): 'if every young man were as tractable, we should no longer lament the want of grey heads upon green shoulders. – 'I hope the grey heads will long continue on the shoulders which they most adorn,' replied Ned; 'but submission to authority, and acquiescence with well-intended advice, become all heads, whether green or grey; and therefore I/ shall pay it.' In the midst of this conversation William entered the room with some letters, one of which Mrs. Waldron announced to be from Lady Cecilia. A deeper crimson glowed on Edward's cheek, on hearing this news; and he could not suppress his impatience while the old lady sought her spectacles, first in one pocket and then in the other, and after all found them in neither. 'Oh! here they are,' said he, as he spied one end of them peeping out of her prayer-book, where she had been reading the psalms appointed for the day. The good lady having adjusted them to her nose, went to the window with her letter; and Edward's eye attentively watched every feature of her face. 'It is all over,' said Mrs. Waldron. 'Dear Madam, what is all over?' said Edward: 'is Lady Cecilia dead?' 'No,' said Mrs. Waldron, 'or she could hardly have written an account of it herself. In good truth, my young friend, I suspect you were born/ among us, or you could not so quickly have acquired the art of bull-making.'[24] Edward blushed. 'Lord Rivers,' said Mrs. Waldron, 'is no more; and his poor father is in the deepest affliction. Lady Cecilia also is a sincere mourner: yet her tears are not so wholly engrossed but she has some left for you, Mr. Evans: but these I hope we shall soon wipe away. Come, I see,' said she, 'your impatience. There, read the letter yourself. Her ladyship never had a thought that might not be proclaimed to all the world.' Ned bowed his gratitude, and took the letter, which trembled in his hand as he read the following lines:

Ravensdale, October 14, 1783.

My dear Mrs. Waldron!

We have at length received the melancholy account of my dear brother's death. He departed this life on the second of this month at the Hot Wells of Bristol,/ worn to a shadow, but sensible to the last. Though this issue of his complaint has been long foreseen, yet I cannot express to you the effect which the confirmation of the event has had upon my father. He has never been out of bed since he heard of it; and I wish to God he ever may![25] My poor brother George's death gave him a dreadful shock; but this seems to have overthrown him altogether, and to have entirely undermined the pillars of his constitution. We expect the body in the course of this week to be committed to the great storehouse of its ancestors; and until this last and melancholy duty is over, I cannot hope for any softening of my dear father's anguish. Ever since George's death he has spoken of Mr. Evans with increased affection; but, alas! here too is another source of sorrow, and our tears are doomed to flow for every one to whom we are attached. No accounts as yet have reached us of this amiable and unfortunate/ young man, whose lot makes me tremble whenever I think of it, and yet is for ever in my thoughts.

Oh! my dear Mrs. Waldron! how much do I regret your absence at this time! It is cruel perhaps to invite you to the house of mourning; yet, if you can stand the scene, there is no presence could so cheer the heart of your faithful and affectionate

CECILIA RIVERS.

The usual lustre of Edward's eyes was softened with a dewy moisture as he returned the letter to Mrs. Waldron. 'What answer, madam,' said he, 'do you mean to give to this request of Lady Cecilia?' 'Nay,' said she, 'I have not thought yet. What would you have me do?' 'It is better,' said he, 'to go to the house of mourning than the house of feasting.[26] I will set out with you this hour.' 'What!' replied she, 'in that jacket and trowsers?' 'Yes,' said Edward,/ 'and without a shoe. I would go the whole way upon my knees if it would give her the least consolation.' 'Well,' said Mrs. Waldron, 'then we will go together, but not to-day. You know you have promised to obey me; and therefore I lay my injunction upon you not to think of quitting these premises till I give you leave.' 'But when will you give me leave?' said Edward. 'When I am ready to go with you,' replied Mrs. Waldron. 'I submit then,' said he; 'and can assure you that in so doing I give you a much stronger proof of my obedience than in refraining from the rocks; but the pleasure of pleasing you shall be my reward; and there is only one greater I could receive on earth.' 'I know well what that is,' said Mrs. Waldron; 'and I will venture to promise that you shall receive it; and no words of mine shall be wanting to express how worthy I think you of it.' 'Now,' said Mr. Evans, 'you do overpower/ me indeed. And great as was the first obligation I received from you, this which you now confer is still greater.'

The heart of Mrs. Waldron now sought to vent itself in private of all those complicated feelings with which it was ready to overflow. Her impression of the near relationship in which she imagined she stood to Edward gained strength in her mind every hour; and her affection for him grew so intense, that, if she had discovered her real grandson in any other person, she would have been disappointed. She anticipated the contending passions of joy and sorrow which she knew would arise in the bosom of Lady Cecilia when she restored to her her beloved Edward; and pleased herself with the thoughts how doubly welcome that present would make her visit. Her first preparation for this intended journey was to procure a proper equipment for Edward, who indeed at present stood in need of every necessary; and therefore she/ ordered William to procure from the next market-town the best materials and artificers that it could furnish. Ned was somewhat surprised, when he came in from his walk, to find a levee[27] of taylors, breeches-makers, shoemakers, &c, awaiting him. And poor David Morgan being now able to crawl about a little, and being equally destitute, he ordered him to be sent for, and they were both taken measure of for every article of dress. Ned ordered for himself a full suit of mourning, as also a regimental frock, with a complete equipment for the saddle, and (excepting the mourning) the same for David. A thousand thoughts arose in his imagination, and filled his breast alternately with hopes and fears – with doubts and with anxiety. If his expectations of Lady Cecilia were presumptuous before, they were now more so by an hundred fold; for, by her brother's death, she was become the first heiress in the kingdom, and, doubtless, would be sought for accordingly/. On the contrary, he had a recent proof that he was still dear to her recollection, and that neither absence, nor the probability of his being never heard of again, had been able to banish him from her heart. Mrs. Waldron's last observation had been a cordial to his soul, and Time seemed to have lost his speed till the necessary arrangements for their journey were completed. In the mean time, however, he wrote a long letter to his father, giving him a full account of his adventures, and particularly of his present situation; and promising that, after he had paid his duty to Lord Ravensdale and his lovely daughter, from whose house he was not above seventy miles distant, he would go to Dublin, and from thence to Holy-head, where he anticipated the joy with which he would be received by his dear parents in that peaceful and sequestered residence, which, if possible, was still more endeared to him by the dangers and the/ difficulties he had surmounted during the three years he had been absent from it.

I will leave it to my readers to imagine with what joy the good parson and his amiable wife received this letter just as they were fitting down to their old and comfortable meal of a Welch rabbit and a tankard of ale before they went to bed. To bed indeed they went in due time, as usual; but sleep they had none; and the whole night they passed in alternate prayers and thanksgivings, talking about their dear boy, and calculating the hours and minutes till they might hope to see him. And now Edward received a letter from the agent of the regiment in Dublin, congratulating him on his return to Ireland, and acquainting him that the regiment was reduced, and he, of consequence, was on half-pay. He inclosed him a remittance of 50l. which he had ordered, and acquainted him that he had still upwards of 300l. in his hands, for which he would/ be ready to account whenever he chose to settle.

These comfortable tidings gave an air of fresh animation to Edward's countenance, sufficiently interesting and animated before; and the different tradesmen having brought home their orders, for which he paid them on the spot, he appeared once more habited as the Officer and the Gentleman,[28] and (like Lothario,[29] though of a very different character) armed for love or war, and able to conquer in either field./

CHAP. LVIII.

In a few days Mrs. Waldron had made all her arrangements, and on Monday the 20th of October they set off together in a post-chaise from Glendemus. They went about five miles out of their road, to set down Miss Walker at her own house, and then proceeded for Limerick, which was about fifty miles of the journey, and where they intended to sleep the first night. David Morgan, who was now perfectly recovered, attended on horseback, and every step they advanced dilated Edward's heart, from the consciousness of its drawing him nearer and nearer to the dear possessor of it. No unpleasing circumstance happened during the day; they arrived in safety at their inn, and the agreeable humour of Mrs. Waldron was never at a loss for conversation./ She drew indeed from Edward the relation of his whole life, and dwelt particularly on the earliest parts of it; but from his relation could discover nothing to strengthen the suspicion she had imbibed. He described his mother as still living, and likely long to do so – as well as his father, who had neither of them been ever out of Wales, except when his father had been at college; and that he was still an unbeneficed clergyman: – but thanks to the generosity of that truly noble earl whom they were now going to see, he had been able to add some comforts to the age of his parents, and was himself, by the aid of the same benevolence, in a way to attain a station which was as much beyond his merits as his expectations. 'If I may judge of your merits by what I have heard and seen,' replied Mrs. Waldron, 'I know of no station beyond them, and hardly any to which I do not suspect them to be entitled: but God will in his own due time bring all things to light;/ for 'there is nothing hid that shall not be revealed, nor covered that shall not be known.' Edward was an entire stranger to the cause of this remark, and at some loss to account for it, but did not think proper to press for an explanation. He replied only in general, that 'the ways of Providence had been in respect to him wonderful; and that he should ever pay a cheerful and ready submission to them, whether favourable or severe.'

It was one of those charming days which in this climate we often experience in October, when mellow Nature robes herself in her richest attire, set off by a golden lustre peculiar to the season, which the declining sun sheds on every

– 289 –

290 *The History of Ned Evans*

object; when, on the second day of their journey, about three in the afternoon, the rich parks of Ravensdale, with their surrounding forests, and the silver windings of the Shannon appeared in view: from amidst the bosom of aged oaks, rose the summits of the noble mansion/ itself, whilst the calmness of the day, the deep silence of the woods, disturbed only by the rustling of some falling leaves, diffused a sober melancholy over the majestic prospect, perfectly in unison with the immediate occasion of their visit. Ned ordered the postillion to stop; they were now indeed on the very spot where he remembered to have stopped three years before to take his last look of Ravensdale, when he left it in company with his dear friend Captain Rivers to embark for America, and where he offered up a mental prayer to be brought back to it again. On the same spot he now offered up a mental thanksgiving, yet chastened with the tender recollection of his departed friend, and of the recent melancholy breach which the family had experienced. A few soft sorrows he on this occasion borrowed from Love to pay to Friendship, and Love was not displeased; for Friendship is his next of kin, and dearest of his relations. A peasant/ now happening to appear in view, they enquired of him about the family at Ravensdale. He informed them that the old lord took on greatly, on account of the young lord's death, whose body was arrived the evening before; but that Lady Cecilia was well. The name of Cecilia vibrated through the heart of Edward, and dispelled all glooms, as the dawn of morning chases before it the shadows of night; and the postillion driving on, soon brought them to the door. A servant in deep mourning opened it; and Lady Cecilia, who heard the carriage coming up the avenue, and supposed it to be Mrs. Waldron, had come down to receive her. She had just entered the saloon as Mrs. Waldron, leaning on Edward's arm, met her. Her ladyship, amazed and delighted, said, 'Mr. Evans! is it possible?' and, overpowered with surprise, and the sudden turn of her thoughts, would have fainted and fallen, had not Edward caught her in his arms. He himself/ was agitated to a degree, that prevented all utterance of speech; he pressed however Cecilia's hand to his bosom, where she distinctly felt the pantings of his heart, with which her own kept time in faithful unison; both ready to burst their habitations, to unite together. Mrs. Waldron saw these mutual emotions with delight; and indeed they were too apparent to escape the observation of the servants; who, however, on their parts were not much less delighted to see Ned return again in safety; for it was impossible for him to be known for any time, even by the humblest menial, without being endeared to him. A few minutes however restored both parties to some degree of composure, at least sufficient to enable them to walk into a drawing room, and sit down. A flood of tears here came to the relief of Lady Cecilia, in which it was doubtful whether those of joy or sorrow were most abundant. At length her ladyship regained that sweet/ and serene complacency, which was the habitual temperament of her soul. 'Oh! Mr. Evans!' said she, 'you must excuse the perturbation in which the joy of this

Volume IV 291

unexpected meeting has thrown my spirits; they have so long been unused to any pleasurable feelings, that I was not able to bear up against the sudden tide which rushed through its deserted channels. I have a thousand questions to ask you, but first, I must go to my dear father, and announce your arrival: if any event can give him pleasure in his present affliction, I know this will.' – 'My dear Lady Cecilia!' replied Ned, 'ever since I had first the happiness to be known to you, the honour of your friendship has been the sovereign cordial of my soul, and the pleasure which I feel after having escaped so many perils, to find myself again in your presence, would perhaps be too intense, if it had not been damped by the affecting situation in which your family at present is placed; and with/ whose unfeigned sorrows I beg leave to mix my own.' A look of the sweetest benignity, illumined perhaps a little by a ray of a more exalted passion, beamed on Edward as she passed him to go to her father: it kindled all the fires of his heart which, fanned by hope, burned brilliant, but did not consume./

'I told you, Edward,' said Mrs. Waldron, when Lady Cecilia was gone, 'that you should get the reward you sought.' 'Oh!' said he, putting both her hands between his, 'I am too happy. To your friendship I can confide my soul. I see her ladyship has not forgot me. I see I am still dear to her, and the rapture of knowing it is almost too much for me to bear.' – 'Edward,' said she, 'you deserve it all. She is a charming creature, to be sure, yet I tell you you are not her inferior. You are worthy of her. Your hearts were formed for each other: they were created to be united, and the will/ of Heaven shall be done.' Poor Edward, who had no conception of Mrs. Waldron's secret meaning, thought this speech only a rhapsody, which her friendship for him had inspired. It came, however, from the bottom of her heart, and the full conviction of her mind, however inscrutable the fact appeared. Lady Cecilia now re-entered the room. 'My father,' said she, 'Mr. Evans, has desired me to offer you his most affectionate congratulations on your safe return to this house. No event that has happened to him for a long time has given him equal pleasure. He has not been out of bed, only to have it made, for upwards of this fortnight past; but his impatience to see you is so great, that he has ordered a fire in the library, and is determined to rise in the evening, to have the pleasure of conversing with you. He desires me to present his compliments to you also, Mrs. Waldron, and to thank you for this kind instance of your attention in/ coming here at this time.' 'We are both under the highest obligations to his Lordship,' said Mrs. Waldron; 'and shall be most happy if our company can conduce to his amusement.' In this sentiment Edward sincerely joined; and now Lady Cecilia, impatient to hear something of Edward's adventures, desired him to relate them. Contrary to the manner of most historians, he began with the conclusion of his tale, and related the manner of his shipwreck, and the interposing hand of Providence, which threw him under the protection of Mrs. Waldron. He acknowledged his having received her ladyship's letter at Charlestown, which

292 *The History of Ned Evans*

was a rich cordial to his spirits after the desperate fatigues of his Indian expedition. He dwelt with a tender, yet a masterly hand on the pathetic circumstances of the death of her gallant brother; and here their tears flowed again in unison. Indeed the whole of his narrative commanded the deepest attention/ from both his hearers, till at last a servant announced dinner to be on the table. A temperate meal, which had the more merit as it was made in the midst of the most refined delicacies, sufficed these virtuous friends, which they made Edward wash down with a glass of exquisite wine, the richest vintage of France. But no pleasures of the table were at any time much prized by him, save only as they contributed to bring friends together, and to promote the genial intercourse of souls. The satisfaction of his heart at this moment arose from feelings which had no grossness in them, and to which the highest delicacies of food could give no addition. In the evening, after tea, Lord Ravensdale's gentleman acquainted Mr. Evans, that his lordship wished to see him in the library. There is perhaps no object more interesting to a contemplative mind than a great and good man in deep affliction: and of all the characters which the pen of any/ writer has ever drawn, the most instructive, and the most affecting, in my opinion, is that of Job.[30] I will not compare Lord Ravensdale to this renowned sufferer; for certainly neither his patience, nor his virtue, would bear to be placed in any degree of competition; but his misfortunes touched the heart of Edward, and added to that veneration which he had for his high rank, his exalted character, and his just sense of the great obligations he supposed himself to be under to him. When he entered the room, his lordship attempted to rise; but Ned, seeing him too feeble, sprung forward, and, dropping upon one knee at his feet, took his hand, and kissed it. His lordship, overpowered with his effort to rise, and with the multitude of tender recollections which filled his soul, sunk back in his arm chair, and was some minutes before he could speak. At length he recovered his voice: – 'In the multitude of the sorrows which weigh down my soul,/ I know no circumstance, Mr. Evans, that could at this time have given me equal satisfaction as that which I now enjoy in seeing you here. The friend of my dear son, in whose arms my gallant George breathed his last, exclusive of all former obligations, must ever be dear to me.' A tremulous hesitation in his speech here stopped his lordship from proceeding; and Edward, at that instant looking up, happened to cast his eye on a picture of Captain Rivers, exquisitely painted, which seemed to look from the canvas with an approving smile as it beheld Edward relating to his father the circumstances of his death. The effect was irresistibly affecting; and a heart much more callous than that of Edward could not fail to have been moved by it. For the space of near two hours he entertained Lord Ravensdale with the recital of the most remarkable events which had befallen him; till his lordship at last, overpowered with the fatigue of sitting up, and still more/ with the agitation of

Volume IV 293

his soul, gave him leave to retire, with assurances of an unalterable attachment of regard, friendship, and esteem.

As he left Lord Ravensdale's apartment, he met Lady Cecilia in the lobby, who asked him if he would take a last look of her brother where he lay in state. Edward complied. Her ladyship led him to the room which had formerly been his lordship's drawing-room, and which was now hung round with black. Having ordered the undertaker, who constantly watched the body, to withdraw, she turned the key in the lock, and Edward and she were left alone. On a raised platform, in the center of the room, lay the body in its coffin, under a canopy of black velvet. It had been embalmed at Bristol, and was to appearance as fresh as in the hour in which it had been separated from the soul. Twelve wax candles of a very large size were burning round it. At the head lay the/ escutcheon[31] of the family with the coronet; at the feet, a large marble urn, containing the heart and bowels of the deceased, embalmed, and which were to be deposited in the vault with the body. The countenance seemed placid and asleep. 'Here,' said Lady Cecilia, 'is what once was Lord Rivers.' Edward wept. 'I too could weep, my Edward!' said Lady Cecilia, 'but I visit this awful object every day.' 'Oh! my Cecilia!' said Edward; 'when I behold this body, and reflect that all that state and wealth it has lost you have gained, my heart trembles at its presumption when it asks you can you still think of your humble but faithful Edward?' 'My Edward! when I behold this body, my soul sickens at worldly pomp. Behold here the sad conclusion of all human greatness! The mind which has this object feelingly impressed upon it, despises wealth; and having food and raiment, may well learn to be therewith/ 'content.' 'Sweet moralist!' said he, as he held her land, while love sat trembling in his eyes; 'and canst thou be content with Edward?' – 'Oh! my Edward!' said she, 'Thou knowest I can be content with thee. Thou knowest my fond heart is all thy own. Give me thy love; and were I mistress of the Indies, they should be thine.' 'Here then, in this awful presence, my Cecilia!' said Edward, 'I devote my heart, my undivided heart, to thee. But why should I devote what is not mine to bestow! From the first hour I saw thee thou possessedst it; and never, never, shall another share it.' A holy kiss, in which their mutual souls hung on each other's lips, sealed this sacred promise; in which they both vowed to each other, that, until the great change should happen, by which both should become like the awful spectacle before them, their hearts should know no other love. For some time they enjoyed the sweet raptures of this/ mutual declaration; and their eyes melting as they viewed each other, beamed unutterable love. At length Lady Cecilia first broke silence: 'My Edward! (for from this hour I shall ever think you mine;) my Edward! let the solemn promise I have made you put your heart at rest, and remain contented with it for the present. Your Cecilia, while she lives, is yours; but the melancholy situation of my father prevents me at this time from avowing this sentiment. Alas! Edward, I behold him fast declining, and I would

294 *The History of Ned Evans*

not do a thing that could add one arrow to the many which stick in his soul, no, not to purchase Heaven. Be patient, then, my Edward! and seek not your Cecilia's hand till she can give it to you without a sigh, without a single reflection that can diminish the rapture with which she would bestow it.' 'Oh! Cecilia!' replied Evans, 'you are too good, too virtuous, too wise for me, ever to dispute your will. My tongue/ has no utterance that can express the sentiments with which my heart glows toward you. Let me then fold you to that heart, and swear by the faithful attachment it has for you, that I live but to love, to oblige, and to obey you.' With these words he again pressed her to his bosom, and their balmy lips breathed into each other the soul of love. They now returned to Mrs. Waldron, who was all this time meditating alone in the parlour; and Lady Cecilia again entrusted to the undertaker the melancholy charge of her brother's remains./

CHAP. LIX.

THE next day was appointed for paying the last sad duty to the deceased Lord Rivers; and as the rector of the parish of Ravensdale was very old and infirm, and entirely unable to officiate, Doctor Burton, as the intimate friend of the family, took the duty upon himself. We have before mentioned the good opinion he had conceived of Edward, and how much he was interested in his favour. It was with extreme pleasure, therefore, as well as surprise, that he learned, on his arrival at Ravensdale, that he was there before him. A very cordial interview took place between them, in which the Doctor pressed Edward to let him see him at Burton Hall – a visit which, indeed, Edward was very willing to make, but deferred at this/ time on account of the distressed state of the family he was with. Lord Ravensdale, who was unable to appear himself, had requested Edward to fulfil the duty of chief mourner, and to do the honours of the house – a task which he acquitted himself of to the perfect satisfaction of a very numerous assemblage of the principal gentlemen of the country, many of whom had never seen him before, but all of whom had heard the beginning of his history, and wished to improve their acquaintance with him, from the specimen of politeness and attention which he this day exhibited before them. After the funeral ceremony was over, they all returned to Ravensdale house, and partook of a splendid entertainment suitable to the dignity of the living lord, and to his affection for the deceased; and in the evening the company departed, impressed with very favourable sentiments of the good sense, modesty, and politeness of Edward. It was remarked, that neither/ of the Mr. Nettlefields was there, though invited. An excuse came from Captain Nettlefield, that his father was ill; but as no word in it was addressed to Edward, the real cause of their absence was imputed to a lurking envy and ungenerous hatred, which both their breasts were suspected of harbouring against that gallant young man. His heart, however, was clear of all resentment, and could not long retain ill will against any creature in the universe; according to the true observation of the poet,

> Forgiveness to the injur'd doth belong:
> They never pardon who have done the wrong.[32]

296 *The History of Ned Evans*

When the sad duties of this day were over, and the tomb closed on the last of Lord Ravensdale's sons, the surviving branches of the family felt a heavy weight removed from them, excepting the venerable peer himself. The ruin of his house, as he called it, wrung him to the soul;/ and being always of a religious turn of mind, he sometimes expressed himself as if he was deserted of God. The piety of his mind, directed perhaps by the native generosity of his temper, induced him to seek the favour of his Creator by the exercise of that godlike virtue which in Scripture is said to cover a multitude of sins; and therefore a few days after the interment of Lord Rivers, he gave to Doctor Burton one thousand guineas, to be by him distributed among such indigent families in the neighbourhood as he knew to be most in need of it. If the blessings of the poor could indeed at any time cure the distempers either of the body or the soul, it is certain Lord Ravensdale would never have felt any of them. But, alas! his disorder lay too deep; and his despondency at times began to be truly alarming. There was no society which at these times seemed so acceptable to him as Edward's. He felt a complacency in his presence, which/ he could not account for: he often kept him for hours together in his room, talking to him of his dear son George, hearing over and over again all the little anecdotes Edward could recollect about him; and not seldom reading his letters, in which frequent mention was made of Ned, in terms of the most ardent friendship. These melancholy interviews, though not quite suited either to Edward's years or disposition, yet he gladly indulged him in, happy in seeing his lordship somewhat relieved by them, and knowing it was the most acceptable service he could perform to Lady Cecilia. But as he had another duty to fulfil, which also lay near his heart, he did at last, with her ladyship's consent, hint to Lord Ravensdale the necessity he was under of going to see his father and mother, who knew that he had now been above a month in Europe, and who were extremely impatient to see him. A visible uneasiness appeared on Lord/ Ravensdale's countenance, when Edward mentioned going away; yet he admitted the necessity of it. At the same time he pressed him to return and spend the Christmas, 'for I know not how it is, my young friend, but I feel a comfort when you are with me that I do not experience on any other occasion.' 'My Lord,' replied Edward, 'there is no circumstance can give me equal joy to contributing to your comfort and consolation. And if your Lordship will permit me to go for a few weeks to Wales, to pay my duty to my parents, I shall return (if God spares me) before Christmas, and pass the winter with you.' This ready compliance cheered his countenance again; and the next day but one being fixed on for his departure, he went to acquaint Lady Cecilia with what had passed.

The candid confessions and mutual vows which had lately been made by each to the other, had removed from their young and/ amiable hearts all the pains and anxieties of love, whilst the sweet hopes of that gentle passion blossomed there as in their native soil. Lady Cecilia, therefore, approved of Edward's going to his father's, but enjoined him to remember his promise, and be speedy in his return. She told him also she expected to hear often from him, and promised that she would herself let him know all the material occurrences at Ravensdale, till she should have the happiness to see him there again. Her ladyship and Mrs. Waldron being engaged this morning about some business between themselves, Ned took that opportunity of traversing some of his old walks, and particularly he wished to visit Doran's mother, who as yet he supposed had not heard of his arrival. He bent his steps therefore towards his door; and entering it some-what abruptly, he found the old woman and her daughter by the fire-side, but thought there was some confusion in/ the young one's countenance, and that just as he entered, he saw something red huddled behind the partition. His sus-picion led him to young Nettlefield, for the girl was uncommonly beautiful; but as her mother was sitting by, perfectly composed, he could not think any thing improper had been passing. He felt however a desire to be satisfied, because he had marked this old woman for an object of his bounty, and did not choose it should be misplaced. She arose as soon as he entered, and expressed her joy at seeing him again; but she did not mention one word about her son.

Edward turning his conversation to the daughter, paid her some compli-ments on her good looks, and asked her if she had not got a sweetheart yet? She blushed, and denied it. 'It is impossible,' said Edward, 'if you are as good as you are fair, that so much comeliness should be overlooked.' 'What say you, dame!' said he to the mother. – /'Indeed, Sir,' said she, 'I hope she is good, and have no reason to think to the contrary, but as for a sweetheart, I never saw one enter the house.' 'Take care dame what you say, I strongly suspect there is one in the house at this instant.' A rustling was at this time heard behind the partition, and there came forward, not Captain Nettlefield, as Ned suspected, but David Morgan, to Ned's infinite surprise, and indeed somewhat more to his satisfaction. 'O ho!' says Edward, 'is it you David!' – 'Yes! please your honour!' replied he, 'it is I, indeed, but not in the character you supposed. It is but the second time I have ever been in the house, and I came only to talk with the young woman and her mother about my old comrade her son, that, as your honour knows, is a brother warrior of your own, among the Indians.'

'Well, David, this is a very good come off, but why did you hide yourself?' – /David looked a little aukward. 'I do not know, please your honour. I was afraid seeing me here, your honour might suspect something and be angry, but I declare both the girl and I are as innocent as the child unborn.' – 'I do not ques-tion the girl,' said Edward, 'but innocence need never hide itself; neither do I see any harm in a young man liking a handsome woman, provided his thoughts are honourable.' – 'God bless your honour!' said David, 'you know soldiers are always honourable.' – 'I know they ought to be so,' said Edward; 'and that I will have no connections with any that are not so.' – 'You shall never have reason to complain of me for that,' replied David, 'and, if Molly here has no objection, I declare before your honour, I will lay siege to her heart according to all the rules of honourable love.' – Poor Molly blushed, and hung down her head. The old woman smiled, and Ned saw that the fortress/ would not be able to stand a long siege. 'Your declaration is fair, David,' said he, 'I shall be one of the neutral powers, but shall wish equally well to both.'

The mystery of the red coat was thus cleared up to his satisfaction. He comforted the old woman with the hopes that she might again see her son, as he had himself left him but a few months before in good health; and with some good advice to Molly not to surrender but on honourable terms, took his leave.

After a little time David followed him, and got up with him just as he entered the grounds of Ravensdale. Ned there renewed his injunctions to him, that if he valued his favour, not to deceive the girl. David assured him nothing was farther from his thoughts; that he thought her a charming girl, and that she had an honest character, and that he thought if she would take him, she would make him happy. 'There is no fear of her not taking you,'/ said Edward, 'only be you faithful and kind to her when you get her. For a little time, however, your courtship will be interrupted; for I shall leave this for Dublin the day after to morrow, and from thence shall go to Wales: but I intend, if it please God, to return before Christmas, and to spend the winter here.'

David felt a little disconcerted that he was so soon to part with Molly; but the hopes of shortly seeing her again, and the pleasure of beholding his father and mother, and relating to his admiring friends his hair-breadth scapes,[33] and hazards in the imminently deadly breach, revived his spirits, and set him on preparing for the journey with alacrity./

CHAP. LX.

SOME part of every day Mr. Evans spent with Lord Ravensdale, whether his lordship was able to rise or not. On that preceding his intended journey, his lordship sent for him up to his bed-chamber; he was exceedingly low, and much agitated by some inward oppression of his mind, which Edward imputed to the shock his nerves sustained from the late deaths in his family. When he spoke of his deceased children, he wept much, yet took a pleasure in dwelling on the subject. Edward, who was no bad preacher, drew some arguments of consolation from religion; but here he found he touched upon a string which added to the sufferings of the unhappy peer, and, instead of consolation, seemed to drive him to despair./

This was a melancholy discovery, since of all mortal miseries religious despondency is the greatest. He had the power, however, for the present, to sooth his anguish, and to divert his mind from its gloomy contemplations. When he announced his departure for the next morning, his lordship said he sent for him on that account, to remind him of his promise to return before Christmas, and to spend the winter. 'God knows,' said he, 'whether I shall live to see you again. In that case, however, Mr. Evans, you will find I have not forgot you.' Edward was embarrassed, but was going to make some reply, when Lord Ravensdale interrupted him:

'My dear friend!' said he, 'I consider you as an adopted child. When my poor George died, he left you to me as a legacy. In this pocket-book,' said he, drawing one from under his pillow, 'is a small sum that was due to him, and which I was intending/ to send to him, when I received the melancholy news of his death. I desire you will receive it as his last acknowledgement for your tenderness and friendship in the hour of his extremity.'

Edward was overpowered, and received the pocket-book with streaming eyes, and greater agitation than his lordship gave it.

'As for your journey,' continued he, 'when you reach Dublin, you will use my house as your own; and to carry you thither, there are a couple of most excellent hunters in the stable, which belonged to my poor son Rivers – I can have no use

300 *The History of Ned Evans*

for them; and though that does not enhance the merit of a gift, yet it may be an inducement to you to accept of them.'

To a generous mind there is no pleasure so great as that of conferring favours; and Lord Ravensdale's was so truly of this temper, that the satisfaction arising from it had a considerable effect upon his spirits, and for a while suspended that despondency/ which had so lately and so grievously attacked him. Edward would have expressed his gratitude, but his lordship would not suffer it. 'Return soon to me,' said he, 'and I shall esteem that the greatest favour you can do me.'

Edward bowed respectfully, and we may be sure renewed his promise, with full intention to keep it; and withdrew from his lordship to confer with Lady Cecilia. Her ladyship was sitting in her own dressing-room; he tapped at the door, and her sweet voice desiring him to come in, he related to her all that had passed. The small red leather pocket-book he opened in her presence, and found it contained five bank notes of one hundred pounds each.

When he mentioned the hint his lordship gave him of having provided for him in his will, 'I am afraid,' says he, 'that will be robbing you, Cecilia.' – 'Never mind that, Edward,' said she; 'I shall contrive to make you give it me all back again.'/

'Dear Cecilia, what is there I would not give you? – Oh that I was an earl, and you a curate's daughter, that I might lay my coronet at your feet, and shew you how disinterestedly I love you!' 'I will give you all credit for the disinterestedness of your love, Edward;' replied she, 'and really believe that if that was the case you would act as you say.' 'Yes! by Heavens would I!' said Edward, 'if I was heir to the crown: but, alas! I am heir to nothing, and all the obligation is on your side: yet I have this consolation, that

> True gratitude, by owing, owes not;
> But stands at once indebted and discharged.[34]

'True,' said Lady Cecilia, 'and on that principle I will in due time give you a receipt in full. – But, O Edward! you shock me with the account of my poor father: what is it that can affect his mind in the manner you mention?' 'Nay, that,' said he 'I cannot tell: whatever affects the nerves generally affects the mind; and where/ the heart has been habituated to religious sentiments, those impressions sometimes take a gloomy turn. But I trust that time, the great softener of sorrow, will apply his lenient balsam to your father's wounds; and as his nerves recover their tone, his despondencies will vanish of course.' 'I trust they will. But, O Edward! I have seen such dreadful effects of similar imaginations, that I tremble only to think of what may be the issue.' 'My dear Cecilia!' replied Edward, 'if you torment yourself with *may be's*, you will never have a happy hour while you live. I have no doubt but that I shall see your venerable father sensible of the blessings of Providence, and of the large portion of them which he may yet enjoy. It is a peculiar pleasure to me, that he seems to like to have me near him. I want not that inducement, my Cecilia! to hasten my return to this happy seat; yet, it shall hasten me; and in the mean time I think it would be advisable for you to ask Doctor/ Burton to spend some time here; for his great erudition, his amiable manners, and his truly apostolic zeal in the duty of his profession, point him out as the happiest resource you could apply to in a situation like the present.' 'I have thought of it some time, my Edward!' said Lady Cecilia, 'and you will not be an hour from the house, till I send to him.' 'I shall count the hours till I return,' replied Edward; 'and I will venture to predict, that I shall find you happier when I come back than when I leave you.' 'You may do that, indeed,' said Lady Cecilia, 'and yet be no prophet: but come, Mrs. Waldron will wonder what is become of us.' So down they marched together, and found the good lady in a vein of such high good humour, as sufficiently indicated she at least thought all was as it should be.

Edward now walked into the stable to view his new acquisition, and to deliver the charge of them to David Morgan. The/ servants indeed had of late been so accustomed to receive all their orders from him, that they began already to consider him as their future master, and whatever he desired was implicitly obeyed. The horses were noble animals, of a dark bay colour,[35] and perfectly matches to each other, well trained for the field, and, as the phrase is, sound in wind and limb. No present could have been more acceptable to Edward, who delighted in a horse above all creatures who wore not the human face divine. He ordered them out into a park, that he might see their paces; when vaulting successively on their backs, naked as they were, with only their halters round their necks, he put them to their speed, and through all their exercises convinced them he would soon teach them to know their rider. Horsemanship indeed was an accomplishment in which he particularly excelled; and when a boy he used to amuse himself with helping David to dress old Blackbird,/ his father's only steed. To David then he now committed the charge of his two coursers, but comforted the old groom, who had hitherto attended them, and was sorry to quit their care, with a guinea. David loved a horse little less than his master, and was as able, though not quite so graceful a rider: he received the charge with transport, as well as the orders to have them ready for their journey at an early hour the next morning. When the morning came, both Lady Cecilia and Mrs. Waldron had risen long before their usual hour, to provide breakfast for Edward, and to bid him adieu. Every parting was in some degree painful to all their hearts; but this less so than any they had yet experienced, from the expectation of so soon meeting again, united to the sweet sensations inspired by mutual love. They saw him to the door; they saw him mount into the saddle; and, with one soft adieu and graceful motion of his hand, they saw him/ shoot from them like an arrow out of

302 *The History of Ned Evans*

a bow. A tear stood trembling in Cecilia's eye, not unobserved by Mrs. Waldron: she soon however wiped it away; and though not cheerful through the day, she yet recovered her usual serenity.

Ravensdale was about 76 miles from Dublin; yet such was the fleetness and the excellent mettle of his horses that he reached Lord Ravensdale's house in Merrion Square before it was quite dark. The house-keeper, who had been apprised of his coming, had every thing in order for his reception, and offered him several delicacies for his supper. He preferred, however, some beefsteaks and roasted potatoes; on which having feasted most heartily, he found himself very well inclined for his bed. David was regaled in the kitchen with several of those dainties which Edward rejected, as also with a bottle of claret after them; for Mrs. Mulroony, exclusive of that general good-will which she always had for/ a handsome young fellow, had remembered David with affection from the last time that he had been there, and kept him up till a very late hour relating to her the disasters of the American campaigns, and the heroic share which his master and poor Captain Rivers (not forgetting himself) had in them. The mention of Captain Rivers brought tears into the good woman's eyes, who lamented how there was now no son to inherit that fine estate. 'Oh! but,' said David, 'there is Lady Cecilia; I will warrant her ladyship will have sons enough if she gets the man she has a mind to.' Mrs. Mulroony now pricked up her ears; and Susan the chamber-maid growing sleepy, or perhaps thinking my lady house-keeper wished her to do so, retired to bed, so that she had full opportunity to ingratiate herself into poor David's confidence, and, with the help of another bumper[36] or two, to get possession of all the secrets he had, some of which she/ no doubt found very interesting. The result of this conference was her assuming a most profound respect for Edward, which she thought on some future occasion might be of use to her; and as David had rather over-slept himself in the morning, she had got Susan to apply to another young man, an acquaintance of hers, to dress the horses, and have all things in order in the stables against Edward rose, which she knew he would do at an early hour. Thus all things went smoothly on; and an excellent breakfast being ready in the parlour against he came down, Edward did justice to her solicitude, and thought himself much obliged to Mrs. Mulroony for her care and attention. After breakfast, he went out with the intention of calling on the agent of his regiment; but passing through Stephen's Green in his way, he met Mr. Grainger, who had so hospitably entertained him when Lord Rivers and he had been overturned in his neighbourhood. His little/ grandson, a sweet boy of about six years of age, was walking with him; they were both in deep mourning, which made Edward forebode the misfortune which really had happened, the death of that beautiful and amiable woman whom Nettlefield had so basely injured. He immediately, however, went up and saluted Mr. Grainger, who at that instant did not recollect him; but, being reminded by Edward of the circumstance of the overturn, and his having passed a night with him in the country, was sincerely rejoiced to see him. 'Alas!' said he, 'Mr. Evans, how short is the time since I had the pleasure to entertain you that night, and yet how many changes have happened in that short period! You and I alone remain of all who passed that night together.' 'I feared as much,' said Edward, 'when I saw you and my little friend Charles, whom I have not forgot, though he cannot remember me, in your present dress.' 'But how long have you/ been in Ireland, and what stay do you make in it?' said Mr. Grainger. Edward then gave him a brief history of his principal adventures, concluding, that he had only reached Dublin the evening before, and intended to go to Holyhead in the packet which was to sail that night; but that he expected to be back again in a month or six weeks. Mr. Grainger then took his promise, that on his return he would spend a day or two with him at his little lodge; and after a cordial shake of the hands, and a kiss of little Charles, they separated.

Edward proceeded to the agent, whom he found in his compting-house; with him he spent above a hour, and received from him the balance of his account in bills upon London, amounting to 336l. some odd shillings. He was also much pressed to stay dinner, but excused himself on account of his intention to sail in the evening. He returned therefore to Merrion-Square, and took a quiet meal alone./

Mrs. Mulroony and Mr. David had another very agreeable tête-à-tête; and about nine at night, the horses being embarked, Edward took leave of Dublin, and set sail with fine weather and a fair wind for Holyhead./

CHAP. LXI.

To one who has twice crossed the Atlantic ocean, the passage between Dublin and Holyhead seems little more than a ferry, and was indeed performed by Ned with almost as little trouble as one often passes a moderate river; for very soon after he got on board he laid himself down in his birth, and gave full scope to those pleasing hopes which could not fail to rise in his mind, whether he contemplated those dear friends whom he was going to see, or those whom he had lately left, and to whom he intended shortly to return. These tranquillizing ideas soon soothed him into sleep; from which he did not awake till David about eight in the morning came to tell him they were just going into the harbour. He was not long in/ jumping upon deck, and once more hailing the sublime shores over which St. David presides. He staid no longer at the Head than to refresh his horses a little after their voyage, and then set forward to Gwindu, intending to breakfast with the good landlady there, Mrs. Knowles, whose house nobody will pass who has once experienced the neatness, cheapness, and kindness of her entertainment. Poor Mrs. Knowles at the time when he arrived there was not able to move farther than from her bed to her easy chair, being confined by a severe fit of the rheumatism, to which she was extremely subject; but when she heard of Edward being there, she invited him into her room, and ordered his breakfast beside herself, that she might not lose a minute of his company while he staid; and indeed she kept him near two hours, hearing his adventures, and entertaining him in her turn with the recent occurrences of the neighbourhood. At last he set forward/ again, and a little before two beheld the venerable brow of Penmanmawr, which overhung his father's dwelling. His heart beat with a quicker motion; a few minutes more brought him to the turning of the road, from whence, between two aged oaks, the humble, but neat and rural dwelling first presents its unobtrusive front. This was the very spot in which he had taken his last lingering look of his dear mother, and in this very spot did the kind fates ordain that she should be at this instant walking, and leaning on the arm of her good and tender husband: their backs indeed were turned, for they had been taking a little walk together, and were now returning home to dinner. They heard the trampling of the horses – they stopped; they turned – they saw their long-

– 304 –

lost Edward, in all the bloom and vigour of health. The mother screamed with joy. She snatched her hand from under her good man's arm, and ran towards her son./ Ned jumped from his horse. – "Tis he! 'tis he! it is my Edward!' she cried, as she strained him to her bosom; whilst honest Evans, with more temperate but not less real satisfaction, first raised his eyes in gratitude to Heaven, and then embraced Edward in his turn. Joy soon communicated itself through the whole neighbourhood. Our honest curate now welcomed David home again, whose father and mother also soon made their appearance, and thought as much of their hero, and not without reason, as if they had been ever so great. David did not think so much of himself, however, as to forget the horses. He and his father put them into the stable, beside old Blackbird, who was still living, and did not seem to relish the intrusion, but who grew better pleased when he partook of the plentiful fare with which the two noble strangers were entertained.

Edward, with his mother leaning on his arm, now reached the house, into which/ the good curate followed; and now another kissing and welcoming took place till Towser, Ned's favourite dog, appeared. Twenty times did he course round him in circles, and jump upon his breast and back, licking his face and hands, and shewing no less faithful attachment than him whom Homer has immortalized in his Odyssey[37] and who knew again his master Ulysses after twenty years of absence. At last the perturbation of sudden joy subsided, and gave place to that calm delight which beamed in the happy countenances of these three dear connexions, who now sat down together to regale on a leg of the curate's own mutton, fed on those flowery downs which are acknowledged to bestow the highest flavour of any part of Britain. Evans and his wife could hardly eat a bit, so completely were they filled with joy, and so intently were their thoughts and eyes fixed on their son; but Edward made a heavy stroke in the little leg, and probably would/ have hid the whole of it, had he not remembered his fellow-traveller Morgan, who certainly was entitled to a share: to him therefore was consigned what remained of it, with a bottle of the curate's best ale; whilst one of excellent wine, long stored for the present happy occasion, was brought out for Ned, who partook of it perhaps with more delight than he had ever before received from any wine whatsoever. Soon after the cloth was taken away, a little boy in a white frock,[38] with the countenance of a cherub, stumped into the room, and immediately took post by Mrs. Evans's knee: he fixed his eyes beaming with lively innocence upon Edward, who, naturally fond of all children whether he was acquainted with them or not, asked whose he was? and was going to caress him. His question was not immediately answered; when his recollection, which, however unaccountably, had been wandering before, immediately returned, and suggested to him/ how near an interest he had in the little innocent, who had now gone to his knee. A tear, whether of contrition or affection I will not say, trembled in his eye, and a blush of the deepest crimson overspread

306 *The History of Ned Evans*

his countenance. His father enjoyed his confusion, which he considered as a sign of grace, but did not let him remain too long under it. 'Yes! Edward,' said he, 'he is your child: his countenance will not let you deny him, for he is the image of what you were at his age. If you have sinned in being the cause of bringing this infant into the world, know that he has the greater claim upon your tenderness; for you have robbed him of the right of an honourable birth. Repay then the injury you have done him, by a closer attention; for, if you neglect him, your last sin will be worse than the first.'

Edward, still embarrassed and abashed, hardly had a word to say. He took the little Edward from the ground, and placed/ him standing on his knee; then folding his arms about him, and pressing him to his heart, 'When I desert thee, O my child! (said he) then may Heaven desert me!'

Let those who are fathers condemn this sentiment if they can. Edward was the child of nature, and therefore he loved his natural child. And surely the Almighty, if he had been so severe against his trespass as some unfeeling bigots represent him, would not have formed the instant in one of his finest moulds; fashioning his limbs in all the symmetry of just proportion, and lighting up in his eyes that radiancy of apprehension which marked the liveliness of that intelligence which resided within.

The maid now coming in for this sweet infant, relieved Edward from some part of his embarrassment. When he asked about the mother, Molly Price, his father informed him that she had been married about a twelvemonth before to a young fellow a farmer's servant, and had lately/ lain-in, and had behaved herself well and decently since he had been away.

The remainder of the evening Ned spent in giving to his father and mother a particular and interesting detail of all his most remarkable adventures; during the relation of which, one might trace all the passions alternately and strongly expressed upon their countenances, according to the circumstances of his narrative. His situation with Lady Cecilia was the only circumstance he did not fully disclose, deeming it a point of honour to keep that to himself until her ladyship should think proper to avow it also.

And now the worthy parson calling his little family around him, according to his invariable custom, closed the evening with thanksgiving to him who loveth mercy, and who had so lately dispensed it to him with liberal hand; and Edward once more pressed that bed, the first on which he remembered/ ever to have slept, and in which he this night experienced as soft and as undisturbed repose as health and innocence were ever blessed with.

In the morning Ned found himself quite at home, and began to betake himself to his old employments. His little round hat and switch, which his mother had so often contemplated in his absence, were still remaining; and with these, as usual, he paid his first visit to the stable. There he found David Morgan equally delighted to resume his ancient duties, and busily employed in rubbing down the two hunters, whose skins shone like a new piece of the most glossy satin. Poor old Blackbird was standing in his usual corner; Ned patted him for old acquaintance sake, and promised him good food, and a writ of ease for his life.

Morgan reminded Edward of the many dangerous hours they had passed together, particularly that day when they were separated/ by the Indians in the woods of America, and how happy the present moment was in comparison.

'True!' said Edward, 'but if we had never been from home, we could neither have been sensible of the happiness of our situation, nor yet have had the means equally to enjoy it.' Morgan admitted this, but declared himself contented with the experiment he had made, and that nothing should induce him to take the field again. Ned did not absolutely make the same declaration, but I believe it was not very remote from his private determination.

The maid, with little Edward in her arms, now came to call Ned to breakfast. The child, smiling, stretched out his little hands to him. Ned took him in his arms (for nature would be obeyed), and, kissing him as he went, carried him into the house. After breakfast the good curate went into his garden, which it was his custom to cultivate with his own hands, assisted occasionally by/ hired labourers. In former times Edward used to spend many of his leisure hours in this useful and healthy exercise, and was happy to resume his labour this day, and assist his father to trench between his asparagus beds, and earth up his celery. Observing a sturdy boy at work, and asking about him, he learned that he was the son of the poor woman who had so hospitably entertained him when he was benighted after leaving the churlish Muckworm's, and that he was happy to repay that kindness by initiating this boy into the practice of gardening, and teaching him to read and write. 'His mother has removed here to be in my neighbourhood,' said he, 'and I hope has not lost the reward of her hospitality.'

'That journey was undertaken upon my account,' said Edward; 'and you must allow me to testify my gratitude also, or at least to assist you in shewing your own.' Evans would have dissuaded him, assuring him that he was himself fully able to administer/ to their comforts; 'for,' says he, 'you do not consider how rich I am through the bounty of the good Lord Ravensdale.' 'Neither do you consider,' said Ned, 'how rich I am through the same source. Look at this pocketbook,' added he, 'and count the contents, and know that they are every shilling at your command.'

When Evans saw the eight hundred pound notes, he was indeed somewhat surprised, and perhaps not displeased, but positively refused to accept a farthing of it, advising Edward to turn it to some account, as it was too great a sum to lie idle. Ned gave into his hands six hundred pounds of it, to do with it as he thought fit, and kept the remainder as a fund for some benefits he meant to bestow, and to defray the extraordinary expenses he might be at on his return to

308 *The History of Ned Evans*

Ireland. And now being near the spot, where, on the morning of his departure, he had planted two suckers, one from a white, and the other from a/ purple lilac tree, with the fond though superstitious imagination of their being emblems of Cecilia and himself; he stole away from his father to take a secret look at them, where he had the satisfaction to find them still thriving, and so grown into one, for they had been twisted together, as to appear but one bush, which in the season bore a profusion of white and purple flowers. The circumstance, though in itself trifling, was yet pleasing, and raised a sensation of tender delight in his heart, softened by love, yet happy in the certain knowledge of that love being sincerely returned./

CHAP. LXII.

For several days Edward amused himself with visiting his old acquaintances, particularly Farmer Watkin, in the neighbourhood; and he prevailed with his father to take a ride over as far as Conway, to see Doctor Jones, who was delighted to find him returned safe to his own country, and to hear such good accounts of Lady Cecilia, for whom he entertained the most affectionate respect ever since she had been his patient. It was on the evening of that day they had been at Conway, a little after dinner, the post from Bangor sounded his horn at Evans's gate, when Edward went out, and received a letter, which he knew to be her ladyship's hand: he retired with it to his own room, and there read to the following purport:/

Ravensdale, Nov. 6, 1783.

My dear Edward!

I sit down to take my willing pen to inform you of the most material occurrences which have happened here since you left us, and hope this letter will find you safe arrived and happy in the embraces of your good father and mother, who will ever be dear to my affections on their own account as well as yours. But when I tell you I take up my willing pen, I must confess to you, it is because I always find a secret pleasure in disclosing my heart to you, let its contents be what they may; and not that I have at this time any thing pleasing to communicate, for, oh! my Edward! my father's situation chills me with horror, as I am sure it will you, when I tell you I fear his intellects are deranged. The very day you left us, I went up to his room, and found him exceedingly low. He asked/ for you. I told him you were gone as you informed him the day before, and that you had desired me to present his lordship with your dutiful respects – 'Lordship!' said he – 'Lordship! – damned title!' – and he gave a deep groan – It harrowed up my soul, for it was the first time in my life I had ever heard an impatient word pass his lips, and I saw no occasion for it at the time. – 'Did he say when he would return?' (said he again, meaning you) – I said you promised to return before Christmas. 'I wish he was come,' said he: 'he would protect me from that fiend.' – 'What fiend, my lord?' said I. – 'Call me not lord! That fiend that tears my soul – he never troubles me when Mr. Evans is near.' I thought it needless to make any reply,

– 309 –

310 *The History of Ned Evans*

but surely I would have given the earth to have had you back again; yet what purpose could it have answered? I sent immediately for Doctor Burton, as you had recommended to me. He was not at home, but he was so/ good as to come the next day. I told him my apprehensions. He was exceedingly shocked, but promised that he would not leave us for some days. Last night he took me aside – 'My dear Lady Cecilia!' said he, 'you must not be alarmed. I hope your noble father will do well, for he seems already better; but he has taken an imagination into his head, which I suppose to be entirely nervous, and the effect of the late misfortunes in his family, which, however, he has disclosed to me in such a collected manner, that for his peace, and yours, I am determined to make enquiry about it, and, if I find any reality in it, to search it to the bottom.' – 'Good God, Doctor!' said I, 'what can it be?' 'It is of a very delicate nature,' said he; 'yet I think it proper to communicate it to you, that you may not be shocked with any imperfect hints of it that might drop from himself. His lordship has taken it into his head that he has usurped the title, and caused the infant/ son of the late Lord Rivers, his nephew, to be murdered twenty three years ago.' – 'Good God!' said I, 'it is impossible! My father is incapable, and has been all his life, of doing a base thing by any mortal – But murder! – it is madness.' – 'Indeed, Lady Cecilia! I think so too. Nevertheless, he affirms that he has done it by the agency of one Laurence Flinn, who lived with the last Lord Rivers at the time, and who now keeps an inn in the county of Clare; and that he not only set him up in that inn, but pays him an annuity of one hundred pounds to this hour to keep the matter secret. I shall go,' said Doctor Burton, 'tomorrow morning to see if there be any such man as this Flinn, and, if there is, to probe this story to the bottom. Lord Ravensdale has desired me to do so, and seemed infinitely relieved when I promised to obey him.' My Edward! he has left us this morning; and though I have not the smallest conception of its being any thing/ else than a chimæra; yet I must lament the state of mind that could create such a horrible fancy, and wait with infinite anxiety the doctor's return. I am uneasy too, in a high degree, about Mrs. Waldron. She is the grandmother of this child; and if she should get any intimation of this strange imagination, it would set her distracted also, or at least make such a noise in the country as I cannot think upon without horror.

Amidst all these disturbing circumstances, I thought I would give vent to my feelings, by disclosing them to you. – Is there a thought in my heart that I do not wish you to know? – No, my Edward! When I learn the whole truth, you shall know it all; and till then I remain
Your ever faithful and affectionate
CECILIA RIVERS.

The contents of this letter filled Edward with astonishment, and also with deep concern. His veneration for Lord Ravensdale/ was almost as unbounded as his love for Cecilia; yet he did not flatter himself as she did, that the whole was a mere chimæra, seeing Doctor Burton thought the circumstances so clearly related, that he undertook a long journey to bring them to the light. Should they prove true according to Lord Ravensdale's own confession, the consequences must be fatal, no less than bringing his head to the block: and what effect so horrible a catastrophe might have on poor Lady Cecilia, who, though innocent as an angel, must yet share in the disgrace, was such as he trembled to think on, knowing her high sense of honour, and the tender and dutiful affection she bore towards her father. For some days these distracting thoughts deprived him both of sleep and appetite, and greatly alarmed his father, to whom he could not impart the cause of them. He was also at a great loss what to say to Lady Cecilia, the subject was so delicate; and he did not, like her ladyship,/ flatter himself that the perturbations of Lord Ravensdale's conscience were merely the imagination of a disordered brain, seeing that on all other subjects he was perfectly collected and composed. To delay writing to her, however, was what neither his love nor his good manners would allow, and he therefore by that very post addressed to her the following lines:

Ti-gwin, Nov. 11, 1783.

Dear Lady Cecilia!

How impossible did I think it, that any letter which your ladyship should do me the favour to write to me, should ever be a cause of uneasiness or regret! yet I confess, that which I this day received has filled me with both. The extraordinary matters it discloses are in the highest degree alarming, in whatever light I can view them; and though I think with you, it is impossible that your noble father could be guilty of what he apprehends, yet the collectedness/ of his mind on other matters seems to justify a fear that it cannot be altogether without some foundation. I wait with the utmost impatience to know the result of Doctor Burton's enquiries; and be they what they may, I am determined to shorten my stay here, and hasten back to Ireland, that in every possible exigency I may be near at hand to yield you all the comfort or assistance that the most devoted heart can give you. O my Cecilia! how often in some of those tender meetings with which you have indulged me, how often have you wished that you had been born in an humbler station, and that even the mountains of Wales had sheltered your cradle! – Cherish the thought! and let those mountains hide in their deepest and most retired bosoms, two hearts which live but for each other, and which, when united, will find all their heaven within themselves. May God preserve you in every trial, and grant a favourable development of the mysterious/ circumstance you have related, and a happy meeting with your most sincere and faithfully devoted
EDWARD EVANS!

312 *The History of Ned Evans*

As soon as Edward had finished this letter, he ordered Morgan to saddle Brilliant, which was the name he had given to his favourite horse, and determined to ride himself to Bangor, to put it into the post-office with his own hands. He had not been gone an hour when a post-chaise drove to the door, in which was a gentleman alone, and seemingly a clergyman. Another chaise waited at the outer gate, in which was a man seemingly an old soldier, between two understrappers of the law. David Morgan happened to be out of the way when the carriage came to the door; and Mr. Evans was therefore obliged to go to receive the gentleman himself. This gentleman was Doctor Burton. Evans soon saw he was a clergyman of distinction,/ and of course asked him to alight. Doctor Burton introduced himself to the worthy curate with that ease which always accompanies men who have kept the best company, and asked if his friend Edward was at home? It was with great regret he heard he had gone to Bangor but an hour before; but as he was expected back perhaps to dinner, or at least in the evening. Doctor Burton accepted of Evans's pressing invitation to stay. He was then introduced to Mrs. Evans, who offered him the refreshment of a glass of wine; and the three persons in the other chaise were invited into the kitchen. As Evans had been well acquainted with Doctor Burton's character by Edward, and his connection with the Ravensdale family, he began with making affectionate enquiries about Lady Cecilia, whose host he had so long the honour to be; and also about the Earl, to whom he lay under so many obligations. Doctor Burton answered in general/ terms that Lady Cecilia was well, but that his lordship, ever since the death of his last son, had been in a very melancholy situation. 'Indeed, Mr. Evans,' said he, 'it is in relation to a most extraordinary circumstance concerning that nobleman, which I beg leave to communicate to your private ear, that I have taken the liberty to call upon you; and I must plead my acquaintance with your gallant and valuable son for my excuse.' Evans replied, that Doctor Burton could stand in need of no excuse for honouring any person with his visit. And Mrs. Evans now withdrawing, the Doctor opened his business in the following terms:

'I have said, Mr. Evans, that an extraordinary circumstance relative to Lord Ravensdale has induced me to call here this day; and indeed it is one so surprising, that no person who knew him so long and so intimately as I have done could have supposed it possible to have happened;/ yet the fact is indubitable, as you shall hear. – His lordship has always been esteemed a nobleman of the most disinterested generosity and unblemished virtue; and, excepting in one instance, which the justice of Heaven seems to be now bringing to the light, he has really deserved this character. But then – that one instance of frailty is a crime of such enormous magnitude, that a whole life of subsequent virtue cannot atone for it. You are perhaps already acquainted, that the last Lord Rivers, who was nephew to the earl we are speaking of, had married contrary to his father's inclination, who in consequence would never see him more; and had the further cruelty to

Volume IV 313

withdraw the allowance suitable to his rank, which he had hitherto given him, leaving him to subsist, with his wife, on the pay of his commission, a captaincy of dragoons. His uncle, the present unfortunate earl, really did all in his power/ to reconcile his brother to his son, but without effect; and when that failed, he supported him himself with a handsome annuity, under certain stipulations of reimbursement when he should succeed to the estate. This event never happened. He died soon after, leaving his wife big with child, who lived only to be delivered of a son, and died also. Lady Rivers had a mother, who is still living, but unfortunately was in a distant part of the country at the time; and Colonel Rivers, as he was then called, happening to be in the neighbourhood, a sudden thought (oh! that it could be blotted out of the registers of the Almighty!) occurred to him, that if the new-born infant could be any way disposed of, so as never to make his appearance in his real character, the injury would be nothing to the child, and the advantage gained to himself would be immense. He ventured to sound at a distance/ one Laurence Flinn, who had been servant to Lord Rivers, and whom, alas! he found too ready to come into his measures, for the consideration of a sum of money – considerable indeed to him, but little to give in exchange for his soul.' 'Alas!' said Evans, 'what would either have gained, though they had got the whole world?' – 'Colonel Rivers returned to his own house; and soon after he was informed that the child had died at nurse; and the same account was transmitted to Mrs. Waldron, mother to Lady Rivers. Here the matter rested; and all the world supposed that the case was really so. When Lord Ravensdale died, Colonel Rivers, as next heir, assumed the title and estate; and has ever since maintained the most noble and irreproachable character that is any where to be met with. But the all seeing eye of Providence discerned this deep-laid train of guilt, and has/ commissioned his great vice-gerent Conscience to bring it to light. Lord Ravensdale has really a deep sense of religion, and a thorough persuasion that there is no darkness nor shadow of death in which the workers of iniquity may hide themselves.' 'It is a true persuasion,' said Evans, 'and a great pity he did not recollect it sooner.' 'Every person must lament it,' said Doctor Burton. 'But to proceed. The late grievous misfortunes in his family he considers, and perhaps justly, as the beginning of Almighty vengeance; and it was under this impression that he unburthened his conscience to me, by disclosing all that I have now related to you.'

A person at this time wanting to speak to Mr. Evans, he was obliged to apologize to Doctor Burton for quitting the room, but promised to be back in a few minutes; and we will avail ourselves, in/ this interval of the narrative, of the opportunity it gives us to reflect by ourselves upon the vanity of all happiness founded on the basis of worldly considerations./

CHAP. LXIII.

THE worthy curate, whose curiosity (as we may suppose) was wound up to the very tiptoe of expectation, hastened to return to the parlour, and the good doctor resumed his narrative. – 'I own to you, Mr. Evans,' said he, 'when his lordship, in the agonies of his soul, made this confession to me, I hardly knew how to believe my ears, and sometimes thought the whole was a mere chimæra of his own brain, formed by the influence of a strong nervous affection: but then he was so clear and connected in all the circumstances, and expressed such a deep and contrite sense of his transgression, that I determined, both for his peace and in pursuance of what I conceived to be my own duty, to search the matter to the bottom. The first step I took was to go to/ this Laurence Flinn, who I understood kept an inn, between sixty and seventy miles away from Ravensdale, in a remote part of the county Clare. I found this man at home; and taking him to a place where there could be no listeners, I told him I came to him through the special agency of God to enquire what he had done with the infant son of the late Lord Rivers. – It is impossible for any language to express the astonishment and confusion into which this abrupt and peremptory question threw him. – 'Tell the truth,' said I, 'and the whole truth, as you shall answer at the dreadful bar of God!' – The fellow was a Papist, and not a little burthened with superstition. – He fell on his knees, and, after two or three crossings, begged I would not hang him. 'What have you done with the child?' said I: 'have you murdered him?' 'No: God forbid!' said he: 'he may be living yet, for aught I know: – I have neither seen nor heard of him these three-/and-twenty-years.' 'Oh! thou agent of Satan!' said I; 'what hast thou done with him? – Thinkest thou that I am ignorant of thy vile collusion with him who calls himself Lord Ravensdale?' – The wretch, trembling and pale as death, confessed, that seduced by the great offers which Lord Ravensdale, then Colonel Rivers, had made him, to put the child out of the way of being troublesome, he had prevailed with his wife, who nursed it, to say it died in a fit; and they actually got a fictitious infant buried as the child of Lord Rivers. In the mean time he gave the real child to one Michael Carrol, a soldier, whose wife was giving suck; and with the child he gave him twenty guineas to carry it to London to put it in the Foundling Hospital,

– 314 –

Volume IV 315

and he told him it was the natural child of a gentle woman who wished it to be concealed, and that it had been christened by the name of Edward. 'This,' added the wretch, 'is all I know of the/ matter, as I shall answer at the day of judgment.' 'A dreadful day indeed it will be to you,' said I; 'but where is your wife?' 'Dead!' said he, 'many years: she did not long survive the loss of the infant.' 'And what is become of this Michael Carrol?' said I: 'is he dead also?' 'No,' said he, 'I believe not: I know a few years ago he was living in Dublin, a soldier in the Old Man's Hospital.' 'Well!' said I, 'Mr. Flinn, you have a great deal to answer for, more than all the Ravensdale estate would make you amends for: but go directly to Lord Ravensdale, who is lying under all the agonies of a guilty conscience for his share in this nefarious business; – go, and comfort him with the knowledge that there is at least a possibility that the child may be yet alive, and that he may not, as he fears, have his blood to answer for.' I wrote a letter by him to the unhappy lord, and I did not quit his house till I saw him fairly set off upon his/ journey. – I set out myself immediately after for Dublin, and enquired for Carrol, whom I found living, as Flinn told me, in the Royal Hospital. I immediately got a warrant for apprehending him, and he was put under the custody of two constables, and these three men are now in your kitchen!' 'Well,' said Mr. Evans, 'and what does Carrol say? What did he do with the little innocent?' 'Carrol acknowledges the having received the child from Flinn, with the twenty guineas, and that he and his wife, who suckled it with her own infant, did leave Ireland with the intention to put the child into the Foundling Hospital at London, as had been agreed; that they came over in the packet to Holyhead for that purpose, and sometimes walked, and sometimes got a list, as it happened: that in going through the village of St. Asaph, it chanced to be a very warm day, and they were both greatly fatigued; when resting themselves under a hedge/ which enclosed a little garden, they saw a gentleman walking two or three times disconsolately, and at last sit down in an arbour, that was at the end of it; he seemed to be a clergyman, and in some distress.' [Here Evans seemed greatly agitated, and wept.] Doctor Burton continued: 'Carrol and his wife thought this a good opportunity to get rid of their charge, and save all farther trouble and expence, by throwing the poor infant on the mercy of this gentleman. The woman, he says, took the infant, which was sleeping in her arms, and gave it to her husband, when she retired: – he took a small slip of paper, on which he wrote the name Edward with a pencil; and, being a Papist also, and as superstitious as you please, he made with a penknife the sign of the cross on the back of the infant's neck, to make it cry, and laid it down just at the back of the arbour, into which he saw the gentleman enter. He retired a few paces to watch what would/ ensue, when presently he saw that meek and charitable stranger come from the arbour to where the child was, and take him up in his arms. 'Whoever thou art,' said he, 'sweet innocent, thou art welcome; I accept thee as a present from God, and thou shalt be my

316 *The History of Ned Evans*

child.' The words were so remarkable, he says, they yet found in his ears; and immediately after the gentleman with the infant returned into the house.' Evans, all whose tender passions were worked up to the highest pitch, could contain no longer; he burst into a flood of tears, to the surprise of Doctor Burton, and, falling on his knees, cried out, 'Gracious God, whose path is in the deep waters, and whose ways are past finding out, I humbly adore thy providence, and thank thee that thou hast made me an instrument of shewing forth thy mercies to mankind' – Rising he said, 'Oh, Doctor Burton! I am the man – I was that afflicted clergyman who found that infant/ in the situation you mention; and Edward, my Edward whom you know, and whom Lord Ravensdale has so long entertained, is that infant himself.' Doctor Burton's astonishment was now not less than Evans's, neither was his joy less than his astonishment. His joy would have been great where-ever he had been able to discover the child; but to find him in the amiable and accomplished Edward, who was already so dear to all the family, was an unlooked-for happiness that seemed to be the peculiar boon of Providence himself. Evans now begged that Carrol, with his attendants, might be brought in: he there related the whole story again circumstantially with his own mouth. Evans went up stairs, and returned with a small drawer of an escritoir in his hand. 'Here, Doctor Burton! here, Michael Carrol! here is a deposit which I have now kept by me these twenty-three years: here is the little frock in which I found my dear Edward, and here is the slip of/ paper with his name Edward written, which I found with it. – See, Carrol, do you know it?'[39] Carrol crossed himself, and said he would know it in any part of the world.

The matter was now sufficiently clear; and Carrol being dismissed, Mr. Evans said, 'Well do I remember, Doctor Burton, that morning, which I then thought so unhappy, but which, by the relation you have now heard, has turned out so fortunate. It was on the seventeenth of July, 1761, about eleven in the morning, a poor little infant, the only one I had, who had been born about a fortnight before, expired in his mother's arms: he had been ill about two days, with what the midwives call inward fits, and I was sitting by his mother's bed side when I saw him breathe his last. We had lost a little girl some years before, who had attained her seventh year, and these two were all the children we ever had. My wife's grief was inexpressibly distressing to me when/ added to my own; and when I saw the child was certainly gone, I went down, as you have heard related, into the garden to get a little fresh air, and retired to that little arbour to shed my tears in secret. There the loss was instantly supplied in the surprising manner you have heard. It struck me at the time as if it was the Lord's doing, and I carried the little babe up in my arms to my wife. 'The Lord,' said I, 'hath taken away, and the Lord hath given; blessed be the name of the Lord!'[40] My wife was amazed; but being naturally fond of children, she accepted the present, and put it to her breast: the child sucked heartily, and looked like a little angel. She saw blood upon its frock; the stain of which you may see still remaining: we then stripped the babe, and found it proceeded from the mark of the cross, which, as Carrol said, he had cut in the back of its neck. The child was a lovely infant, apparently about two months old, in high health and/ vigour, and soon found the way to endear itself to my wife, and, I may add, to myself; so that if he had been ten times our child we could not have loved him better. From that hour to this we have had nothing with him but pleasure; and surely it is needless to tell you, that a more beautiful figure or a more virtuous mind can hardly meet in man. He himself knows nothing of his destination. He believes himself to be our child, but I will venture to engage that he will fill the high station to which he is entitled with as much grace and dignity, as he has the humble one to which he has been accustomed with cheerfulness and contentment.' 'I know enough of him,' said Doctor Burton, 'to vouch for all you say, and to assure you that I think it the greatest blessing that could have befallen him, that, unknowing of his rank, he has been educated under your care.' Mrs. Evans now came into the room; she had got some intimation of/ the discovery from the people in the kitchen, and her husband and Doctor Burton explained it to her fully. 'But how,' said she to Doctor Burton, 'did you not meet Edward (for I must still call him so) by the way? did you not come from Bangor?' 'No,' said the doctor, 'I came from Conway. We had been at St. Asaph, expecting that Carrol would have brought us to the very gentleman, or at least the house, where he had deposited the infant. He did indeed bring us to the house, but no person there could give us any information about the matter: however, upon enquiry, an elderly woman who kept a shop told us, that at that time we mentioned, the house was inhabited by you, and that possibly you might give us information about any matter of consequence we might desire to know. It was also my intention to call here in my way back, for, as I sailed from Dublin to Parkgate, it was not in my power to do it before; but no circumstance could/ give me equal satisfaction with finding in this house the end of all my enquiries in the person of that amiable youth you have hitherto called your son, and who will always honour and respect you both as if you were indeed his parents.' This conversation had hardly ended, when Edward himself arrived. He had rode hard from Bangor, and the air and exercise had contributed to enliven his spirits, and recall the animated glow of health and cheerfulness to his countenance, which Lady Cecilia's intelligence had somewhat abated. When Morgan told him Doctor Burton was in the parlour, and had some great news to disclose to him, he flew like lightning to the house, impatient to be informed of his dear Cecilia, and not dreaming that he himself was the object of the intelligence. When he entered the room he immediately advanced to his reverend and respected friend, who saw in his open countenance and beaming eye the sincerity of that pleasure with/ which he took him by the hand and welcomed him to the humble hospitality of Ti-gwin.

318 *The History of Ned Evans*

It was agreed between Evans and Doctor Burton not to mention any thing to Edward of his exaltation, till after dinner. His enquiries therefore about Lord Ravensdale and Lady Cecilia were answered in general terms; by which, however, he had the satisfaction to be informed that her ladyship was in perfect health, and that some events had taken place which were likely to restore his lordship too – an intelligence in which Ned expressed the most heart-felt satisfaction, and which enabled him to play his part at the neat and plentiful meal which the good Mrs. Evans now ushered in, with all his accustomed appetite and cheerfulness./

CHAP. LXIV.

AFTER the cloth was removed, and a glass or two of excellent old Oporto had gone round, the conversation about Lord Ravensdale was renewed, and Edward expressed much anxiety on his account; particularly as he acknowledged to have heard from Lady Cecilia that the state of his mind was highly alarming. 'Pray, Doctor Burton,' added he, 'can you give me any new information upon that subject?' – 'I can assure you,' replied the doctor, 'that Lord Ravensdale is at this time in perfect health, both of mind and body.' – 'God bless me!' said Edward, 'you surprise me. How is that possible, doctor? It was but within these few days I received a letter from Lady Cecilia, assuring me the very contrary, and that you had left Ravensdale-/house on some important business relative to his illness, of which, however, I am ignorant. How then can you tell me that his lordship is in perfect health?' – 'All this is very true,' replied the doctor; 'yet I still solemnly vouch for the fact. Lady Cecilia does not know Lord Ravensdale as well as I do – nay, she was not with him at the time she wrote that letter.' – 'My good doctor!' said Ned, 'if his lordship's complaint has any thing of phrensy in it, I am afraid he has bit you in some of your communications together, and has infected you with his disease.' – 'No!' said he; 'I appeal to my venerable friends here, Mr. and Mrs. Evans, if I am not perfectly correct, for his lordship is in this house at this instant.' – 'Oh! where?' said Edward, and he looked at the worthy curate for an answer. Doctor Burton rose, and with a benignant, but yet serious aspect, said, 'Thou art the man.' 'Yes! truly,' said Mr. Evans; 'my Edward, your real/ name and designation is Edward Rivers, Earl of Ravensdale.'

Mrs. Evans rose, and folded him to her bosom, and said, 'We do not jest or deceive you, my Edward! I am not your mother, though I have a mother's affection to you; you lost your mother the day you were born; you are really whom we tell you, the true Earl of Ravensdale.'

Edward was for a few moments thoughtful and silent. He saw both Mr. and Mrs. Evans in tears, yet tears that did not seem to flow from sorrow, but from tenderness and satisfaction. 'My father!' said he, 'my mother! for I know you by no other names, nor ever shall forego the blessings I have received from that dear connection; I look to you and to Doctor Burton here, for the explanation

– 319 –

320 *The History of Ned Evans*

of this strange mystery, which, if true, however advantageous it may be to me in a worldly view, will hardly compensate to me the regret with which I am informed that I am not your son.'/

'My Edward!' said Evans, 'for I must still call you so, do you recollect the morning that I parted with you at Holy head, when you first went to join your regiment?' – 'Yes,' said Edward, 'perfectly; I never can forget it. – I remember well, that just before I went down to the shore to embark, you took me by the hand, and told me you had something to reveal to me which might some time or other be of consequence to me, but at that time could be of none, and therefore you suppressed it. And I also well remember, my father, the present that you made me immediately after, and the promise which I gave you relating to it, and which I trust I ever shall perform.'

'Well!' said Mr. Evans, 'the circumstance which I intended to reveal to you was, that you were not my son – but as I at that time did not know to whom you were indebted for existence, nor never indeed till this day, that the providence of God/ has so wonderfully brought it to light, had any information on the subject, I thought to acquaint you with the circumstance would at that time have served only to afflict you, and therefore I suppressed it. But now I have to give you joy of it with the most heart-felt satisfaction, as the fact is indubitable, and all the circumstances which led to the discovery, such as singularly point out the all directing finger of Providence, whose eyes are on the ways of men, and who spieth out all their goings.'

Mr. Evans now gave Edward a minute detail of all those circumstances relative to his first finding him, with which the reader is already acquainted; and Doctor Burton related Lord Ravensdale's contrition and agony of mind, and the active part which he himself took in searching out the matter to the bottom, which was now elucidated beyond all doubt, and for the happy issue of which he sincerely added his congratulations;/ 'and I trust,' added he, 'that your lordship will long live to enjoy your hereditary honours and great estates, so as even to surpass the illustrious ancestors from whom you are descended.' 'Gentlemen!' said Edward, 'the circumstances you have related are so extraordinary, that if I had heard them from any less authority I could not have given credit to them; and even now, cannot help finding myself very highly embarrassed by them. I beseech you, therefore, not to call me by any title which I have not been accustomed to bear, and which I certainly cannot believe I have any right to, until it is recognised by the legislature of the kingdom. My father,' said he, turning to the good curate, whose eyes were glistening in tears, 'let me be your Edward still, and not lose the endearing appellation of your son (to me the most grateful title I shall ever bear) until there shall be a necessity for doing so.' 'My Edward!' said Evans,/ 'you will be ever dear to me, by what ever title you are called; nor can the splendour of rank add any thing to the affection which I felt for you when all

Volume IV 321

your possessions were a linen frock. If you take a pleasure in still calling me your father, surely I must have both pride and pleasure in calling you my son.' 'Such,' replied Edward, 'I am, and such I ever desire to remain. The father to whom I owe my body I never saw, and the unfortunate mother who brought me into the would, only beheld me, and lost sight of me for ever. Here is the mother (taking Mrs. Evans by the hand) on whose breast I hung, the first face I ever beheld with attachment. Here is the father (taking Evans in his other hand), who, owing me no duty, fulfilled all the most tender parent could perform. To my natural parents I indeed owe my body, who, however, never had it in their power to bestow on it a single comfort. To you I owe my mind. You formed my heart;/ nay, you also cherished that body which I received from others, and which, but for your care, would never have attained the strength or stature of a man. To you then am I justly indebted for both; and every faculty, both of my body and mind, shall be exerted to repay the immense debt of duty, love, and gratitude which I owe you.' Edward, who was still holding both their hands, with these words raised them to his lips, and, impressing upon them alternately the warm kiss of true affection, returned to his seat. The graceful manner in which the noble youth expressed these endearing sentiments, and the calm tranquillity with which he received the sudden intelligence of his great and unexpected elevation, confirmed Doctor Burton in the high opinion he had before formed, both of his virtue and his understanding, and raised in him the most justifiable expectations that he would be an honour and a blessing to the country which was going to claim/ him. Evans and his wife were melted into the softest tenderness by the affectionate sweetness of his behaviour; and they were all in danger of growing too serious, had not Edward filled a bumper to the health and perfect recovery of peace and happiness of the old Earl, whom he declared that, next to Evans, he loved and revered of all men living. This was followed by another bumper to Lady Cecilia; and the glass beginning to circulate again freely, carried round with it mirth, freedom, and good humour. They continued their hilarity as long as they could within the bounds of that perfect temperance which neither Evans not Doctor Burton ever transgressed; and as soon as the glasses were taken away, Edward went out to look after Brilliant and Belisarius,[41] his two hunters, for whom he had conceived a very warm affection, and did not think them unworthy of being sometimes rubbed down even by an Earl. He was actually amusing himself/ with this employment when David Morgan entered the stable. Edward perceived an unusual shyness in David, who stood at a distance with his hat off, and neither said nor did anything. 'What's the matter with you, David?' said he: 'have you got any bad news from Moll Doran?' 'No, God bless your honour! but I hear your honour is a lord.' 'Well, and are you afraid of a lord? or are you sorry if I should be one?' 'No, please your lordship! but I did not know as how whether your lordship would choose to speak to such a poor man as I.' 'Is that the way

322 *The History of Ned Evans*

you would serve your old friends, David, if you too should turn out to be a lord?' 'Lord help me!' said David, 'how could I be a lord?' 'Nay, I do not know,' said Edward; 'I am sure I thought as little of being one two hours ago. But know this, David, that whether I be a lord or not, I never shall forget that I am a man, nor be unmindful of those who/ have assisted and shared with me in the distresses which man is liable to.' 'Now, God bless your lordship! for I with your lordship was a king.' 'I suppose you think that would be better for you.' 'I should hope so,' said David. 'Indeed, David, it is a great doubt whether it would or not; but I have no doubt but that it would be much worse for myself; nor do I believe, David, that I can be happier in any station, or under any name, than I have been under that of Edward Evans, by which name I desire you will continue to call me until I tell you that I am entitled to any other.' 'Why, and are you not then a lord?' said David. 'I am told so, I confess,' said Edward; 'but I do not know it; and till I do, I shall content myself with the name I have always borne, and which I never wished to change: and so, David, finish the horses, and prepare for a visit to Moll Doran, for I think we shall soon be for Ireland again.'/ Ned then returned to the house; and David wondered at the indifference with which he treated his title and 16000l. a-year. If I had got (thought he) but the sixteen hundredth part of it, it would have put me out of my senses – surely master has a soul that cannot be changed either by the happiness or the misery of this world.

When Edward returned to the parlour, Doctor Burton and Mr. Evans were still talking of the train of wonderful incidents which led to the interesting discovery they had made; in which nothing appeared more extraordinary, nor more clearly manifested the interference of a particular providence, than that when Ned had suffered shipwreck, and been saved almost by miracle, he should have been carried to the house of the nearest connexion he had in the world, and sheltered in the bosom of one who did not know she was giving protection to the child of her daughter. 'Are you certain, Doctor Burton,' said Edward,/ 'that Mrs. Waldron did not know or suspect that I was in any way related to her?' 'I believe not,' replied the Doctor; 'I left her at Ravensdale, and never heard of her ever having intimated anything of the kind.' 'I cannot be certain either,' said Edward; 'but she has several times expressed herself to me in terms somewhat enigmatical, which, I confess, at the time they were spoken, I did not entirely comprehend, but which lead me to imagine that by some means or other she had information that I was her grandson.' 'This is truly extraordinary,' said Doctor Burton, 'for I cannot conceive by what means she could have any such information, unless it were by some divine communication.' 'That I cannot pretend to say,' replied Edward, 'neither can I believe that Heaven in these days dispenses miraculous communications, especially where the object does not justify the interference: but certain it is that she has more than once made/ use of sentiments and expressions to me, when alone, that now convince me that she has had some knowledge of the matter, though I cannot form any idea by what means she attained it.' 'This will be a very interesting enquiry,' said the Doctor, 'which I shall not fail to make as soon as I have the pleasure to see Mrs. Waldron again.' 'I agree with Edward,' said Mr. Evans, 'that communications strictly miraculous are never now indulged by Heaven to mankind for any purpose whatsoever, and far less for one merely secular and private; but to a being who has all the events that can possibly happen in the universe absolutely in his power, and at the same time who possesses the most perfect knowledge of every thought of every heart that ever was or ever will be – I cannot conceive it difficult for such a being so to direct the ordinary occurrences of things, as to suggest what ideas he pleases to the mind, and this, strictly speaking, without/ any miraculous interference; and something of this sort may have happened to Mrs. Waldron; but as you say, Doctor, it is an enquiry that to us, at least, must be highly interesting.'

The tea-equipage being now introduced, put an end to this disquisition. Ned, as usual, handed the kettle and the bread and butter. After tea the Doctor and the good Curate took a hit at back gammon, and Edward sought in his own room a short retirement to reflect on the surprising change in his situation./

CHAP. LXV.

THOUGH Edward had betrayed no visible emotion on being made acquainted with his great elevation, we are not to suppose that he was indifferent about it, or by any means insensible to the many advantages of high birth and a great fortune. He must of necessity then have felt a very considerable degree of internal complacency and satisfaction in the intelligence which had that day been communicated to him; but the circumstance in it which he contemplated with the greatest delight, was the situation it placed him in with respect to Lady Cecilia, on whom he could now confer a higher title than that which she had been accustomed to enjoy; and instead of receiving from her disinterested love the possession of a great estate, he could manifest/ the sincerity of his own, by laying that very estate at her feet. These were the contemplations which filled his heart with sensations of the purest and most lively joy, and which he was indulging alone with all the secrecy of silent rapture, when his meditations were suddenly disturbed by the noise of a carriage and horses driving to the door. Mr. and Mrs. Evans were surprised who this new visitor could be; and Edward went out to see: he met a lady just alighting from the chaise, whom, as it was night, he did not immediately discover; but whom, as soon as she approached the parlour, he found to be Mrs. Waldron herself; it was in the same moment she first discovered that it was Edward who conducted her. She turned instantly to him before she spoke to any other of the company. 'Oh! Edward!' said she, 'my son! my son! my Ravensdale! thou precious remains of my dear Lætitia! let me fold thee to my bosom.'/ 'My mother! my benefactress!' replied Edward, 'it is but this day that I have discovered the tender relationship in which I stand towards you.' After a mutual embrace, which nature demanded without any regard to the forms of ceremony, Edward continued. 'Here, Madam, is the only mother whom till this day I have ever known; here are the parents who fostered my helpless infancy, and reared me up to the state of manhood in which you now see me.'

Mrs. Waldron could not behold the nurturers of her grandson without the tenderest emotions; she thanked them over and over again with tears of gratitude, and blessed God, who, by restoring Edward to his long lost rights, would enable him to repay their piety and affection. She now saluted Doctor Burton,

– 324 –

whom she always revered, and whom she was particularly rejoiced to find there; and being somewhat overpowered with the variety, and the/ greatness of her emotions, she sat down. – Mrs. Evans ordered back the tea-things, and would not permit Edward to fatigue Mrs. Waldron with answering his enquiries until she had taken some refreshment. 'You know,' said she, 'you have been accustomed to obey me, and I will not give up my authority the first moment that another puts in their claim to it.' 'My dear mother!' said Edward, taking her by the hand, 'your authority shall not lose its weight with me while I live. I cannot express the joy my heart conceives in seeing the two to whom I am most indebted upon earth, now sitting together for the first time.' 'My Ravensdale!' said Mrs. Waldron, for I can assure you, Edward, that title belongs to you, 'my joy in this meeting is not inferior to your own; for I must ever feel myself bound by ties of unutterable gratitude to those who have sustained my child for three-and-twenty years, and now restore him to me, every thing my heart/ could wish.' The tea now again made its appearance, and Edward resumed his assistance, whilst the two ladies viewed him with eyes of equal transport and affection.

When this second tea-drinking was over, Ned ventured to resume his enquiries about Lady Cecilia and Lord Ravensdale.

'Cecilia,' said Mrs. Waldron, 'is well; but as for Lord Ravensdale, you must no longer give that title to the hoary hypocrite who has usurped it – that title, Edward, is your own; and God be thanked that I have lived to see his justice manifestly displayed in restoring it to you.' 'That the title will be mine, my mother, I cannot doubt, after all that I have heard; but if you regard my feelings, I beseech you not to call me by it, until it is recognized by parliament; and far less to reflect on that venerable character, for whom I must ever retain the most heartfelt gratitude and affection; who was a noble friend and benefactor to me when I/ stood in need of both; and who, if he erred in assuming the title, has made ample amends by the open and candid manner in which I understand he disclaims it.' – 'Why yes, Edward, he does disclaim it; and I can tell you he is prepared to acknowledge you as the true possessor of it.' – 'How did that happen?' said Edward; 'it is but this day that we have known it here ourselves.' – 'To tell you the truth, my Edward, I did suspect it from the first day I saw you at Glendemus; and though I could not account for it, I did communicate my suspicions to Miss Walker, and in some measure even to yourself.'

'Yes, my mother!' said Edward, 'I did indeed take notice of some expressions which seemed to cover some mysterious meaning which I did not comprehend, and which you did not think proper to reveal; and it was but this evening that I was mentioning them to the present company; and/ I am sure you will gratify both them and me extremely if you will explain the cause of your surmise.'

'Until the day I saw you, Edward,' said Mrs. Waldron, 'I always conceived the story so artfully obtruded on the world of my grandchild's death to be a

326 *The History of Ned Evans*

genuine truth; and I felt myself, as I conceived, infinitely indebted to what I thought a noble generosity, which conferred upon me a pension after my poor Lætitia's death, which had been settled upon her: but now I find all this generosity was a bribe to Heaven to cover the most atrocious iniquity, which, however, the justice and the purity of Heaven would no longer conceal. The first day I had the pleasure of seeing you at my house (Oh! may that day be blessed! and blessed be the power who saved you from the boisterous element, to put you under my protection!) – the first day, my Edward, that I saw you, recovered from your fatigue, and shining with manly/ grace, though disfigured in a jacket and trowsers, that day I was struck with the surprising resemblance which I thought I beheld in you to my poor deceased daughter Rivers. You chanced to take up a guitar which had once been hers, and sang a Scotch air, which you accompanied on the instrument. It had been a favourite air with her; and allowing for the difference between a man's voice and a woman's, there were so many turns which strongly reminded me of her, that here again I was impressed, even to astonishment. I know not whether there are any secret instincts of nature, which by some inexplicable sympathy can draw the affections of a parent to an unknown child; but I am sure I felt something like this, and conceived a tenderness for you, which I never felt for any other being, except my daughter. I was no stranger to the gallant services you performed for her whom we used to call Lady Cecilia Rivers – to/ your passion for that amiable girl, nor to the unbounded and disinterested love with which she repays it. Her brother dies; and then I found you likely to succeed to all that property by your union with her, which had my grandchild lived, would have been his of right. Surely, thought I, he is my child, and God, in his own way and time, is restoring him to his inheritance. This was an abiding impression on my mind, which I neither could, nor indeed desired to get rid of; but the matter was of so delicate a nature, and involved in it so many important consequences, that until I had more conviction, I thought it imprudent to say any thing upon the subject. I determined, however, in my own mind, to take a journey to this place, to enquire from my new and ever to be valued friends, if you were indeed their son. Whilst this was in my thoughts, the stings of conscience disclosed to my reverend friend here, Doctor Burton, that secret/ iniquity which it could no longer bear, and the circumstances of which I first learned from the vile agent in the business, Laurence Flinn. This was farther confirmed by the letter which Doctor Burton wrote from Dublin immediately upon finding out Michael Carroll; relating the circumstance of the child's having been dropped with a clergyman in Wales, and his intention of immediately going thither to enquire about it. This poor Cecilia in the candour of her heart confessed to me; and never were my ears blessed with such joyful sounds, for then the whole mystery was unravelled, and I in my turn acknowledged to her the suspicions I had for some time entertained, and filled her with inexpressible delight when I assured her that our Edward here was the man.

Upon the strength of this, she conducted me to her father. I own I went filled with resentment, and determined to upbraid him with his perfidious supplanting of/ my child, and depriving me for so many years of the consolation of a mother. – But when I beheld the miserable shadow of him whom I used to contemplate with reverence and affection; when I saw sorrow and contrition deeply marked upon his countenance; and above all, when the beautiful and amiable Cecilia was standing by my side, bathed in tears, I own my resentments were disarmed, and I told the old man, 'I am come to speak peace to your soul, and to bring you forgiveness both from God and from myself.' I then related to him all my own surmisings, before his own uneasiness of mind had disclosed any thing of the matter, and assured him he might console himself with the firm belief that he would find in Edward the only, yet the certain remedy to heal his broken heart. A visible gleam of joy brightened his countenance at these words. 'God grant it!' said he; 'that young man has been long/ dear to me; and if he should turn out to be the child I have injured, I shall no longer lament those whom God has taken from me, but consider this new gift as a sign of pardon and returning favour.' The ease that this information gave him has considerably recruited his strength and spirits; and when I told him that I was coming here directly to search this matter to the bottom, he determined himself to set off for Dublin the next day with Cecilia, where, I make no doubt, they now are, impatiently expecting to see us all return.

Edward, with some eagerness, whispered Mrs. Waldron, 'Have you no word from her ladyship for me?' – 'No,' replied she, 'not a syllable; Cecilia's situation is now changed; and it will henceforth belong to your lordship to bestow those great advantages which her generous and faithful heart was once willing to confer on you; and which I am sure she would not receive/ from any other hand.' 'Oh! that I was at her feet,' said Edward, 'to make offer of myself and all that I shall ever possess on earth!'

'You must soon be so,' replied Doctor Burton; 'this alliance was indeed sometimes talked of in the country, and I for one always wished it success; but now it becomes indispensable; for the marriage seems to have been already made in heaven.' 'We will consummate it on earth then,' said Edward, with a smile; to which both the reverend gentlemen replied, 'Amen!'

Evans now related to Mrs. Waldron all those little circumstances relative to his first finding Edward which she had not yet heard, and brought her the little frock which he had on when he first saw him. Mrs. Waldron looked at it, and wept. – 'This frock,' said she, 'is my own work; it was one of many others which I made/ for my poor Lætitia against her lying-in. – Here,' said she, 'I could swear to the stitching of these gussets in any part of the world.' Some tender emotions

328 *The History of Ned Evans*

which the sight of this frock, and the recollections connected with it caused, now visibly appeared in Mrs. Waldron's eyes, which Edward endeavoured to divert, by begging her to keep the frock for the little lord whom Cecilia should in due time present her, adding, 'it was a pity such beautiful work should have been so long concealed.' This turn restored her to her spirits, and enabled her to spend a charming evening, when Edward sung, after supper, some delightful Scotch and Welch airs, and joined with Doctor Burton and Evans in several catches and glees; so that perhaps this was the happiest night that several of the company, though advanced in years, had ever passed. To Edward himself, it certainly was so, though far short of many which we hope fortune/ has yet in store for him, and to the enjoyment of which we shall conduct him with all the speed that is compatible with the necessity of letting the good Doctor Burton and Mrs. Waldron repose a little after their journey./

CHAP. LXVI.

In the humble dwelling of Ti-gwin, there was some difficulty in finding accommodation for all this good company who had so unexpectedly met together. Mrs. Evans however contrived it some how or other, packing Edward with her husband, whom he still (and probably ever will continue to do) called his father, and to whom as he told as he went to bed, 'that he was glad of that opportunity to introduce his new coronet to his old night-cap.' Evans replied, 'he was sorry his coronet should keep such bad company, but hoped soon to turn his night-cap into a mitre, when they would be fitter companions for each other.' – Thus did these two dearest of friends manifest how little they were to be intoxicated by any worldly advantages, and/ soon sunk into that state which, next to death, is the greatest leveller of distinctions, and which prefers a night-cap both to a coronet and a mitre.

In the morning the same happy company met again to breakfast, refreshed with their night's sleep, and perfectly in health both in mind and body. It was determined to continue that day at Ti-gwin, and all of them to set off the day after for Dublin, the presence of Mr. and Mrs. Evans being necessary to ascertain the great discovery they had made. Carroll, with his attendants, was sent off that same day, to be still however detained as witnesses, but with an assurance that no evil could happen to him, as there really did not appear in him any guilt.

And now Edward having some visits which he wished to pay, ordered his horses, whilst Evans took Doctor Burton to shew him his garden, which he cultivated with his own hands, and Mrs. Evans entertained/ Mrs. Waldron with a thousand anecdotes of Edward's sweetness from his earliest infancy even to that day; to which she listened with that secret rapture, with which we may suppose a mother to be delighted on the first discovery of her child. Whilst the good Mrs. Evans was thus fondly descanting on Edward's virtues, and particularly dwelling on his early piety and just sense of religion, fortune, which is always a slippery jade, played her a trick, and sent the little Edward into the room, to the great surprise of Mrs. Evans, who had strictly charged the maid to keep him out of sight. The child, to be sure, looked as beautiful as any that nature ever sent from her hand, and Mrs. Waldron, who loved all children, ran to embrace it. 'Whose is

– 329 –

330 *The History of Ned Evans*

this pretty creature?' said she to Mrs. Evans. Mrs. Evans blushed, and was silent. The child called her grandmama. – 'Oh!' said Mrs. Waldron, who was quick in discerning countenances, 'I believe, my dear/ madam, that our friend's sense of piety and religion has not always been equally uniform.' 'It is true,' said Mrs. Evans; 'in this one instance he has erred, and I believe from my soul in this one only. He confessed this to his father, as the dear youth then thought Mr. Evans; and this little creature was born a few months after he left us; I took him as the memorial of my Edward, whose perfect image he is; and I intend never to part with him.' – 'You must part with him a few minutes to me, however,' said Mrs. Waldron, who took him up in her arms, and almost devoured him with kisses. 'We cannot approve of these children, to be sure,' said she; 'but oh, nature! who is able to resist your laws?' She then enquired about the mother, and it was agreed between her and Mrs. Evans that she should take no notice of having seen the child to Edward; she, however, enquired for the servant who took care of him, and gave her five guineas to/ encourage her in her attention. Poor little Edward was remanded to his retreat, and the maid, who perhaps brought him into view with the very expectation which so well succeeded, went with him perfectly pleased.

In the mean time Edward arrived at the cottage in which poor Molly Price, the mother of his sweet infant, resided; she had heard of his great exaltation, as indeed news so extraordinary is seldom flow in finding wings, and almost despaired that he would now bestow a thought upon her – but when he entered the door, she beheld the same sweet countenance which first won her virgin heart, and which received in return the same tribute of maiden innocence. The meeting was tender, as was suited to both their natures, and virtuous as became the relative situations in which they were both of them now placed. Molly indeed was employed when he entered, in the tenderest office of nature, suckling the little/ infant she had borne about two months before to her husband. Ned asked how he behaved to her, and whether she was happy? She replied, that no husband could behave better, that he gave her all his earnings, and that she would be as happy as perhaps any in her station could be, if she could forget – 'Alas, Molly!' replied he, 'rather say, if you could forgive.' – 'Forgive!' said she; 'whom have I to forgive?' – 'Me,' said Edward; 'Oh! Mr. Evans!' said she, 'if I do not mistake in calling you by that name, I have no complaint to make of you; it was my own heart betrayed me; and if you did wrong, I surely was alike to blame.' – 'The fault,' said Edward, 'perhaps was mutual; but to repair it as far as I can, with respect to you, must be my part.' He then sent her to fetch her husband, and with that condescending sweetness which characterized all his actions, rocked the cradle in which she had just laid her infant, till she/ returned. The husband, whose name was Richard Parry, was a strapping young fellow about his own age, well enough featured, and cast in that mould which nature wisely thought best suited to his condition. Edward told the young man, he had sent for him because he wished him well, and because he wished to see him and his wife together, as he knew he had had a regard for her before he had married her. Richard replied, he was not ignorant that Molly had had a misfortune, which many another honest girl had as well as she; but that she made him a good wife, and as he did every thing to make her happy that was in his power, he hoped she would be grateful, and remain true to him. Edward commended the sentiment, and added, that it should be his care to supply them with some of the ingredients which in the general opinion of the world were essential to happiness.

He then briefly told them of his being to/ return to Ireland the next day, where he had the prospect of a considerable property; and that, as he did not intend immediately to take the child over, he would commit it to the care of its mother, sending with it however a servant; and to enable them to do this with care, he told down fifty guineas, which he presented to Molly, in the presence of her husband. Neither Richard nor Molly had ever seen so much money before at one time, and were expecting nothing less than to be the owners of such a sum; they received it with expressions suitable to their surprise and gratitude, and Edward took leave of them, promising to be still more permanently useful to them, as long as their good conduct should entitle them to his regard. From Molly's Ned went to the old veteran her father, whom he had not yet seen since his return. They had been ancient friends, Ned having spent many an hour in his days of boyhood, listening to his harp, and learning/ from him to touch the strings himself. When old John heard that he was in the house, he inwardly rejoiced, for he loved Edward in his heart, though he could not help charging him with somewhat of unkindness for the tune he had played with his daughter. Ned made the best excuse he was able, which he strengthened by a powerful argument, similar in kind, though less in force, with that which he had just used with Molly, and thus regained the friendship and good wishes of the old man.

He invited John up to the house, to get his dinner and a cup of good ale in the kitchen, and ordered him to fetch his harp, which the good old soul immediately set about tuning, that he might give them a specimen of his performance. In his way home he called upon Mr. and Mrs. Watkin, who however were absent at their daughter Colebroke's, she having lately lain in, and her first child, a boy, was to be christened. Ned was sorry that by this accident,/ and his unexpected return so soon to Ireland, he missed seeing them at this time, altogether; and so, without prolonging his ride further, he went home. When he got in, he found his mother, that is Mrs. Evans, busily employed among her trunks. The journey she was next day to undertake, appeared to that good woman like a voyage to the East Indies; nor is it to be wondered at, since the circuit of her whole travels might be comprised in a circle of forty miles diameter. To quit Wales therefore, was in some degree to her like quitting the world; and was a journey, which on

332 *The History of Ned Evans*

her own account nothing would have tempted her to undertake; but to which she looked forward with less dread, when she reflected on the great object that was to be accomplished by it, and that she should be accompanied by all she held most dear in the world. When Edward saw her preparations, he could not help smiling; he prevailed upon her, however, to undo/ all she had been doing, by assuring her she would have no occasion for any thing but her body linen, and a couple of gowns; as all the rest she held most valuable she would find of no use but to make pin-cushions or work-bags of; and that in future she must look to him for all things necessary. He then told her he had seen Molly Price, and that he had determined to leave the child with her, till there was a more proper time to take it to Ireland. Mrs. Evans agreed in the propriety of this, though she was determined to come back and live with it, rather than want it; but Edward assuring her she should have it at her own disposal, she was easy; and having replaced all the things in their repositories, where many of them had lain unmolested for thirty years, she packed up those only which Ned recommended, and then went to superintend the dishing of the dinner.

Farewel ye temperate and simple meals, as delicious as ye were wholesome! farewel,/ ye mountain flocks, able to please the palate of Apicius![42] farewel, ye savoury steams of toasted cheese, converted to a rabbit by the power of a toast and nutbrown ale! This is the last day we shall be allowed to regale upon your simple luxuries. But often amidst the pomp of plate, and of attendants; often amidst the puzzling variety of unknown dishes, shall we remember with regret the pleasant though small parlour of Ti-gwin, its neat though unadorned sideboard, its hospitable though simple entertainment.

Perhaps the thoughts of this being the last dinner they might ever eat together in that room, which for more than twenty years had witnessed the happiness of their domestic intercourse, might in some degree have depressed the spirits of our honest curate, and his amiable wife, notwithstanding the brilliancy of those scenes which were just opening to their view. But Ned, aware of this effect, called in the all-/powerful aid of music, to chace away all melancholy. And having seated Price in a corner, supported by a noble flaggon of ale on his right hand, and David Morgan to help him to it on the other, and pushing with unusual gaiety at his own table the warming juice of Oporto's grape,[43] sorrow was banished from all hearts; and the hours, winged with joy, and beguiled by music, flew uncounted. Poor Price himself, contrary to his usual custom, was the first that tired, but not till such an hour as justified all in thinking of their repose. The honest old fellow had no reason to repent his evening's entertainment; he was well paid for the amusement he afforded, and the good-natured curate lent him old Black-bird to carry himself and his harp home under the guidance of David Morgan.

Volume IV   333

In the morning two chaises, as ordered the day before, were ready at the door by eight. It was however ten before the good Mrs. Evans had adjusted all her concerns,/ and given the important charges she thought necessary to David Morgan's father and mother, whom she left to take care of the house; her last business was to steal up to the room in which little Edward stayed, and to water his little cheeks with her tears: but the thoughts of soon either sending for him, or returning to him, consoled her; and after being twice or thrice called for by the good curate, she at last went down, and was handed by Edward into the chaise, where Mrs. Waldron had been seated ten minutes before. Doctor Burton and Mr. Evans went in the other chaise; and Edward and David Morgan, mounted on Brilliant and Belisarius, drew up the rear.

They continued their journey without any accident, and arrived at Holyhead time enough to get a tolerably comfortable dinner before the packet sailed in the evening. About six they were informed it was time to go on board. It was dark, and the weather rather squally. Mrs. Evans was/ frighted, and would have gladly turned back again for Ti-gwin; but Mrs. Waldron assuring her that no packet had been lost within any person's recollection, she suffered Edward to conduct her on board; and the two ladies being accommodated with one of the state rooms, they went immediately to their births together./

CHAP. LXVII.

IT was said of the old duchess of Bedford, that being asked on her return from Ireland (where her husband had been Lord Lieutenant), how she liked that country? she replied, 'there was one good thing in it, there was always a fair wind to carry you out of it.'[44] Her Grace's assertion could not be contradicted by the experience of our present voyagers. The wind certainly blew from that kingdom, and seemed determined to give them all the opposition in their approach to it, that was in its power. Edward, who was now so well accustomed to the sea, as not to be incommoded by its highest rage, as long as he was in a good ship, and had sea room,[45] would not have minded its present turbulence, but for the terrors of all the female/ passengers, and the sickness with which both Evans and Doctor Burton were affected. He passed the whole night in assisting them, and indeed every person else in the cabin, and in soothing all the ladies, whose terrors at the perpetual cry of 'luff! luff!' and the thumps which the vessel received as she buffeted the waves, were often expressed in screams, which he did all in his power to compose; at length towards morning the wind abated, and grew somewhat more favourable, so that about two o'clock the next afternoon they passed the bar, and in less than an hour were landed at the Pigeon House. Here they soon got a coach, which they ordered to drive to the Marine Hotel.

Edward profited by his experience in his first voyage to Ireland, so as not to be a second time taken in by the officious impostors who never fail to surround strangers on their first landing, and conducted Mrs. Waldron and Mrs. Evans, with the/ good curate, into the house, where he got them a comfortable room and some refreshment. Mrs. Waldron and Doctor Burton went together in a coach to Lord Ravensdale's, to acquaint him and Cecilia, with the arrival of Edward and the Evanses, and the happy and important discovery they had made. Edward remained with Mr. and Mrs. Evans to allow time for this communication, and that they might get themselves a little in order after their voyage, before they should be introduced to his lordship. In about an hour Lord Ravensdale's coach came for them to the hotel, and Evans and his wife were, for the first time in their lives, seated in a carriage with a coronet. Edward got in after them, and I will leave it to my readers to imagine the feelings of his heart as

Volume IV   335

they turned into Merrion Square, and approached Lord Ravensdale's house. The carriage stopped, and the porter opened the door. Two footmen in laced liveries were behind the carriage. Edward alighted/ and handed Mrs. Evans up the steps; the good curate followed, and Doctor Burton met them in the hall. In the drawing room they were received with all the emotions of the sincerest friendship by Lady Cecilia, who took Mrs. Evans by both her hands and kissed her, and who conferred the same favour on Evans himself. The worthy curate was somewhat abashed, and endeavoured at a bow in the best style he could. Edward smiled, and just got a glance of Cecilia's eye, which dropped and trembled as it met his. He was going to approach her, when Doctor Burton whispered to him, that the old Lord wished to see him in his dressing room. 'Will you come with me,' said Edward? 'Yes,' said the Doctor; 'I mean to accompany you.' As he went out, Ned turned his face towards Cecilia, whose eyes again met his. The intelligence they communicated was instantly understood by both, and more expressive than/ any language could convey. When Edward entered the room, the old Lord rose, visibly in much emotion. Edward advanced towards him, and dropped upon one knee at his feet: the old Lord clasped him in his arms, and wept aloud. 'Weep not, my Lord!' said Edward, 'I hoped that my return would have wiped away all tears from your eyes.' 'They are tears of joy,' said the old man, 'tears which wash away from my soul a burthen which has oppressed it for more than twenty years. Come then to my arms, my deliverer! and let me restore you to those riches and honours, of which I basely wronged you; which have well nigh brought me to perdition, but which will sit light and easy on their true possessor.' 'My Lord!' said Edward, 'I request' – 'My Lord Ravensdale!' interrupted the other, 'I beseech you no longer to call me by a title which it was my shame to have been ever known by; but which I here resign with ten/ thousand times more pleasure than I assumed it, which truly belongs to your lordship, and which I have already taken steps to put you in the legal possession of.' 'How then am I to call you?' said Edward. 'Call me Rivers, call me what you please, call me any thing but Lord Ravensdale,' 'Oh!' said Edward, 'there is a name which if you would allow me to call you by, would fill up the measure of my happiness, and without which all the honours and riches you are showering upon me, will be but splendid misery.' 'Say then what is it?' 'Let me call you father. Let me lay these new acquired possessions at the feet of your charming daughter, who has long been the mistress of my soul, and let me have your sanction to request her sharing them with me.' 'My Lord! (said colonel Rivers, by which name we must in future call him) if any circumstance could increase the satisfaction which I feel this day, in restoring to your/ lordship your long usurped rights, it would be the happy alliance you have now done me the honour to propose.' Edward, or rather Lord Ravensdale, which title he from henceforth must assume, was going to express his gratitude, when the old colonel interrupted him, by proposing to

336 *The History of Ned Evans*

go down directly to the ladies, to introduce him in his proper character, and that he himself might be introduced to Evans and his wife. 'My Cecilia!' said he, as he entered the room, 'let me present to you the Earl of Ravensdale, who by coming to that title, has somewhat abated the rank which you have been accustomed to move in, but who, with a gallantry inseparable from a great spirit, entreats your acceptance of a higher.' Cecilia blushed, but yielded her willing lips to the fervent kiss, which the young Earl then impressed upon them. As all the company were now connected in the dearest ties either of friendship, or of consanguinity; this happy disclosure/ of the intended marriage was received with mutual congratulations and fervent joy. Mrs. Waldron and Mrs. Evans gazed on Edward, in whom they thought they had an equal claim, with rapture, and joined his hand to Cecilia's with the most heart-felt satisfaction. Indeed the marriage might have been solemnized on the spot, as there were two clergymen present, and all the parties were agreed, but the colonel wished first to have the matter of the peerage settled. The parliament was to meet in a few days, and on the first day of it, Edward's claim to the title was laid before the house. As the whole matter had been previously made known to the chancellor and the other law lords, there was little difficulty in ascertaining it, and he took his seat as Earl of Ravensdale, a few days before the Christmas recess. On that same day the bishop of Limerick,[46] who had long lived in habits of the greatest intimacy with the Ravensdale family, and in whose/ diocese the estate of Ravensdale lay, went home from the house with colonel Rivers, in order to be introduced to the new Earl, and dined with him. Cecilia did the honours of the table, and looked like beauty itself. Doctor Burton had been long acquainted with the bishop, but Evans had never seen him before, and was now introduced to his lordship by the colonel, with that eulogium on his character which it justly deserved; and the bishop received him with every token of respect. His lordship was the only person present that was not of the family; and after the cloth was removed, and a long and happy enjoyment of his titles and estate drank to the new Lord, who had that day taken his seat, he rose, and expressed his desire, that as he then really felt himself, for the first time, to be the possessor of those titles, which he had been accustomed to revere and love in those who had formerly enjoyed them, he wished to crown the happiness/ and justice of that day, by laying those titles and possessions at the feet of her who had long possessed his heart, and by restoring to her that rank in society which he had been so unexpectedly the cause of her losing. Colonel Rivers seconded the motion, while Cecilia, covered with blushes, was yet too ingenuous to invent delays, for what had been already agreed on, and which she had so often confessed to be the wish of her heart. The bishop claimed the right of performing the ceremony. 'I,' said his Lordship, 'gave her her first name, and I shall rejoice still more to add this new title to it.'

Volume IV 337

Cecilia retired with Mrs. Waldron and Mrs. Evans, and a little before tea came down to the drawing room, arrayed in a simple gown of white muslin. Her lovely tresses were bound with a string of oriental pearls, and hung down her back in natural curls, glossy as the richest silk; unstained with powder, and unconstrained by the disfiguring/ art of the hair-dresser. The young Lord Ravensdale, in whose countenance the sweetness and modesty of Ned Evans still beamed with unaltered lustre, stood up beside her, and exhibited a person which no painter or statuary would have disdained to study, as a model of male beauty. The bishop read the service with all dignity suited to so solemn and sacred an obligation, and a little before seven pronounced that blessing, which joined in holy union two bodies, whose souls were united long before, and whom Heaven itself by its almost miraculous interference seemed to have created for each other.

No marriage that was ever solemnized seemed to give more perfect satisfaction to all concerned; the old colonel recovered all his usual gaiety and spirits; joked with Lady Ravensdale and the other ladies with a flow of humour which he had not exhibited for many years, and prolonged the festivity of the evening with the bishop and/ the two reverend gentlemen to a late hour; long after that which admitted Edward to the paradise of Cecilia's arms.

These important events being all happily adjusted, and the Christmas recess approaching, the young Lord Ravensdale and his bride wished to go down to their seat in the country, to dispense at that rigorous season of the year, the blessings which ought always to accompany the festival, among their tenants and dependants; and to enjoy, amidst the shades of Ravensdale, those serene raptures for which both their bosoms were formed, but to which the noise and parade of the capital were little accommodated. Colonel Rivers joined most heartily in this intention, for he was always fond of a rural and retired life, and seldom went to Dublin except when his parliamentary duties called him thither. Of these he had now taken leave for ever; for though he might command a seat in the house of commons, yet having been so/ long a member of the house of lords, he thought the situation would be somewhat awkward. His intention was to live in future at his own seat of Riversfield, about nine miles from Ravensdale, excepting the time he might spend with his daughter, and which both she and her lord desired to be as much as they could prevail on him to bestow. In the disposal of their affairs they had no occasion for the interference or delay of lawyers. The Colonel surrendered all the Ravensdale estates, together with a great sum of money which he had saved out of them, to the young Lord, together with the house in Dublin and all its furniture, his horses, carriages, &c. and all the family plate. He reserved to himself his own paternal estate, which he had improved to be worth near three thousand pounds a-year; and this too at his death was to go to his daughter and her children.

338 *The History of Ned Evans*

The next day but one after the marriage, the whole family took leave of Dublin./ Lord and Lady Ravensdale went in their own travelling chaise and four, attended by David Morgan riding Belisarius, and leading Brilliant. Colonel Rivers and Evans, with Mrs. Waldron and Mrs. Evans, went in a post coach which had been his before, and was now also Lord Ravensdale's. Doctor Burton remained in town for a few days, but promised to be at Ravensdale with Mrs. Burton and Lady Ravensdale's dear friend Sophia, very shortly after they got there. At so late a season of the year, the journey could not well be performed under three days. The tenants had notice of their approach, an innumerable crowd of whom met their young lord at the gates of Ravensdale Park, and taking out the horses, drew his carriage to the house. They paid the same compliment to the Colonel, whom they always loved, and whom they cheered with three huzzas as he got out of the carriage. The whole company stood a few minutes/ on the steps, where the young lord expressed his gratitude for the affectionate reception they had given him, and the satisfaction he felt in observing the esteem and regard they manifested to their late master, in whose steps it should be his pride and ambition to walk. He presented to them Lady Ravensdale, whom they had long known and revered in another character, and whom they now welcomed with the loudest acclamations. Her ladyship made them a low and graceful curtesy, and they were all invited into the great hall, where a barrel of strong ale was broached, which they emptied with flowing cans and sincere hearts – to the health and prosperity of the House of Ravensdale./

CHAP. LXVIII.

WE might here have closed this narrative, having brought the hero of it to the summit of earthly felicity, by means which discover the secret direction of Providence in the affairs of this world, and how his almighty hand can make the unruly passions of sinful men subservient to the most righteous purposes; and events seemingly trifling and accidental, yet in the great chain of causes and effects to lead to the most important consequences. This indeed is a truth which we have long had occasion to observe ourselves, and which we have endeavoured in this story to impress upon the minds of our readers. Before we take our final leave, however, it may be pleasing to some, to know what became of those who/ have appeared as subordinate characters in this work.

Among the first visitors who came to pay their respects at Ravensdale-house, was Captain Nettlefield, who perhaps could not have induced his proud and envious spirit to pay any compliment to Edward in his new character, did not the necessity of his affairs require it. He appeared before him with all the servile awe with which conscious wickedness is always overwhelmed in the presence of virtue. Edward knew his character well, and always despised it; he had himself received the basest of injuries from him, but he nobly thought that it did not become the Earl of Ravensdale to remember the wrongs offered to Ned Evans, and he therefore shewed him a greater civility and respect than he would other-wise probably have been tempted to do, and asked him to stay dinner. Nettlefield accepted the invitation, and in the evening, when his heart had been somewhat/ warmed by a bottle of the best claret, he desired to speak to Lord Ravensdale alone. His lordship took him up to the library, where he usually sat in the morn-ing; and Nettlefield began by professing his extreme contrition for his conduct towards him in America, which he acknowledged to be base and unmanly, but which he begged his lordship to ascribe to the effect of sudden rage, which was an unfortunate disposition interwoven in his constitution, and not to any premedi-tated malice, which his soul abhorred: – that besides this, which had long lain upon his mind, there was another business which made him solicitous for the honour of this interview, and which he had his father's commands to lay before him, and this was the unhappy situation of his affairs. He then entered into a

340 *The History of Ned Evans*

detail of the incumbrances, which amounted to near ten thousand pounds, to be paid out of an estate of six hundred pounds per annum. Mr. Nettlefield concluded with/ stating, 'that as six thousand pounds of this money was due to his lordship himself, and as there was no possibility of satisfying the other creditors without bringing the estate to an immediate sale, his father thought it his duty to make the first offer of it to his lordship, in which he entirely concurred, and had therefore presumed to wait upon him for that purpose.'

Lord Ravensdale replied, 'As to what passed between us in America, Captain Nettlefield, I have long since forgotten, as well as forgiven it; and I desire to shake hands with you upon this subject, and never to let a syllable about it escape from either of your mouths again. As for the derangement of your affairs, they give me great and real concern, as I do not see that if your estate is sold, there can be any reversion adequate to the maintenance of the family.' 'It is true, my lord,' replied Nettlefield, 'but there is no alternative; a small reversion there will be, and I must/ remain at home, and assist my mother and my sister with my pay.' 'I am happy to hear from your own mouth,' said Lord Ravensdale, 'a sentiment so full of dutiful affection, which gives me hope that you will acknowledge the propriety as well as the necessity of what I shall now take the liberty to propose to you –

'I have the honour to be the intimate friend of Mr. Grainger, the very mention of whose name I see covers you with confusion; his amiable and innocent daughter is no more, but a beautiful and lovely boy remains, of whom no parent ought to be ashamed. If, Mr. Nettlefield, you will do justice to the memory of that unfortunate and much injured lady, and acknowledge your child, I will find means to save your estate, and to extricate your father from his difficulties.'

'My lord,' said Nettlefield, 'I am indeed covered with confusion; I stand before you self-convicted, and self-condemned./ I acknowledge the unbounded generosity with which you have treated me, and I beseech you to believe that my heart is not so depraved but that I can love and esteem virtue, though I have never yet been able to practise it. From this moment I beg leave to surrender myself to your lordship's disposal, entreating of you only to command me what to do, and I will do it.' – 'Do as you would be done by,' said Lord Ravensdale; 'there is no other command necessary: and let me assure you, Mr. Nettlefield, that if you will make this command the rule of all your future actions, you will find yourself not only more respected, but also much more happy than you have ever hitherto been.' Nettlefield bowed, and withdrew.[47]

Three years have now elapsed since his lordship took possession of his title and estates; and since his happy union with the beautiful and virtuous Cecilia, as many lovely children have crowned those years,/ a boy to inherit all his father's virtues, and two girls, the lovely likenesses of their all-accomplished mother. Nor is there any reason to doubt, but that, if Heaven shall please to spare the parents,

Volume IV   341

many more young scions shall arise to continue the name and the virtues of the family.

Colonel Rivers is still living, and spends much of his time with his daughter and her children. The most cordial friendship and affection subsists between Lord Ravensdale and him; nor does his lordship ever take an important step either in public or in private life without consulting his experience.

For two years the worthy Evans and his wife lived entirely at Ravensdale house, experiencing the same affection and the same dutiful attention from Lord Ravensdale that he had ever shewn them when he thought himself their son. Last year the old vicar of the parish died, and the bishop immediately presented Evans to it. It is/ worth a good six hundred a year; and he bids fair to be as much loved and respected by his congregation in Ireland, as he had ever been in Wales. He is at present busily employed in making great additions to his garden, which are to connect with Lord Ravensdale's pleasure gardens, so that he will have an extensive range of the most beautiful scenery, in a manner within his own premises. The good old man continues to work himself in his garden, in which wholesome exercise Lord Ravensdale often delights to share, and assists him with the same pleasure as when he called him his Ned Evans. The old woman and her son, who had been so hospitable to him the night of his disappointment at Muckworm's, he has brought over from Wales, and they now live with him. John is a stout lad of about sixteen, and he educates him for a gardener.

Mrs. Evans has assumed no new airs upon the great change in her situation; she attends/ as usual upon her domestic concerns, and retains that happy evenness of temper which long endured poverty without repining, and now enjoys affluence without being extremely elated. Her chief care is indeed directed to the sweet little cherub whom she calls her grandson; who lives entirely with her, and who is an exact counterpart, both in features and disposition, of what her Edward was at his age. This circumstance has endeared this child to her in an extreme degree, and she seems to have transferred to him that tenderness of maternal affection, which she felt so intensely for his father. Nothing can place Lady Ravensdale's heart in a more amiable point of view than her conduct to this child. It was by her express desire, and without her lord's knowledge, that she had him brought over from Wales, who never was more astonished than when he saw him in her ladyship's arms. It was an endearing compliment she paid him, when she presented/ the infant to his lordship, and requested him for her sake to provide for him as if he was hers. Lord Ravensdale is now in treaty for the purchase of Ti-gwin estate, which is worth about five hundred pounds a-year, and which he intends to settle on the little Edward.

Mrs. Waldron spends part of every year with Lord and Lady Ravensdale, but passes the summer for the most part at her own house of Glendemus. It is a charming retreat, and exquisitely convenient for seabathing. The children are

342 *The History of Ned Evans*

usually sent there for a couple of months, to reap the advantage of that wholesome practice;[48] and Lord and Lady Ravensdale usually go for them, and bring them and Mrs. Waldron back to Ravensdale house. His lordship has increased the annuity which Mrs. Waldron enjoyed, to five hundred pounds a year – a sum which is fully adequate to all her wants and wishes. David Morgan renewed his addresses to Molly Doran, and/ was too handsome a fellow, and too advantageous a match for her, to be long in gaining her consent. Lord Ravensdale has set him up in a farm, of which he has given him a lease for his own life, and two sons, whom Molly has already born him; and he is likely to succeed well. The old woman, his mother-in law, lives with him, and she had last year the consolation to see her son return from America. Doran immediately waited on Lord Ravensdale, who received him as a brother warrior. He related the extreme grief of Awattahowee, when the time had elapsed for his return without his appearing: but the season having turned out very fine for hunting, and Awattahowee being uncommonly successful, he imputed it to the intercession of his dear friend Warbishcondar with the great spirit, and the whole nation got drunk at a grand feast of bear's broth and dog's flesh, which he had given in gratitude to his memory. Lord Ravensdale was well pleased/ to hear this account of his friend's faithful attachment, and has placed Doran in a lucrative station about his own person. Captain Nettlefield has kept the promise which he made to Lord Ravensdale, and acknowledged his son Charles. His contrition appears so sincere, that Mr. Grainger has been induced to see him, who has now built a small house in the village of Ravensdale, to be near his lordship, whom he justly considers as his dearest friend, and to superintend the education of his grandson. Old Nettlefield died of a paralytic stroke, about a year ago, by which his wife and daughter have been relieved from a most oppressive tyrant, and they are happy in the affectionate attention of their son and brother, who since his reconciliation with Lord Ravensdale seems entirely reformed, and endeavours, within his sphere, to form his manners after his example. By the united exertions of his Lordship and Mr Grainger, all other creditors of the estate/ are paid off, and the land is settled upon Charles. Under the wise and œconomical management of these trustees, the estate will be clear before he comes of age; whilst an annuity is reserved for the family, on which they live with much more comfort and respectability than ever they did before.

Doctor Burton and his family are frequent visitors at Ravensdale house, where Sophia in particular spends a great part of her time. An old attachment between her and Nettlefield is suspected by some to be reviving; and if he continues to behave with as much propriety as he has done for these last three years, it is probable they may one day be united. He has many qualities to recommend him both to man and woman, to which if he could add virtue, he would be wholly unexceptionable.

Volume IV 343

And now, reader, having throughout these pages endeavoured to amuse your/ mind without injuring your heart, I trust I have in some degree succeeded; and that the events here artlessly related, some of which have really happened, and none of which transgress the bounds of nature or probability, may lead you to believe that the eyes of God are on the ways of men, and that he spieth out all their goings; that his Providence can, and does direct their minutest affairs, though without any miraculous, or visible interference; and that (as we are assured by the highest of all authorities), 'though five sparrows are sold for a farthing, yet one of them shall not fall to the ground without our Father, who is in Heaven.'[49]

FINIS.

EDITORIAL NOTES

Volume I

1. *O'erstep not the modesty of Nature*: Hervey takes her motto from the scene in Shakespeare's *Hamlet, Prince of Denmark* where Hamlet addresses the players;

   > Be not too tame neither, but let your own discretion be your tutor. Suit the action to the word, the word to the action, with this special observance – that you o'erstep not the modesty of nature. For anything so ov'rdone is from the purpose of playing whose end, both at the first and now, was and is to hold as 'twere the mirror up to Nature to show Virtue her feature, Scorn her own image, and the very age and body of the time his form and pressure. Now this overdone, or come tardy off, though it make the unskilful laugh, cannot but make the judicious grieve, the censure of the which one must in your allowance o'erweigh a whole theatre of others. O, there be players that I have seen play, and heard others praised – and that highly – not to speak it profanely, that neither having th' accent of Christians, nor the gait of Christian, pagan, nor man, have so strutted and bellowed that I have thought some of Nature's journeymen had made men, and not made them well, they imitated humanity so abominably.'

   (Hamlet III.ii.16–34).

2. *Evan Evans*: a stereotypically Welsh name, but also that of a real-life clergyman residing near Snowdon in the 1760s and 1770s. The *Oxford Dictionary of National Biography*, which notes his 'bardic' name of Ieuan Fardd and his dates (1731–88), describes him as a scholar and poet who, like the figure in Hervey's novel, never progressed further than curacies and who resented the imposition of English clergymen on Welsh parishes. He may have been the author of two books, *Some Specimens of the Poetry of the Antient Welsh Bards* (1764) and *The Love of our Country, a Poem, with Historical Notes* (1772). The name of Ned Evans suggests the figure of Edward Evan or Evans (1716–98), a nonconformist minister, poet and harpist who together with Iolo Morganwg (Edward Williams) was deemed to be one of two true heirs to the 'Ancient British Bards' (see the *Gentleman's Magazine*, November 1789). The poems of Edward Evans were first published only in 1803, but he was a popular and well-known figure in Glamorgan and may have served as a partial inspiration for the harp-playing, poetical Ned.

3. *a beneficed clergyman*: that is, one who holds a church living himself rather than simply fulfilling the duties of the incumbent for a tiny stipend as Evans does.

4. *quarrelled with the parishoners about his tythes*: in parishes which had not been reorganized under parliamentary enclosure, clergymen were entitled to one-tenth of everything

– 345 –

346 *Notes to pages 3–23*

produced (including crops, livestock and even, in some cases, bricks and tiles) but their attempts to claim it often resulted in disputes and litigation with their parishioners. In Austen's *Pride and Prejudice* the rebarbative Mr. Collins talks of the difficulty of making 'an agreement for tythes as may be beneficial to himself and not offensive to his patron', J. Austen, *The Novels of Jane Austen*, ed. R. W. Chapman. 3rd edn (London: Oxford University Press, 1980–2), vol. 2, *Pride and Prejudice*, p. 101.

5. *a cure*: the spiritual charge or oversight of parishioners or lay people; the office or function of a curate.

6. *Winifrid*: St Winifred or Winefride is patron saint of North Wales. The daughter of a Welsh chieftain, she was roughly wooed by Prince Caradoc. Finding his attentions unwelcome, she sought sanctuary in a church to which Caradoc followed her, striking off her head. St Beuno replaced her head, bringing her back to enjoy a long and successful life. The spring at Holywell marks the place where her head came to rest. The name perhaps foreshadows the number of doublings which feature in the novel.

7. *lowness of his finances*: Ned's 'wonderful' accomplishments are similar to those spontaneously attained by another character raised in rural isolation in Wales, Emmeline in Charlotte Smith's *Emmeline, or, the Orphan of the Castle* (1788), and mocked by Austen at the beginning of *Northanger Abbey*. Smith's heroine is eventually revealed as the rightful owner of the family property and comes close to marrying her first cousin, who has long been considered heir to it. These motifs, of course, also appear, somewhat modified, in *Ned Evans*.

8. *the month of November in the year 1779*: this gives us a starting point for the main narrative, which ends around Christmas 1783. Hervey's dating is consistent, to the extent that in Volume 4 she gives an exact date for the abandonment and discovery of the infant Ned.

9. *Towser*: a common name for large dogs.

10. *covert*: a hiding place.

11. *Hungary water*: rosemary flowers infused in wine or some other alcohol.

12. *Welsh rabbit*: not simply, as nowadays, cheese on toast, but a far richer dish consisting of cheese and butter melted together, mixed with ale, then poured over buttered toast.

13. *if I had been there with young maister*: an attempt at rendering a Welsh lower-class accent, though some characters – notably the harper Price and his daughter Molly – are spared this.

14. *woundily*: excessively, extremely, dreadfully.

15. *pallet*: a straw bed or mattress, generally a temporary or inferior place to sleep.

16. *Sherlock upon Death*: presumably *Practical Meditations upon the Four Last Things* by Richard Sherlock (1612–89), published posthumously in 1692.

17. *not a regular physician*: that is, he is not one of the elite, who studied for a degree at Oxford, Cambridge or one of the Scottish universities, but like the majority of medical practitioners combines the roles of surgeon and apothecary, providing drugs and carrying out treatment and surgeries.

18. *wine whey*: 'whey' is a general term for any drink taken medicinally, wine whey generally being a mixture of wine and milk.

19. *Oh! ye great ones of the earth*: Hervey numbered several bishops among her acquaintance, including the Bishop of Salisbury, at whose house she often stayed.

20. *without enthusiasm*: in the eighteenth century 'enthusiasm' was used to denote misdirected or excessive religious display, often in the context of nonconformist religion.

21. *answerable*: equivalent, corresponding.

Notes to pages 23–43 347

22. *her education was confined*: Hervey contrasts Miss Watkins's purely domestic education unfavourably with the more liberal one which Lady Cecilia has received. The education of young women was a popular topic for writers throughout the 1780s and 90s. Hannah More's *Essays on Various Subjects, Principally Designed for Young Ladies* (published anonymously in 1777) and *Strictures on the Modern System of Female Education* (1799) insist on the benefits of training women for domestic duties while Mary Wollstonecraft's *Thoughts on the Education of Daughters* (1786) suggests the advantages of a broader education. Though Hervey's children were boys and were educated at Eton, she helped oversee the education of her motherless Beckford nieces and may well have been familiar with the terms of the debate.

23. *I do not, indeed, think it necessary ... equally unnatural and disgusting*: this passage serves as a development of the novel's motto and despite the extravagancies of Hervey's plot she adheres to it for the most part. She uses letters to avoid what she terms 'distracting' leaps between different countries and takes care to make the details of dates, journeys, clothing, etc. seem plausible. This may perhaps be a reaction to *Modern Novel Writing*, which was published in the same year as *Ned Evans* and in which her half-brother William Beckford viciously parodied the excesses of sentimental novels.

24. *poppies*: opiates.

25. *The wretched and gloomy look ... universal horror*: the grim state of the prison at Conway would not have seemed unusual to Hervey's readers. Prisons were notorious during this period, particularly for their treatment of those who had not yet had their case heard, though by the time of the novel's publication the work of the prison reformer John Howard was beginning to bear some fruit. Howard describes the county prison at Caernarvon, from where prisoners were also sent to the sessions at Conway, in his compendious 1777 work *The State of the Prisons in England and Wales*. He states that the rooms are 'incommodious and dirty' and notes that the jailer helps himself to a portion of the money allotted to feed and clothe the prisoners (p. 462).

26. *bob*: a common abbreviation for bob-wig, in which the bottom locks are turned up into 'bobs' or short curls.

27. *honest cock*: here 'cock' is an affectionate term for a male.

28. *subaltern myrmidons of the law*: more properly Myrmidons, the elite warriors who, in Homer's *Iliad*, accompanied Achilles to Troy; used to denote a bodyguard, retinue, or group of assistants.

29. *I know that Father Dogherty ... absolution for half-a-crown*: references in the novel to Roman Catholicism veer between the openly anti-papist and the more sympathetic. The more aggressively anti-Catholic expressions are generally placed in the mouths of characters and thus do not necessarily represent the feelings of the author herself. Hervey's husband's cousin, Frederick Augustus Hervey, who was Bishop of Derry as well as Earl of Bristol, was strongly in favour of easing the penal laws against Catholics.

30. *pen-case*: hard pencil case.

31. *blisters*: anything applied to raise a blister.

32. *It happened that they were one night at the theatre ... an alarm in the house, of fire*: in a letter to her half-brother William Beckford of July 1789, Hervey describes a fire at the opera house which might have been a partial inspiration for this scene, though she treats it comically; 'The papers have informed you, that the Opera house is consumed[?]; it was (though a dreadful Catastrophe to the owners) a most glorious sight, the eruption resembled that of Vesuvius, the flames were seen at Windsor – And it was a very comical spectacle to see the attire of Alexander and Cleopatra, and all the apparatus of the

348   *Notes to pages 43–55*

Gods & Goddesses hanging in tattered fragments in St. James's square. Such a tawdry assemblage of finery never was seen before – All the Signors and Signora's are squalling out their grief for their particular Robes.'

33. *possessed a jointure from her husband of 300l. a year*: the term 'jointure' was loosely used to describe any kind of property to which a wife became entitled on the death of her husband. Hervey notes that £300 is a tolerably sufficient income only because Mrs Melville has no children and resides in Ireland, spending much of the year at Ravensdale.

34. *Merrion-square*: near St Stephen's Green and Leinster House and hence one of the most desirable areas of Dublin.

35. *Berkeley-square*: a square in the West End close to Green Park, a very fashionable address by the 1790s though perhaps a little less so in the 1770s.

36. *Ranelagh*: public pleasure gardens in Chelsea, a fashionable place of leisure with a large rotunda at the centre.

37. *esculent herbs*: edible vegetables.

38. *battle of Fontenoy*: a battle in the War of Austrian Succession fought on 11 May 1745, in which the British and their allies were defeated. The Irish Brigade, which served as part of the French army between 1690 and 1792, was particularly active during the battle, meaning that this may be meant as a somewhat obscure reference to British–Irish tensions. This *curriculum vitae* seems to leave a period of around twenty years unaccounted for.

39. *defluxion*: effluence, emanation.

40. *I have sometimes heard it played upon in Ireland ... by some blind woman*: the harp, which had previously been associated with the Protestant Ascendancy, was reincarnated as a symbol of Irish nationalism and the United Irishmen during the late 1780s and early 1790s (see the introduction for a more detailed discussion of the significance of harps in the novel).

41. *dulcimer*: a musical instrument composed of strings stretched over a box or sounding board which is struck with hand-held hammers; essentially an early forerunner of the piano.

42. *Strada's nightingale*: Famiano Strada (1572–1649) Jesuit and author of a poem narrating the duel between a harpist and a nightingale, in imitation of the late Roman poet Claudian. It was translated or adapted by a number of seventeenth- and eighteenth-century English poets, among them William Cowper, whose version of the poem, first published only in 1803, is as follows;

> The shepherd touch'd his reed; sweet Philomel
> Essay'd, and oft essay'd to catch the strain,
> And treasuring, as on her ear they fell,
> The numbers, echo'd note for note again.
> The peevish youth, who ne'er had found before
> A rival of his skill, indignant heard,
> And soon (for various was his tuneful store)
> In loftier tones defied the simple bird.
> She dared the task, and, rising as he rose,
> With all the force that passion gives inspired,
> Return'd the sounds awhile, but in the close
> Exhausted fell, and at his feet expired.
> Thus strength, not skill prevail'd. O fatal strife,
> By thee, poor songstress, playfully begun;

Notes to pages 55–82 349

> And, O sad victory, which cost thy life,
> And he may wish that he had never won!
> (3.226)

Cecilia, though, must be recalling an earlier translation of the poem, though I have not been able to discover which one.

43. *casimir*: possibly cashmere. A frock is a frock coat, one with wide 'skirts'.

44. *petrifactions*: rock formations.

45. *'Twas thus,' said Evans ... with the company of angels*: the first of many references to John Milton's poem *Paradise Lost*. Before the fall Milton's Adam and Eve subsist solely on fruit, on which they regale the archangel Raphael in Book 5 (lines 309 ff.). The 'oranges and dried fruits' and the water scooped up in 'a deep scollop shell' which Ned proffers for Lady Cecilia's refreshment recall the lines, 'the savoury pulp they chew, and in the rind / Still as they thirsted scoop the brimming stream' (4 lines 332 ff.). Cecilia's indignation is, in the circumstances, entirely understandable.

46. *sublime and beautiful*: Cecilia is showing her knowledge of Edmund Burke's *A Philosophical Enquiry into the Origin of our Ideas of the Sublime and Beautiful*, first published in 1757.

47. *Salvator Rosa*: Salvator Rosa (1615–73) was an Italian painter whose work enjoyed renewed popularity in England in the last quarter of the eighteenth century. Again, the reference demonstrates Cecilia's excellent liberal education and the fact that it is not merely confined to the slightly conservative pictures which hang in her father's Dublin town house (see Volume II, note 17, p. 352 below).

48. *the ox which treadeth out the corn should not be muzzled*: Deuteronomy 25:4.

49. *escritoir*: writing desk.

50. *Mr. Muckworm*: 'muckworm' is a derogatory term for a miser.

51. *horsed upon the back*: that is, Evans was raised on Muckworm's back to facilitate the flogging he received and, of course, with the intention that it would serve the dual purpose of punishment and warning.

52. *turned methodist*: according to Derrick Knight, Hervey's mother, who died in 1798, became a Methodist towards the end of her life, D. Knight, *Gentlemen of fortune: the Men who Made their Fortunes in Britain's Slave Colonies* (London: F. Muller, 1978), p. 114.

53. *piling up light guineas, which he separated from those that were weight*: coins which are 'weight' are those weighing what they ought to, indicating that, unlike 'light' coins, they had not been shaved or adulterated. This was by no means an unusual practice.

54. *I did not hide my talent in a napkin*: the word 'napkin' was sometimes used to translate the word 'sudarium'. It appears far more often in Tyndale than in the King James Bible and Muckworm's use of it may be intended as a nod to his non-conformist religious beliefs.

55. *one of those Italian fellows from London, one Squallini*: Sir Thomas Spendall's generosity, his lavish building projects and his intimacy with a Latin singer suggest that he may be intended as a portrait of Hervey's half-brother William Beckford. The correspondence between Hervey and Beckford often makes reference to the latter's charities, while work had finally begun on Beckford's long-nurtured plans for Fonthill in 1796, the year of the novel's publication. Beckford also lived on terms of intimacy with a musician, Gregorio Franchi (1769/70–1828), the Portuguese-born son of an Italian singer, to whom he gifted an annuity of £400 in 1795 (*ODNB*).

350   *Notes to pages 83–102*

56.   *ad unguem*: 'to the fingernail', to a nicety.
57.   *Often did he wish for the power of Elijah … nor her cruise of oil be diminished*: the story is told in 1 Kings 17:10–16, where a poor widow's meagre store of food is made miraculously inexhaustible as a reward for her generosity to Elijah during a famine.
58.   *were married for half-a-crown, by a gentleman who was preaching in a field to a great congregation*: until the so-called Hardwicke Act came into force in 1753, such questionably formal marriages were both common and legally-recognized.
59.   *distraining*: seizing and selling other property in order to obtain satisfaction for a debt, particularly for arrears of rent.
60.   *grass plat*: a small patch of ground for grazing.
61.   *mode cloak*: possibly a cloak which accords with current fashion.
62.   *eldest ensign*: senior ensign (ensign being the lowest commissioned infantry rank and traditionally the standard bearer, as Ned is in the Battle of Eutaw Springs).
63.   *his eyes sparkled with unusual fire from the … foe*: this appears to be a loose translation of a passage in Book Four of Virgil's *Aeneid*, 'ostroque insignis et auro | stat sonipes ac frena ferox spumantia mandit' (ll. 134–5). In Dryden's 1697 translation;

> Her lofty courser, in the Court below
> [...]
> Proud of his Purple Trappings, paws the Ground;
> And champs the Golden Bitt; and spreads the Foam around
>   (*Aeneid*, Book 4 ll. 190–3)

    It is the first of several references to the *Aeneid*, a Latin poem of the first century BC which deals with looming civil war and nation-building.
64.   *Irish tabbinet*: tabinet is a watered fabric of silk and wool resembling poplin and associated with Ireland.
65.   *Farewell to Lochaber! and farewell my Jane*: a relatively well-known folk song throughout the eighteenth century and one with a particular application to Ned's situation. According to *A selection of favourite catches, glees, &c. as sung at the Bath Harmonic Society* (1797), the words are:

> Farewell to Lochaber, and farewell my Jane,
> Where heartsome with thee I have many days been;
> For Lochaber no more, Lochaber no more,
> Maybe to return to Lochaber no more.
> These tears that I shed, they are all for my dear,
> And not for the dangers attending on war;
> Though borne on rough sea to a far distant shore,
> May be to return to Lochaber no more.

Notes to pages 106–21 351

Volume II

1. *cutting two suckers ... he twisted them together*: a motif which appears in various versions of the story of Tristram and Isolde. Sometimes it is hazel and honeysuckle which grow together, more often a rose and a vine growing from the respective graves of the lovers intertwine. Lilac is associated with youth and the first emotions of love. Like Lady Cecilia, Iseult/Isolde is Irish.
2. *Molly Price*: in his review of the novel Coleridge called Molly Price a poor copy from Fielding's Molly Seagrim but she is by no means a promiscuous character.
3. *He then gave her five guineas ... went into the house*: It is notable that Hervey allows Molly Price to end the novel happily married to a man who knows of and accepts her past, something that is seldom permitted in novels to women who have lost their virtue. Miss Grainger, meanwhile, who does marry with the consent and connivance of her mother, though admittedly in a legally questionable Roman Catholic ceremony, is repudiated by her husband, young Nettlefield, and ostracized by society before dying.
4. *won it unfairly ... honour*: According to Todd's *Dictionary of British and American Women Writers* (p. 162), Hervey's second husband, Lieutenant Colonel William Thomas Hervey, was addicted to gaming and was forced to leave England when his debts became impossible to manage.
5. Corruptio optimi est pessima: 'corruption of the best is the worst'.
6. *flagitious*: deeply criminal.
7. *Cromwell and his saints may serve for a specimen of the one ... popery abounds with examples of the other*: 'Cromwell and his saints' refers to Oliver Cromwell and his parliamentary supporters. The 'Sicilian vespers' is the War of the Sicilian Vespers, which began in 1282, when the island rebelled against Charles I of Naples who had taken it over in 1266 with papal blessing. 'The massacre of St. Bartholomew' was the large-scale killing of Huguenots in Paris in 1572. Since Cromwell's behaviour in Ireland was notorious, reference to him slightly undercuts Evans's anti-papist message.
8. *the comfortable little inn of Gwindu*: there was by all accounts a good inn at Gwindu. John Ferrar recommends it in his *A tour from Dublin to London in 1795* and Edward Lloyd mentions a hostess in his 1781 *A month's tour in North Wales, Dublin, and its environs*, suggesting that Mrs. Knowles may well have been a real-life individual.
9. *his honour*: an attempt to imitate Irish speech patterns.
10. *shame-faced*: bashful, shy.
11. *the Duke of Leinster's*: now the Irish Parliament. As discussed in the introduction, Hervey strongly encourages her readers to identify Ned with Lord Edward Fitzgerald, but this specific reference to the Fitzgerald family's Dublin house seems meant to distance them from their fictional counterparts.
12. *Stephen's Green*: St Stephen's Green, the principal park in Dublin.
13. *In the Beauwalk ... the island of Cythera*: the Beaux Walk was the name for the walk on the north side of the green, so called because the gentlemen's clubs were in the street overlooking it. The 'island of Cythera' is claimed as the birthplace of the goddess Venus.
14. *the equestrian statue in the centre of the field*: John van Nost's statue of George II, blown up by the IRA in 1937.
15. *the work of Phidias*: a Greek sculptor of the fifth century BC, generally considered by far the greatest in the ancient world. He created the famous chryselephantine (gold and ivory) statute of Zeus.
16. *answerable*: comparable.

352   *Notes to pages 121–52*

17. *Titian, Guido, Correggio, and Tintoret ... Claude*: Tiziano Vecellio (d. 1576), Guido Reni (1575–1642), Antonio Allegri da Correggio (1489–1534). 'Tintoret' is Jacopo Comin, commonly known as Tintoretto (1518–94) and 'Claude' is Claude Lorrain (d. 1682). Reference to these artists indicates that the Rivers family are both wealthy and established, and that they have excellent, if conservative taste. Claude was particularly well-known for the tranquillity of his rural scenes, a speaking contrast to some of the Irish rural scenes later in the volume.

18. *Angelica*: Angelica Kauffman (1741–1808), Royal Academician and portrait painter. She did indeed pay a visit to Dublin in the early 1770s. The Rivers family also appreciate the best modern art.

19. *Diana ... on the banks of the renowned Eurotas*: Diana, twin sister of Apollo, is the virgin hunter goddess and goddess of the moon. The River Eurotas is renowned because it flows through the city of Sparta. No such picture by Kauffman is known to exist, but the fashion for mythological portraits was well established by the end of the eighteenth century.

20. *piddled*: toyed with his food, nibbled. His meal is a highly spiced stew of sweetbreads and oysters.

21. beau garçon: a handsome fellow or, when used negatively, a fop.

22. sans souci: carefree.

23. sed credat Judæus: 'sed credat Judaeus Apelles, non ego', literally, 'But let the Jew Apelles believe you, not me', a modern equivalent might be 'tell it to the marines'; a proverbial Latin phrase, to be found in a number of classical authors.

24. mauvaise honte: false shame or modesty, extreme shyness.

25. *shotten herrings*: thin herrings that have spawned and are not good to eat.

26. *six years ago come All-Saints*: the woman's reference to the festival of All Saints (1 November) is a strong indication that she is Roman Catholic.

27. *Nor did he much admire the statue itself, which he thought unworthy of the great hero it represented*: Irish nationalism has generally disapproved very strongly of William III, and Ned's apparent admiration for him is somewhat peculiar. This statue, the work of Grinling Gibbons, was blown up by the IRA in 1929 after several unsuccessful attempts.

28. *gone to the house*: the parliament.

29. *Oh spirit of the immortal Burgh*: Walter Hussey Burgh (1742–1783), politician, orator and Irish patriot. He enjoyed huge success, being made head of the governmental party in 1777, a post he resigned in 1779 to join the opposition. According to Grattan's memoirs his resignation speech included the prophetic words; 'Talk not to me of peace; Ireland is not in a state of peace; it is smothered war. England has sown her laws like dragon's teeth, and they have sprung up as armed men' (*ODNB*).

30. *Lord Jehu*: a Jehu is a fast or furious driver, ultimately from the Jehu in 2 Kings 9.

31. *bucked*: boiled in an alkaline lye; bleached.

32. Infandum jubes renovare dolorem: 'infandum, regina, iubes renovare dolorem', 'O queen, you command me to renew an unspeakable grief', the words with which Aeneas begins the narration of the fall of Troy and his long wanderings around the eastern Mediterranean to Queen Dido's Carthaginian court (*Aeneid*, 2 l. 3).

33. *young Nettlefield, of Nettlepark*: Hervey likes to use suggestive names for her more minor characters, such as Lord Squanderfield, Sir Thomas Spendall and Mr Muckworm. Nettlefield's name, though, seems to imply that he belongs to the class of negligent Ascendancy landowners identified by Arthur Young in his *Tour through Ireland* (see introduction).

34. *dulcinea*: the name given by Cervantes' Don Quixote to his mistress; hence, sweetheart, mistress.

Notes to pages 158–73 353

35. *Oh happy plains ... taste and opulence*: Hervey's word-picture of Ravensdale seems to combine elements of Arthur Young's description of Carton and Milton's Eden in *Paradise Lost*:

'the park ranks among the finest in Ireland. It is a vast lawn, which waves over gentle hills, surrounded by plantations of great extent, and which break and divide in places, so as to give much variety. A large but gentle vale winds through the whole, in the bottom of which a small stream has been enlarged into a fine river ... there is a great variety on the banks of this vale; part of it consists of mild and gentle slopes, part steep banks of thick wood; in another place they are formed into a large shrubbery, very elegantly laid out, and dressed in the highest order, with a cottage, the scenery about which is uncommonly pleasing: and farther on, this vale takes a stronger character, having a rocky bank on one side, and steep slopes scattered irregularly, with wood on the other'.

(*A Tour through Ireland*, vol. 1., p. 23)

A happy rural seat of various view;
Groves whose rich trees wept odorous gums and balms
Others whose fruit burnished with golden rind
Hung amiable, Hesperian fables true
If true, here only, and of delicious taste.
Betwixt them lawns, or level downs, and flocks
Grazing the tender herb, were interspersed
Or palmy hillock or the flowery lap
Of some irriguous valley spread her store,
Flowers of all hue and without thorn the rose.
Another side umbrageous grots and caves
Of cool recess, o'er which the mantling vine
Lays forth her purple grape and gently creeps
Luxuriant: meanwhile murmuring waters fall
Down the slope hills dispersed, or in a lake,
That to the fringed bank with myrtle crowned
Her crystal mirror holds, unite their streams.

(Milton, *Paradise Lost*, 4, ll. 247–63)

36. *tittle*: a small stroke or point in writing or printing.
37. *grand climacteric*: a particularly critical year in one's life, generally held to be the sixty-third. It was, however, also used more loosely.
38. *reynard*: the fox.
39. *cotters*: a cotter was, in Ireland, a peasant who rented a small holding under cottier tenure, under which land was leased out annually in small plots at a sort of public auction. It was an extremely insecure form of tenure, and led to extremes of poverty.
40. *his desire to study Hoyle*: probably *Hoyle's Games Improved: being Practical Treatises on the Following Fashionable Games*, which appeared in 1775. There are a number of other treatises on gaming which appear connected with the name Hoyle from the middle of the eighteenth century up to the present day.
41. *like Jephtha sacrificing his daughter*: Judges 11:29–40.
42. *ecclaircissement*: (eclaircissement) a mutual explanation or clarification.

354   *Notes to pages 174–202*

43. *a mountain of a singular form ... kept by constant care in the highest order*: from the description, this seems to be a drained bog. Like Maria Edgeworth, Hervey seems doubtful about the effectiveness of the agricultural improvements carried out by Ascendancy landlords. See introduction for a further discussion.

44. *The horses ... seconded his rider's views*: A similar incident occurs in another novel of 1796, Robert Bage's *Hermsprong, or, Man as he is not*, where the eponymous hero rescues the heroine after a startled carriage horse bolts with her. There are a number of other minor similarities, including the radical views of the hero, who is the rightful heir to an estate which is currently held by his usurping uncle.

45. *concentred*: brought to a centre, concentrated.

46. *choused*: cheated, tricked.

47. *like Eve in her days of innocence, she had been visiting her shrubs*: leaving Adam to dispute with the angel, Eve 'went forth among her fruits and flowers / To visit how they prospered, bud and bloom, / Her nursery; they at her coming sprung; / And, touched by her fair tendance, gladlier grew' (8, ll. 44–7). The passage immediately precedes Milton's encomium on the happiness of the union between Adam and Eve, and on Eve's beauty.

48. *the trumpet of Bellona*: Bellona is a minor Roman goddess of war, not particularly associated with trumpets. Hervey may be confusing Bellona and Allecto, both of whom are mentioned in Book 7 of the Aeneid. Bellona is described as the 'pronuba', the bridesmaid of Lavinia, while Allecto is sent by the goddess Juno to stir up war amongst the Latin tribes, blowing a horn at the end of the book.

Volume III

1. *an opportunity of rising when it offers*: that is, by purchasing a higher rank when it falls vacant.

2. *like Andromache, δαχρυεν γελἀσασα*: a misquotation or misprinting of δακρυόυεν γελἀσασα, 'laughing through her tears', 'crying and laughing together'; Hervey is referring to the touching scene in Book 6 of Homer's *Iliad* where the Trojan hero Hector, seeing that his baby son is scared of the nodding plume on his helmet, removes it and dandles the child in his arms before passing him back to his mother, Andromache (ll. 482–5). The passage emphasizes the disjunction between the grim world of war and the intimate and loving space of the family.

3. *promethean fire*: according to Hesiod's *Theogony*, Prometheus brought fire to humans. The term was also used to designate an early kind of match which seems a more probable meaning; at any rate, Cecilia's eyes spark and glow.

4. *our country*: that is (probably) county, as in Austen.

5. *to put on the whole armour of God*: Ephesians 6:11–13, 'Put on the whole armour of God, that ye may be able to stand against the wiles of the devil. For we wrestle not against flesh and blood, but against principalities, against powers, against the rulers of the darkness of this world, against spiritual wickedness in high places. Wherefore take unto you the whole armour of God, that ye may be able to withstand in the evil day, and having done all, to stand.' A very suitable verse for Lord Ravensdale to quote but a suggestive one given the novel's temporal setting to the early 1780s, when there was an upswell of patriotic and nationalistic sentiment in Ireland.

6. *flung*: 'fling' can mean to emit, send forth, give out, or diffuse.

7. *ton*: cask, barrel.

Notes to pages 207–22 355

8. *Neptune and the Naiads*: Neptune is the Roman god of the sea, but naiads are specifically freshwater nymphs. It is the nereids who are sea-nymphs. This is a very minor error, however, and may belong to the printer, though it appears in other editions of the novel.

9. *one Saturday evening ... drinking with the captain in the cabin, to the health of their wives and sweet-hearts*: the traditional toast in the Royal Navy for a Saturday.

10. *before she could be wore into stays*: turned around to sail back.

11. *As to those who sail ... For many a league*: a misremembering or deliberate misquotation of part of the passage from Milton's *Paradise Lost* describing Satan's journey to Eden.

> –As when to them who sail
> Beyond the Cape of Hope, and now are past
> Mozambic, off at sea north-east winds blow
> Sabean odours from the spicy shore
> Of Arabie the blest, with such delay
> Well pleased they slack their course, and many a league
> Cheered with the grateful smell old Ocean smiles.
> (Book IV, ll. 159–65)

12. *an halbert*: the rank of a sergeant.

13. *But Satan, envious of the felicity of this second Eden ... to obey it*: yet another reference to Milton's *Paradise Lost*, though a less specific one.

14. *liberal use of bark*: that is, quinine obtained from the bark of the Cinhona tree.

15. *Mars ... fortune*: Mars is the Roman god of war and Bacchus of wine. Fortuna is the Roman goddess of luck and hence of games of chance.

16. *Bobadil*: Bobadil is a braggart character in Ben Jonson's *Every Man in his Humour* (1598) and, like Nettlefield, an impoverished and plausible soldier.

17. *came on the tapis*: a semi-translation of the French phrase *sur le tapis*, meaning to come under discussion. Horatio Gates (*c.* 1727–1806) was a godson of Horace Walpole and an officer in the British Army. In 1772 he moved to Virginia, offering his services to the revolutionary army at the outbreak of hostilities. After early successes, his campaign in Carolina was a disappointment and he was soon replaced by Nathaniel Greene (1742–86).

18. *The important victory at Camden ... over General Gates*: the Battle of Camden, a major victory for the British which took place on 16 August 1780. Hervey's dating is admirably precise.

19. *allowed to reside there on their parole*: that is, they have given their word of honour that they will not engage in combat.

20. *sent off to Augustine*: presumably St Augustine, which lies on the Florida coast around a hundred miles south of Charleston, and which was under the control of the British.

21. *videttes*: mounted sentries.

22. *on the eighth of September, they were attacked ... South Carolina*: this is the Battle of Eutaw Springs in which, like Ned, Lord Edward Fitzgerald was injured in the leg before being rescued from where he lay on the battlefield. It took place on 8th September 1781.

23. *a miracle little less striking ... by the ravens*: Elijah is miraculously fed by ravens in 1 Kings 12:16–17. This was evidently a favourite passage, since Hervey cites verses 10–16 in Volume I (see note 57).

24. *underwood*: undergrowth.

356   *Notes to pages 223–60*

25. *the stock-dove*: the wild pigeon, which is known for nesting in the hollows of decayed trees.

26. *gins*: generally, any devices by which game can be caught but here probably intended more specifically to denote snares of some sort.

27. *the Agigua tribe, a branch of the Cherokees*: the Cherokee Indians sometimes refer to themselves as *A-ni-yv-wi-ya* ('Ah nee yuhn wi yah') and Hervey's 'Agigua' is perhaps a misliteration of this, or alternately a misprinting. I have found it nowhere else.

28. *their inhuman masters tied them all together ... before them*: These descriptions of Indian life seem to be lifted almost wholesale from James Adair's *The History of the American Indians* (1775), a somewhat esoteric text which combines anthropological detail with the claim that the American Indians are descended from the Jews. As Hervey glosses the Indian words I have not troubled to do so. Tim Fulford's *Romantic Indians: Native Americans, British Literature, and Transatlantic Culture 1756–1830* (Oxford: Oxford University Press, 2006) details other popular European treatments of American Indians during the eighteenth century; Hervey's depiction of the Indians is fairly typical, though a degree more sympathetic than some.

29. *loaden*: perhaps a printer's error, though 'loaden' indicates that the pair are not merely laden but heavily laden.

30. *his manes*: the spirit of a dead person, in the context of worship.

31. *bits of lightwood*: in the southern United States, lightwood is resinous pinewood.

32. *calumet*: according to the *Oxford English Dictionary*, a tobacco-pipe with a bowl of clay or stone, and a long reed stem carved and ornamented with feathers.

33. *hurdled*: wattled, woven of wood.

34. *feudal oppressions*: a two-layered phrase which might refer either to the old-fashioned rural system which prevailed in the Scottish Highlands, forcing the majority of its inhabitants to eke out a precarious living on an insecure land tenure, or to the legal restrictions which came into force after the '45 rebellion and the early examples of what are now called the Highland Clearances, both of which combined to drive thousands of Scots to settle in America. Eric Richards's *Debating the Highland Clearances* (Edinburgh: Edinburgh University Press, *c.* 2007) provides more detail.

35. *metheglin*: a spiced or medicinal type of mead.

36. *submitted to be inoculated*: this episode, in which Edward innoculates the Agiguans against smallpox is by no means anachronistic. Edward Jenner perfected vaccination in 1796, the year the novel was published, but a more primitive method of innoculation by variolation had been popularized in Britain by Lady Mary Wortley Montagu, who had seen the practice being carried out in Turkey. It became increasingly commonplace from the 1720s onwards, but carried greater dangers than Hervey suggests here.

37. *He reverenced that truth and intense affection ... gentle savage*: many European authors stated that American Indians never exhibited emotion (see Fulford, *Romantic Indians*, p. 43) but Hervey allows Sheerasta a moment of heroic pathos.

38. *spunk*: makeshift touchwood or tinder.

39. *the Chickesaw nation*: when first encountered by Europeans, the Chickasaw were settled in Mississippi and in South Carolina.

40. *The cruelties which he exercised ... his father's house*: The sympathetic – if somewhat patronizing – treatment of both slaves and unwilling slave owner is interesting given the fact that the fortune Hervey brought her first husband had been secured on the proceeds of Oldfield's Bog, an estate which was certainly run on slave labour.

Notes to pages 262–8 357

41. *the strange paradox ... than the civilized*: Jean-Jacque Rousseau's *Discourse on the Origins of Inequality* (1755) and the Abbé Raynal's *A Philosophical and Political History of the Settlements and Trade of the Europeans in the East and West Indies* (1776) together formed the kernel of the image of native Americans as 'noble savages' subsisting in an ideal state of society, a notion which was repeated and developed by William Godwin and in the Pantisocratic writings of Samuel Taylor Coleridge and Robert Southey.

Volume IV

1. *the Quarter-house*: probably the Quarter House Tavern, which lay around six miles north of Charleston. As Hervey explains, this was used as a military base during the Revolutionary War.

2. *the redoubts and the palisadoes*: redoubts are generally features within the main fortifications, though here Hervey may use the word to mean 'detached redoubts', small separate fortifications guarding the approach to the main one; palisades are pointed wooden stakes fixed in the ground, marking off a defensive enclosure and making passage across it extremely difficult.

3. *pale phantoms of hatred*: the phrase 'phantoms of hatred' appears in the title of a poem by W. B. Yeats, *I see Phantoms of Hatred and of the Heart's Fullness and of the Coming Emptiness*. It is also used in Goldwin Smith's *Irish History and Irish Character* (2nd edn 1862) to describe the public reaction to the events of the 1798 United Irish Uprising. It seems possible that Yeats may have unconsciously picked up on Smith, and Smith – perhaps – on this phrase of Hervey's.

4. *prayers to shut the lions' mouths, and deliver you from the fangs of those ferocious tigers*: a reference to Daniel 6:22, 'My God hath sent his angel, and hath shut the lions' mouths, that they have not hurt me: forasmuch as before him innocency was found in me; and also before thee, O king, have I done no hurt.' The word 'tiger' was sometimes used to denote a particularly savage or bloodthirsty person.

5. *the Hot-Wells of Bristol*: Bristol Hot-Wells or Hot-well lay about a mile and a half from Bristol proper. According to *A Picturesque Guide to Bath, Bristol Hot-Wells, the River Avon, and the Adjacent Country* (London, 1793), the first effects of drinking the waters were unpleasantly like intoxication (pp. 169–70), so that Lord Rivers, in his 'declining state', may have received little benefit there.

6. *She expects to come back here soon lady lieutenant ... is put under his subjection*: the new Lady Squanderfield anticipates that her husband will be made Lord Lieutenant of Ireland, a position which combined the roles of viceroy and head of the Irish executive. One of Hervey's husband's cousins, George William Hervey, second Earl of Bristol, was nominated to fill this post but never did so. The last few pages of the novel, in which Hervey details the fate of her other characters, are mute on when Lord Squanderfield takes up the role, if he ever does so, making it impossible to firmly identify him with any of the individuals who in fact held it. However, a loose identification with Charles Manners, the fourth Duke of Rutland (1754–87) may be intended, since he was a very young man when made Lord Lieutenant in February 1784. Like Squanderfield, Rutland was a notorious and largely unsuccessful gambler. He was a man of more parts than the fictional Squanderfield, but as Lord Lieutenant he promoted Pitt's plans for Ireland, which were geared towards union, and he encountered opposition from those who wished to cement Grattan's reforms, including the Duke of Leinster, eldest brother of Lord Edward Fitzgerald, and Hervey's uncle the Earl-Bishop.

358 *Notes to pages 271–81*

7. *the gulph stream*: eighteenth-century mariners were well aware of the Gulf Stream and often exploited it to accelerate voyages from Europe to America.
8. *in the best trim possible*: the best arrangement of sails.
9. *laboured*: pitched and rolled.
10. *biscuit*: a particular type of thin crisp biscuit used as a substitute for bread on long sea-voyages.
11. *hogshead*: a large cask.
12. *boisterous*: of the weather, rough.
13. *outrageous*: mad.
14. *boatswain*: the person in charge of sails and rigging.
15. *to tack*: to sail against the wind.
16. *huzzas*: cheers.
17. *somewhat past her grand climacteric*: a euphemistic way of saying that she is in her late sixties or early seventies.
18. *her life being in the lease, she held it for that term*: it was very common for the length of an eighteenth-century lease to refer to lives. Thus a contract might mention the life of a child, a member of the royal family, or, as here, a wife or widow and stipulate that the lease would last as long as that person lived, ceasing after they died. In certain circumstances this was far more practical and economical than a lease lasting for a fixed period.
19. *wine whey*: see Volume I, note 18, p. 346, above.
20. *she fancied she discovered in his countenance a strong resemblance of her dear daughter*: this is more overt than the reference in Volume II and, as discussed in the introduction, Hervey emphasizes its unlikeliness. The uncannily close resemblance of parent and child is a common motif in sentimental novels of the period, often helping to reveal romantically hidden parentage. It is parodied by Austen in *Northanger Abbey*, where the portrait of the late Mrs Tilney perplexes Catherine, who, 'had depended upon meeting with features, air, complexion that should be the very counterpart, the very image, if not of Henry's, of Eleanor's; – the only portraits of which she had been in the habit of thinking, bearing always an equal resemblance of mother and child. A face once taken was taken for generations', J. Austen, *The novels of Jane Austen*, ed. R. W. Chapman, 3rd edn, 6 vols (London: Oxford University Press, 1980–2), vol. 5 *Northanger Abbey and Persuasion*, p. 191.
21. *Will you gang to the ewe-bughts, Marion*: a Scottish folk-song with a strong anti-military theme.

> Will you gang to the ewe-bughts, Marion?
> An wear in the sheep wi' me?
> The sun shines sweet my Marion!
> But nae ha'f sae sweet as thee.
>
> Thus Sandy sang sweet to his Marion,
> As we sat by the wimpling burn;
> But Sandy has left her, no caring,
> In sorrow his absence to mourn.
>
> Tho' wi' gowd now his garters be glaring,
> An siller on his bonnet ajee,
> Nae joy can that gie to his Marion,

Notes to pages 281–95 359

Himsel' 'twas gae pleasure to me.

His hose, an his plaid, look sae gaudie,
The red coat I like nae to see,
They've stown the young heart o my laddie
Far, far, frae the ewe bughts an me.

Ilk blythe ,bonny laddie, maun leave us,
Seeking Honour, an' Fortune afar;
While we lanely lasses maun grieve us,
To think on the horrors o' war.

Then haste, wi' your sweet smile, sae cheery,
Nor langer leave Marion to mourn;
Ilk spat 'bout the ewe bughts looks eirie,
Till Sandy dear Sandy return.

22. *heir*: inherit.
23. *a huge cavern, not unaptly termed the cathedral*: there is a fairly well-known and spectacu-lar sea-cave called the Cathedral, but it is in County Antrim, a good distance from the Limerick setting of Glendemus.
24. *the art of bull-making*: a bull is a self-contradictory and nonsensical statement, and the making of them was at this period strongly associated with the Irish. Maria Edgeworth's *Essay Concerning the Nature of Bulls and Blunders* suggests that many apparent 'bulls' are in fact examples of peculiarly Irish English.
25. *I wish to God he ever may*: a slightly incoherent construction, perhaps intended to dem-onstrate that although Cecilia is made an heiress by her brother's death she is nevertheless deeply affected by it. Cecilia, of course, hopes to God that her father will leave his bed rather than remaining there to die.
26. *It is better ... to go to the house of mourning than the house of feasting*: Ecclesiastes 7:2, 'It is better to go to the house of mourning, than to go to the house of feasting: for that is the end of all men; and the living will lay it to his heart.'
27. *a levee*: an assembly of visitors.
28. *the Officer and the Gentleman*: appearing most often in handbooks of regulations and court martial proceedings, the phrase 'the Officer and the Gentleman' denotes the military ideal.
29. *Lothario*: Lothario is the name of several literary characters, but here certainly a reference to the character in Rowe's *Fair Penitent*, who in one speech explains that;

> ... love and war take turns, like day and night,
> And little preparation serves my turn,
> Equal to both, and armed for either field.
> (Act 4)

30. *Job*: the archetypal sufferer.
31. *escutcheon*: coat of arms.
32. *Forgiveness to the injur'd doth belong ... who have done the wrong*: 'Forgiveness to the injured does belong; / but they ne'er pardon who have done wrong', John Dryden, *The Conquest of Granada,* Part 2, 1.2 ll. 5–6. The play centers on the period of the Recon-quista, when Ferdinand and Isabella were attempting to drive the Moors out of Spain.

360   *Notes to pages 298–336*

33. *scapes*: escapes.
34. *True gratitude, by owing, owes not; But stands at once indebted and discharged*: Milton,
     Paradise Lost:

> a grateful mind
> By owing owes not, but still pays, at once
> Indebted and discharged; what burden then?
>   (Book IV, ll. 55–7)

35. *dark bay colour*: bay is reddish-brown.
36. *bumper*: a cup or glass filled to the brim, and, commonly, this drunk as a toast.
37. *him whom Homer has immortalized in his Odyssey*: the episode occurs in Book 17 of
     Homer's *Odyssey*. When Odysseus returns home after a twenty-year absence, his dog
     Argus recognizes him. In Pope's translation:

> He knew his Lord; he knew, and strove to meet,
> In vain he strove, to crawl, and kiss his feet;
> Yet (all he could) his tail, his ears, his eyes,
> Salute his master, and confess his joys.
>   (17, ll. 360–3)

38. *a little boy in a white frock*: little boys were dressed in frocks until the age of around 5 or
     6, when they were 'breeched'.
39. *I found my dear Edward ... do you not know it:* The revelation of Ned's identity echoes
     that in Fielding's *Joseph Andrews*, where the evidence of a tinker and a strawberry-shaped
     birthmark on Joseph's chest provide the proof. Abraham Adams, who accompanies
     Joseph on his adventures, carries with him a copy of the plays of the Greek tragedian
     Aeschylus, whose play *The Libation Bearers* (458 BC) features an improbable recognition
     scene. The scene was wickedly parodied by another Greek tragedian, Euripides, in his
     Electra. Hervey was extremely well-read and it is not impossible that she intends an allu-
     sion to these other texts.
40. *The Lord ... hath given; blessed be the name of the Lord*: a deliberate reversal of Job 21:1,
     'Naked came I out of my mother's womb, and naked shall I return thither: the Lord gave,
     and the Lord hath taken away; blessed be the name of the Lord.'
41. *Belisarius*: Belisarius was a general of the sixth century AD, and the subject of several
     plays and novels, including a 1724 play by William Philips, John Downman's *Belisarius*
     (1742) and Jean-François Marmontel's *Bélisaire* (1767).
42. *the palate of Apicius*: a proverbial Roman gourmet who lived during the reigns of Augus-
     tus and Tiberius. A Roman cookbook, the *De Re Coquinaria*, was erroneously attributed
     to him.
43. *the warming juice of Oporto's grape*: port.
44. *It was said of the old duchess of Bedford ... always a fair wind to carry you out of it*: Lady
     Gertrude Leveson-Gower (1718/19–94), second wife of John Russell, the fourth Duke.
     Her husband served as Lord Lieutenant between 1756 and 1760.
45. *had sea room*: that is, was away from the shore, or anything against which the ship might
     run.
46. *Bishop of Limerick*: strictly the Bishop of Limerick was also Bishop of Ardfert and
     Aghadoe, but it seems plausible that he is meant for a portrait of Hervey's husband's

Notes to pages 340–3   361

cousin, who was Bishop of Derry as well as being Earl of Bristol. As discussed in the introduction, the Earl-Bishop was a political ally of the Duke of Leinster who, though more moderate than his brother Lord Edward Fitzgerald, was sympathetic to the aims of the United Irishmen.

47. *Nettlefield bowed, and withdrew*: This episode, in which Nettlefield agrees to manage his estate as Ned directs, should be understood as a symbolic restructuring of the Irish constitution under which the Ascendancy is controlled and improved by a nationalist Irish government.

48. *convenient for seabathing ... that wholesome practice*: sea-bathing was still considered slightly outré at this time, though it rapidly gained in popularity after around 1810. Lord Edward Fitzgerald and his siblings, raised along Roussevian lines, were frequent sea-bathers.

49. *though five sparrows are sold for a farthing ... Heaven*: Luke 12:6, 'Are not five sparrows sold for two farthings, and not one of them is forgotten before God?'